The song came to an end. The tape whirred a little. A few preliminary chords were struck. Over them, a voice whispered: 'Listen closely, Anna.'

Before she could wonder whose voice it was, or why it had spoken, the vocalist came in. She frowned, jabbing at the rewind button then replaying the tape.

There it was again: 'Listen closely, Anna.'

Not Hannah. Not her name. But one that she had been called over the years, either by people who did not listen carefully enough, or by people unfamiliar with the less used name.

'*Every move you make, I'll be watching you,*' the singer declared. '*Every vow you take, every claim you stake, every move you make, I'll be watching you.*' They were intended as words of obsession, of love. Given that three-word introduction, they became sinister and menacing. Pushing at the buttons, once again Hannah rewound the tape and then replayed it. Again the voice admonished her, anonymous, androgynous, impossible to decide whether it was male or female.

The Italian Garden

Susan Moody

CORONET BOOKS
Hodder and Stoughton

Copyright © 1994 Susan Moody

First published in Great Britain in 1994
by Hodder & Stoughton
First published in paperback in 1995
by Hodder and Stoughton
A division of Hodder Headline PLC

A Coronet paperback

The right of Susan Moody to be identified as the Author of
the Work has been asserted by her in accordance with the
Copyright, Designs and Patents Act 1988.

10 9 8 7 6 5 4 3 2 1

British Library Cataloguing in Publication Data

Moody, Susan
Italian Garden
I. Title
823.914 [F]

ISBN 0 340 60915 X

Printed and bound in Great Britain by
Cox & Wyman Ltd, Reading, Berkshire

Hodder and Stoughton
A Division of Hodder Headline PLC
338 Euston Road
London NW1 3BH

For Jonathon, Timothy & Benedick

NOW

1

Outside the railway carriage, the night flows backwards, smooth as a river. Hannah's windowed reflection lies like a ghost on the glass. Through her insubstantial self, she stares into the blackness outside.

The carriage lights are bright and dispassionate, unforgiving of tired eyes, wrinkled skin, scuffed shoes. Under one of the seats ahead of hers, an empty soft-drink can rolls with the motion of the train, hitting table legs with a soft ping again and again until someone, a man in a fawn raincoat, leans forward and sets it upright. Although the voices of the other passengers are muffled, in the seat behind hers a young couple is bickering gently about the film they have just seen: whether the plot stood up, what the director meant by the last enigmatic shot of the hero. 'Don't patronise me, Mike,' the girl says. 'I don't need that kind of shit.' Mike murmurs at her, his words caught in the plush covering of the seat back, overlaid by the sound of the wheels beneath the train.

Once again Hannah looks at the reflected face beside hers. Her own face. Etched on the glass. Her but not her. Middle-aged, middle-class, unexceptional. No one would pick her out in a crowd; she is indistinguishable from a thousand others, a paradigm of all she has laboured so hard to be. No one, should their passing eye rest briefly on her, would think: *there* is a woman responsible for a man's death.

She looks tired, the line of her cheek drooping, her mouth turned down, dissatisfied, almost disagreeable. Occasionally, she knows, she appears younger than she has any right to do, but now is not one of those times. It is late and this is the last train home from London. All day she has been shopping – Christmas is only days away – and the concert started late, the train was delayed. She wants desperately to sleep, to shut out the world.

Behind her, the girl says sharply: 'Look, Mike. I know who I am, OK?'

Mike murmurs again. Hannah senses that he has reached out a hand to his girl and had it thrust away.

I know who I am, OK?

Has there ever been a time when Hannah knew who she was? Perhaps once – but then she was too young to consider that she might not be what she appeared to be.

The train slows, moving at half-speed through some unmemorable station where it will not stop. There are white lights, benches against brick, an empty waiting-room. On the platform three or four people stare at the passing train without expression, pale-faced, unconnected to it and its passengers. The further lengths of concrete are left behind, dark and deserted. Blackness thickens against the window again, and she sees nothing within it, no lights, no suggestion of other people. Only the frail semblance of herself.

She closes her eyes. She is exhausted, she must sleep. But behind her eyelids jump images she dare not face. Not here, not now.

Not ever.

Either you believe in ghosts or you don't.

Hannah does not.

Therefore, there has to be a rational explanation for what she saw tonight. What she *thinks* she saw. Which, she tells herself, was only a similarity of expression, of bone structure, of colouring. Nothing more than that. After all, it is twenty-five years since she saw him for the last time. He would, given the chance, have changed. He would no longer be young, handsome, full of life; he would not be like whoever it was she saw through the glass frontage of the Festival Hall tonight.

His head was thrown back; he was laughing as she had seen him laugh so many times. For a moment the burden she has carried with her for so long was lifted. For a moment she was able to believe that she might not, after all, be guilty. Expectation, impossible though it was of fulfilment, buoyed her, made her smile: she could see the smile reflected in the tall windows. But of course, it could not have been him.

Besides, the one on the other side of the glass was altogether too solid, too corporeal for her sudden unrealisable hope to do more than evaporate almost before she had recognised him. Or, rather, *not* him. Had it been *him*, he would have been more substantial, less of today; he would not have been wearing that unstructured jacket with rolled-up sleeves, that open-necked shirt and loose trousers. He would have been weighted down with the years.

And anyway, this subjunctive mode has no meaning: it is impossible for it to have been him. A fleeting resemblance, she tells herself again, as the train rushes north through the empty suburbs towards the dull provincial town in which she lives.

She is lying. She has lived so long with the lies she tells others that sometimes she almost comes to believe in them herself. But in the end, however easy it is to deceive others, it is impossible to deceive oneself. Hannah knows that the resemblance was *not* fleeting. It was striking. His hands – those thin, elegant hands she remembers so often, and with such pain; the angle of his head as he leaned to speak to someone with him. They were *his*.

Briefly, she had thought his eyes met hers through the glass. Those unmistakable eyes. Was it her imagination, or did they widen in some kind of recognition? She tells herself it was impossible, that he could not have seen her standing out there in the rain, that even if he had, even if it was *him*, he would not have recognised what she has become.

What she now must decide is: did she dream him, or did he really exist, there, behind the tall windows? Have her thoughts, her memories, so long repressed, packed down over the years, hardened to such an extent that they can persuade her of something which she knows cannot be? Walking across the wet concrete terrace between the river and the concert hall, she saw him flanked by the reflections of the lamps behind her, white globes laid like communion wafers on the black glass, and between them, that face, *his* face.

Has the past finally caught up with her?

On the seat opposite hers an old woman sits asleep, head nodding in time with the train's movement. Faded skin, mottled hands clasped on her lap, all the lines and wrinkles which age imposes. She opens her eyes and stares sideways at Hannah, not seeing her. Her eyes are grey, blurred with old age, unfocused. What lies behind them? Another secret life? Did she once know passion, excitement, adventure? Or has she lived serenely, marrying, producing children, watching them grow and have children in their own turn? What griefs, what quiet happinesses, have brought her to this moment on a train, among strangers, while time streams past the windows? She stirs, her foot touching Hannah's momentarily. What would she feel if she knew she had touched the shoe of a woman capable of doing what Hannah did? A woman responsible for the death of another?

Perhaps she would feel nothing. Perhaps she too has been implicated in someone else's dying. Perhaps she too knows what it is like to be begged for mercy and to show none. Perhaps, in the hidden existences of all the people on the train – the man in the raincoat, the young couple behind – there lies violence and blood.

As the railway track beats beneath her like the rhythm section of some half-heard rock group, Hannah tries to decide if she is upset by what happened tonight. Or has she so schooled herself into imperturbability that she is incapable of feeling anything beyond standard love, ordinary pleasure, occasional depression?

They travel onwards, Hannah's twin and Hannah, two faces set towards the north, drawn onwards into the dark together, seeing nothing of their shared destination.

Yes.

The thought explodes in her mind. She *is* upset by the face she saw tonight between the suspended lamps. And as she thinks this, she thinks, too, what a meaningless word 'upset' is, what a mealy-mouthed, suburban substitution for real feeling. All her life, parents, teachers, friends have whipped her with that word. Mouthing it, using it as though it had meaning. It has none, it says nothing, is deliberately chosen to bleach out emotion.

She should not blame them. She does not understand what moves her, any more than they did or do. On the cold window, her reflected image gives away nothing.

Another station. Bleak platforms, benches of gaudy steel where nobody sits, an unmanned ticket-barrier, rain driving against the high white lamps. The name flashes by, too fast for her to read. She could be anywhere. Or nowhere.

If he really had existed there, in that moment before he turned away and was lost in the concert-going crowd, who was he? The one person he seems to be is the one she knows he cannot be. So who is he? How can she find out? And if she knew the answer to that question, she would have to ask another: does she *want* to find out?

For somehow she has won through to a sort of peace. She lies curled up at the heart of the world she has created for herself, like a pearl in an oyster. Like a worm i' the bud.

Since she knows who he cannot possibly be, how can she find out who he *is*?

She stares through her image into the dark and realises the futility of the question. An anonymous face glimpsed briefly in a crowd. Hopeless.

The train slows again. Stops. More midnight-black platforms, yellow lighting, empty waiting-rooms. A few passengers descend. Including Hannah. Doors slam. The train sighs deeply, pulls itself together, moves away with gathering speed into the darkness.

Outside the station, rain sweeps across the forecourt, across the black curves of taxis, the white dividing lines of parking slots. Wind shakes the emaciated skeletons of rosebushes intended to show the human face of rail travel, just as the red-painted lampstands and moulded seats on platforms along the line are designed to bring cheer to the daily commute, though they only succeed in reinforcing its dreariness.

Hannah finds her car. A sudden buffet of wind sends rain sliding between her hair and the collar of her coat. The ends of her good silk scarf slap against her jawbone as she scrabbles for her car keys and then drops them into a garish, oilslicked puddle, tarnished rainbows caught in the light from the lamps. As she straightens up, her breath is squeezed from her in an involuntary ouf! Under her dress, her stomach strains at the waistband of her tights. She is middle-aged, middle-class, mother of two. The Invisible Woman. The age, the sex, the class which nobody listens to, nobody notices. She knows who she is, OK?

Who she *appears* to be.

Yet, despite the blurring lines here and there, the sag of breasts and stomach, the lines beneath her eyes and around her mouth, she also knows she is still an attractive woman. Her legs are good, her dark hair shines, she has kept some, most, of her figure. The raincoat she wears is fashionably long, the skirt beneath it fashionably short. Men still find her – not to put too fine a point on it – sexy.

Why should she care, she wonders? Why should sexiness still seem a desirable state? Why is she so much a child of her generation of women that, however much she fights against it, she still measures herself against the light in the eyes of the men she comes into contact with? She smiles as she drives down the main road, past the Social Security offices, the High School, the prison, the overcrowded windows of estate agents, late-night fish and chip shops. Rain slams against her windscreen, too heavy for the wipers to cope with efficiently, so that for a moment she drives in semi-blindness. Lights from cars coming in the opposite direction brighten the edges of the semicircular swirl. Waterdrops bounce up from the metal hood. An old man pauses uncertainly by the traffic lights and then, as they change to green, starts to cross.

She drives slowly past the contemporary repetitions of suburban life: the Woolworths, the Dewhursts, past Dolcis, Boots, W. H. Smith, Radio Rentals. An unboxed cassette is lying on the passenger seat and she reaches for it, pushes it into the car radio, presses the button. It must be one of her son's compilation tapes, she realises as, expecting Mozart, she gets Phil Collins, his voice almost lost in a mess of nearly-musical sounds. '*Take, take me home,*' he croons, and a ghostly audience inside the dashboard applauds the start of the song.

Briefly Hannah wonders why this is in her car. Was it there earlier, when she drove to the station car park? She does not remember. It can only belong to Adam, her son, but he has been away at university since October. '*I've been a prisoner all my life,*' says Phil, '*take me home,*' and as she turns on to the busy main road, she remembers that Adam was briefly at home last weekend, for a local friend's birthday. The tape is a recorded concert and as the singer's voice fades, the audience takes over, echoing the cry, and she imagines their hands lifted above their heads, a forlorn forest of waving arms. She knows they do this at concerts, she has seen them on the television. *Take me home*, they keen and she wonders how many of them have still to learn that, as the man said, you can't go home again. But the song does not involve her; she turns off the tape.

The shops give way to a church set in a square surrounded by the Town Hall, a couple of pubs, the Tourist Information offices, the Corn Exchange, a bookshop. Green and red raindrops roll down the windscreen as she passes a pizza parlour and turns, discarded wrappings and styrofoam trays crunching under the tyres of her car, on to the road which runs parallel to the river. After weeks of rain, the water is high, brimming the banks. Brown, churned by the insistent rain, inching towards the houses which face it, fingers of water reaching on to the pavement.

Already there have been flood warnings. Sandbags have been delivered to those houses most at risk, nearest the impetuous river, Hannah's among them. Sandbags. She wonders just how effective they would be in holding back the rising water. What it would be like to come down in the morning to find the stairs leading into flood water, carpets squelchy with mud, the walls wet, her possessions – books, telephone, furniture – floating about the rooms. But despite the sandbags, the possibility seems remote. That is one of the reasons she still lives in this town: because the chance of drama is so minimal. She has learnt to distrust drama. Street lamps are tangled among the bare branches of the plane trees which stand along the embankment pavements. Shapes float on the shaken surface of the river: Canada geese, swans, mallard of various kinds, asleep under the willows.

She pulls up alongside her own house, turns off the engine, the lights, fits the car-thief deterrent to the steering wheel. She is like that now, cautious, careful, unimpetuous. Unexceptional.

There is a light glowing dimly somewhere behind the curtains of the front bedroom. She opens the front door, feels the house reach around her, smells its familiar scents of flowers (dying, she notes: they must be replaced tomorrow), smoke from the fireplace, a memory of cooked food. On the chest in the hall, the red light of her answering machine winks quietly, on-off, on-off, promising her the voices of friends, of family, loved ones, promising that she is not alone.

As she removes her raincoat and shakes it, reaches for a hanger in the closet, she presses down the flickering button.

'Welcome home, Hannah,' says the machine. 'I hope you're all right, not too tired after all that shopping, and that you haven't bankrupted yourself buying presents. I only wanted to say goodnight, we'll talk tomorrow, I miss you, sweetheart. I love you. Sleep well.'

Marcus's voice. Strong, loving. He says things she wants to hear but can hardly allow herself to believe. Who, after all, could love her? He says things she says back to him. Saying them is as exhilarating as strong drink; for years she has not dared to unzip her heart and set free an emotion such as love. She knows how dangerous love can be. Often she wonders if she means the things she tells him.

At first sight, Marcus seems no more than the steady, reliable kind of man which women are supposed to want – and how much more a woman like herself, a woman weighed down by the past, a woman seeking anonymity, craving safety? Marcus, a jobbing hack, as he describes himself, lives in the north. Under different names, he writes newspaper columns on everything from antiques to country matters. But there are contradictions: from things he has told her, she understands that in the past, his life has been one of activity. He holds a helicopter pilot's licence, served in the Army, has driven overland to Russia, lived in Peru. He reviews books for newspapers, teaches journalism at a nearby polytechnic which has lately been granted university status. A former foreign correspondent for a Fleet Street newspaper, he has recently turned his hand to the writing of fiction, so far without success. It is a good thing, he often says to her cheerfully, that he has other sources of income, though he has not yet told her what they are, and, aware of her own hidden life, it would never occur to her to inquire into his.

Marcus has many secrets.

He lives in a stone cottage on the edge of the moors, the vista from his haphazard Welsh-dressered kitchen encompassing heathered hills, wide skies, sheep, and at the same time a small, stone-walled garden full of holly trees and evergreens, small stone paths which meander between disordered lavender bushes and leaking clumps of thyme, the crushed leaves of which, when trodden on, bring back memories of winter stews and Provençal hillsides. Marcus and Hannah have been friends for eighteen months or so – she smiles, remembering how they met – but only recently have they also been lovers. He seems to be everything that Hannah wants, needs. Yet she suspects there are inscrutabilities in Marcus, just as there are in her. She suspects, for instance, that the apparently calm existence he lives is as much a front as her own, that behind the stability there is a wildness, a perilousness, which he can sometimes barely keep in check and which reveals itself in sudden unexplained angers, a brutal bark into the telephone, a redness of the eyes as though rage exploded behind them. Sometimes she wonders if he knows what he is getting, with her, and whether he suspects that she too might not be everything she seems.

A mechanical voice intones: 'Saturday, December 14th, twelve thirty-five a.m.' The machine whirrs, beeps.

She goes upstairs, parts the curtains, stares out into the night. The river shines greasily in the cold light of the street lamps, flat and potentially powerful. Someone once told her that when river waters rise like this, bodies float to the surface, the disintegrating corpses of people who disappeared earlier in the year, sad souls who drowned themselves from who knows what unregistered despairs.

Across the road, the park waits. She can only make out the branches of the nearest trees; when there is snow on the ground, even at midnight she can see right across to the other side where houses begin again. There are owls hooting, their long cries wreathing the darkness like streamers. Getting into bed, the mattress is firm beneath her body, the sheet she lies on matching the extravagant roses of the duvet cover and the curtains which shut out the dark. Polished furniture, the gleam of mirrors, porcelain bowls, scent bottles: they are small securities, but at the same time, the solidity of these things usually helps to reassure her that she has successfully managed to lay the ghosts of the past.

Tonight, she reflects that they make flimsy bulwarks.

She is restless. The evening's encounter – if such a one-sided recognition can be so described – has unsettled her. Her heart beats too rapidly, setting up vibrations in the mattress springs. She tells herself that were she to have approached the man, if she had perhaps spoken to him, she would have seen at once that he bore no resemblance to anybody she once knew.

Nonetheless, she wishes now that she had run back into the Festival Hall and confronted him. Instead, she has let her old ghosts rise again. She moves about the bed, remembering Anthony. There are, she thinks, compensations in living alone. This is one of them, this possession of an unshared bed, this being able to burrow into the comfort of pillows or mattress and not be brought up short by another's back, another's elbow. Which is not to say that she does not enjoy sharing a bed with Marcus – a bed and many other things, for Marcus is a surprisingly inventive lover.

Outside the window rain spatters with sudden viciousness against the glass and the wind knocks frenziedly, surging round the house with a howling roar, catching the house beneath the eaves and, momentarily, threatening to lift it bodily from the ground. Though she is not in the least ancraophobic, the sound is terrifying and she pulls the covers more tightly round herself. Then, realising she has forgotten the floods, she leaps from her bed and looks out between the curtains but cannot tell if the waters have risen since she got home. Edged with straw and twigs, the river sprawls at the end of the road, a jungle creature beautiful in repose, waiting to pounce.

The telephone rings. Nervous, she snatches it up. As before, Marcus asks, when she answers: 'Are you all right?'

'I'm fine,' she says, knowing that in the sense he means, she is not.

'You sound – different.'

'I'm not,' she says. 'I'm the same as always.' The trouble is, the same as always is not what he thinks it is.

'I just wanted to check that you got home safely.'

'Yes, as you see, I did.'

They talk for a while. 'I love you,' he says.

She does not give the right response. She does not say that she, in her turn, loves him. 'What the hell is love?' she says unfairly, harshly, disliking herself for her response to this enigmatic but needful man. She listens to the silence at the other end of the phone before putting down the receiver.

When it rings again, she does not answer. She remembers that summer in Italy, the long days of unbreathable heat, the violence in the air, the nights full of fireflies and the afternoons of explosive, prohibited love. She is reluctant to put out the light, knowing that she will wake in the early hours of the morning, mind still thumping with the images of blood among the trees, night insects calling, and the sickening shine of water on dead flesh, pale streams of blood, empty eyes, an agonised mouth.

As, indeed, she does.

When she wakes again, it is barely light enough for objects to achieve solidity within the gloom: the chest-of-drawers, her dressing-table, the bulk of an armchair. Peering out at the river, Hannah sees that during the night it has stealthily advanced. In her dressing-gown she invades the gale-blowing dawn day and heaves sandbags about, stacks them along the sill of the front door, wondering what good they would do were the water to reach her house. Very little, she suspects. Shivering, she runs upstairs and back into the warm burrow of her bed. It is too early for tea, or the Sunday papers, too late to attempt sleep again. She tries to recall the face she saw last night.

How can she find out who he is? Reason tells her she cannot. Reason points to the impossibility of finding one anonymous body in the vast churn of London. She has nothing to go on, no clues which could fix him as belonging to an identifiable group. Even his presence in the Festival Hall means nothing: he could have been meeting friends, just passing through. Yet the unreasonable desire to know him, to – yes – touch him, increases rather than diminishes as the grey day breaks and the wind moans across the swollen river.

She thinks of Anthony, her former husband. She thinks of dying. She does not wish to die in this dull town. She does not want to find herself on her death-bed regretting the cowardly impulses which kept her here, the tamped-down life she has deliberately chosen to lead. She knows only too well that there are richer lives where risks are taken and breath comes short, where blood is still red rather than the slow, grey stuff which she imagine fills her own veins. The world, she tells herself, is her oyster. Technically she is a wife abandoned, yet she feels much more like a wife set free. To have been abandoned implies loss and betrayal, angry voices and slammed doors. There were none of those in her abandoning. She can go anywhere, do anything she likes. She knows she will not.

Anthony is a large and genial man. He skims across the surface of life's sea, preferring not to notice the floating bodies, the protruding spars of wrecked ships, the arms of those sinking for the third time. Preferring not to hear the cries for help. Theirs was a safe marriage if by 'safe' Hannah means that they rubbed along comfortably enough, raised their children, entertained and holidayed together, occasionally shared a pleasant but unexciting sex-life. Looking back, she is not sure how much they mattered to each other. For her part, she fretted mildly when he had to fly abroad, worried if he did not arrive home at his usual time, planned treats for him, was marginally happier when he came through the front door. But she often felt that if one morning she dissolved and was swept away with the bath water, he would scarcely notice, or, if he did, would hardly mind.

Clearly he felt the same about her. She found his letter one evening, almost a year ago, left for her on the kitchen table, weighted with a pot of his favourite black cherry preserve. He had met Someone Else – the capitals were his, for Anthony has always been alive to the irony of a cliché – and really didn't think she would care that much if he went off with her, that in any case he felt their marriage meant little to either of them, and the children were grown now. I am, he added, rejuvenated by love, a Young Lochinvar again. He knew she would understand.

At the time, she felt that she did not. But although she envied him, she could not blame him. She was not surprised when he went. She had waited for this to happen, knowing that one day it would. The pain she felt at his departure was made all the worse because she could feel so little pain at learning of it.

Sometimes she lifts the lid of the piano downstairs, neglected now that Lucinda is so rarely home, and presses the keys, eyes closed, remembering windows leading on to gardens where roses blew, bright air full of bird song, green waves rolling in from distant horizons. The clichés of youth and promises, implicit bliss, which she has forfeited. She feels that she deserves what she has, and no more.

THE DIARY

. . . It seems so long since the Dr suggested I might start feeling better about myself if I tried to write it down. He was right: I do. But it's like lancing a boil: even though a lot of the poison has gone, there are still ugly things I have to squeeze out of my memory, still pus I've got to drain from the past if I'm going to be able to function properly.

I've lived like this for so long and it never seemed to matter. But now that I've met T . . . Everything's changed. I've got to get things sorted out.

Sometimes I literally want to die. Not from despair, simply because the effort of living seems too great. Waking in the morning, I find myself saying aloud: Take me home, *as though it were a mantra – but I* am *home, this* is *supposed to be home. What do I mean?*

Images come to me sometimes. Pain, for instance, heavy as water: I can feel it inside me, behind a kind of curtain of non-remembering.
    And blood.

Is it mine or someone else's?

. . . Woke from a dream I've had before. A nightmare, really. There is something frightening about the fact that however hard you try to sweep it clean, the brain doesn't want to get rid of the debris that's shut in there, but likes to take it out, sort through it like an old bag lady sifting her gleanings, put it back and bring it out again another time.

Why do I keep dreaming the same things? The Dr says it's my memory, trying to kick-start me into remembrance. I don't want to remember if it's this sort of shit.

I thought writing it all down would clear things up, but I was wrong. It was OK for a while, but all the old turmoil is starting up again. When I'm awake, I have that sense of seeing myself through a heat haze, shimmery and not quite real. Like a mirage.

In the dream, I'm running through these tunnels of green, like the toy I had when I was little, a long metal spiral covered in cloth, which you could stretch out into a tunnel, or fold flat. Funny thing is, I'm thinking about that fold-flat tunnel, even in the dream. Something is running behind me – or in front or alongside: it varies – but I never see it. A beast of some kind. It pants, deep, regular pants like a heart-beat, on and on, never faster, never slower. I can hear the sound of its footsteps thudding on the ground. Impossible to describe the terror of that unseen companion. It makes me think of the book I used to have as a child: Where the Wild Things Are ('The night Max wore his wolf suit and made mischief of one kind and another, his mother called him "Wild thing"—' I love that!), and though I've never seen it, I know this wild thing, this beast, with its slobbering mouth and pointy teeth and claws, will get me unless I run and run, keep running for the rest of my life. And all the time, I can hear screaming.

The beast with two backs.

Somebody said it once, years ago, can't remember who. I know what it means. But at the same time, it means something else, much more terrifying. What does a beast with two backs look like? It sounds almost apocalyptic. It pants. It shudders and groans. And screams. The screaming cuts through my head like a sword.

2

As the flood waters abated, so did Hannah's remembrance of the face of a familiar stranger which she had glimpsed behind the lighted windows of the Festival Hall, and her certainty. What else could it have been but imagination, exhaustion, *hope*? Christmas came and went in the usual hectic flurry of cards and presents, food and drink, friends and relations. In the New Year Adam went to Portugal with some university friends, while Lucinda and her boyfriend were travelling round Italy on a student rail-card. Hannah herself spent a few days with her lover. Although she had asked him, Marcus had not wished to spend Christmas with her, nor did he talk of where he had been. She thought he had family somewhere – a sister, grown children? He was thrifty with personal details.

She had not thought she would ever feel again the passions she had known in her youth. Marcus had rekindled in her both passion and desire so that they had often spent whole days in bed together, each intoxicated simply by the naked nearness of the other, the sensation of flesh on flesh, mouth on mouth. And more. Much more. Hannah recognised that she was lucky. Yet now, still unsettled by the emotions aroused by the incident on the South Bank, she found herself keeping him somewhat at arm's length, both in bed and out of it. His evident anger, although he laboured not to show it, added to her guilt.

As always, she found a measure of needed peace in the long horizons of the Dales. Standing in the garden of Marcus's stone-built cottage, she could see only the fells, green close at hand, fading to straw-coloured and then to hazy-grey and purple, where the heather began. On the third day of her visit, snow fell during the night and they woke to a white landscape dissected by dry-stone walls and the occasional rectangle of barn or shed. They stayed in bed for most of the morning while, outside, snowflakes dropped heavily past the window and the hills disappeared, blotted out by snow-weighted clouds. In Marcus's arms, Hannah could sometimes glimpse the fact that the past could no longer hurt her, that if recompense was to be paid, she had more than discharged her debt; implicit in his lovemaking was a promise of haven which she found hard to resist. Yet, away from him, the old doubts and hesitancies always returned.

Lying tangled together, secure in the warmth of the old-fashioned feather mattress, she wondered lazily about his wife. Without thinking, she said: 'What happened to your wife?' and realised too late how abrupt and insensitive the question must appear.

He tensed. She put a hand on his bare chest. 'Don't tell me if you don't want to.'

'It's all right,' he said. He rolled on to his back. 'It's a while ago now, I suppose.'

'It doesn't matter. I shouldn't have asked.'

'You have a right to know, if anyone does.' He breathed deeply, his ribs rising and falling under her hand. 'She was – kidnapped.'

'Kidnapped?' The word was brutal. For a moment, it had no meaning; after all, kidnap happened to strangers, to characters in crime thrillers, not to people one almost knew. 'But . . . how?' She lifted herself on to an elbow, clutching the covers round her. The little bedroom, startlingly cold, was filled with a harsh white light.

'She was taken away from me,' Marcus said, sounding desolated. 'Stolen away.'

'But that's—' Hannah said. She could tell he did not wish to talk about it. She pressed her hand harder against the soft skin of his belly, thinking she could feel his pain. 'Who took her? Was she—' She could not bring herself to ask if the missing wife had been returned, whether she had been murdered, where she might be now.

'I lost her, but the person who . . . took her didn't get away with it,' Marcus said, and it would be months before the obliquity of his reply occurred to her.

'It – it wasn't sexual, was it?'

He did not answer. Inside his body something fluttered, like a trapped bird trying to escape.

'I shouldn't have asked that,' Hannah said and added, before he could reply, 'Do you mind talking about it?'

'Yes,' he said. He sat up. 'Even after all this time. Even with you. I mind.' As he spoke, his fist pounded the coverlet over his knees; she could see the angry blood spread up his neck and into his face. 'What kind of a man would I be if I did not?'

'I'm sorry. I shouldn't have—'

'It's *thinking* about it that hurts.' He spoke through gritted teeth. 'Thinking about the bastard who—' With a visible effort, he calmed himself. He touched her breast, and sighed slowly. 'Yes, it was sexual.'

Hannah bit her lip as his hand moved down her stomach, came to rest between her thighs. Voluptuously, she gave herself up to him, and tried not to think of a woman's body (naked? clothed?) slack beside a road, spread thighs, blood, a face battered beyond recognition. Where had it happened? Marcus had lived in Rio de Janeiro and Rangoon: had it been there? Or was it a snatch off the streets, as the wife walked home from an evening class, from shopping, from some innocent daily activity?

18

Perhaps she'd been taken from her own home, in broad daylight, the neighbours busy with their own concerns, the children at school, no one around to see who took her or where they went. She asked no further questions, but now the picture of the vanished wife was added to her own images of violence and blood.

Walking hand in hand with Marcus along the snowy village street the next morning, a car screeched to a skidding stop behind them and for a moment she heard again the screams which she would never be able to forget, even if sometimes she was able to push them from the forefront of her mind. In the afternoon, filling a basket with logs from the stone barn with which to feed the fire, from the corner of her eye she caught a glimpse of something drifting, moving slowly on the surface of red-tinged water, and for a moment her heart pounded, her mouth went dry, before she turned her head and saw only a galvanised-iron water-tank beside the barn, where a leaf floated on reflections of the wintry setting sun. Carrying the logs back to the house, she dumped them beside the hearth and knew Marcus was watching her, though he said nothing.

On her last day, just before she left to go home, she went into his study. Computer screens glowed in the dark light of a winter morning. She loved this low-ceilinged, book-lined room with its stone window surrounds and double aspect across the dale. She stood by the window, staring out at the round hills.

'Hannah,' Marcus said, getting up from his work-table. He touched the back of her neck.

She did not want him to ask if she was all right. There was a pile of books beside one of the word-processors. 'What are these?' she said.

'They've just come out in the States,' he said. 'People send them for review. Take one if you want. Hannah—'

Without looking, she picked up the top one.

'Thanks.' She leaned forward and kissed him on the mouth. 'Darling,' she said. She smiled, in the hope of deflecting him from whatever else he intended to say.

He pulled back. 'Something's wrong, isn't it?'

She did not deny it. They were both too old for the games and subterfuges of youth. 'Yes.'

'Do you know what?'

'Not really.' Behind him, she could see her reflection in the glazed cupboard where he kept his guns.

'Can I help?'

She shook her head, leaned forward, touched his cheek. 'Thank you, but I think not.'

'If I can—'

'If you can, I'll ask,' she said. 'I promise.'

They walked into the hall and as he picked up her bag, she saw the muscles harden in his upper arms. She had felt them before, many times, as he held her close to his chest; for a man of his age he was surprisingly strong.

'Hannah—' he began, as though about to tell her something important. He broke off.

'Yes?'

'Ring me as soon as you get home,' he said abruptly, and she wondered, negotiating the little stone bridge across the beck and turning left towards the A1, what he had really been going to say.

It was early, the day still coming into fullness; although the roads were clear, there was a forecast of more snow to come. She listened to the soothing tones of the Radio 4 presenters as they catalogued the day's news items, and kept the car radio tuned as *Today* gave way to *Start the Week*. The curious camaraderie established between people who in the normal course of events would never have met always fascinated her; the ability to call total strangers by their first names seemed to be a premier requirement for appearance on such programmes. It was an ability which she knew she did not possess. Halfway home, she groped among the litter of cassettes she had put on the passenger seat and found the one she had played the evening of the concert at the Festival Hall. She pressed it into the player, rewound it, again heard Phil Collins pleading to be taken home. The song came to an end. The tape whirred a little. A few preliminary chords were struck. Over them, a voice whispered: 'Listen closely, Anna.'

Before she could wonder whose voice it was, or why it had spoken, the vocalist came in. She frowned, jabbing at the rewind button then replaying the tape.

There it was again: 'Listen closely, Anna.'

Not Hannah. Not her name. But one that she had been called over the years, either by people who did not listen carefully enough, or by people unfamiliar with the less used name.

'*Every move you make, I'll be watching you,*' the singer declared. '*Every vow you take, every claim you stake, every move you make, I'll be watching you.*' They were intended as words of obsession, of love. Given that three-word introduction, they became sinister and menacing. Pushing at the buttons, once again Hannah rewound the tape and then replayed it. Again the voice admonished her, anonymous, androgynous, impossible to decide whether it was male or female.

Ahead of her, a square blue P sign indicated that in a quarter of a mile, there would be room to pull off. Reaching it, she turned off the roadway and pulled up, putting on the hand-brake. Had she really heard that voice, had it really used her name? She rewound the tape again, replayed it, once more heard the voice telling her to listen closely, using her name. Involuntarily she looked into the driving mirror. No one had pulled in behind her.

'*Every move you make, I'll be watching you.*' What did it mean? She knew that it was a song from one of the groups her children liked: the Eurythmics? The Police? She picked up the tape and studied the writing on the label. *For Anna*, it said. She did not recognise the hand any more than she recognised the voice. How had this tape come to be in her car? Who had left it there, and why? Was it some joke of Adam's? Looking down at her hands, she saw that they were trembling. What was this all about? She knew she ought to play the rest of the cassette but instead, she pressed the button and pulled it out, replacing it with a Mozart clarinet concerto. She still had a way to go and needed to concentrate on driving.

By midday she was home, parking the car outside her house. Taking her bag from the back seat, she glanced around. *Every move you make, I'll be watching you*— The park opposite was empty, the trees motionless, reduced to their elemental patterns by lack of leaf. To her left, the river lay unrippled between its banks, smooth and opaque as a slab of toffee except where the ducks kicked up water as they chased each other. There was no one about. Could the tape have come from one of her neighbours? The only time she left the car open or unlocked was when she was heaving supermarket groceries from the boot into the house. Had one of them sneaked out of their own door and put this tape on the seat for her to find later? It was certainly possible. Equally, it was inconceivable that they should have done so. Most of them were known to her by sight; they exchanged smiles, even, occasionally, conversation. They were like herself: ordinary, unexceptional. And, like them, she did not indulge in unneighbourly behaviour. Her children did not set the adjoining house thumping with heavy metal music in the small hours; neither of them had motorbikes which they revved up loudly at unsuitable times; she herself did not entertain a constant succession of undesirable men. She glanced up at the windows on either side of her own house but no face at the window stared hostilely down.

Every move you make—

While she was taking her coat off, she pressed the winking button on the answering machine. Messages: from Adam, from friends, from a fellow-musician in London, from someone returning a call she had made days earlier. The machine clicked and whirred. Another voice. Light, happy. Lucinda, her daughter.

'Hi, Mum,' Lucinda said. 'We're back from Italy. Sorry to miss you. How're things going? Hope you enjoyed your dirty weekend up north. We had a *fabulous* time in Rome. Dropped in to see Susie, on the way back – looking much better than she did at Carlo's funeral, thank goodness. She sent loads of love – I'll tell you about it when we speak. We're going up north for the weekend: Tom said we could use his parents' cottage. Last chance before term starts – and the run-up to Finals. Oh my *Gaaahd*! I'll give you a ring on Monday evening. *Ciao*.'

Hannah stood for a moment, as the answering machine lumberingly composed itself into silence. Lucinda sounded so happy, so carefree. Was I ever like that? she wondered. Did I ever sound as she does?

She felt a sudden ache for her daughter. Despite the security which had been wrapped round Lucinda since birth, despite the fact that her generation of women was far more at ease with itself than previous ones, Lucinda was still heartbreakingly vulnerable, far more so than her brother. Men are so armoured, thought Hannah, so much less prey to their emotions than women.

'*We're going up north—*' Idly Hannah wondered when she was going to meet the current paragon. The longer she had to wait, the better, she reflected wryly, walking into the kitchen. The emotional expenditure involved in taking each of Lucinda's young men to her heart was exhausting. How many times had she not only made a tremendous effort to like some frightful man she could see was entirely wrong for her precious daughter, but also agreed that yes, he was really nice, yes, he was *super*, no, she wasn't just saying that, she really meant it, she had really *really* liked him, only to be greeted a month later, after a tentative enquiry about the well-being of Damian or Andrew or David, with cries of disgust and derision, nearly always followed by Lucinda wondering whether it would be all right if she brought this really nice chap home next weekend?

The young always think they can see the road plain ahead, just as it stretches clear behind. What they cannot see or plan for, are the unexpected obstacles along the way. That summer, that catalyst summer, they had all believed they knew where they were going. Lucas, for instance. Susie, Hannah and Faustino, Tristan. They came together unware of the road-blocks already being placed in their paths.

The house settled comfortably around her as she put down the accumulation of letters which had been waiting for her, set water to boil, found coffee beans and ground them, took butter from the fridge, sliced a crust from the wholemeal loaf she had brought with her from Marcus's local baker. Although these were the calming routines of every day, for once they failed to produce their usual illusion of serenity. The tape in her car was, to say the least, unsettling. And at some point she was going to have to give it thought.

Sitting down, she sorted through the mail. There were a few bills, which she put to one side, some junk mail which she threw away. Other envelopes were from friends clearly less organised than she herself was who had been late in sending Christmas greetings.

Later that evening, with the curtains drawn against the storm outside, she picked up the book she had borrowed from Marcus.

The book smells of carpet cleaner and has that faintly alien look which characterises publications printed in countries other than one's own. It crouches on the table in front of Hannah like some new life-form, waiting to step into and take over her life. Stylised trees hang over a green pool, their branches stabbing upwards into the plain black letters of the title. *Hurled by Dreams*, she reads, by Max Marsden.

For a moment Hannah feels light-headed, as though the contents of her skull have suddenly been sucked out by some powerful force. She blinks, aware of the rapid beating of her heart, the sweat in her palms as she turns the book over to read the hype on the back:

This poignant powerful novel of despair and revenge . . . [she reads]
. . . a romantic novel which nonetheless has something serious to say.
A tragic love affair . . .
. . . obsession . . . betrayal . . . revenge.

The words pass like ticker-tape through her eyes and into her brain. She flicks through the pages, stopping to read here and there, alarm growing inside her as certain lines, certain scenes, bring back brutal memories. Words form sentences, paragraphs make pictures:

Anna ran down between the trees. Pale afternoon shadows shifted across the walls of the house. From the balcony, Ivo watched her flight, laughing. He was naked, peeled, like a tree stripped of its bark.
Anna tore at her clothes, dropped them, dived into the pool. Silently, Ivo came down from his room and went after her. He stood among the bamboo stems, smiling as she plunged again and again beneath the dark water, trying to wash his traces from her skin. She touched the face of the faun at the edge of the pool.
'Ivo,' she said, and there was no love in her voice, only resignation.
Watching her, Ivo no longer smiled. His face, patterned by leaf-shapes, wore a cruel melancholy; like the faun, he looked beyond this time, this place, this woman. After a while, he turned and went away, back to the house. Anna had not seen him arrive. She did not see him go.

Reading this, a chill spreads from some point near Hannah's chest until she is shuddering with cold. Who is Max Marsden? There is no photograph of him. The name is unfamiliar to her and the blurb on the inside back cover merely informs her that this is the author's first book and that he is currently resident in the United States. But Hannah does not wish to read any more.

She places both hands flat on the table and closes her eyes, deliberately relaxing the muscles of her shoulders, aware of the tension in them. She is not willing to plunge into the dark waters of the past; she is not sure that she is even able to make such a deliberate leap. For years she has buried her yesterdays deep: is she now capable of exhumation?

She tells herself it is time she sloughed off the past, that what happened was a long time ago, that, in any case, despite her guilt, there was probably very little she could have done to halt the march of events. That is what Marcus would say, were she to confide in him. And he might even be right. But Marcus is something of a scientist. He deals with the tangible, the factual. Objective analysis and logical deduction are the tools by which he proceeds from one certainty to the next. Where there is ambiguity, Marcus would seek to dispel it. Where there is hypothesis, Marcus works to make it sure or else to eliminate it. There is little place in Marcus's world for ghosts. No place for fear.

Hannah picked up the book again and, opening it at random, began tentatively to read. She could feel herself holding back, her mind not ready to be embraced by it, frightened of what she would find. The page in front of her described in careful detail an evening picnic on the shores of a lake. Although she was perfectly well aware than any lakeside picnic was going to be very similar to any other, there were certain particulars about this one which Hannah recognised, sentences she knew had been spoken, impressions she herself had registered. But how was it possible? She found herself blushing, her body pricking with embarrassed sweat. Had this Max Marsden also been present at the picnic? If not, how could he have known about any of this? Had she actually known him under a different name? Only a handful of other people could have had any knowledge of some of the things which the book described; only one knew all of them, and she knew, with terrible certainty, that he could not have written this book. So who had? And how could he be so intimately acquainted with what was her own story and no one else's? Except Lucas's. And Lucas was dead.

The question was deeply disturbing to Hannah.

On impulse, she called International Inquiries and found out the telephone number of the American publisher of *Hurled by Dreams*. Before dialling she paused, uneasy, feeling that once she had done so she would have embarked on an enterprise from which there could be no turning back. But she had no other choice. Max Marsden – whoever he was – had told a story which was not his alone to tell, and the events he described did not belong only to him.

She pressed down the buttons and, with an ease which astonished her, found herself talking almost immediately to the switchboard of the book's New York publishers.

'I'd like to speak to the editor in charge of *Hurled by Dreams*,' she said firmly.

'One moment, please.'

Another voice came on the line, hard-edged, heavy with overwork. 'Shauna Pollack. Yes?'

'My name is Hannah Carrington,' Hannah said. 'I'm calling from England.'

'Oh, right.' She could hear Ms Pollack's interest in her unknown caller shift gear from uninterested to marginally intrigued.

'I've just read a copy of Max Marsden's book,' said Hannah.

'Great, isn't it? We're really pleased with the way it's going.' Clearly Shauna took her for a critic, an organiser of literary festivals, someone in the book trade, even, perhaps, someone on a prize-awarding committee. 'If you're interested in any kind of a—'

'No,' Hannah said. 'I'm just a . . . person.' It sounded odd. Is that what I am? she thought. A person?

Ms Pollack's voice changed again, became edged with bad temper. 'What exactly do you want to know?'

'The thing is, I was there.'

'There?'

'Where the book is set.'

'Is that right.'

'And the stuff which happened – the plot – really did – I mean, I was involved.'

'This is a work of fiction, Mrs – uh – Faringdon.'

'Carrington.'

'Whatever. A very fine work, but not one which seeks to present the reader with recorded fact.' Ms Pollack was wary now, and impatient. Some nut wanting to exchange reminiscences, Hannah could feel her thinking. Some loony convinced she too could write a best-seller.

'In fact the story as Marsden tells it almost exactly mirrors my own experience,' said Hannah. 'Too much so, I would have thought, for it to be entirely coincidental.'

A pause. 'What exactly did you want to know, Ms – uh—?'

'I wondered where I could get hold of Mr Marsden. I'd love to talk to him.'

'I'm afraid we cannot divulge details of a personal nature about our authors,' the unsympathetic voice said, slipping easily into mechanical refusal mode. Hannah could see Shauna Pollack raising her eyes to heaven, doodling on a pad in front of her, looking down at her schedule and wishing this head-case calling from England would stop wasting her valuable time.

'Can you suggest any way I might get in touch with him?' Hannah asked.

'If you write a letter care of us, I can promise you it would be forwarded,' Pollack said.

'But that could take ages.'

'Right.' Pollack's attention was audibly slipping.

'Is Marsden his real name?' Hannah said quickly.

'I'm afraid we cannot divul—'

25

'Surely you can tell me if he is writing under a pseudonym,' said Hannah.

'I'm afraid we can't give—'

'Could you just tell me where he lives?'

'Ms Carrington, it is company policy not to give—'

'—out personal information on your authors, yes, I understand that. But I do assure you I'm not going to try and file a paternity suit on him,' Hannah said lightly. 'Nor am I a psychopath with a desire to bump him off.'

'Really?'

Too late she remembered that irony is not an American habit. 'It just seems to me,' she said, 'that he must be someone I once knew and I really would like just—'

'Send us a letter, Ms Carrington. I promise it'll be sent on.'

There was a click and Pollack disconnected.

Having once worked briefly in the publicity department of a publisher's office, Hannah had not really expected much more help than she had been given. But if the publishers would not tell her, was there any other way of finding out what she wanted to know? She thought of Marcus. He must have connections still, contacts in the newspaper world, access via his computers to – she was vague about it – cuttings libraries, bulletin boards, information services. Someone, surely, must know. She dialled his number, but there was no reply.

At six o'clock, she poured herself a drink, dry martini and gin, and drank it quickly. Normally she liked to savour it, but tonight she was impatient for the quick kick.

The book waited for her. The black branches on its cover leaped upwards. In the sky between the branches was a sickle moon, even though there had been no moon that night. Though it was no more than a drawing of an imaginary place, for Hannah it held a terrible reality.

She poured another drink, stronger than the first. A sense of doom hung over her, a sense of events rushing to a conclusion and herself caught up in the flow, unable to stop them. Turning on the television, she watched a mindless game-show involving minor celebrities and lettered squares, something on gardens in Scotland, something else about children in Belfast. The news came and went, comedy succeeded earnestness: she watched it all and took none of it in, the coloured images passing through her brain without in any way impinging on it.

What she really needed, above all, was to talk to Susie again. She wanted to say: 'Susie, was I really to blame? And if so, when can I begin to forgive myself?' Something like that she should have, would have said.

But it was impossible. Had been, ever since the events of that final summer's night in Italy. As though it were yesterday, and not twenty-five years before, Hannah remembered that current of abuse and hysteria, the hatred, the ugly words, and beneath them, like a terrible undertow, the real anguish.

Since then, though the two of them had patched up their friendship, they had spoken of that night only briefly and unsatisfactorily a couple of times, and not at all since Susie's marriage to Carlo. If she had other questions, Susie did not ask them; in any case Hannah herself had no answers. Why had she behaved as she did? What had happened to the Hannah she had, until then, been? For nearly a quarter of a century the facts had remained unsifted inside her, solid, accusatory, growing ever larger because she had tried so hard to ignore them. At first, they had simply been too terrible to discuss; later they had become a stone, a rock, a boulder, far too heavy to remove, something she had to skirt around in order to survive.

She parted the curtains of the sitting-room and looked out into the night. What wild beast lurked out there? What human agent spied on her?

Every step you take.

Every move you make . . .

At the end of the street the river moved, fingers of muddy water stretching into the road, and above it the bare willow branches shook. She was overpowered by the feeling that, despite all her efforts, the peaceful refuge she had made for herself had changed, had suddenly become an inimical jungle full of thorns, where creatures with sharpened teeth and razor claws waited for a false step, a straying from the path.

THE DIARY

. . . This diary: it's getting away from me, I can't hold on to it. I write about places, for instance, but they are not topographical locations, somewhere you could pinpoint on a map, towns with a recognisable geography, buildings and streets with names and numbers, they come out of my head, they bear no relation to anything I thought I knew.

People appear on the pages and I don't know who they are. Is this memory creeping up on me? Do I 'remember' the things I write about, or simply create them? Are they real *– whatever that means?*

I wish I knew.

I 'remember' details, mostly: the wall of a white house. Stone pots in a line. High tunnels. Water. A wide staircase. A house which was a toy yet not a toy. I remember sun on particular grass. Butterflies.

And screaming. And blood.

. . . Yesterday, I was stuck in the express line behind some old bitch with about twenty items in her basket. I nearly exploded. 'Look, lady,' I said, using my best hoodlum-from-hell snarl. 'Can't you read? It says five items only.' I was shaking. I wanted to grab her horrible fat arms and squeeze them until blood came out through the pores. 'Bitch,' I said.

Luckily the other people in line were so anxious to get through the checkout that they didn't see how close I was to complete meltdown. Or maybe they just chose to ignore it.

I know anger's supposed to be good for me. Anger drives out fear, all that crap the Dr keeps giving me. He doesn't realise just how angry I get: it's like a bar of slippery soap inside me, impossible to grab hold of, until it comes bursting out of my mouth in words. Terrible words, and sometimes worse things than words.

I've tried to tell him about this but he always seems more interested in the bits I can't remember, and at the moment, I feel I've done enough remembering. I'm tired of remembering.

Control. It's all about control.

Most of the time, I'm good at control. Most people see me as calm, well-balanced. Nobody looks beneath the surface I present to them. Sometimes I think I could get away with murder – if I wanted to.

. . . It's three o'clock in the morning, but I wanted to write this down while I remembered. I woke up, and was lying there in the dark, wondering what could have woken me, when a name came into my head, just popped in.

Anna.

Where did it come from? Who is Anna?

The name rattles round inside my skull like a pebble in an empty can. Anna. Anna. Saying it aloud, I almost see the past, almost hear. Memories stir, like some monster heaving itself out of the mud.

In spite of this, the name doesn't mean anything. Yet I'm convinced it's bound up with the stuff I can't remember, whatever it is that I'm blocking. Auto-amnesia, the Dr calls it. Says, when I want to remember, I will. When I'm ready.

I say, Hey, listen, Doc, I'm ready, OK? but he just smiles and shakes his head. God, if he only knew how much that pisses me off, that know-all shit he hands out all the time.

Anna's not much to go on. Must be millions of them in the world. I wonder if M would remember. But I don't want to bring it up: I remember what it was like, all those years ago, when we first came here. All the weeping and stuff. There's always F, I suppose. I could ask him what he thinks.

3

Hannah loved the pretty Edwardian house, four-square and solid under sloping eaves, its paintwork a smart moss-green, its dark front-door shiny with polished brass. Everything about it spoke of a more peaceful era, a time of certainty, of fulfilled expectation. She knew that the golden summer of those years between the death of Queen Victoria and the onset of the Great War was no more than a myth; she had read too much about the period not to be aware that there was no more social unrest, inequality, lack of justice, adultery, war-mongering and crime today than there was then, for human nature does not change very much. None the less . . .

She looked inside the drawing-room of the Gentleman's Residence, imagining someone in trailing white passing round sandwiches, imagining croquet on the lawn, late afternoon sunshine, neat housemaids bearing silver jugs of hot water upstairs to richly furnished bedrooms.

The owner – Major Perowne – was ill at the moment, suffering the effects of a disease picked up in India while he served out there with his regiment. She touched the elaborate curlicues of the silk-covered eiderdown on his bed. Beside it she placed a pedestal table whose surface was an inlaid chess board. She set up a game, moving the ivory pieces about the highly-polished surface. White had taken Red's Queen, she decided. Red had just captured one of White's Rooks, and thereby put one of his Knights in jeopardy. Carefully, she placed the pieces: the set had taken one of her craftsmen almost six months to produce.

Did Major Perowne play chess? Or would it be better to put the chess table downstairs again? Yesterday a girl had come into the shop and displayed a range of miniature objects, including a set of false teeth. Put those in a glass tumbler beside the bed, along with a pipe and tobacco pouch, a tiny fob watch, a Bible . . . but if old Major Perowne was a Bible reader, it would alter the whole feel of the house.

She sat back on her haunches, considering the matter. The Major had just hobbled to the bathroom with the help of his nurse, a saucy piece who although she had only been in the family's employ for two days, was already making eyes at Major Perowne's younger son Harold. Definitely no Bibles, Hannah decided – unless she brought in a maiden aunt who occupied one of the spare bedrooms. An aunt who had A Past, perhaps. An aunt who was Not What She Seemed.

The Major's brother's wife? Or his own or his deceased wife's sister?

She put a dog in a basket on the floor of the Major's bedroom, then put the dog on the eiderdown. Major Perowne was definitely a doggy man; the sort who in his youth strode across tussocked downland with a yellow Labrador at his heels, or sat by log fires on winter afternoons with a spaniel flopped across his brogues.

The decision to buy the shop had been serendipitous. No other word for it, the legacy from some hardly-known aunt of her mother's coming just after Anthony's departure. Seeing the For Sale sign, she had gone in, and before she could stop to think or to worry, had agreed to buy.

It had been called Miss Muffet's Miniatures, the name spelt out in pink letters on a white ground and enwreathed with tiny blue and pink cornflowers. Inside it was crowded with doll's houses, some painted and wall-papered, ready for occupancy, others still unvarnished and empty. The architectural range was eclectic, everything from Queen Anne to early 1950s, taking in hat shops, florists, butchers and thatched country cottages along the way. Seeing it all for the first time, Hannah had felt a wave of something close to happiness.

I'll be the boss, here, she had thought then. For the first time since that summer, I'll be in charge.

'I'd be deceiving you if I let you think you could make much of a living from it,' the owner had said dourly.

She was an angular woman, very tall and thin, with hair parted in the middle and dragged fiercely back across a narrow skull. Her large dark eyes were set in bony sockets and burned with the repressed fire of a Victorian spinster about to abandon her clergyman brother and throw in her lot with a desert sheikh. Taking out her cheque book in order to leave a deposit, Hannah had thought to herself that if this was Ms Muffet in person, it would take a hell of a big spider to frighten *her* away.

'I'm prepared to take that risk,' Hannah said, she who never took risks if she could help it; she had glanced round the shop with a feeling of proprietorial pride. She had often wondered since whether she would have had the courage to take it if Anthony had still been around. Going against Anthony's wishes had always been difficult, and she had long ago learned that life was only bearable if, at every point where there was a question of wish or choice, one of them gave way. That one was always herself.

'Poor you,' her friends had said, when she told them that Anthony had gone. 'You poor poor thing. What are you going to do? How are you going to manage?' And she had been unable to tell them that her main feeling at his defection was one of deep relief. No longer did she have to have the second bath when the water was never quite hot enough, holiday in Dorset when she longed to go to France, eat beef when she preferred chicken, sit with her back to the room when they went to restaurants, let Anthony drive when she knew she was a better driver than he would ever be.

No longer need she blame herself for marrying him.

She did not tell them these things because they would not have believed her. Anthony was amazingly handsome, and that seemed to equate in most people's minds with being a good husband and a loving father.

Even less would they have believed her relief at no longer having to have sex with him. Repressed. It was Anthony's favourite adjective for her, usually flung after sex. It was not that she refused to do anything he wanted her to: it was simply that she had never had an orgasm with him, and however hard she tried to fake it, he always knew.

'Frigid,' he would say. 'Bloody repressed. Don't blame me, for God's sake, I've spent hours trying to arouse you.'

And seeing this as part of the price she paid, she had never pointed out that merely knowing he regarded lovemaking as some kind of chore to be got through made orgasm impossible.

Besides, she had probably used up her ration of ecstasy.

'Coffee's ready,' Zoe, her assistant, called from the tiny kitchen, and Hannah squeezed towards the back of the shop past a display cabinet containing tiny objects made of copper and brass: door handles, fire-tongs, coal scuttles, jelly moulds.

Zoe Griffin had been helping in the shop three days a week for the past couple of months. In her late twenties, with a degree in business studies, she had not hesitated to tell Hannah that she only wanted part-time work while she looked around for a job commensurate with her qualifications.

'I don't really think I need anyone, thank you,' Hannah had said, amused by the girl's forthrightness.

'You do. I've been studying this place for a while,' Zoe had said frankly. 'You don't need anyone full-time but you could certainly use a bit of extra help. So why not me?'

'For that matter, *why* you?'

'Because I'm efficient. I'm suitable. I *adore* doll's houses. And it suits me, for the moment, because of my child, to work part-time.'

'I can't pay very much,' Hannah had said doubtfully.

'That's OK.'

Looking at her, Hannah had seen someone who, while not in the least resembling Lucinda, none the less reminded her of her daughter. A vulnerability beneath the businesslike exterior. The sense of a person who had not yet found the road she wished to tread. And there was something else, a wildness which Hannah sensed – and since then, had occasionally glimpsed – which spoke of someone still at odds with themselves.

'All right,' she had said. 'A month's trial period, a month's notice on either side. All right?'

'Cool,' said Zoe. Her urchin air was increased by the faint American accent she occasionally assumed, the Hollywood colloquialisms she sometimes came out with.

Now, she glanced up when Hannah came through the curtain and handed her a mug. 'We've had heaps of orders in the post this morning,' she said. 'And three left on the answering machine.'

'What does "heaps" mean?'

'At least eight,' Zoe said happily. 'And one of them wants that chess table.'

'I've just set it up beside Major Perowne's bed,' Hannah said. 'I'll be sorry to let it go.'

'I don't think the old boy's up to chess any more,' Zoe said. She shook her head sadly. 'Brain's going. He may have been chess champion of Sambalphur District back in 1934, but Ludo's more his speed these days.'

Hannah laughed delightedly. One of the things she enjoyed about Zoe was the fact that she liked embroidering the backgrounds of the various inhabitants of the miniature houses as much as Hannah herself.

Anthony had scoffed when she told him she was now a business-woman; he predicted bankruptcy, citing all the times she had found herself overdrawn at the bank, all the bad buys, all the extravagances – frowning in that special worried way of his. But so far she had proven him wrong. Calling the shop by her maiden name had somehow set the seal on her independence, as though Mrs Hannah Barlow no longer existed. Carringtons, the name painted in brown on cream, had done amazingly well, tapping into an obvious need, so much so that she was considering buying the shop next door when its lease next came up, and turning it into a tea shop. Her customers always lingered, always gratefully accepted a cup of instant coffee from the battered kettle behind the curtain. Why not cash in on that? She saw cakes with proper names on stands: Chelsea buns, Eccles cakes, Sally Lunns. Nursery teas, cheerful girls behind teapots, a sense of vanished safety.

A big old-fashioned roll-top desk had come with the shop, part of the fixtures and fittings. It stood squeezed into the space between kitchen and showroom, and she sat down on a chair, swivelling round to smile at Zoe.

'Anything else in the mail?' she said.

'Pretty straightforward stuff, really,' Zoe said. 'We'll have to put in an order for more of those upmarket kitchen dressers in stripped pine: we're almost out of stock.'

Hannah made a note. 'Any word from Mr Winter on when he can produce another chess table?'

'I rang him as soon as I opened the letter from the woman who wants to buy,' Zoe said, and not for the first time Hannah reflected that, if she herself were suddenly to disappear, Zoe would probably be perfectly capable of carrying on the business without her.

'And?'

'He said he's almost finished another one, and he's also been working on a backgammon set,' said Zoe. 'Can you imagine? Walnut and ebony for the board, and matching pieces? Doesn't it sound wonderful?'

'Did you tell him to send one so we can see it?'

'As a matter of fact, I told him we'd buy as many as he could produce. We already know the quality of his work, and it seemed a pity to waste time.'

'Well done.'

To Hannah's left stood a row of glass-fronted cabinets containing pygmy pieces of furniture of every possible kind, from rush-bottomed kitchen chairs to drawing-room sofas. Displayed among them was minute bric-à-brac: Crown Derby dishes and hand-painted Japanese screens, stuffed birds under glass domes, cross-stitch samplers, diminutive silver candelabra, walking sticks. An entire world of Lilliputian consumer durables, mirroring the larger one within which it existed, but without the chaos. Doll's-house washing-machines never went wrong, the gutters did not clog up with rotting leaves, the teapots did not leave ugly stains on the tables, the occupants did not quarrel and throw things at each other.

People weren't murdered.

She remembered a museum she had visited with Anthony. A rainy afternoon up north, the children with Anthony's mother. For once he had been in a good mood, ready to indulge her desire to see the small collection of antique doll's houses on the upper floors. In one, there had been evidence of disturbance; in the dining-room a butler lay prone on the floor surrounded by tiny glasses and bottles of wine.

'Drunk again,' Anthony had said lugubriously and the two of them had laughed so hard they had been forced to leave.

'It was the beatific expression on his face,' gasped Hannah in the car park, eyes streaming.

'Obviously been at the port,' said Anthony, his voice accusatory. He had taken her hand. So rare. Hannah forced the memory from her mind.

Two middle-aged women came into the shop and began sorting through a box of wallpapers printed with patterns that had been scaled down to suit shoebox-sized rooms. Before Hannah could move, Zoe had hurried out to see if they needed help.

Hannah turned to the already opened letters. More than fifty per cent of the business was with foreigners, Germans and Americans mainly, with some high-spending customers in the Gulf states. For the most part the shop was not selling toys; although she carried a cheap range of do-it-yourself houses and the furniture to go with them, most of her stock was not intended for children to play with. The Heirlooms of the Future, she put in her brochure.

Zoe had steered the two customers towards a rack of curtain fittings: wooden poles with turned ends, brass rods, tie-backs. The women were exclaiming.

One said: 'I didn't even know the shop was here.'

'We're fairly new,' Zoe said smoothly. 'As a matter of fact, we're planning an open house party later in the spring, to kind of put ourselves on the local map.'

'That sounds fun,' one of the women said.

'Why don't you give us your addresses and we can contact you nearer the time?'

'I've got a couple of friends who'd really be interested,' said the other woman. 'I'll give you their names too, shall I?'

'Terrific,' said Zoe.

The two women eventually left, clutching bags containing three times as many purchases as they had intended to make. 'I never realised what a very narrow dividing line there is between the con-artist and the saleswoman,' Hannah said admiringly.

Zoe wrinkled her brow. 'How do you mean?'

'If you started selling fraudulent time-share schemes or flogging shares in non-existent copper mines, you'd make a fortune. You're very convincing.'

'I prefer things that are real.' Zoe sounded prim.

'And you think doll's houses are?'

'They do actually exist—' began Zoe.

'Yes, but they're a dream-world,' Hannah said. 'Most of our customers are women, and dissastisfied in some way with their lives, trying to recapture the safety of the nursery. Otherwise, they wouldn't have started collecting in the first place.'

'Some of them are men.'

'Husbands pandering to their wives' hobby. The point about these houses is that they provide the women who furnish them with control.'

'Control?'

'Yes.' Aware that Zoe was staring at her, Hannah could feel her neck going red. 'You might not have any control over your life or your environment, but when it's a miniature house, you suddenly become God.'

'Maybe that's why I like working here,' Zoe said.

'I know it's why I do. After the way my life's gone—'

'Your divorce?' Zoe said sympathetically.

'Mmm.' In the few weeks she had known Zoe, Hannah had never before spoken so intimately about herself, though she often talked about Adam and Lucinda, answering Zoe's many eager questions about the two: their interests, their holidays, their ambitions, their likes and dislikes. 'Trouble

40

is, I sometimes worry that all this—' she gestured at the shop and its contents, 'is a denial of life, rather than a celebration of it. A form of escape.'

'What's wrong with that? If your own reality is pretty awful, why shouldn't you escape?'

'Is that why you came in here to ask for a job? As an escape?'

'In a way,' Zoe said. She did not meet Hannah's enquiring gaze. 'Did you have a doll's house when you were little?'

'Heavens no. My parents didn't believe in toys. I was a university student before I ever came across a real doll's house.' The enchantment of that well-stocked miniature world, the order it had contained . . . 'How about you?'

'I had one for a while. It was almost as big as I was. I loved playing with it.'

'What happened to it?'

Zoe shrugged. 'We moved.'

'The one I remember wasn't a doll's house exactly, it was a miniature of the owners' house, a replica complete with kitchen and plants and the same pattern curtains, all exactly the same as their own.'

'Where was that?'

'In Italy, as a matter of fact. In a place where I once spent a summer.'

Zoe nodded, her wide-eyed gaze fixed on Hannah.

'This one I'm talking about had everything duplicated, right down to the stone urns on the terrace, and the furniture in the bedrooms.'

'Yeah,' Zoe said again. There was an impatient look to her and Hannah said quickly:

'Sorry. Am I going on?'

'Course not. I just wondered what you were telling me this for.'

'I was just thinking, the other night, do you think we could start a service, using our own craftspeople, making replica houses? People really love their homes: it would be like a souvenir, especially if they had to move.'

'Be kind of expensive, wouldn't it?'

'For people who are seriously into doll's houses, expense is usually no object.'

'It might work.' Zoe considered the proposition. 'Yeah, it might work very well indeed. We'd need breakdowns on the time and the cost involved. You can't have a range – it's got to be precise and in scale, if it's going to take off. But—' She stared ahead, childish hands clasped to her chest. 'Think of it: wedding presents, for instance, for the bride to take with her to her new home. Or wedding anniversaries. You'd have to make sure it didn't all take too long to produce because otherwise you might find it wasn't cost-effective, or that the profit margin didn't justify the effort. But if we could crack that, yeah, I think it could be a great idea.'

'Thank you,' Hannah said humbly.

'Maybe we could start with your house,' Zoe said. 'I mean, maybe as a present for Lucinda next year.'

'Next year?'

'She leaves university, doesn't she?'

'Yes. Yes, she does.' Hannah smiled a little crookedly. 'Clever of you to remember.'

'I remember everything,' Zoe said.

At three twenty Zoe left, grabbing at her belongings and stuffing them into a brightly-coloured rucksack, exclaiming over her lateness, the shopping she still had to fit in before she picked up her son – Orlando, Hannah recalled – from school, bemoaning the lack of time to do anything these days. At the door, she turned. 'See you tomorrow,' she said.

'Of course.'

'Everything all right, Hannah?'

'Why do you ask?'

'It's just that since Christmas, you've been a little bit – well, withdrawn, I suppose. Disturbed, even.' Zoe tugged at the floppy beret of patchwork squares which she had pulled down over her auburn curls.

'Disturbed? What on earth do you mean?' Hannah looked down at her desk to hide her expression.

'Jumpy.'

'Am I?'

'Getting – well, upset about tiny things. You know.'

'I'm sorry. I—'

'No need to apologise. I'm just worried about you, that's all.'

'Are you really?' One of the squares of Zoe's beret was cream with tiny green leaves all over it. It reminded Hannah of something . . . something she could not remember but thought she probably did not want to. She stared at it. Leaves, water—

'Yes, Anna. Believe it or not, I am.' Zoe, about to reach forward and put a hand on Hannah's arm, drew back.

'What did you call me?'

Zoe stared at her. 'Hannah. That's your name, isn't it?' She frowned. 'Are you OK?'

Hannah rubbed a hand across her forehead. 'Sorry. I must admit I'm a bit frazzled.'

'Is Lucinda coming home soon? Or Adam?' Zoe said. 'Or your . . . boyfriend up north – couldn't he come down and look after you for a bit? Perhaps that's what you need.'

'It's simply that I haven't been sleeping very well recently. And I've been getting these awful headaches.' Hannah smiled up at her assistant. 'I expect that's it. Headaches.'

Dreams. That was what it was. Dreams of the past. Dreams of things which were better forgotten. Of things she thought she had forgotten. Around her the little houses sat quiet, some propped open to display parquet flooring, mahogany banister rails, marble fireplaces, others shut up, windowless and empty. Even if they were the stuff of which escapist dreams were made, they none the less provided satisfactory proof that she had achieved something; it was all she required.

Or had been, until now.

Zoe had been right. She was disturbed. Had been ever since she'd seen him out there, a couple of weeks ago. He had been standing across the road, staring at the shop from the shelter of a doorway. At first, she had not believed it was him. It couldn't be him, of course. She knew that. But if it wasn't him, it had to be his twin. Or his doppelgänger. But you only found those in unconvincing thrillers: doppelgängers. It had been after dark, the lights on in the shop, turning the front window into a sheet of black mirror. She found herself irrationally perturbed by the way her own image had been superimposed on his reality. She had seemed transparent, insubstantial, looking at him through herself, as though she did not exist, as though she were made of water or air and only he had any solidity.

There had been people in the shop, buying things, asking questions. By the time they had gone, so had he.

If he'd ever been there in the first place.

She ran a finger across a roof beam and was reassured. This was solid, this was real. Except that, of course, it was not, being no more than an illusion of a home, a pretence. No emotion would ever crowd these perfect rooms; no passion inform these hand-embroidered pillowcases and carved four-poster beds.

Which might well be why she found some peace here.

Unusually, Zoe had left the desk in a mess. Straightening up the papers lying on the leather top, before pulling down the old-fashioned roll-top and locking it for the night, Hannah saw a book lying face down among the papers.

Branches. A blood-tinged pool. A purple sky above.

How could it possibly have got here?

Marcus had said it was not yet published in England, so where did Zoe get a copy from? Her own copy she had hidden at the back of a cupboard in Adam's room. Heart pounding, Hannah now paged through the book. Scenes leaped out at her. Scenes she knew intimately, people she recognised, even though the names were different:

'*Did you know there's a mole on the back of your right thigh?*' he murmured.

Lying on her stomach, Anna leaned towards him. 'I've never in my whole life even thought about the back of my right thigh, let alone looked at it.'

'Heart-shaped,' said Ivo.

'The mole?'

'Your beautiful bottom.' He put his hands on either side of her waist and straddled her. His toy, his plaything. His unwitting destroyer. As dangerous and unsuspected as a bomb in a shopping basket. He bent his head and licked the perspiration below the line of her buttocks. 'A perfect heart.' He bit at the mole, teeth closing painfully so that she struggled to get away. He held her against him, his erection leaping, its shadow lying across her back like a scar, like a knife. No premonition marred the gliding moment; the sheets gave back only the scent of their own sweat, not of the grave, as sun danced in through the half-open shutters.

'Let me go,' Anna said, half-fearful, half-anticipatory. 'Ivo, don't.' But already her hips were lifting to meet him . . .

How was it possible? The scene jumped into her mind, complete with sounds – the tiny tap of some bird pecking at the lichened terrace, the pipes gurgling as a tap turned on somewhere in the house – and smells, the heat lying on her skin like butter, the feel of his hand on her hip, his dead hand—

Nausea rose in her throat and holding her hand over her mouth, she pushed into the tiny lavatory which lay through an outer door. For a long time she half-sat, half-lay on the cold floor, gasping over the bowl. It was freezing in there, the place only a concession to the Health and Safety officers, a former outdoor loo without heating, damp causing the paint to peel off, making ugly tide marks of crumbling plaster just above the skirting board.

There were two choices, she reflected later, cupping her hand under the cold water tap at the little hand-basin and rinsing out her mouth. She could ignore it. She'd done that successfully for all these years: no reason why she shouldn't go on doing so.

Or she could investigate. Contact some of these people whose real names she knew. But why bother? What did it matter, so long after?

But it did, it did.

It would always matter, until expiation had been done.

There had to be a connection between this book and the appearance of the man from the Festival Hall who had appeared across the road the other evening. She should have ignored the customers, should have dashed out into the street and confronted him. A thought struck her. Was it him who had put the tape in her car?

The book, the man, the tape, all within a week when – except the sour stew of her own thoughts – there had been nothing for years. No mention, no meeting – except with Susie, no repercussions. Was it some kind of warning? Some greater force pointing out that, whatever she might think, she had not yet paid the proper price?

Should she do something about it?

THE DIARY

. . . *It used to jump about on the end of a lead. A yellow lead. A puppy. How could I have forgotten for so long? Or is it another 'creation', rather than a memory of something real? Whichever, it was a little brown thing, so small that it hadn't yet learned to bark and uttered these kind of chirps instead.*

I loved it. I used to run through the woods with it. At least, I think I did.

Where was *that? Where did the puppy come from? Where did it go? Can't remember anything else about it except an associated feeling of hate and extreme rage.*

4

'Mum?'

'Darling!' Hannah smiled, even though Lucinda, at the other end of the telephone line, could not see her. 'How are you?'

'Fine, thank you.'

'Oh dear.'

'What?'

'When my daughter says "Fine, thank you," in that downbeat way, I know something's wrong.'

There was a silence.

Hannah had been teasing; it was obvious that something was upsetting Lucinda. She had been thinking in terms of lovers' tiffs. Now she felt sharper alarm. 'Lucy, what's the matter?' she demanded.

'Nothing really. It's just—'

'Just *what*, darling?'

'There've been one or two things recently.'

'What sort of things?' From the expression in Lucinda's voice, it was reasonably serious. Hannah's mind raced with a parental sinking of the heart through drugs, drink, rape, missed periods . . .

'Hassle, mostly,' Lucinda said. 'I told you somebody broke into the house, didn't I?'

'But that was some time ago.'

'It's happened again. But this time, they only took *my* things. That opal brooch Granny gave me. My little television set. And—' Lucinda stopped and Hannah sensed she was close to tears.

'What, darling? What is it?'

'You know that new dress Susie bought me when I was in Rome?'

'The one you told me about?'

'Whoever broke in has – has – Oh God, it's revolting.'

'Urinated over it, do you mean?' Hannah kept her voice calm though she felt sick at the thought of some swine, some man (it had to be a man, didn't it? It always was) making free in her daughter's bedroom, besmirching, despoiling.

'Worse than that. They've poured blood all over it.'

'Blood?'

'That's what it looks like. Animal blood, I should think. It's not ink or ketchup or anything.'

'*Blood*? But that's horrible.'

'I know. And then someone's been tampering with my work-notes – tearing them in half and mixing them all up together.'

'Why haven't you told me about it before?'

'I'm telling you now, aren't I?' Lucinda said, unaccustomedly sharp. 'And on top of that, there's this—' Again Lucinda broke off.

'This *what*?' The panic Hannah had managed to subdue for the past two or three weeks now rose again. And with the panic came fury. She didn't mind for herself. She could cope with anything, had, indeed, done so for years. But to have her child threatened . . . atavistic angers churned.

'Nothing really. What I don't understand is *why*?' Lucinda's voice was beginning to wobble out of control. 'Why is someone coming on to me like this? I mean, it's got to be directed at me, hasn't it? It's *my* TV that's been taken, *my* dress which has been ruined, *my* notes destroyed. Someone obviously *hates* me.'

Hannah tried to be soothing but Lucinda wasn't listening.

'Who is he? What does he want? Is it someone I used to go round with? Some bloke I gave the push to? It's like something out of *Cape Fear* or something, where some raving lunatic terrorises you before he – he . . . I mean, you read about cases like this in the *news*papers.'

Hannah had rarely heard her usually poised daughter sound so upset, so unsure of herself. 'How long has this been going on?' she asked.

'Since the beginning of term, I should think. It's difficult to be sure because I didn't think anything of it at first.'

'Have you reported it to anyone?'

'You mean, like the police?'

'Of *course* like the police, Lucinda.'

'Get real, Mum. The police are far too busy hassling the local black kids to take any notice of me,' Lucinda said bitterly. She had happily lived for nearly two years in an inner-city area which made Hannah sweat whenever she thought about it.

Determined not to be drawn into political arguments, Hannah said firmly: 'What about the university authorities?'

'I thought of going to them, but the trouble is, there isn't anything much to report. They'll just think it's one of my friends playing silly games. Or some nutter. Thanks to the policies of this bloody penny-pinching government, there's hundreds of people wandering round here who've been shoved out into the wider community and just can't cope on their own: you see them all over the campus. Most of them are harmless, really.'

'But not all. Anyone who's gone to the trouble of getting into your house and pouring blood on to a dress is *not* harmless,' Hannah said. 'You've got to speak to someone about it.' She could tell that Lucinda had been thrown badly off balance. Which in itself was upsetting, since

Lucinda was not easily rattled. Hiding her own sense of worry, she said: 'You have checked with your friends, have you?'

'Of course. It's not them, I'm sure. Besides, even if they were the sort who went in for spiteful games, none of them've got time, not with Finals next term.'

'What does—' Hannah tried hard to remember the new man's name, but failed, 'your boyfriend think?'

'He says it's part of the problem of being a pretty woman.'

'Does he, indeed?' Hannah said drily. Whoever he was, he did not sound very supportive.

'But worse than that . . .' Lucinda said dismally.

'Tell me.'

'I'm certain someone's been watching me.'

'What makes you think so?'

'That's the problem. It's only a feeling, nothing I can put my finger on. But you know how there's the recreation ground on the hill just at the back of my house? I keep getting this absolute sense that someone's out there, waiting for me, watching . . . it's horrible, Mum, it really is.' Lucinda laughed awkwardly. 'Perhaps I need HRT or something.'

The two women were silent for a moment. Hannah felt as though a crater had just opened at her feet. So far she had managed to ignore the cassette tape in her own car, dismissing it as some joke of Adam's, however much she knew that if it were a joke, it was not Adam's style, and besides, it was a joke which had no point.

But the uncertainty in Lucinda's voice was a stress she could hardly stand. 'Do you want me to come up and get you?' she asked. 'Do you want to come home?'

'I'd like to, but I've got essays, lectures, all sorts of stuff.'

'Look, none of that's important if you're frightened, Lucinda. You can always study at home for a bit. Being away from the distractions of university life might even help you concentrate.'

'It's a nice idea, Mum, but I don't really think so.'

'How about moving to another place?'

'I can't. We signed the lease on this house for a year, and the landlord will never give us back the deposit if I try to back out of it.'

'Don't be ridiculous,' Hannah said briskly. 'If it's a question of your being in any danger, of course you must move, whatever it costs. Naturally I'll pay anything necessary: you can't be expected to cover it out of your student grant.'

There was another silence. 'I'll think about it,' Lucinda said. She sighed heavily. 'One more stress, on top of all the others . . .'

'Which others?'

'You know. Essays to get in on time. Someone's borrowed my portable typewriter and won't give it back. And . . .' Lucinda's voice trailed away.

'And what?'

'Just . . . *things*—'

'What kind of things?'

'Oh, nothing special.' Hannah could tell her daughter was lying: Especially when she hurried into a gabble about one of the people sharing the house with her. 'He's the most unbelievable slob, Mum. Smelly feet, unwashed hair, never does his share of the washing-up, has fry-ups and leaves the stove for us to clean up. You know. Small things, but they add up, especially with Finals coming up.'

'Yes,' said Hannah.

'Susie rang up the other day, said she was coming over on a flying visit some time soon,' Lucinda said, in an obvious attempt to brighten the conversation. 'She said it would be the last chance she'd have to see me before I leave university.'

'That should be fun for both of you.'

'Yes.'

'Did she say whether she'd have time to come down here for a visit as well?'

'She didn't, but I'm sure she will.'

In the pause which fell, Hannah wished desperately that Lucinda would share whatever other worries she had, but compared to some of her friends with teenage daughters knew herself to be lucky that she was told even as much as this. Maybe she would talk to Susie, her godmother, Hannah's oldest and dearest friend.

'I'm going to try and go up north weekend after next,' Lucinda said. 'Get away from the hassle. I went a couple of weekends ago – it's so peaceful there, you simply can't imagine.'

'This is to your friend Tom's cottage, is it?'

'His parents' place, really. It's beautiful up there, really restful. Just what I need.'

'Did you go . . . alone?' Hannah asked delicately.

'No,' said Lucinda.

'With— ?'

'Yes, Mum. With *him*.'

'I'm doing my best not to pry,' Hannah said bravely, 'but is this one – is he . . . English?' Lucinda seemed to have a penchant for foreigners: so far there had been an Australian, a New Zealander, a charming Indian, a totally laid-back Brazilian. Hannah had nothing against any of these nationalities except the distance they lived from England, and the possibility that they might one day sweep Lucinda away to some inaccessible corner of the globe.

'Not really,' Lucinda said.

'What does that mean?'

'Actually, he's American. Born in the Deep South, Mississippi or somewhere really civilised like that.'

'Oh.' Immediately Hannah saw her child involved in some dissident anti-civil rights group, the Ku Klux Klan, bombs being thrown, crosses burned on some innocent victim's lawn, her daughter ending up sullen and manacled in a heavily-guarded courtroom . . . 'Do we know what he does?'

'*I* do, Mum,' Lucinda said teasingly. 'Honestly, what a question. You mean, you're burning with curiosity, don't you? Absolutely desperate to know whether he's a suitable partner for your daughter.'

'Anything wrong with that?'

'No. It's just, your generation can't seem to believe that men and women can be friends, without necessarily wanting an engagement ring and a mortgage after the first date.'

'Rubbish.'

'Talking of which, he's an unemployed refuse collector.'

'A *what*?'

'There you go. Immediately assuming he's not good enough for me.'

'I didn't say that.'

'You didn't have to, Mum. Anyway, if it makes it any better, he's actually a freelance journalist.'

Did that make it better? Probably. 'Good,' Hannah said inanely, thinking how strong the young were, how powerfully they were able to block out even the most tentative parental enquiry.

Once the phone has been been replaced, Hannah pours herself a stiff whisky. She became pregnant almost casually, never for a moment anticipating the overwhelming, self-consuming love she would feel for the two children she produced. That fierceness had become so much part of her she seldom thinks about it, any more than she questions whether she breathes or eats. It lies dormant, a force always ready to spring into aggressive action but seldom called upon except for minor irritants: an unsympathetic teacher, a bullying older child, a less than flattering remark about the general perfection of Adam or Lucinda.

Now, it roars. The break-ins at Lucinda's house, the thefts, even the sense of being watched: any one of these she could have handled. The realities of modern living mean that there are always the furtive watchers, the petty thieves; near a university campus, a houseful of young women would be a particular target. But coupled with her own harassment, matters have taken a more sinister turn, for someone has clearly targeted not just Hannah, but now Lucinda as well. Someone has been watching, spying, learning. For how long? *Every move you make*, Hannah thinks. She goes to the window to pull the curtains tighter, knowing the gesture to be pointless. Whoever is engaged in this nasty little exercise already has the information he needs.

The question is: what is he after? Why is he doing this? What is the point? Clearly, in the short-term, the aim is to frighten, to make uneasy. Equally clearly, there must be a long-term objective. Someone has given time and effort to this enterprise, first finding Hannah, then tracking down Lucinda. What is behind it?

She pours another whisky. The first crouches inside her, fuelling the fear and anger which already consume her. She holds out both hands in front of her and is amazed by their steadiness. She does not feel steady. The skin is no longer the soft supple stuff of her youth; unstretched, it begins to remind her of her mother's hands, quiescent on the white sheets of her death-bed. The physical contrast between Hannah-now and Hannah-then, Hannah as she once was, is suddenly poignant. Last week she watched some of the ciné-film taken when the children were young, recently transferred on to video. There she was, Hannah young again, rounded, smiling at the camera with a baby in her arms, a toddler clutching her knees. So young, so . . . *tender*.

Who was I then? she asks herself now, the whisky warm inside her. Where did I go, how did I get here, where I never meant to be? I am nearly fifty, with more than half my life gone: what happened to it? What have I done with it?

On the table in front of the sofa lies the book. *Hurled by Dreams*. She picks it up, holds it for a moment, then puts it down. Between its covers, she know, waits that Italian summer. It is ridiculous to imagine that there is a link between the events of that time and what is happening now, twenty-five years later.

And yet . . . she glances round her sitting-room, at the colours, the china, the pictures, the freesias in a narrow silver vase, the fire in the grate. Once it was safe; tonight she hears a jungle sound. She tells herself that the possibility of there being any connection between what happened then and her life now is pure fancy.

But she is not convinced.

THE DIARY

. . . Went into the town today. Difficult to do, all those stores standing there like mouths, waiting to suck me in and swallow me up. I found myself wanting to cross the road in order to avoid the supermarket, but made myself keep on. Maybe I'm not as well as the Dr keeps telling me I am. If I'm to get away, get started on my quest for the past, I've got to cope with things like shops. Occasionally I feel as if some great force has taken me by the shoulders and is pulling me backwards up off the earth so that I can look down on streets and houses and see them receding, smaller and smaller, ants' nests full of people with big mouths and staring eyes.

I hate the supermarket because often when I'm in there the most paralysing blankness comes over me, I can't remember who I am or what I came to buy. Supermarkets are too big; they make me feel so insignificant that I'm afraid I'll lose myself in there. I panic. I start to sweat and tremble, just grab anything from the shelves, in order to look ordinary and in control. Went home once with twenty-four cans of processed peas and a twenty-five-pound bag of dog biscuits. We haven't even got a dog and I hate canned peas.

M and O would have thought I was mad if I'd tried to explain how I'd suddenly had this terrible feeling that any minute the floor was going to tilt and I wouldn't be able to stop myself sliding across those shiny tiles towards the potted plants and the vegetables, past the household cleaners and the home baking supplies, past shelves full of meat and frozen corn, past smoked salmon and nan bread, preserves and detergents, until I reached the onions and eggplants, how I'd been afraid I would somehow fall into the interstices between the mounds of earthy potatoes, choking on the dust, crushed by those plump and dirty ovoids, and no one would find me for weeks, by which time I'd just look like a bit of rotting vegetation caught in the bottom of the display bin.

All I wanted was a newspaper.

. . . 'Can I read it?' he said today.

'Diaries are supposed to be private,' I said.

'My, my,' he said. 'We're being very British today, aren't we?'

'Well, it's true,' I told him. 'Diaries aren't written for general consumption.'

'Don't you want to be cured?' Typical trick. Never answer a question, ask another instead. He looked at me over the tops of his glasses, these half-moon things he always wears which make him look as though he's a hundred years old.

'What the fuck kind of question is that?' I said. One of the things I really enjoy about visiting the Dr is the way I can be as foul-mouthed as I like and he can't say anything, not if he is to hold on to that professional unshockability of his. 'Why do you think I'm here if I don't want to be cured?'

Didn't go on. Don't want to sound pathetic. Fact is, I not only want to be cured but I need to be cured if I'm going to get my life in gear. If I'm ever going to get it together with T. I've wasted so much time – there's a lot of catching up to do. But I can't get started until I remember.

I don't want to tell the Dr about T. It's still too new, too precious.

I said: 'OK. You can read it. But I don't want any literary criticism, thank you. I don't want any snooty remarks about style or grammar or stuff.'

He raised his eyebrows in that supercilious way of his. 'You're being very defensive,' he said. 'This diary of yours is only a psychological tool, a way of enabling us to leap over the fences you've erected around your memory.'

'Kind of a mixed metaphor there, Doc,' I said. Truth is, to me, the diary has become something more than a tool or an aid. Much more.

'We could always do it through dreams, if you prefer,' he said.

I said: 'No thanks, I'll stick with it, now I've started.' Didn't tell him, but I'd hate to stop writing now.

. . . Wish I could talk to O about things – about T – but I can't.

I love reducing my – ha ha – nearest and dearest to mere initials. For one thing, initials are safer than names are, they're containable. Names are words and words can drift away from you before you know it, they can squeeze out between the gaps, however tightly you hold on to them. Initials are like those blue butterflies I used to catch and hold fluttering in my hand. I had absolute power over them: I could let them go or I could simply squeeze my hand shut and kill them.

There is something quite stirring in the idea that, in a metaphorical sense, I can, within the pages of this diary, hold O and M and F, even the Dr, in my power, and do with them as I please.

Sometimes I worry about my dependency on the Dr. Last time I went in there, he had a different pair of glasses on. It completely threw me. He didn't look like my Dr. God, I hate that, hate sudden changes, I wanted to lean forward, tear them off his face, demand that he put those half-moon ones on again. I wondered if he'd done it deliberately to make me nervous. To make me angry.

I held on to myself. Breathed deeply, in . . . out, in . . . out. Looked straight at him. At them. 'New glasses, Doc?' I said.

'Yes.' He took them off, twiddled them around in his hand. Without them, he seemed weak and defenceless, like a fledgling before its feathers have grown. For the first time, I wondered which of us two was the strongest.

I know that at the very heart of myself, I'm strong. Sometimes I know I could do anything, if I put my mind to it. In spite of the terrors, the dreams, my dependency on him . . .

THEN

5

'You'll come, won't you?' Susie said, looking up from the letter she was reading.

'Come where?' The two girls were at Hannah's house, Susie back from Bristol, where she was studying natural sciences, Hannah down from Cambridge for the Easter break.

'Ma's house in Umbria.' Susie looked up at Hannah who was wrapping her newly-washed hair in a dry towel. 'She says I can have it for the whole of the summer since Pa's got to go to South America to look at installations or something, and Ma's going along for the trip.' Her face splintered into an ecstatic smile. 'The whole summer! That's *marvellous!* Oh God! Isn't life heavenly?'

It was one of her constant cries, and for her, so it was, Hannah often thought. 'I've never been to that part of Italy,' she said.

'Which is why you absolutely have to come with me. Quite apart from anything else, I need to have you along. Ma says I can't go unless I've got a quote sensible unquote friend like quote Hannah unquote with me.'

'I can't say I'm exactly thrilled to be described as "sensible", thanks all the same.'

'She means level-headed.'

'Is that any better?' Hannah raised her eyebrows.

'Compared to mad old me, darling, you're as steady as a rock.'

'Humph. Anyway, yes, please. I'd love to come.'

'It's ridiculous that you've never come before,' Susie said.

'Music-camps,' Hannah said. 'Every bloody summer until we left school. I must have carted that damn cello of mine to more European venues than even Pablo Casals. No wonder my knuckles scrape along the ground like a gorilla's.'

'At least you had those years off when we did India and Mexico,' Susie said. She clapped her hands together. 'I shall invite everyone I know to come and stay with us in Italy. And one of the best things is that my cousin Lucas is going to be around at the same time.'

'My God, am I finally going to meet this paragon you're always going on about? I can hardly wait.'

'Don't try to seduce him away from me while we're out in Italy, will you?'

'Fat chance. With these arms, who's going to look twice at me when you're around? Or even once.'

'Hannah Humble.'

'Just as a matter of interest, does lovely Lucas know that you plan to marry him?'

'He could hardly not, since I've never made any secret of my adoration. I've wanted to marry him from the moment I first realised what boys were for. Before that, really: ever since I could talk.' Susie made a face. 'Not that he ever seems particularly enthusiastic about the idea.'

'Dear, oh dear,' said Hannah.

'I'm not worried. I've told him he'll come to his senses one of these days. And I'm always pointing out what wonderful children we'd have – I know he wants children.'

'What else did you tell him: their sex and names? What schools they'll go to?' Hannah chuckled. 'The Secret Life of Susie Wilton – the smallest book in the world.'

'Get out of here,' said Susie. 'You don't know anything about my secrets.'

Italy. When she told them about her plans for the summer vacation, Hannah's parents were as enthusiastic as she had ever seen them. After a hellish winter of blizzards and snowstorms, this was the first warm day of the year and the two of them had been working in the small garden which went with their dark flat in Islington. It was not a garden like the one Susie's mother had created, full, it always seemed to Hannah, of profuse roses and creamy clematis, lilacs heavy with bloom, huge copper chrysanthemums.

This was just a rectangle of lawn stretching towards a timber shed, with prim herbaceous borders on either side, containing orderly shrubs with dark-green leaves, the occasional daffodil in springtime, golden rod in the autumn, three or four tidy rose trees. A *constipated* garden, Hannah often thought; it typified her elderly parents and the dull lives they led.

Today they had been pruning things, scratching at the soil with hoes, pottering about together in the companionable way they had, which always included but never succeeded in embracing their only child.

Now, as they sat round the slatted garden table, its surface wiped clean of the winter's accumulation of dirt and twigs, they cast complicit glances at each other. 'Italy, eh?' said Professor Carrington, roguishly, and Hannah saw, for perhaps the first time, a hint of the younger man he must once have been. 'Do you remember, Cordelia?'

'Indeed, yes,' said Hannah's mother, with unaccustomed warmth. 'Fra Angelico. Giotto.' She bared her big yellow teeth in a smile. Whale's teeth, Hannah used to think them, perched as a child uneasily on her mother's bony knees.

'Venice,' said her father, throwing a sly look at his wife from over the gold-rimmed half-moon glasses which sat halfway down his nose. He turned to his daughter. 'I can certainly recommend you an hotel in Venice.' It was a measure of his dry academicism that even in casual conversation, hoisting a scone laden with clotted cream and raspberry jam to his mouth, he should still use the correct indefinite article.

There was a pink flush on her mother's cheeks. Hannah had a sudden vision of the two of them in a room where dappled light from a backwater canal danced on the ceiling and the distant cries of gondoliers and seagulls on the Grand Canal pierced the slow heat of the afternoon. She had always shied away from thinking of her own parents engaged in the kind of activity which had brought herself into being. Here, in the garden, with traffic pounding the road beyond the garden wall, it was marginally easier to contemplate that parental coupling. Square continental pillows in starched linen covers, the huge *matrimoniale*, clocks silverly sounding the passing hours, hands reaching for another's hands . . .

'We shan't be in Venice,' she said. 'Susie's house is in Umbria.'

'Ah.' Her father nodded. There was a flaky patch of psoriasis on the back of his left hand and he touched it once, gingerly, with the middle finger of his right hand. Neither of Hannah's parents would have dreamed of such vulgarity as enquiring after the state of the Wilton finances, but she knew he was wondering when he added vaguely: 'How many homes do the Wiltons own, exactly?'

'Three,' Hannah said. 'The house in Cornwall, the London flat, and this place in Italy. And they have access to a company apartment in New York, I think.' She was conscious of an urge towards cruelty as she said this, a desire to point up the contrast between Susie's parents and her own.

'James, did we go to Umbria?' Her mother's earnest spectacles blinked as she turned her head.

Under his battered panama hat, her father smiled. 'Oh yes,' he said. He leaned out of the creaking basket chair and patted his wife's hand. 'Yes, indeed we did.'

Pity brought an ache to the back of Hannah's throat. Poor things, she thought. Poor awkward, ugly things. Her mother's shapeless body in its unbecoming cotton dress, her father's psoriatic homeliness, carried with them an underlay of grief of which she had been aware all her life and which she passionately did not want to share. To be so unlovely must have been a constant source of sorrow to them. Nearly twenty-three years old, but still unaccustomed to reality, the thought occurred to her that, sadly, the unattractive must experience exactly the same longings, the same despairs, as the beautiful.

Yet, looking at the two of them, she also acknowledged that she had never once doubted the strength of the feeling which lay so palpably between them. Any more than she could deny the alienating nature of their self-sufficiency. Why had they never taken her to Italy? To *any*where? Why had they not shown her the worlds they themselves had once enjoyed and presumably, in their quiet way, still did? Why had they never *shared* anything with her?

They were neither defeated nor depressed; both of them were successful academic anthropologists, much admired in their own sphere, yet she could not remember either of them ever giving vent to an expression of enthusiasm or delight. Although she was their child, they had never really belonged to her; all her life she had stood outside the haven they provided for each other.

'What you've got to remember is that my Italian grandfather came from the south,' Susie said.

'Why must I remember?'

'Because it will make so many things clear to you when we arrive at the Villa Giulia. People from the south of Italy are like elephants: they never forgive.'

'I thought it was for*getting* that elephants were supposed never to do.'

'Grandfather never did either, actually. What happened was, his friend, the local grandee, got married to a woman who also came from the south.'

Today the two girls were drinking wine in the big, cluttered kitchen of Susie's house. ('A planning session,' Susie had called it, summoning Hannah over from Islington by telephone. 'So we can sort out what clothes to take and which books, and stuff like that. I mean, we're going for three months or so. And apart from food, the shopping will be pretty basic, so we have to organise ourselves. You don't want to forget your Tampax, for instance; the village *farmacia* has never heard of such things, and anyway, it's a mile and a half away up a hill.')

'So you're talking about irresistible forces and immovable objects, are you?' Hannah asked.

'Grandfather and the old Contessa? Definitely. From what they say, she was certainly irresistible. And *he* was absolutely immovable.'

'A recipe for trouble.'

'A recipe for dis*ast*er.' Susie tipped back her head and swallowed the last drops of wine in her glass. 'This is rather good, isn't it? Do you think Pa'll mind if we open another bottle?'

'I shouldn't think so.' To Hannah, the idea of opening even one bottle of her parents' wine – always supposing she could find a bottle to open – was completely alien. Susie's easy relationship with her parents – her American father and Italian mother – was one of the things which captivated her about the Wiltons. 'And if he does, he'll only make you replace it.'

'Do you think so?' Susie peered doubtfully at the label on the empty bottle. 'You know Pa and wine: this probably cost thousands of pounds.' Which did not prevent her opening the second bottle she had earlier carried up from the cellar. 'Anyway,' she continued, pouring unsteadily into Hannah's glass. 'This disaster has lasted for two generations so far, and'll probably go on unto the third and fourth as well.'

'Sounds like a vendetta or something.'

'It *is*. The old Contessa's still alive and kicking.' Susie got up and took down one of the glittering knives which hung from a magnetic rack on the wall. 'Which means we don't speak when we meet in town, nor do we have each other over for dinner. It's all frigid bows in the bakery and frosty nods over the artichokes. And that's on a *good* day.'

'What happens on a bad one?'

'*Then* we sweep past, ignoring them and gazing witheringly into the middle distance, probably curling our lips in a contemptuous sneer as we go.'

'I'm not sure I can manage to sweep and sneer at the same time.'

'Don't worry: you'll get plenty of practice. And need it, too.' Thick-fleshed green peppers lay on the kitchen counter, umber-skinned onions, bursting scarlet tomatoes, cloves of garlic flushed faintly with purple. Susie began slicing one of the onions. 'As a guest of the Wiltons, you automatically get tarred with the same brush as us.'

'Heavens,' said Hannah. 'What happens if I make a mistake and actually talk to one of these people, not realising who they are?'

'Someone in a cloak will probably run you through with a rapier,' Susie said cheerfully, 'not that it'll come to that. It's a small enough town for people to know which are the strangers and who they're staying with.'

'Suppose I'm in an accident and this gorgeous hunk steps forward and rescues me from beneath the hoofs of a runaway horse,' said Hannah. 'When I discover he's one of *Them*, am I supposed to do this sweeping and sneering, or can I at least thank him for saving my life?'

Susie frowned, as though giving the question serious consideration. 'I should think thanks would be all right. But don't get too effusive, OK?'

'Should I be taking notes?'

'If you want. Actually, as soon as this hunk realised you were from the Villa Giulia or the Villa Diana, he'd probably shove you straight back under the horse.' Vigorously Susie seeded the peppers and began to chop them.

'Does anyone remember what the original quarrel was about?'

'A land dispute, I think. With Italians, it usually is.'

'Not an affair of the heart, then?'

'Could be. I'm sure Aunt Diana in her time must have had it off with one or other of the Contessa's sons. And as for Lucas . . . Here, do the garlic for me, will you?'

Susie gave Hannah three cloves of garlic, a tiny chopping board and a knife. Wiping her hands on her apron, she went out of the room. When she came back, she was holding a picture frame. 'Look at this. My grandfather.'

Hannah studied the old-fashioned photograph, which showed a stern man of swarthy appearance, his skin touched with the oily translucence which photographers gave to their subjects fifty or sixty years ago. Under formidable brows, he stared out at the world from strangely pale eyes. 'He looks very like you, as a matter of fact.'

'Thanks a lot.' Susie plunged a fork into a tomato, then held it over a naked flame until the skin began to blacken and split.

'He's very handsome.'

Susie leaned over the back of the chair to look over Hannah's shoulder. 'He's also got a beard and a pair of eyebrows which can only be called beetling, neither of which, in case you haven't noticed, *I've* got.'

'Not yet.' Hannah grinned. 'What did he do for a living?' The face in the picture was an unusual, even a compelling one.

'He was a diplomat of some kind and then he went into politics,' said Susie, 'but if you think he's handsome, wait until you meet my cousin Lucas.'

Hannah groaned. 'Not Lucas again, please.' On the stove behind her, onions seethed in olive oil, filling the kitchen with their promising smell. 'Have you got a photograph of *him*?'

'No, but he's the spitting image of the old boy,' Susie said.

'Beetling brows and all?' Hannah peeled the garlic cloves and began slicing them finely.

'The lot,' said Susie.

'Since you're practically engaged to him, shouldn't you be carrying his portrait around next to your heart, or in a locket round your neck?'

'Haven't got one. He hates having his photograph taken. And anyway, I don't see him that much. He's not really in my parents' good books.'

'Why not?'

Susie grimaced. 'He's a bit of a . . . a womaniser is the word, I suppose. And two or three years ago he—'

'He *what*?'

'Had a rather ghastly car accident. The woman in the car with him was killed. He was flung clear but she was trapped and he couldn't get her out. He had to watch her burn to death.'

Sobered, Hannah said, 'How awful, Susie. You never told me about this.'

'It gets worse.'

'How?'

'Lucas was driving much too fast, it was all his fault. What's more, the woman was the sister of one of his friends, and married to someone else at the time.'

'Lord.' The two girls stared at each other.

'I know.' Susie gave a kind of shake.

'And you still plan to marry this . . . this *rakehell*, do you?'

'Certainly.'

'If it's not a rude question,' Hannah said carefully. 'Do I take it you aren't – uh – saving yourself for the wedding night?'

'If he can philander,' Susie said in an airy way, 'so can I. He womanises; I man-ise.'

'*Please*,' groaned Hannah. 'That is a truly *terrible* joke.'

'Who says I'm joking?'

Hannah frowned. 'Do you love him?'

'Love? I don't know about that. I'm certainly hooked, though. He's got this way of – kind of getting inside your head. Like hypnosis. All I know is that all I've ever wanted is lots of children, lots of money – and Lucas.'

'Good luck.'

'Lucas's bit of the family is frightfully grand. As you know, my aunt Diana never did things by halves.'

'Ah.' Thinking about flighty Aunt Diana, Hannah lost concentration. She felt nothing when the sharp little vegetable knife cut into the fleshy part of her finger. Only when blood oozed thickly, staining the chopped garlic, running down the blade, did she realise what she had done. She dropped the knife and pushed away from the table, nausea rising in her throat.

'Susie—' She lifted her other hand and put it over her mouth.

'What is it?' Turning from the stove, Susie took in the blood-soaked garlic and Hannah white-faced, paralysed, shaking.

'I can't stand the sight of blood,' she whispered. 'I just can't—'

'Don't look then, while I wash it,' said Susie, efficient. 'You've never seen my Florence Nightingale act, have you?'

Eyes shut, Hannah shook her head.

'They're twins, you see. Giulia and Diana: my mother and my aunt.' Susie lay back in her chair. 'God: I'm absolutely stuffed.'

'Me too.' Hannah patted her stomach. 'I always eat like a pig when I come to your house.'

Susie raised her eyebrows. 'I hope that's a comment on your eating habits rather than my culinary ability.'

'Anything's delicious, after my mother's cooking.'

'Does she do it deliberately?' asked Susie. 'No one could be such an awful cook by accident.'

'I think she works at it. Lies awake devising ever more disgustingly inedible dishes. If it wasn't for coming here,' Hannah said gloomily, 'I'd probably starve to death.'

'Your father's so good about it, too.' Susie chuckled. To Hannah's eyes, one of Susie's many lovable qualities was the way she had accepted Hannah's parents for what they were, an old-fashioned, well-meaning couple, who were not cut out for parenthood and remained slightly bewildered by the unexpected appearance of a child in their bookish, ordered lives. And they in turn seemed to accept Susie, the way they had never accepted Hannah; even her occasional wild moods when she would twirl about the house laughing, singing, chattering madly about anything and everything, they tolerated with no more than a raised eyebrow and a smile.

Susie teased them, thrust the latest feminist publications – *Sexual Politics*, *The Female Eunuch* – at them, fulminated against the Americans in Vietnam, the war in Biafra, told them if they had any conscience at all they would be marching to Aldermaston alongside Hannah and herself. She played the Beatles, Diana Ross, T Rex, the Stones, rather than Beethoven and Vivaldi, once even tried to teach Professor Carrington to do the twist. She encouraged Hannah to wear flared jeans, mini-skirts, have her ears pierced, chew gum, and all without any apparent consciousness that Hannah's parents were in any way different from her own.

'My mother thinks food is just fuel for the body,' Hannah sighed, clearing plates away and stacking them in the dishwasher.

'So does mine, really.'

'So how come you get four-star and I end up with diesel?'

'Anyway.' Susie swirled the remains of her wine round in her glass. 'Giulia and Diana are identical twins. But only in looks, not in temperament.' Picking up one of the serving spoons, she thoughtfully licked it clean. 'Despite the differences, my grandfather doted on them both, and when they were twelve, he bought this estate from the Contessa, just because it had once belonged to some ancestor of hers who'd also had twin daughters and had built them these identical houses.'

'What else do you do when they get too old to be dressed in identical frocks?' Hannah murmured.

'Quite. The thing was, she – the Contessa – had fallen on hard times and wanted to sell off some land. But *not* the villas. So Grandfather simply badgered and bullied and bribed her until she gave in and sold them to him. And then he promptly changed the names to the Villa Giulia and the Villa Diana, which caused huge offence.'

'Sounds as though the diplomatic service lost a winner when he took up politics.'

'Exactly. Since Wicked Aunt Diana was last widowed, she's been living in Barbados most of the time, so the Villa Diana is usually empty, unless Lucas goes over there. Which he does a lot in the summer.'

'Including this one?'

'Right. When I phoned him, he said he'd already organised some housekeeper to look after the place.' Pressing buttons, Susie set the dishwasher going and poured out the last of the wine. 'The most awkward thing, given the fact that the old Contessa doesn't speak to us, is how close we are to her place. Her land backs right on to ours. In winter you can even catch a glimpse of their top windows. And if they're sitting on the terrace, you can sometimes hear their voices.'

'That must make her grind her aristocratic teeth a bit.'

'You'd think so.' Susie giggled. 'Her grandchildren come for the summer quite often and she's forbidden them even to go into the grounds, in case they catch sight of one of us and get contaminated by our filthy English ways. Not that they take any notice. One of them, a girl called Marina, used to come and swim – Lucas fancied her like anything.'

'Funny how wherever the conversation starts, it always ends up with bloody Lucas, isn't it?'

'Hannah Hootilo,' said Susie. 'Honestly, I promise you'll like him.'

'What happened to the girl   Marina?'

'They married her off pretty damn quick, the minute they realised she'd been spending time with us. To some doctor in Rome.'

'Your grandfather's dead, isn't he?'

Susie nodded. She poured shiny black beans into an electric coffee grinder and whirred them for twelve seconds, counting aloud. Finally she said: 'About five years ago. A heart attack or something. I . . . really loved him. Ma was pretty upset. He was staying with us in Cornwall at the time. He got up after lunch and said he didn't feel well. Then he just . . . died.'

'Oh Susie—'

'I was in the room with him. I'd never seen anyone dead before.'

'I never have.'

'The awful thing is that I can't remember what he was like before. I only ever see him lying there on the carpet, dead. Sort of colourless. Definitely dead; not a bit as if he was asleep, whatever they say in books.'

'Poor you.'

'One thing about having elderly parents like yours,' Susie said, 'is that they do tend to get all that sort of thing – grandparents dying, I mean – out of the way before you show up.'

She smiled at Hannah, visibly changing the subject. 'At least there's a lot of woods and trees between us and the Contessa. And my ma has this amazing overgrown garden, very melancholy and shady.'

'Sounds like the sort of place I love.' Hannah closed her eyes. Sun on dappled leaves, sly pagan faces peeping through branches, fountains falling into porphyry basins . . .

'We'll have a wonderful time.'

'Should be a summer to remember,' Hannah said.

6

'Heaven.' Susie sighed with satisfaction. 'Isn't life absolutely heaven?'

The two of them were standing on the arcaded stone veranda which ran round three sides of the Villa Giulia, the fourth being an open terrace. All around them was the misty violet of distant hills, ochre villages, towers, the landscape darkly speared by the occasional thrust of cypress and poplar.

Nearby lay fields of drifting poppies; across vines and sunflowers, a terraced hill rose out of the landscape. At its feet clustered a little town, no more than a collection of umber walls and terracotta roofs; it was crowned with the ruins of a castle complete with a campanile of dusty-pink brick. The road from the town to the nearest city ran past the gates of the Villa Giulia. Half a mile further on was the driveway – ('Lucas *always* keeps the gates locked, though nobody else ever does') – leading to the Villa Diana and, nearer the town, the houses of other people, many of whom, according to Susie, were ex-pats, mostly British, some American, some German or French.

The day after they arrived Susie developed a stomach virus. She lay about groaning and asking to be left alone. Apart from brewing hot tisanes, which were all she could keep down, Hannah was left to her own devices.

She explored. The Villa Giulia must once have been imposing; now it lay largely empty, a house of bare, shuttered rooms and sepia shadows. Remnants of grandeur clung like cobwebs to walls and ceilings: elaborate cornices, carved mantels, dim, gilded looking-glasses. Every now and then, a fine chair or dusty commode inlaid with splitting marquetry would rear briefly out of the gloom. Side tables topped with elaborate arrangements of dried flowers – giant artichoke heads, plumes of delphiniums in washed-out pinks and mauves, silvery leaves which disintegrated at a touch – stood here and there, only reinforcing the faded magnificence.

With her friend ill in bed there was nothing much for Hannah to do. At Susie's feeble insistence, she found a heavy black bicycle of old-fashioned shape in one of the outbuildings and cycled along dusty roads for two or three miles to buy food at market stalls or in pungent one-roomed shops. Briefly, hurrying through the little town, she glimpsed narrow, stone-paved streets, a church, a small central piazza lined with shops and a café. She would have examined it more closely but, worried about Susie left on her own, did not linger.

Heat crawled from the corners of the rooms and hung below the ceilings, not yet overwhelming, but giving due notice of what to expect. At night, having checked Susie, she ate alone in the kitchen – slices of mortadella, blood-red salamis, big tomatoes sliced and scattered with herbs and oil, hard rolls, soft yellow cheese – listening to tap-drip and clock-tick. There was no television, no wireless. Hannah sat in the *salone* and read, wrapped in a blanket since the evenings were cold. Sometimes the dim, yellow bulbs flickered and died for an hour or two, and then she would walk down the long drive to the road and back again, past glossy evergreens and whispering poplar trees, or go to bed.

Time trickled by, noiselessly, like the dust which dropped endlessly in the rooms, unseen except where sunlight squeezed through the shutters and made semi-solid lines across the space between floor and ceiling. Hannah's favourite room was the empty ballroom which opened on to the terrace and was lined with fly-blown mirrors in crumbling gilt frames. The ceiling was painted with dim garlands of fruit and flowers, pink-tinged clouds, roguish *putti*; damp had penetrated the plaster, blotching the pouting mouths, leaving patches of mildew on pear and plum. Watching her reflection as she walked across the parquet floor, fragile as a moth in the ghostly glass, she asked herself: *Who am I? Where am I going?* and wondered whether, twenty-five years from now, she would have an answer to the questions.

The daytime sun was already fierce, despite the chilly evenings. It leaned on the house, powerful, imperious; one day, under the onslaught of that heat, it seemed probable that the bricks and mortar, the curved tiles and tall shutters, would grow dryer and ever dryer until finally they baked into dust and slowly crumbled back into the earth.

The house was surrounded by acres of decaying gardens. Once, they must have been magnificent. Now, neglected, they had reverted to a state of overgrown unkemptness. Exploring, Hannah would stumble across crumbling balustrades, arched grots almost invisible under giant ferns, half-hidden statuary of entwined figures, satyr faces peeping from wild masses of neglected yew, naked youths in athletic stance. Mossed stone steps led down to choked-up fountains, niches held bird-spattered vases of marble or earthenware, ivy covered everything like tapestry. Below the villa's urned terrace, an area of grass and shrub was kept clear by Antonio, a slow-witted man, who arrived on a rusty moped once a week to run an ancient mower over it. Beyond that, untrimmed box hedges marked out the remains of more formal flower-beds. Otherwise, the garden was left to grow as it pleased.

'Ma likes it like that,' Susie had explained. 'She does the same in our Cornish house. She loves the melancholy of it.'

So did Hannah. The garden was full of the past. And of surprises. Pushing her way through pathways obscured by years of unswept leaves, pulling aside the branches of bushes which, when disturbed, left an aromatic dust in the air, she would find herself at the edge of tiny rush-choked ponds, or in sudden clearings where sunshine, silted down through the dense cover of leaves, filled them with a green underground light while, above her head, unseen birds called.

Once she came across what might originally have been a little chapel. Derelict, its four tumbledown walls stood open to the sky, only an arched gothic window left to indicate the purpose the building used to have. The floor was a tangle of creeper and fern and fallen leaves. From the remains of window-sills and piles of fallen stone grew the gnarled stems of some purple-blossomed shrub round which bands of small, fierce coloured butterflies hovered, enticed by the heat trapped in the stones.

The vehemence of the sky, framed by those ruined walls, was seductive. Hannah felt she had never known what passion was until she looked up into that cloudless sky. This was not the insipid blue of an English heaven; above the derelict gardens it blazed bluer than peacocks, softer than velvet. Staring up into it, it was easy to imagine her soul shaking free of her corporeal self and dancing like a swallow in that illimitable air.

Susie recovered. Their shared days passed slowly. Nearly every morning the two girls cycled into the little town to drink coffee in the piazza at one of the two small *trattorias*, before shopping for red peppers, strings of garlic, damp white cheese, tomatoes the size of suns, ominous sausages. Otherwise, Susie sat on the terrace, chewing pencils and staring distractedly at her chemistry notes. In the autumn they would both be going back to their last year at university, and she was already beginning to panic about her finals. Hannah too had brought books with her but found it impossible to settle down to them.

The heat was enervating; the garden lured her. Enticed into its shady depths, she gradually found herself losing all ability to act, to think. She gave herself up entirely to the sensual pleasures of leaves brushing against her skin, leaf mould beneath the bare soles of her feet, the sun's seduction. For hours, she simply did nothing.

She was not used to inactivity. School, university, cello lessons, music camps, exams: her life had been one of insistent bustle, constant imperatives. Even on previous visits to Italy, there had been the language to learn, sightseeing to accomplish, culture to absorb. Here, now, she revelled in the luxury of torpor, somnolent under a sun which had become a separate element, one in which she became what she might always have been meant to be, a creature wholly given up to the rich sensations of the flesh.

One afternoon, pushing back from the table which she had set up on the terrace, Susie said: 'There's a pool thing. Have you discovered it yet?'

'Lily pond, do you mean? There's several of those.'

'The one I'm thinking of's bigger than that. Perhaps you missed it because it's on Lucas's side of the boundary. You know how law-abiding you are.'

'Am I?'

'Let's go and find it.' Susie stood up.

'Is it big enough to get into? I'd adore a swim.' Hannah yawned, stretched. Sweat lay along her arms; languidly she sniffed at the smooth brown skin, the delicate smell of herself.

'We used to swim there when we were younger, but that was years ago,' warned Susie. 'God knows what horrors lurk in the depths. The Italian equivalent of the Loch Ness monster at the very least.'

Indeed, the pool did not look inviting when they broke through a jungle growth of rhododendron, clambered between broken railings which marked the end of the Villa Giulia's terrain and the beginning of the Villa Diana's and found it. Greened with waterweed, it lay beneath a canopy of arching trees, a long rectangle surrounded by stands of rustling bamboo. White marble slabs marked the edge; at one end there was a stone bench, at the other, a lustful stone face – satyr? faun? – held a jutting verdigris pipe between its thick lips. A couple of archaic marble pillars gave it the spurious air of a classical ruin. Yellow buds of water-lily lay on the surface, between flat, dark leaves, and shoals of minnows darted in and out of patches of sunlight which dappled the water. A pair of dragon-flies hovered.

Hannah stirred the surface with a stick, disturbing the tiny circles of waterweed which covered most of the pool, and the two of them looked down into the murky water.

'It doesn't look as though anything's come out of that pipe for centuries,' Susie said.

'It's probably only blocked by leaves.'

'Do you think we could get Antonio on to it?' Susie looked vaguely round the clearing.

'Not if we want actually to *swim*,' Hannah said. 'Antonio's still on Lesson Two in his *How to Master Breathing* manual.'

'He's not that bad.'

'He's worse, if anything.' Hannah took off one of her sandals and put her foot into the water. 'It's nice and cool.' She began unbuttoning the front of her cotton shirt.

'Hannah, you *can't* go in,' Susie said. 'It's revolting.'

'It won't be full of old mattresses, like it would at home,' Hannah said. She stepped out of her shorts.

'Tetanus,' said Susie. 'Cholera. Dysentery.'

'I'll risk it.' Hannah pointed at the centre of the pool, where a mild turbulence stirred beneath hanging clouds of gnats. 'Look.'

'What's that?'

'It could be some kind of underground spring,' said Hannah. 'Maybe there's a conduit leading up to that pipe which is supposed to recycle the water.'

'Lucas used to go in,' Susie said, 'when we were younger. And some of the others.'

'Which others?'

Susie looked round at the enveloping trees. 'Some of the other properties round here slope down towards us. There used to be great gaggles of us, we spent most of the summer down here – it was away from the grown-ups, we could smoke, even drink. The others were always leaping in and out of the water, but I could never bring myself to: it always looked far too slimy.'

'It's not, though. The green stuff is only weed on the surface.' Whipping off her T-shirt, Hannah said: 'Look out for splashes: I'm going in.'

She leaped into the air. For a moment she hung there, untethered as a bird, floating through leaves, sky, filtered sunlight. Then she was under the surface of the pool, eyes open to a green opacity, the watery equivalent of the overgrown paths and the drifts of sunlight. Ripples slid like fish against her skin as she swam to the middle of the pool where the surface riffled gently. Turning over, she lay on her back and stared up at the devouring sky, the glitter of sunshine through the overarching leaves. Against her shoulders she could feel the movement of some subterranean welling.

'Don't swallow any,' Susie said, watching from the edge.

Hannah turned again and cupped the water in her hands. Small particles of forest matter floated between her palms, and a stray tiddler wriggled, blunt head butting at her fingers. 'It only looks dark because of the trees,' she said. 'I think it's pure. It's certainly clear.'

The water-lilies rocked gently on the far side of the pool as she allowed herself to sink until her feet were ankle-deep in mud. Moving them about in the ooze, she felt something hard, the mud agitated by the sluggish movement of water. It was like standing on a half-open plug hole. 'There's definitely a spring here,' she said. 'It's blocked up with silt but it only needs clearing out. There's years of muck and stuff down there but even so, it's managing to push through.'

Lazily she swam back to where Susie waited. 'And look, there's even some steps here. They only want cleaning.' Clambering out, she began casting about in the undergrowth round the pool. 'And I bet you that there's some sort of gutter or pipe where the spring feeds down into this faun thing as well as an outlet in the centre, to keep the water circulating.'

'Gosh! How do you know about things like that?'

'Basic commonsense, my dear.' Hannah looked at the reflection of the pillars in the dark water. 'It's obviously been copied from the ancient Romans.'

Susie, brushing at Hannah's wet shoulders, said: 'You look like a water-sprite or something, all covered in tiny green stars from that weed.'

Finding a small garden fork left by Antonio in one of the big stone urns along the terrace, Hannah took it down to the chapel. When she dug down into the matted floor, she felt it strike stone. Clearing away a little of the accumulated mould, she discovered coloured mosaic: a black eyebrow above an almond of brown eye.

Reclamation became a holiday task more congenial than her books. Each afternoon she worked there, unscabbing the mosaic of its natural carpet and watching the past slowly emerge. A head, noble and Roman, eyes raised, a hand offering a dish, a white-draped shoulder. She had assumed that the worship which had once taken place here was sacred; as time went by, she wondered if she had mistaken the purpose of this tiny building hidden among the trees. A rounded thigh, a naked breast, grapes purple and fecund: had lovers dallied here on languorous afternoons? If so, who were they: the Contessa's ancestors? If the property had been in her family for generations, Hannah entirely sympathised with her anger at the high-handed behaviour of Susie's grandfather in changing the names of the two villas. In one corner she came across a brass circle set flush into the floor and wondered what it could have been meant for; since the area round it was clearly more of the border of acanthus leaves and grapes which she had already painstakingly uncovered, she continued to clear towards the centre.

Susie, sociable, spent the evenings renewing old acquaintances, mostly among the local ex-pats. Some of these were permanent residents, bringing up children, working locally, usually at some artistic or creative endeavour, for the town was beginning to become a little colony of artists and writers; others arrived, like Susie's family, in the summer. Many of them had been coming for years, so that they all made up a close-knit mutually-acquainted community.

Hannah dutifully accompanied her or dispensed drinks and food to those who called at the Villa Giulia. Faces passed before her like a blur: afterwards she could remember, not what any of these people looked like, but only identifying details: the woman writer with the purple moon-face, the interior designer who wore yellow corduroy trousers, the London barrister whose little finger was missing its top joint. They were hospitable, kind, accepting her for Susie's sake but, although they always made her feel welcome, Hannah was conscious of the effort they had to make to include her in conversation which seemed to wind in and out of a long-established pattern of names: Dorian, Chloe, Hugo and Kim, Tristan, Helena, Toby. Knowing none of these people – and brought up by her parents to consider the discussion of others as the height of vulgarity – Hannah had nothing to contribute.

Together with Hugo and Emma – an engaged couple, friends of Susie's, who'd arrived to spend a few days at the Villa – they were at the house of the Trevelyans, American ex-pats who lived on the outskirts of the town. Lew Trevelyan was a big, bluff man, red-cheeked and overweight, intensely proud of his Cornish ancestry; his wife, Nancy, was an attenuated blonde with a perpetual frown of worry between her eyebrows. They had children, a boy and two girls: occasionally they burst into the room to demand hamburgers or French fries, or to ask whether Mom could *puh-lease* make Jerry stop switching channels when they were trying to watch *I Love Lucy*, it wasn't *fair*.

Seated on a long, low sofa between the London barrister and a woman who designed tapestry cushion kits, Hannah heard the name Lucas dropped into the conversation. Was this Susie's cousin, the Lucas she was so keen on? Looking across the room, she guessed it must be for Susie wore an expression of elaborate indifference. She sat on a stool by the open hearth, hugging her knees with an intensity which spoke of emotions barely reined in. Hannah was startled. She was always teasing her friend about her handsome cousin Lucas; now she saw that perhaps Susie had not been joking when she said she intended to marry him.

The conversation veered towards another regular visitor to the area. 'Sure,' Lew said. As always, he wore jeans and a loose dress shirt of striped cotton. 'We had a card from Tristan just yesterday. Said he's leaving Morocco any day now.'

'Morocco? I thought he was in Rome,' Susie said.

'He was – but he decided to take a quick fortnight over there, as I understand it, before he goes back home.'

'Is he still planning to come here on his way?' Susie asked.

'Oh, I think so,' said Lew.

'What about his friend Mark?' Emma asked. She turned to Hugo, who sat beside her: 'Remember we met up with them in Paris a few years ago, when we went to visit Bungo and Min? Mark and Jane. We liked them, didn't we?'

Hugo nodded. He was a morose young man, some kind of civil servant, though Hannah had not established what exactly he did.

'Oh, my dear, haven't you heard?' someone exclaimed.

'Heard what?' Emma looked round the company. 'No, we haven't heard anything.'

'Mark and Jane split up last year,' the person said, lowering her voice.

'That's dreadful.' Emma seized Hugo's hand. 'They seemed so much in love, didn't they, Hugo?'

Again Hugo nodded.

'There was a child, too, wasn't there?' pursued Emma. 'Oh, that's terrible.'

'We met Mark once, in Cornwall, years ago,' said Nancy, 'but we never met his wife. He's a good friend of Tristan's.' She turned to Hannah. In the kindly way they all tried to prevent her from feeling left out, she said: 'This Tristan guy we were talking about lives in Cornwall, near where Lew's family came from.' She held a carafe of red wine enquiringly over Hannah's glass; Hannah nodded. 'So we sometimes see him when we go over to England to visit Lew's cousins.'

'I think I've met him,' Hannah said. For once she knew who they were talking about.

'Is that right?'

'I stayed with Susie at her parents' place down there, when we were about sixteen.'

'Nice guy, Tristan.'

'Yes,' Hannah agreed. He had walked in through the kitchen door one lunchtime, followed by a dog, and she had been surprised to see that though he was a young man, with a young man's firm, bright-eyed face, Tristan Carrick's thick hair had the colour of old age.

'All the Carricks go grey early,' Susie had said later. 'Ma told me that his father was exactly the same.'

None the less the unseasonable white hair made Tristan – eight years older than herself – seem to Hannah immeasurably ancient, especially as he was already through his university studies, had qualified as an architect, was someone who travelled the world. He seemed to belong to her parents' generation rather than her own. Tristan's eyes had met hers when he first came in and she had felt the strength of that meshing glance long after Susie had leaped up from the kitchen table and rushed over to hug, to exclaim, to adopt an exaggerated Mummerset accent as she greeted him.

'Ar, et do be moy liddle maid come woam,' he had said, holding her at arm's length, sounding like any stage West Countryman, but it was only to humour Susie, for after that he spoke without further trace of accent.

Later, they had been invited to lunch by his parents and had walked across the cliffs to the crumbling Georgian house, three or four miles from the one Susie's parents owned near Mullion Cove. Hannah could still remember the spectacular view over the sea, the big buttercup-yellow drawing-room, the copper beech at one side of the house.

For the rest of their time in Cornwall he had remained remote, saying nothing to Hannah, although they came across him several times, the three Carricks coming to a reciprocal lunch; the two girls invited, along with Susie's parents, to dine amid tarnished silver candlesticks and beautiful not-quite-clean dinner-plates, hand-painted in gold and blue and crimson. Nor did Hannah feel any deprivation at not seeing more of him. There had been too much to do: walking the dogs, picnicking, swimming, bicycling through high-hedged lanes to play tennis or visit the old fleapit cinema.

'Let's eat, folks!' Nancy said now, and led them towards basil-flavoured tomato soup, pasta, cold lamb in a rosemary sauce, fruits and cheeses.

Tearing at roundels of bread, Lew said: 'Say, Susie, did you know Tristan was thinking of setting up for himself?'

'No,' Susie said.

'He's trying to set up his own design company at home,' said Lew. 'His parents hadn't been too good, health-wise, in the couple of years before they died and he thought he ought to move nearer them.'

'Gosh,' said Emma. 'I hope our children are as devoted as that to us when *we're* old, don't you, Hugo?'

Hugo nodded.

Lew poured wine from coarse green carafes, while his wife passed plates of artichoke and sausage. 'There's some tie-in with some people in New York,' he said vaguely. 'Computer graphics or something. It's a bit over my head, really.' He grinned round at his guests. 'I'm just an unregenerate reactionary slob, strictly computer-unfriendly. Still using my Remington portable, I'm afraid.' Lew wrote science fiction, under a pseudonym, and did it well enough to ensure a pretty comfortable life for his family.

'That'll change,' someone said. 'Bet you won't be able to do without a personal computer ten years from now. Especially here, so far away from New York and London.' The talk became technical.

'Where will Tristan stay when he comes?' Susie wondered.

'I don't suppose either of us will know until the last moment,' said Nancy. 'You know how he is.'

'He's so gorgeous, I do hope he comes to your place, Susie, and that we're still there,' said Emma. She had straight blonde hair held back from a high, pale forehead with a velvet Alice-band. Hannah found it difficult to believe that she was a barrister. 'Don't you agree, Hugo?'

'Frankly, no,' Hugo said. 'But then I'm not in the habit of finding other men gorgeous. Absolutely not.'

'You Brits are so uptight,' Nancy said.

'If you want uptight, have you met the Swedes who just bought that little place on the other side of the town?' someone asked. 'Typical Scandinavians.' The conversation moved towards national types, how Germans always had loud voices, the Italians drove like idiots, the French complained all the time . . .

Looking across the table at Susie, Hannah found herself wondering about the unsatisfactory-sounding Lucas. Did Susie genuinely want to marry him, or was it just her usual exaggerated fashion of talking? Yet how many times had Hannah heard her say it – 'all I ever wanted is to marry Lucas and have lots of children!'? Certainly enough to think she meant it. Especially about the children. The only flaw in Susie's otherwise perfect life was the fact that she was an only child, an omission she compensated for by treating Hannah like a sister. But the man she had chosen did not sound likely to make her a good husband. And Hannah had never once heard her say she loved him, only that he hypnotised her, that she was hooked. It always seemed an odd choice of word.

And anyway, the thought of Susie married was not comforting. She would be occupied, taken up, no longer just Hannah's friend but also someone else's wife, with all the concomitant responsibilities and imperatives that entailed. Perhaps Susie would feel the same about Hannah marrying. So far, Hannah had kept to herself the contents of the letter from Anthony which had arrived two days ago.

Please marry me [he had written]. *You know I wanted to ask you when we had dinner together before you went to Italy. You know I love you, darling Hannah, and I think we'd be terribly happy together. I'd certainly see it as my lifetime's work to make sure that you were. Everything I have I give to you. If you want it. Darling Annie, I do so hope that you do.*

She had not told Susie about this proposal because she knew that Susie, always practical, would immediately demand to know whether she had slept with him. If not, she would not only want to know why not, but also point out that Hannah must be crazy if she was seriously contemplating marrying a man with whom she had not gone to bed.

That was exactly the point: Hannah was *not* seriously contemplating marrying Anthony Barlow. He was extremely good company, amusing and witty, already established as a junior partner with a firm of accountants in a provincial town north of London. She enjoyed being with him and waited with impatient anticipation for their meetings; she felt a melting inside her when he kissed her. Yet she sensed in Anthony something not quite rooted, something uninvolved, a flimsiness of attitude. So far she had not introduced him to her parents, knowing that despite his calling, they would dismiss him as a lightweight. What she had not yet worked out to her own satisfaction was whether she shared that opinion or not. And if she did, whether it mattered.

What she really wanted to keep from Susie, however, was not Anthony, but her own virginal state. What mattered most, she knew, was love; unversed, she still did not know whether she loved him or not.

Three or four days later a car pulled up on the yellow drive below the terrace. Voices called. Hannah, drowsing by the pool, heard them dimly through the muffling undergrowth: male laughter mingled with the lighter voices of women. Apprehension filled her. She was not good in company, she knew that. Social chit-chat, dinner-table banter: it was a foreign language she had never mastered. In her own home, her parents spoke earnestly together of new textual interpretations, academic articles, discoveries in German libraries or forthcoming symposia in Prague. Occasionally they lofted a remark in her direction and then both of them would wait politely, looks of interest on their faces, while she answered. Even as she did so, she was aware that mere good manners prompted the questions and that they were not in the least interested in her replies.

With these new arrivals, she would, she knew, seem even more out of it than usual. All Susie's friends seemed to know each other; all had a wide network of other interconnected friends. Seemingly, none of them had ever known what it was to be shy; all of them were cared for, beautiful, well-dressed.

Yet she could not despise them for frivolity, which might have been a comfort. They did serious things with their lives, worthwhile things, creative things. All of them seemed terrifyingly competent. Some were solicitors, some worked for publishers or taught in single-sex schools or were medical students. Some had their own businesses: antiques or interior design or bed-and-breakfasts. One even farmed, by herself, a hundred and fifty acres in Lincolnshire. The ability to drive a tractor or tell the difference between a Georgian silver snuff-box and a fake, or provide hungry businessmen with three-course lunches, impressed Hannah deeply.

Saying this to Susie once, she had been surprised by her friend's reaction. '*They're* all frightfully impressed by *you*!' she had exclaimed.

'Me? Why?'

'For one thing you're amazingly brainy,' Susie said forthrightly. 'Scholarships all over the place. Awards. Prizes. Plus you're practically a professional cello-player.'

Hannah snorted derisively. 'Of course! I turned down an invitation from the Philharmonic only the other day.'

Susie ignored that. 'And, as I'm always telling you, you're beautiful, too.'

'Me?'

'Let's face it, your parents aren't exactly Mr and Mrs Gorgeous

Couple,' Susie said, forthrightly. 'Frankly, it always amazes me how two people like them ever produced you.' She surveyed her friend critically. 'There must be Mediterranean blood in you somewhere. Perhaps an Algerian corsair captured one of your ancestors and after clapping her up in his harem, impregnated her.'

'I say, steady on, old girl.'

'Look at you.' Susie pulled her over to a mirror which hung on the wall. 'That ballerina face, that dark hair and *huge* eyes. And that tiny, tiny waist. Oh God,' groaned Susie, pinching her own hips. 'I'd *kill* for a waist that size.'

Hannah was amazed. She genuinely felt herself at a loss in the world which Susie inhabited and, bringing up her own inadequacies, had expected, at most, a piece of encouraging advice: smile more, hold your head up, think of three interesting questions to ask when you go out to dinner with a bloke. It was the sort of thing Susie was good at.

Huge eyes, Susie had said. She stared at them later, leaning into her own reflection. Were they huge? They just looked like eyes, really. And her waist . . . she put her hands on either side of it. It *was* quite small. But did it matter? Was it important in any way, compared to the much more serious fact that she could never think of anything to say in company?

Remembering this conversation, but taking no comfort from it, she reluctantly began to make her way back to the house, her bare feet dragging in the soft mulch of the secret pathways through the undergrowth. Her hair caught in a hanging branch and she stood with arms above her head to untangle it, while all around her the earth breathed heat, and cicadas ticked in the white noonday heat beyond the leafy corridors. Somewhere, a tap, long ago rusted into almost-dryness, dripped ponderously into a leaf-silted marble basin, all that was left of a fountain.

Coming out between overhanging bushes of bougainvillaea into the brightness of the sunlit lawn behind the house, she could not see the others in the shade of the roofed veranda which ran across the back of the house, though she could hear them talking, their voices subdued by the heat. She crossed the grass towards them, feeling sweat break out under her arms, knowing that they were all watching her. Ineffectually she brushed at her skirt, belatedly aware of leaf-mould under her fingernails, dried waterweed clinging to her legs.

And then one of them got up and came down the stone steps to meet her. He wore pale trousers and an open-necked white shirt with the sleeves rolled up. A straw hat shaded his face. He walked with the grace of an athlete and as he came nearer to her, he smiled, teeth white in his tanned face, holding out a hand.

'We haven't met before,' he said. 'I'm Lucas. Susie's cousin.'

'Hannah,' she replied. 'Hannah Carrington.'

He took her hand and held the fingers lightly between his own. 'Hannah,' he repeated softly. 'Ah yes. Susie's friend.'

Things were never ever going to be the same. She knew that instinctively, looking up at him, and she shivered suddenly in the blazing sunshine. She sensed disaster in the future, pain, anger. He was Susie's, and she wanted him. Never in her life had she felt naked desire for anything; she felt it now. In that split second before she pulled her hand from his, she knew the recklessness which drove on Héloïse and Abélard, Romeo and Juliet, Lancelot and Guinevere. All the doomed lovers.

Was it a coming-together of twin souls, clashing like waves at the foot of some storm-bound cliff? Long afterwards, acknowledging that it had not been, she was to wonder whether the spell Lucas cast over her in that first meeting was so powerful simply because, opened like a flower under the hot Italian skies, she was ready to be enchanted.

'I thought you were a naiad,' he said, 'or a dryad or something. Some kind of wood nymph.'

'Oh?'

'Definitely sylvan.' His voice was intimate, warm. He smiled down at her. 'There are wreaths of laurel crowning your hair.'

'Wreaths?' She tried to laugh, to sound collected and confident; he bent towards her so that she could smell clean skin and cool cotton and the faint tang of fresh perspiration.

'Laurel leaves, certainly,' he said. 'Or at least, *one* laurel leaf.' He picked something from her hair, his hand grazing her face as he held it towards her. 'Bay – that's the same thing as laurel, isn't it?'

'I—' She cleared her throat. 'Yes.'

'Proof enough, I think, of your nymph-like status.'

From the veranda, someone lazily called his name; he took no notice. Someone else laughed, and Hannah flushed: were they laughing at her? Was the effect he was having on her so obvious? She felt as though there was a golden streak where he had touched her cheek.

'Very suitable,' she said, taking the stiff green leaf from him, crushing it in her hand. She held it towards him and he bent his elegant head to smell the pungency in her palm. 'Did you know that the nymph Daphne was changed into a laurel tree in order to escape the amorous attentions of Apollo?' She was surprised at how much in command she sounded.

'Apollo. The sun god.'

'That's right.'

'If I were to pursue you,' he said lightly, 'would you try to escape?'

'That depends. I certainly wouldn't want to spend the rest of my life as a bay-tree.'

'Could be boring,' he agreed. His eyes crinkled at the corners.

'On the other hand,' said Hannah, 'it might be better to be bored to death as a tree than burned to death by a sun god.'

'Possibly.'

'So I'll just have to watch out, won't I?'

'Yes,' he said soberly, holding her glance. 'If you don't want to be scorched.' He had strange eyes, cat's eyes, opal-coloured, which glowed in the dark bronze of his face.

His intensity was unnerving. Carefully she stepped away from him and began walking towards the house, very conscious of him at her side. He was extraordinarily good-looking; to Hannah, who had spent most of her life with ugly people, he was undoubtedly the most beautiful human being she had ever encountered. Did his beauty make him attractive, she wondered? Or was he merely another object to be admired, as she might admire a Botticelli portrait, a Michelangelo statue, a jewelled snuff-box?

As she reached the foot of the shallow steps up to the veranda, he said softly behind her: 'Beware, Hannah Carrington.'

7

'You'll come over to lunch tomorrow, won't you?' Lucas said, as he and his friends were leaving.

'Love to. Wouldn't we, everybody?' Susie looked round at her own house guests. 'We'll bring things with us – tell your housekeeper not to worry.'

'My housekeeper, as you call her, has got other things on her mind than a crowd of layabouts like you lot,' Lucas said cheerfully. 'However, I'll tell her what you say.'

Although Lucas addressed his cousin, his shaded gaze was on Hannah. Had Susie noticed? It seemed not. But then she never seemed to be aware of the fact that Lucas always appeared totally indifferent to her.

'There,' Susie remarked, when Lucas had gone. 'Didn't I say he was handsome?'

'You did, and you were right because he is. Very. But a bit disappointing.'

'Why?'

'You told me his eyebrows beetled, and they didn't at all.'

'What about those weird eyes of his?'

'They're certainly unusual.'

'Poor Lucas. We feel terribly sorry for him.'

'Why?'

'Didn't you notice how twitchy he was?' asked Susie. 'He's was in another car accident recently. And he's always being mugged.'

'Always?'

'At least twice in the past six months.'

'Not much fun for him.'

'Plus, Ma and I are convinced he's nursing a Secret Sorrow.'

'Isn't that part of his charm? That air of mystery?' And doesn't, Hannah thought, he trade on it? Now that he was no longer there, it seemed astonishing that she should have allowed him, in some indefinable way, to take her over – and even more so that she should so easily have surrendered.

'Probably. Ma thinks he's got some unsuitable mistress in Maida Vale or wherever it is they keep mistresses these days. Someone he can't marry in case she taints the purity of the bloodlines.'

'What bloodlines? And anyway, I thought *you* were going to marry him.'

'I am, when I'm ready. Which I'm not, at the moment. So he might as well sow some wild oats.'

'Getting married is the opposite of wild oats, isn't it?'

'Whatever,' Susie said casually. 'Married or not, it won't make any difference, once I make my move.'

'Honestly, Susie, that's the most immoral thing I ever heard. Incidentally, does he know about these speculations of yours?'

'Of *course* he doesn't. And I wouldn't dare ask him about *any* of them.'

'Why not?'

'Apart from anything else—' Susie gave a melodramatic shiver. 'I'm scared stiff of him, even if he *is* my own cousin.'

'Not exactly a good basis for a long-lasting relationship, you know.' Hannah thought about Anthony Barlow. Even though she could not imagine herself married to him, there were a number of points in favour of such a union. One of which was how well they got on together. How could you want to spend the rest of your life with someone of whom you were, to quote Susie, 'scared stiff'?

'Quite apart from anything else, like I've said before, he kind of . . . gets inside your head, if you're not careful,' Susie said.

'What *are* you talking about?'

'Difficult to explain, really.' Susie lowered herself on to one of the cushioned chaises on the veranda, and said sleepily: 'We'll just have to do our best to keep poor Lucas cheerful while we're here, won't we?'

'I suppose so.' Why did Hannah have a brief, hopeless vision of herself, white-robed and garlanded, led out like a heifer to some pagan altar, a virgin sacrifice?

Although the two villas were built to an identical plan, Hannah found that Lucas's house, the Villa Diana, had been added to and altered in minor ways. The gardens were better maintained: the hedges were trimmed, there was a formal parterre, box hedges enclosing roses with sandy paths between. The house too was much more ornate than its twin. The furniture was massive and polished, the rooms fully furnished; armies of maids were implied, putative butlers presided.

In his own surroundings, Lucas was authoritative. Seated halfway down the long table spread outside, under a grape-vined arbour, Hannah glanced surreptitiously at its head, where he sat. If his mother spent most of her time in Barbados, was he solely responsible for the upkeep of this impressive home? He seemed young to have shouldered such a burden.

There were about a dozen guests, disposed around the trestle table; they drank wine from goblets of grainy-green glass and ate cold salamis, pasta, a complicated garlicky salad. Above their heads, the sun peered, nudging aside the leaves every now and then, landing like a red-hot spider on exposed skin. The talk was the sort Hannah had come to expect of such gatherings: inconsequential, rambling – Chappaquiddick, Kent State, Harold Wilson's defeat at the polls – and incestuous in its plaiting of names already familiar to her. Kim, Chloe, Helena, Dorian . . . She leaned back against the wooden chair and half-closed her eyes, mind blank, thinking of nothing, giving herself up to the pleasures of wine in her mouth, the marbled floor beneath her feet, the scent of leaves, the food . . .

'*Hannah.*'

She looked up, startled. From his seat at the top of the table, Lucas had just spoken her name, almost shouted it, as though to gain her attention; she could still hear its echo in her head. Yet when she leaned forward, eyebrows raised enquiringly in response, he was talking to Emma, on his right. Then, as she was about to sit back, he slowly turned his head.

For Hannah, that point at which his glance met hers was, for the rest of her life, to remain seminal; she could still, then, have retreated, closed herself off, barricaded herself against him. But, unaware that the shape of her future swung on that pivotal moment, she looked back at him. And was lost. There was a slow convulsion in her chest, as though he had reached in and taken hold of her heart; with a jolt which shook her, she thought: is *this* love?

'*Hannah.*' The voice belled in her brain and although his mouth had not moved, she knew it was Lucas, drawing the will from her, pulling it out of her soul as a magician pulls ribbons from a hat. '*He kind of gets inside your head* . . .' Susie had said, and Hannah had never understood. Now she did.

She looked away. 'Beware,' Lucas had told her. She had wondered what he warned her against.

Through the exquisite green of the grapevine, she could see the sunlit lawn and, beyond it, the box hedges. A child suddenly appeared, short fair hair bleached almost white; one moment it had not been there, the next it stood beside the fountain in the middle of the laid-out garden, staring towards them, its arms hanging by its sides. It seemed at once close to, so that Hannah could see the golden hairs on the tanned arms, and at the same time, distant, so that she could not tell whether it was a male or a female child. Almost she imagined she could see the flower-beds through the insubstantial body – and then, from beyond a screening hedge came a low call, and suddenly the child was gone again, darting like a bird, vanished.

Hannah closed her eyes. Was it the effect of the dazzling light, or the wine they had drunk, that made everything seem so clear and, at the same time, so hallucinatory? Why, when she looked at Lucas, did she feel a torment which was not yet hers?

At her side, an English voice brayed inanities: 'History at Cambridge, I think Susie said – met Prince Charles, have you?'

'Not yet.'

'Still, you must be fearfully brainy—' and she spoke again, and smiled politely, all the time seeing inside her head, as though through the wrong end of a telescope, the child, the white light, the unbroken line of the box hedge.

'Child?' Susie said later. 'I didn't see one.'

'It wasn't there for very long,' Hannah said apologetically.

'It probably belongs to Lucas's housekeeper,' Susie said.

'Is that the woman who lurked?'

'I didn't see anyone lurking.'

'You must have done. She lurked like anything, while those Italian girls were loading up dishes and carrying trays. Didn't you see her, watching Lucas, hidden in the shadows? It was like something out of a movie. All burning eyes and brooding stares.'

'I didn't, actually. I suppose she's a local widow or something.'

'Why would she brood over Lucas?'

'You probably imagined it,' said Susie, half asleep.

'Is it her who keeps the house so glossy-magazinish?'

'Her or the maids. It certainly isn't Lucas,' Susie said. 'I doubt if he even knows where the kitchen is, let alone the furniture polish.'

'What does he do?'

'Merchant banking or something,' Susie said vaguely. 'When he's not farming the ancestral estates.'

'He doesn't look like a farmer to me.'

'My dear, when you're that wealthy, who does?'

'Did you say he lived in Cornwall?'

'Much of the time, though I know he has a flat in London as well. It's the twin-thing again. Ma has a house there so Diana has too. Or did. That's how we met Tristan, actually; his family are old friends of Lucas's family.' Susie looked round at the shabby covers of the Villa Giulia's salon. 'This is very different from the Diana, but I feel a lot more at home here than among all that splendour, don't you?'

Hannah lay on her back, naked in the waterweed. Above her head circled two dragon-flies; were they the same pair she had seen before? Did they mate for life, like swans? They hung in the air only inches from her face so that she could see the unimaginably delicate tracery of their wings, the gorgeous blue on either side of the long, jointed bodies.

She should have been thinking about Reform Bills, Castlereagh's foreign policy, the Irish Question. Instead, she thought of Lucas. These days, she did little else. What did he do all day: walk on the hills, visit friends, sight-see? Did he ever think about her?

Sometimes he appeared at the Villa Giulia, his face reddened by the sunshine, his thick, fair hair already bleaching white at the ends. She would watch, pretending she did not, his hands, wondering at the thick white scars across the knuckles, wondering what they would feel like if he were to – and she would hastily remind herself of the Industrial Revolution, the Boer War, the first Home Rule Bill, anything, so that he could not pick up on such thoughts.

He never talked about his own doings, preferring to sit stretched out in a chair listening to the others – for another carload of Susie's friends from university had recently arrived. He did not speak to Hannah, but they communicated. Sometimes she would look up and find his long eyes resting on her; sometimes he would call to her, '*Hannah, Hannah,*' soft whispers which leaped from his mind to hers and made no earthly sound.

There were long lunch parties, picnics, swimming expeditions. When she could, Hannah got out of going, preferring the melancholic pleasures of the neglected garden, the empty rooms.

In the evenings they all sat together in the big *salone* which Susie's mother had filled with old sofas covered in faded rugs. The ceiling was beamed and planked in dark wood; the thick, uneven walls had been washed in a dull raspberry-pink which bathed the big space in a warm glow. At night, with candles lit, the rooms seemed Rembrandtesque, painted in unobtrusive crimsons, soft browns, golds, which gleamed softly when caught in the leaping flames of the fire it was still necessary to light once the sun had gone down. In her mind they always appeared as though frozen in a posed tableau: Helena leaning against Dorian, Mungo reaching towards Charlotte, Susie, herself.

The days plodded by, fiery, languid. The visitors changed, always similar if never quite the same. Toby, Charlotte, Kim and Lucy, Dorian, Helena, Philip. But never Tristan. They sat listlessly on the back veranda, fanning themselves, complaining about the heat and the flies. Sometimes they roused themselves to drive to places of interest, beauty spots mentioned in guide books, the houses of acquaintances near by. Sometimes Hannah joined them, but increasingly she felt isolated from them. A difference of attitude was reinforced by a difference of expectation. They knew what they wanted, where they were going; Hannah did not.

They had none of Hannah's shyness about their bodies. Unashamedly, they bathed with the door open as they chattered to each other, showered, walked naked in and out of each other's rooms. It was too hot for any but the lightest clothing: everyone wore as little as they possibly could. Sometimes the girls went topless; Hannah averted her eyes from those thin breasts, those flaunting nipples. Casually they wondered aloud why she did not do the same as they but did not press the point when she shook her head.

Sexually too, they were uninhibited, liberated, moving in and out of each other's arms and beds in a flutter of blown kisses, shared hugs, intimate looks. Hannah was intrigued: as an only child, the daughter of parents such as hers, the sexuality of others was as much a mystery to her as her own.

Did Helena go with Mungo; were Dorian and Charlotte a couple? Was Lucy about to part with Kim and take up with Philip, or possibly Dorian? The interchanges fascinated her. Observing, listening, especially at night, when music drifted from open windows, crackly old recordings of *Tracks of My Tears*, and *You've Lost That Lovin' Feelin'*, hit songs left behind from the previous summer, Smokey Robinson, the Miracles, throbbing into the darkness, and the empty corridors magnified even the slightest noise, she felt her hold on herself slipping. Sex, lovemaking, which she had hitherto perceived as some kind of test or ordeal, some major rite-of-passage, was obviously easier and sweeter than she had imagined. She felt she had missed out on something; she thought of Anthony and wished she had not always deflected his questing hands and mouth.

She thought of Lucas.

At night their contemporary faces took on a different, almost mediæval look. Voices softened and blurred. Was it only the wine so freely drunk, Hannah was to wonder later, or did the atmosphere of the place catch and hold them, transform them from their daytime personae into images from another earlier time? She was not used to alcohol; her austere parents occasionally drank sherry when their tall, stiff colleagues came to call; on special occasions they might open a bottle of something which even ignorant Hannah knew was not particularly good. She was not, therefore, prepared for the effect on her of the warm local wines, the way they could soften the edges of things so that the room and the people in it seemed somehow to liquefy, like the melting wax of the candles, reducing their complicated selves to single elements: laughing mouths, the shape of an ear, dark profiles against the pink walls, a hand pale in the gloom.

Through the open windows came moths, large, softly furred, drifting under the ceiling like unquiet souls before, always, they fluttered towards the candles. Briefly they would dance among the flames until, inevitably, their grey wings caught fire and, with a tiny incandescence, their bodies fell to the floor. Hannah, observing, felt as though she was on the verge of a major discovery, that she had stumbled on some metaphor for life. Was the dance worth that final flaming plunge? Did those who danced always have to pay the price?

*　　*　　*

By now, she had uncovered two or three square feet of the mosaic floor of the ruined chapel. Every afternoon she patiently removed more of the accumulated mulch. The brass ring was clearly set into a trap-door which led to storage space beneath, but although she tried several times to lift it, she was unable to do so. She concentrated instead on clearing the mosaic. It was difficult to guess what the whole scene would eventually portray. So far, she had the heads of two men, one elderly, a wreath of leaves around his grey curls, the other younger, his brown hair tied with a black band, his expression eager. A priest and his acolyte? Saints? Both of them looked towards something which, for the moment, remained obscured: would it be an altar, a Christ figure martyred and bleeding, the finger of God? Desire to know drove her on despite her inadequate tools and the sweating toil involved.

Each afternoon she bathed in the pool.

'A nymph,' Lucas had called her; she had sensed some kind of promise in his words. Wrongly, as it turned out. None the less, as she floated naked beside the lily-pads, she was keenly aware of the analogies with classical mythology, of the lusty gods and fleeing dryads who might once have sported in these glades.

When did she first begin to wonder, as day followed day, if someone was watching her? Certainly, she had for some time had the feeling that behind the sheltering leaves there were eyes, that fingers had gently reached forward to part the branches, that behind them there lay a kind of breathing expectation. She put it down to the imperatives of the place and her own classical education, all the precedents of dreaming maidens surprised while bathing.

Listening to the rustle of bamboo, the languid murmur of leaves, it was all too easy to see how some of the myths of ravishment and metamorphosis might have originated in the slanting bars of sunlight, the movement of a tree.

At what point did she become certain that the hidden watcher was neither godling nor satyr, but real and human? Was, in fact, Lucas? What gave him away: a shuffle of feet, a softly cleared throat? Or was it the intermesh between them which caused her, one afternoon, to hear his voice – 'Hannah. Hannah' – lapping at the edges of her mind, and feel the heat of the sparks which burned deep in his eyes as she floated in the shadowed water?

Knowing he watched, she turned so that her breasts lay rippled, aqueous, a mermaid's breasts. Her usual shyness had vanished; she felt no sense of shame or wantonness. The sun, dappling through the trees overhead, had burned through her and left only the ashes of her inhibition; she had, in the days since her arrival here, undergone some kind of pagan metamorphosis. She swam towards the mossy steps and climbed out, her body liquidly expectant, already prepared for his touch. He waited for her, shirt open at the throat, hands in pockets. Under the wide brim of his straw hat, his eyes were expressionless. Though she smiled hesitantly at him, he did not return her smile. Never in her life had any man seen her naked; she trembled slightly, her nipples hardening as he looked at them. In a moment, he would start to undo his shirt, he would take her in his arms. In anticipation she felt the heat of his sun-flushed skin against the coolness of her still-wet body.

'Hello, Lucas,' she said shyly.

'Hannah.' It was the same whisper which sometimes invaded her mind as they sat in the *salone* watching the fire while the others laughed and chatted.

For a moment they stared deep into each other's face. Then he sighed.

'What is it?' she asked, naked in front of him.

'I think you . . . endanger me,' he said slowly.

'How?'

'I don't know. But I think you will be my downfall.' His face was sad. Slowly, he bent his head and kissed the white skin of her breast. His mouth, lingering, had the heat of fire. He straightened, then looked away from her.

She took his hand. 'Kiss me again,' she said.

As though the movement was difficult, he brought his eyes back to hers. 'It wouldn't be wise,' he said. 'Believe me, it would not.'

'Why?'

'You are an innocent,' he said. 'I don't want to hurt you.'

'Then why have you been watching me?'

He frowned. 'You knew I was there?'

'Not for sure – not until this afternoon.'

'Why didn't you say something?'

'What would I say?' She shivered. 'What *is* there to say?'

Slowly, as though moving through water, he put out a hand and touched the skin along her jaw. 'Nothing.' His voice was low, almost inaudible. 'Nothing at all.'

Standing on tiptoe, she leaned closer to him so that his mouth was almost touching her own. 'Kiss me,' she whispered. 'I know you want to.'

Again he frowned. He held her away from him. 'Hannah, please don't.'

She flushed at the rejection, feeling a tide of embarrassed blood surge up her body, wanting, in that moment, to die. Hastily she moved away, acutely conscious of her nakedness. 'I'm sorry,' she said.

'Why are you sorry?'

'I really didn't mean to push myself at you.'

He held her wrists. 'Don't be an utter fool.'

Pulling violently away from him, Hannah picked up a towel and held it against herself. She wondered at her own boldness in urging him to

– to what? Make love to her? Confusion seized her: did he think she wanted more from him, some kind of commitment before she would lie down with him, some promise to share the future? She was aware of hurt, and knew it was not just hers.

'I'm not a virgin,' she said, her voice brusque, hoping he would not sense the lie.

'Do you think I care?' he demanded. 'Do you think I give a shit whether you've had it off with half the Brigade of bloody Guards?'

The rudeness was stunning, like a blow. She supposed that in his world, the world of the experienced women – cool-eyed, long-legged, sophisticated – who visited the Villa Diana, he was always being propositioned, and took her to be no more than one of them.

'I – I don't know what you—' There were lines round his eyes and his mouth which made her realise that he was older than she had suspected.

'Of course you don't.' He pushed at her, roughly, so that she stumbled. The towel fell, and she heard him draw in a breath. 'For God's sake get some clothes on,' he said.

Stung, angry now, she contemplated jumping back into the pool and from there, telling him to sod off and leave her alone. Yet something about his expression evoked pity more than anger. She dressed as quickly as she could, her clothes catching on her damp skin; they walked together to the house, without speaking.

At the foot of the steps leading up to the terrace, Lucas stopped. 'You should wear a bathing suit when you swim,' he said.

She stared at him coolly. 'Should I?'

'I'm not the only one who's been watching you.'

'I suppose you're going to try and make me believe that you've been spying on me in order to save me from a fate worse than death,' she said scornfully.

He raised uninvolved eyebrows. 'Something like that.'

Swinging past her, he went on up the steps while she watched, feeling the last shreds of self-confidence shatter. How could she have been so bloody stupid as to think that he wanted to make love to her? How *could* she? He must have been laughing himself sick when she flung herself at him – or even worse, been thoroughly embarrassed.

Suddenly, she was running, snatching up one of the bikes which lay haphazard below the terrace and pedalling clumsily away between the trembling poplar trees which lined the long drive. Oh *God*. How could she have been such an *idiot*? Her face flaming, she turned left into the road, away from the town, past the closed and padlocked gates of the Villa Diana, and out into the wilder country, cycling past neat fields of pruned vines and fruiting trees. Poppies blew on the grass verges. Puffs of white dust rose from under her wheels and floured her feet, hanging for a moment in the sultry heat before settling again.

There were ditches on either side, crammed with some kind of broad-leafed weed which sprouted a thick, white flower and gave off a strange scent. A heat fiercer than the sun made her perspire as she relived the past half-hour. She had stood there *naked*; she had rubbed her boobs up against him, she had behaved exactly like a back-street tart. Rage and shame burned her. There was only one thing she could do now and that was to pack her bags and leave. Susie would protest, but that was just too bad.

She cycled for what seemed a long time, not sure where she was going, only aware that her humiliation was gradually subsiding. She turned off the road on to a dirt track; after a while the fields gave way to a stand of sweet-smelling pine trees which dropped a resiny scent into the air beneath their spread branches. The track dipped downhill. She stood up on the pedals with the wind in her hair. For a few yards, she soared. Then the front wheel hit some obstruction, the bike veered to a violent stop and she was falling, hitting the hard-packed dirt. At the same time, a car-horn sounded behind her, long and angry. She rolled away, reflexively covering her head with her hands, expecting to be crushed. But the car pulled up with a screech of brakes; she heard the squeal of unoiled hinges as the door was opened and someone got out and walked over to where she lay. A man began to shout at her. She could have got up; it seemed easier to lie there in the white dust. She hoped he would think that he had killed her. Then a hand grabbed her arm and she was jerked roughly to her feet.

'Idiot! Cretin! Lunatic!' he yelled, in Italian.

She was all those things and worse. She slapped at her jeans, brushed dirt from her T-shirt, aware that she wore no underwear and hoping that he was not. 'I'm sorry I got in your way,' she said.

'You *do* know you're trespassing, don't you?' he said icily, switching to accented English.

'I didn't, as a matter of fact,' she said. 'Should I have obtained written permission or something?'

He hesitated, wondering whether she was being serious, then shook her head. 'No,' he said. 'That isn't necessary.'

He was much taller than she was, with a head that reminded her of the famous bust of Alexander the Great. Behind him rolled the elements of a classical landscape: blue sky, cypress trees, the town embedded in its hill. 'You nearly ran me over,' she said.

Instead of answering, he reached towards her. She flinched, thinking he was about to slap her face but instead he gently touched the skin under her eyes. 'You have been crying,' he said. 'Why?'

More tears welled. The bamboo grove, the weed-speckled pool, the naked girl: she saw them as though she studied a painting on a wall, the precise arrangement of the composition: the subtlety of skin tone, the varying greens, the play of light and shadow. She looked away from him, trying to blink the tears from her eyes.

'What has made you weep?' he said.

She sniffed. 'I'm sorry if I was trespassing.'

'Is there anything I can do to—'

'Nothing, thanks.' Violently she shook her head and more tears flew, prismed with rainbows by the sun.

'I cannot bear to see a woman cry,' he said. He pulled her towards him and looked down at her face. 'Especially a woman like you – a bruisable woman.'

'Oh, *please*,' she said wearily. Breaking away from him she picked up her bike. 'Look, I apologise for being on your land.'

'Not mine. My wife's.'

'Hers, then.' Hannah looked up at the pine trees. 'It's beautiful here: I can see why you don't want strangers trampling all over it.'

Before he could say anything further, she had mounted the bike and was pedalling away from him, the white dust clouds rising.

8

'Fuck it,' Susie said. '*Fuck* it.'

'Language, old girl.' Hannah was lying in the hammock slung between a corner of the house and a handy tree. The heat had increased; even the nights now were almost unbearably warm, sleep difficult.

Susie slammed the garden table with her clenched fist. 'Damn them to hell.'

'For heaven's sake.' Hannah tried to sit up. 'What on earth's the matter?'

'My bloody parents.' Susie scowled at the letter which had arrived that morning from her father. 'It looks as though I shall have to go to Rome after the weekend. *Fuck* it.'

'Why?' Although she kept her voice unconcerned, Hannah could already feel a flutter of tension in her stomach. Susie was building up into one of her spectacular rages.

'Why? Because my *bloody* parents have made an appointment for me to see someone, that's why.' Susie spoke through gritted teeth.

'What about?'

'Nothing much.' Furiously, Susie scraped her chair back and then, with slow deliberation, grabbed the edge of the table at which she had been sitting and tipped it over, sending the remains of their breakfast flying. Crockery smashed, fruit and bread were showered with shards of broken porcelain, a juice glass rolled to the edge of the grass.

'Calm down, Sooz,' Hannah said, without any hope that Susie would do so. When she was really angry, she was like some elemental force, completely out of control.

'On top of that, Pa wants me to talk to his lawyers about something. Which, knowing Italian lawyers, could take days. Even weeks. And Rome'll be bloody *sweltering* at this time of year.' Susie stamped the ground and then, her face clearing, looked suddenly hopeful. 'Why don't you come with me?'

Hannah groaned inwardly. The last thing she wanted was a hot drive down to the crowded city. 'Do I have to?'

'Pa can damn well pay for the hire of a car. We could drive down together, make a trip of it.'

'I'd much rather stay here.'

Susie frowned, face contorting with anger, then shrugged. 'OK. Suit yourself.'

'I've got masses of reading to do.' Hannah did not add that, so far, she had scarcely opened her books. 'With you away, it'll be a good opportunity for me to get on with it. Finals next term and all that.' She had no wish to spend time in the enervating heat of Rome, nor did she wish to get caught up in any more of Susie's rage than she had to, knowing from experience that it would take hours to simmer down. Then she reminded herself that Susie was her friend. Hastily, she added: 'I'll come if you really want me to, of course.'

'Not if you don't want to,' Susie said. 'Actually, now I think about it, it might be quite a good idea if I went alone.'

'Why?'

'Because, my dear, much as I love you, there are times when two's company and three's a crowd.'

Hannah tried to sit up, the hammock rocking dangerously beneath her. 'I see. And where will you be staying in Rome, might I ask?'

'Ma's got this cousin with a flat near the Colosseum.'

'And is this cousin young, male, gorgeous and loaded?'

'As a matter of fact, *she*'s ninety-two and looks like a cross between the Hunchback of Notre Dame and one of the Ugly Sisters.'

'Is there a young, gorgeous, loaded male living on the premises? Or close by? Or somewhere in Rome?'

'Since you ask,' said Susie, 'there just might be something of the sort.'

'All I can say, old girl, is jolly good luck to you.' Relieved, Hannah lay back again in the hammock and swung herself slowly back and forth. Used to solitude, she could almost taste the pleasure of being on her own in the Giulia, with its echoing rooms, its dusty sunlight and dim, grey mirrors. And lying beneath that pleasure, there was, too, the tingle of some not-quite-acknowledged anticipation which she did not care to examine too closely.

After Susie had left, she went to the kitchen to make a mug of coffee. A majolica bowl lay shattered on the floor; frowning, Hannah found a broom. Susie must have come in here before she left and flung it violently at the wall. Her rage of the other day had not abated over the intervening weekend, then, though she had managed successfully to conceal it after her initial outburst. She wandered slowly through the empty house, drifting across the polished floors while swirls of dust rose like moths in her wake. Standing on the balustraded terrace, she looked between the big urns towards the town. It was noon. The sun burned; the fields of ripe wheat glittered. Later, when the long shadows began to move up from the plains, the scene would change, the colours turn from fawns and terracottas to shades of cinnamon and chocolate.

A hot breeze stirred. She watched it shiver among the leaves at the edge of the grass and die down. Overhead the air was milky, a blue so fragile that if she were to reach up and touch it, the whole sky might shatter and fall about her in dagger-sharp fragments, like the majolica plate.

Sweat rolled down her back, under her thin blouse. It was cooler in the house, but the pool, deep among the trees, was more inviting. Crossing the grass, she pushed between the shrubs, leaves stroking her skin. Heat waited even in the green tunnels; where the sun penetrated, it burned like a flame. It was too hot to do anything more than endure, lie comatose like a lizard and simply wait for the dark.

The surface of the pool was warm, almost hot, but cool and shadowed underneath. Ripples moved across the black water and stirred the water-lily leaves; the fat buds rocked, bamboo rustled and whispered.

She caught a glimpse of white in the shrubs which crowded behind the two marble columns. Someone was watching her again. Lucas? Or some archaic spirit of the trees? In the melting heat, she felt herself to be at one with all that was around her. It did not matter who watched; they too were part of the green woods and black water.

Towards evening, when the sun had moved lower in the sky, she cycled along the flat roads towards the town, to buy bread and fruit. The shadows were longer now; behind the castle on the brow of the hill, a ghost-white circle of moon hung from the cloudless sky.

In the piazza she saw Lucas slouched at a table, a cold beer in front of him. He raised a hand and called her name; she pretended not to have heard him. Since the afternoon at the pool she had managed to avoid him, pleading a series of headaches, saying she had work to do, or was tired. Carrying a disc of crusty bread, she hurried away from him between high, pink walls. In the coolness of the dairy, she waited while they wrapped the creamy cheese which was a speciality of the region. She bought fat tomatoes, gleaming purple-black aubergines, yellow capsicums. She hoped he would not follow.

But, as she was choosing wine in the dark little grocer's shop, she felt a hand on her shoulder.

'You can't run away for ever,' he said, behind her.

Hannah did not reply. He was close enough to her that she could feel his voice against the back of her blouse. He touched one of the knobs of her backbone with a finger; she arched away as though singed by a flame.

'You're too thin,' he said, and his breath brushed the side of her neck.

'Am I?'

'Much, much too thin. Let me take you out to dinner tonight.'

'No thank you,' she said hastily, bending her head, reaching for a bottle, any bottle so that he would not realise how awkward she felt.

'Why not?'

'I just . . . couldn't.'

'Of course you could.' He took the bottle from her, taking her hand, turning her round so that she faced him. 'I wouldn't buy that – it's quite disgusting.'

'Oh.' He burned like a candle in front of her.

'Look. I know you're all alone at the Villa Giulia – Susie rang and told me she was going to Rome. She asked me to look after you, see that you were all right.'

'I'm perfectly capable of taking care of myself, thank you.'

'I know you are. So will you come for my sake? I too am alone at the moment.'

'I'd really rather not.'

'Please, Hannah.'

She turned her back to him, considering. She did not wish to have dinner with him; the memory of his rejection still flooded her with embarrassment whenever she thought of it. And she knew, without analysing exactly how, that if she went with him, she also would be, as he had said, endangered.

Yet he sounded as if he wanted her to come. And it might be fun. And he was a—

'*Hannah* . . .' The unspoken word rang inside her skull.

'All right,' she said. She turned to face him. 'What time?'

'I'll come for you at eight.'

How easily the wrong road was taken.

The moon was almost overhead when they came out of the restaurant, round and golden against a sky splattered with stars. Hannah had enjoyed herself. Lucas was an entertaining and informed companion; his knowledge of the classical myths was at least equal to her own. And he had never once given any indication that he remembered her unsolicited advances beside the pool, never glanced at her mockingly or suggestively, not even touched her.

She stared up at the dark as they walked towards Lucas's car. 'Look at those stars.'

'Glorious. Seeing them, I realise why I never feel quite at home in England.'

'It'd be chilly by now, if we were there now,' Hannah said. 'The air's still warm here, even though it's so late.'

'Careful,' Lucas said. 'You nearly bumped into that car.' He took her hand.

Hannah did not pull away. They walked in silence. In the car, instead of starting the engine, he sat with his hands on the steering wheel, staring ahead. Then he sighed: 'I must take you home, Hannah.'

'Yes.'

The road out of the town wound uphill for a while before dipping down to the plain. The huge, sombre-faced moon was sometimes behind them, sometimes ahead. At the top of the hill, Lucas pulled to the side of the road.

'Look,' he said softly.

Up here, the moon seemed flatter, paler, pasted against the sky rather than hanging from it. Beneath it lay a landscape smoothed out by darkness, sheened like silk. The moonlight was not silver but grey, as though a blanket of cobwebs had been spread over it. In the middle of the vast flatness, riding the dark fields like a boat, reared a small ridge crowned with a pink four-square house which looked out over the lonely countryside all round it. The windows were shuttered; there were four trees, one at each corner, black in the pearl-grey light. The scene had the simplicity of a child's painting.

'Oh,' Hannah said.

'Isn't it beautiful?'

'I wonder who lives there.'

'A friend of mine,' Lucas said. 'A good friend. She's – the house is empty at the moment.'

Hannah turned to him. In the strange light, his eyes were almost opaque, the colour of the moonlight itself. 'Listen,' she said.

'What to? I can't hear anything.'

'Exactly. There's no noise. Absolutely nothing.'

'Cicadas,' Lucas said.

'But no traffic, no sense of other people. Not even night sounds, like owls.' Beads of green fire hung in the air around them. 'Fireflies,' whispered Hannah.

'Magical, isn't it?' Lucas was still staring at the pink house under the moon; momentarily, the long lines of his face seemed to deepen. He was so still that he seemed not to be breathing.

He shook himself and turned towards her.

Hannah. She heard the word, though his lips did not move.

He reached across the car for her, lifting her face to meet his. She knew she ought to resist, but could not.

As his lips touched her mouth, images of regeneration and metamorphosis filled her mind; butterflies and chrysalises, ice and water, buds and flowers. He stared down at her; she could feel herself disintegrating under his sombre gaze, her old self tearing like paper, transmuting into something new and shiny. Under the pressure of his mouth, she groaned.

He took a deep breath. When he took her into his arms, the material of her dress touched her breasts and the sensation filled her with a peppery excitement. It was the heat, she told herself, nothing more than that, the will-sapping heat. But still, she yearned. She wanted to lose herself, take his hand and push it into the hot moist place between

103

her legs, feel his hands opening her, his mouth learning her. Proprieties dissolved. The wine, the candles, the slow flicker of the fireflies, the stunning heat and in front of them, the ghost-coloured fields spreading away towards the black hills: there was an urgency in the night to which, although unconversant, she longed to respond.

Then, remembering his rejection of her by the pool, she forced herself away from him. 'You'd better take me back,' she said. Her voice was not quite under control.

'Yes. I suppose I had.'

She looked at him from under her lashes. His profile was black against the moon which seemed so close that it could have been lying on the windscreen, staring in at the two of them. He turned his head and their eyes met. Were hers as full of longing as his, she wondered? Did they contain the same expression of regret, of might-have-beens, of something precious which had slipped from their grasp?

'Some things are not meant to be,' he said quietly, and searching her mind for a response, she could not come up with one and so remained silent.

'And some things which are, should never have been,' he added, his voice harsh.

She did not ask what he meant. Her hands ached to reach out to him, her mouth longed to feel his again. She wished she was like those others, those girls who so lightly swapped their beds and their men. She wished she could enjoy sex as they did, without needing the complications of love.

He dropped her at the foot of the terrace steps, and then turned in a spin of sandy gravel and drove back down to the road which led to his own house. He had not kissed her again.

She was sitting in the piazza two days later, trying to make sense of the local paper, when someone stopped at her table.

'At least today you are not trespassing,' a voice said and, looking up, she saw the man who had almost run her over a couple of weeks before.

It was a slight remark, and one to which, in view of the heat, she could scarcely be bothered to reply. None the less, she smiled and, when he asked if he could join her, pointed to a chair.

'You are English,' he said, after ordering a *cappuccino* from the waiter, 'yet you look like an Italian. Much too—' He clicked his fingers in the air, searching for a word, 'too skinny, of course. But you have the colouring of the women of our country.'

'Just because I have dark hair—'

'It's more than that,' he said. He looked her over and she felt herself begin to blush. 'Even in that terrible dress, you have a kind of – of excitement about you. A . . . sexiness.'

'Thank you very much.'

'You are not pretty, but when you are old you will be beautiful.' He leaned back and put one hand in the pocket of his slacks.

'Hasn't anyone ever told you that it's very impolite to make personal remarks?' she said.

For a moment he looked at her with a puzzled expression on his face. Hannah could see that he did not know how to react. Then he laughed, throwing back his head.

'You are right.' He reached quickly across the table to touch her hand. 'I have been very ill-mannered—'

'And it's not the first time, either,' Hannah said prissily. 'You were pretty bloody-minded the afternoon you ran me over.'   .

'*Almost* ran you over.' He laughed once more. 'But you see, there I was, driving along on my own land—'

'I thought you said it was your wife's land.'

'It is the same thing,' he said carelessly, 'and what do I see in front of me but a girl on a bicycle. A very furious girl.'

She wondered how old he was. Ten, maybe fifteen years older than herself? He was dark, tanned, handsome, his body full of energy. 'How could you tell?' she asked.

'Every line of your body registered rage,' he said. 'And not only were you furious, but you were wavering about—'

'Do you mean weaving?'

'Weaving is with a—' He mimed the actions of someone at a loom. 'To make fabrics, no?'

'Yes. But it's also teetering from side to side, like a – like a drunk.'

'Exactly. Like a drunk. This girl, I say to myself, this stupid girl, is not only furious, but also drunk, and I must be careful.'

Hannah giggled.

'And possibly crazy as well,' he continued. 'This, I say to myself, is a girl to avoid.'

'Except that you *didn't* avoid me.'

He spread his hands. 'I had no choice.'

'You practically ran me over.'

'Believe me,' he said, 'no one could be more thankful than I that my brakes were in such good condition. And when I say that, I am not joking.' His face was serious; although she knew that what he said was no more than the gallantry which came with being Italian, inside Hannah something contracted for a moment, as though her heart had been squeezed like a sponge and then wrung out. He leaned towards her. 'It is good to see you laugh, rather than cry.'

She watched a cat stalk across the sunny square, its tail held high, and settle down in the shade of the plane trees. 'My parents will be pleased to hear that you maintain your car so well,' she said lightly.

'Ah. Your family. Tell me about them.'

She spoke of her parents and as she did so, the two of them, awkward and dull, assumed a gentler outline, time or distance softening their angularities, lending them some distinction. They were both eminent in their field; were she not their child, she might well have seen them as parents to be proud of. Susie was always saying that she would never inflict the misery of being an only child on another human being: would her own inner loneliness have been assuaged by a sibling? It was one of those questions to which there could never be an answer.

'And your house,' he said. 'Tell me how you live. I am anxious to know.'

'Why?'

'Because you seem to be a fascinating woman, a woman of contrasts. And I ask myself: what makes a woman like this, why is someone so lively at the same time so afraid? How can a woman be so full of fire and yet so frozen?'

Before she could answer, he smiled. 'But perhaps you will accuse me once more of making personal remarks. I am sorry.' He put out a hand. 'Perhaps I should introduce myself: my name is Faustino Castelli.'

'Hannah Carrington.'

'Anna Carrington. Good.'

'Hannah,' she corrected. 'You said you live in Rome.'

'We have a flat,' he said. 'A big apartment near the Via Veneto.'

'And how often do you come down here?'

'My wife is often here in the summer. I come once or twice. I have work to do, patients to see. Besides, I prefer the city to the country.' With a kind of bow at her, he added: 'But now I have met you, perhaps I shall change my opinion.'

'But of course,' Hannah said, her voice sardonic. 'You're a doctor, are you?'

'A psychiatric doctor, yes.'

She stood on the balcony of her bedroom. Overhead, fierce stars burned. As she watched, one detached itself from the sky and rushed across the darkness in a thin trail of fire. Ignorant of the night skies, Hannah could only identify the Plough. It seemed wrongly positioned here and – or did she merely imagine it? – brighter than in England. Behind her, in the bedroom, there was a sound and she turned. In the glimmering half-light she could see a figure standing just inside the room.

She should have been afraid but was not. 'Who's there?' she said calmly. And heard his voice calling her across the room, beating like a moth against her brain.

Hannah. Hannah.

'Lucas.' For a moment she stopped breathing, seeing again a

composite set of images: white breasts, green water, the long leaves of the bamboo.

'I had to come,' he said. 'I couldn't . . . not.'

He had been leaning against the wall. Now he came slowly towards her. She was powerless. Even when he pressed a hand against the small of her back, almost lifting her from the ground, she could not move, or speak. She wanted to lie down with him among flowers, under warm pine trees. She wanted him to linger over her naked body, to kiss the secret moistness of her. She wanted to make love with him. As if in a dream, she felt him lift the dress over her head; she raised her arms like a child when he asked her to. Slowly he began to undo his shirt and somewhere at the back of her mind, she asked herself: *do you really want this?* But body and mind seemed dissociated as he ran his hands down her back to her buttocks. The soft places in her melted. She felt as though she had been poured full of sunshine as he laid her down on the bed.

Why did she yield so easily? It was a question which, afterwards, she was never able to answer. At the time, it seemed to her that there was nothing else in the world except the two of them and the heat of the empty house, the sheets beneath.

'Hannah,' he said, and this time she felt the tender movement of his mouth against her shoulder.

It was as though she no longer had a will of her own. Lucas called to her, and his voice was compelling. Helplessly, she would stop what she was doing and walk through the hanging leaves, down the mossy paths towards the pool. Sometimes he was there waiting for her; he would take her without speaking, open her, stare deep into her eyes as he slowly entered her. At other times, ducking between the tumbledown railings which marked the boundary line of the villas, she would make her way along the paths between the bushes here, at the Diana, kept raked and sanded – up to his house.

Sometimes he would be on the terrace, naked, his body white, already erect. Sometimes he would draw her after him, up the marble stairs to his bedroom, the twin of hers, and then make her wait. Sometimes she would see him standing between the half-closed shutters of his room, watching as she made her way towards him across the grass. Always, after that first time, she went to him.

He rarely spoke. He used her body like a piano, playing her like someone for whom the sounds he drew from his keyboard were memories of raptures once experienced, all the joy he would ever know. Eyes half-closed, their secret fires hidden, he would watch while her body sang for him.

'Lucas,' she would sigh, moan, scream. But he did not answer her, nor did he call her name. She was transfixed by him, melting, arching, clasping; whatever he wanted, she let him do. Sometimes he would take her almost as soon as they came together. At others, he would lie above her, tracing the line of her body, skilfully arousing her with his fingers, his mouth, his tongue. Through him, she learned the secrets of her own sensuality, discovering herself as he discovered her.

Once, she felt tears on his face.

And when it was over, when his sweat had dried on her body, she would stand and dress herself in silence, turned away from him, afraid that if he looked into her eyes, he would see that despite the totality of her yielding, she was none the less able to keep back one small piece of herself, a tiny corner of her mind where she did not allow him to enter. Then, leaving him on the bed, she would walk along the passage to the top of the sweeping stairs and go slowly down them, his juices still oozing from her, and out of the terrace door into the violent heat. He never offered to accompany her; she never asked that he should. She was aware, occasionally, of doors quietly closing as she passed, of eyes which watched from the end of passages, of corners just turned; sometimes, looking back, she would see a shape at one of the windows.

Reaching the pool, she would take off her clothes and plunge into it, up to the neck, to rid herself of Lucas. Sometimes there was a violence about him which hovered on the edge of being perilous. She did not question why she allowed him to use her as he did, to turn her into nothing more than an object, but away from him she could always see that what they did together was altogether degrading. Until the next time he called.

Need me, she begged him silently. *Want me. Ask me for something.* He made no emotional contact with her. She felt unclean, yet the pleasure he gave her was intoxicating, a drug whose habit she had acquired.

'Need me,' she said once, standing over him after he had rolled away from her and her body had regained its normal pulses.

'What?' He turned on the damp sheet and looked up at her from under tousled hair.

'You use me, Lucas.' She shrugged into her cotton shirt and began to do up the buttons.

'Don't you like it?' He reached out a hand and caressed her hip.

She stepped away from him; his arm dropped to the side of the bed and his fingers trailed on the floor. 'You know I do. But I hate the – the impersonality of it. Surely there ought to be something more than just—'

'Just fucking?' He laughed. 'Isn't that enough?'

She pressed her lips together for a moment. 'Not for me,' she said quietly.

He hoisted himself up on one elbow. 'Come on, Hannah. You're a grown woman.'

'Am I?' She did not feel it.

'You know what it's all about.'

'I suppose I do.' But she did not. Fucking without feeling: she had supposed that even so there would be murmurs, kisses, whispered sweetnesses. She had not thought it would be this brutal. Or this lovely.

'Please, Hannah. You aren't going to talk about—' he paused, '*love*, are you?'

'Of course not.' She reddened. 'I just wish you—'

'What?'

'*Needed* me more than you do.'

He sat up. 'Oh, I *need* you, Hannah. Don't make any mistake about that. I really do need you. In fact—' he glanced down at himself, 'if you come back to bed, I'll show you just how much.'

She did not wish to. But he reached out and pulled her towards him, holding her wrist so tightly that the small bones grated. He lifted her shirt, kissed the base of her stomach. She felt his tongue caress the slippery places of her and her body yearned towards him. 'No,' she said faintly. 'Not like that.'

But it was too late. He threw her down, kneeling between her legs, kneeing them apart, wider and wider, before coming into her in a series of violent movements which had her shaking with ecstasy.

'I need you,' he said. 'Do you believe that?'

'Yes,' she said, exploding around him. 'Yes, I do. Yes.'

Afterwards, it seemed pointless trying to explain that that was not what she had meant at all.

He showed her how to manipulate the padlocked gates, in case she wished to cycle to him by road. 'Why do you keep it shut like that?' she asked. 'It must be fearfully inconvenient.'

'Less inconvenient than unwanted visitors would be.'

'We never get strangers turning up at the Villa Giulia.'

'Don't you?' was all he said.

Sometimes, when she left him, the child would be hanging about. Occasionally it was outside Lucas's bedroom, playing with a huge doll's house which stood on the galleried landing. One afternoon, stooping over its shoulder, smelling the half-rank odour of childish sweat, she realised that the rooms were all replicas of those in the Villa Diana. At other times the child would be outside, watching her from under a straw hat, and Hannah would smile, hunch towards it as she might towards some half-wild kitten, but the child only stared at her, expressionless. Once, Hannah said, in Italian: 'Do you like it here?' and then, when she received no answer, asked again, in English: 'Do you like living here?'

The child did not reply. Reaching down, it scratched at an insect bite on its leg, still staring at Hannah, then tugged at the faded red shorts and ran off.

Hannah saw it once, running across the carefully tended lawn with a puppy on a slender yellow lead; it seemed a different child then, more fluid, freer. But later, when Hannah asked what the puppy was called, whether it had a name, the child backed away, as though Hannah's voice spelt danger.

Another afternoon, stepping quietly through the long windows on to the terrace, smelling of Lucas, of lovemaking, she heard the child talking, murmuring in a mixture of Italian and English, and knew then that it was not, as she had begun to think, dumb. It was on the grass below the terrace, quite still, holding up its hands. Even as she watched, it caught one of the powder-blue butterflies which hung in clouds above the grass. For a moment, it examined its prey, then flung it back into the air to join its fellows. About to come down the steps, Hannah paused as it caught another, and without hesitation, clapped its palms together before letting something flutter limply to the grass.

Susie rang from Rome. 'Are you all right?'

'I'm fine.'

'Are you sure? You sound . . . different.'

I *am* different, she wanted to say. 'I don't know what you mean,' she said.

'I hope Lucas has been looking after you,' said Susie. 'I told him to.'

Did you tell him to make love to me? Did you tell him to kiss my hitherto unkissed breasts, to hold me up against the wall in the library and fuck me? Did you ask him to be sure to bend me over the sofa in the *salone* and take me from behind, to lay me naked in front of the mirrors in the ballroom which is the twin of ours, and screw me till I screamed, while all the time I watched my ghostly self in the grey glass, Hannah thought? 'Yes,' she said quietly. 'He's been looking after me.'

'So you're OK?'

'I'm just *fine*, I told you. Why do you keep asking? Do you want to stay down in Rome a bit longer?'

'I do rather.'

'I take it the gorgeous loaded made is doing his stuff.'

Susie paused. Then, sounding unusually guarded, she said: 'You could say that.'

'Have a good time,' said Hannah. 'Stay as long as you like.'

Yet part of her wanted to call for help, to demand that Susie come back; she was afraid that only Susie's return would rescue her from the situation in which she found herself.

9

With the advance of summer, the light began to change. It had been golden when they first arrived, silky and yellow, staining the sky, almost palpable. Dandelion mornings, saffron evenings, the days lying like butter on roofs and fields. Imperceptibly, as the weather grew dryer, the light became brighter and more dazzling. The yellow tones burned out, giving way to a white as intense as snow, harsh and unyielding. The sun became an enemy, predatory, lurking beyond shadowed walls, leaping unexpectedly through windows, battering its way past defences put up against it.

It became too hot to work or eat, almost too hot to breathe. Sometimes Hannah thought she would go home, back to England, but the heat made her listless and the effort of packing, the business of buying tickets, organising taxis, seemed too much. It was easier to sit it out. She no longer worked at uncovering the floor of the chapel; even under the screen of overhead leaf and branch, the air was suffocatingly hot and the slightest movement made her break out in a sweat. The pool began to shrink away from its sides, leaving a green rash of long-haired weed which clung to the edges before drying into faded beige wisps. The spring at the centre grew more sluggish; now she could wade to the centre and the water only came up to her heart.

Occasionally she thought she ought to clear it, to free the water which must obviously be waiting underground for release. But it was too hot, and besides, the pool would have to be drained first. Every day new buds thrust up between the flat lily-pads, plump and yellow; the flowers looked like praying hands, each petal tipped with a faint pink flush. She tried to pick one, but the stems were surprisingly strong, slippery as rubber tubing, impossible to grip.

At night, she lay with the windows wide open, looking out at the burning stars, even a sheet too hot for comfort. Yet, uncovered, she felt vulnerable, sacrificial, as though she offered herself to some huge insatiable god. It was impossible to sleep for more than an hour or two at a time; often she would get up and lean on the balustrade of the balcony, grateful for the cool stone under her arms. Outside, the whole dark landscape seemed to pulse; she could almost hear the throb as it held itself together, cautious, waiting for the cooler weather to return. From the garden below, the scent of roses and camomile mingled to produce a perfume far sharper and richer than during the day.

Sometimes, desperate for relief, she slept out on the balcony. The day's heat lingered longer inside the house now; even after the incandescent sun had dropped down behind the town, the shuttered rooms baked, the air in them difficult to breathe. Studying herself in the mirrors as she passed, she could see she was shrinking, slipping away, each day less corporeal, subsumed, somehow, in the spirit of the house. Her eyes grew bigger, her face smaller; she was aware of bones here and there about her body which she had not known existed.

'You are too thin,' Faustino told her one afternoon, coming across her in the town. He touched her shoulder. 'Are you eating?'

Hannah shook her head. She wore a straw hat and a loose cotton frock. Their weight seemed almost more than she could bear. 'It's too hot to eat,' she said.

'Come with me.' He took her hand and led her towards a low, dark doorway set a step down from the cobbled street. There were four or five rough wooden tables, napkins in a chrome container, bulbous Fanta bottles each holding a single carnation on the tables.

He ordered pasta. 'Five different kinds,' he said, ticking them off on his fingers. '*Carbonara, con pesto, marinara, alla bolognese, alle vongole.*'

It sounded like an opera. Although Hannah protested that she could not eat a thing, none the less when the dishes came she found she was hungry. For days she had eaten nothing more robust than fruit and occasional chunks of bread, snippets of the local cheeses. Her clothes were beginning to hang from her as though she were anorexic.

Faustino watched, sipping from a glass of red wine. 'Good,' he said occasionally, with approval. 'Very good.'

When she laughed, he nodded again. 'I like to see you laugh,' he said. 'For someone so young, you are too sad.'

'Absolutely right,' she said, and laughed again, though it seemed no laughing matter.

When she swore she could eat nothing more, he walked back with her to where she had left her bicycle. 'And now you go back to your villa?' he asked.

'Yes. And thank you very much for feeding me,' Hannah said. She was conscious of her wrinkled dress, of the white dust along her legs. 'I feel much better.'

'And look it, too,' he said.

'I've obviously not been eating enough.'

'Perhaps, Anna, you will—'

'Hannah,' she said.'

'Perhaps one evening you will permit me to take you out to dinner.'

'That's very nice of you,' she said politely.

'Not nice,' he said, shaking his head at her. 'Simply that I should not like your death from starvation on my conscience.'

Cycling back to the Giulia, she wondered about his wife. He always spoke of 'I' rather than of 'we' yet she knew he was married, that the wife came down more often than he did, that she owned a house somewhere near by. Presumably this was where Faustino stayed on his visits here: it seemed odd that they were never together.

Freewheeling down the hill from the town one afternoon, she heard a car behind her and pulled towards the side of the road. Faustino. He stopped beside her and got out. 'I am going to put your bicycle into the back of my car,' he said.

'Why?'

'Because I wish to show you something.'

'But I don't want—'

He put a hand on her mouth. 'Why do you English girls always argue so much,' he said. He looked down at her, then bent and kissed the tip of her nose. The two of them were suddenly still, eyes not meeting, bodies held apart. Her pulses flickered.

He pulled up the back of his car and manhandled the bike inside; the boot was neat, vacuumed, empty except for a first-aid box, a set of tools, and a piece of shiny steel curved like a bow. She climbed into the front beside him. Were Faustino to try and make love to her, she would not reject him. Did that make her a slut, or merely someone anxious to make up for lost time? She thought: what have I become? What has Lucas made me? Or is it the heat which induces this sense of having been laid bare, stripped naked by the sun?

Faustino drove for some time in silence, passing the entrance to the Villa Giulia and, further on, the locked gates leading to the Villa Diana.

Eventually he struck off the road on to a dirt track, and stopped under some pine trees. 'Here,' he said. 'You will like this place.'

He walked along a path between the pines and she followed. It was cool here, the ground slippery with pine needles. She could smell them, faintly tarry, like a newly surfaced road. A kind of sparse fine grass pushed up between the trees, brightly green, and fallen pine cones lay here and there, crunching when she stepped on them.

'What do you think?' he said over his shoulder.

'Lovely,' she said. The sound of occasional traffic from the road had receded. The ground was springy, each footstep resonating with a kind of shudder. The silence became more intense.

Finally, he stopped.

She looked round. The thin grass had given way to velvety green moss. The thick growth of pine kept it damp; the air was as cool as water. There was a tumble of white rocks and, beyond them, lines of almost solid sunlight slanting between the tree trunks, as though she looked out from a barred cave into another world.

Faustino knelt. 'There's a spring here,' he said. 'That's why it stays so green.' She stood behind him and saw a bubbling of clear water. 'It drains away further down the valley.'

Hannah knelt too. This must be the source of the water which fed the little pool at the Villa Diana. The moss was soft under her knees, it sprouted a miniature forest of golden hairs, each one crowned with a black head. Tiny beetles staggered between the stems; red spiders, flimsy as tears, wandered over the unnatural green.

Faustino was very close, close enough for her to see the fine skin of his tanned face, the dark line where eyelash emerged from eyelid, the wrinkle at the corner of his mouth. He turned his head and she saw herself reflected in his eyes, convex, vulnerable.

'You are very beautiful, Anna,' he said softly. Tenderly he stroked the moss, the fine hairs bending under his hand.

She leaned back on her heels. 'You told me I wasn't pretty. And it's *Han*nah, not Anna.'

He shook his head. 'When will you unromantic English learn the difference between a beautiful woman and a pretty one?' Leaning forward, he touched a mark on the side of her neck. 'You have a lover,' he said.

'Do I?' Hannah was caught in confusion.

'I think so.' For a moment he regarded her gravely. She expected him to kiss her again but he stood up, brushing at the knees of his trousers. 'Look, Anna. I will show you something.' He walked fast into the deeper heart of the trees and she went after him, her sandals slipping on the pine needles.

The wood suddenly thinned and they were standing on the edge of a rise, looking down across a valley to a ridge crowned with a pink house. Was it the same one Lucas had shown her? From this angle, with the sun high overhead so that the shadows were eliminated, it was difficult to tell. From here she could see how close it must be to the edge of the land belonging to the twin villas.

'That is my house,' Faustino said.

'You're lucky to live there: the views must be marvellous.'

'They are,' he said. 'And sometimes surprising too.'

There was a definite significance in his voice; she flushed. Surely he didn't mean – he couldn't possibly have been . . . the thought of Faustino, of *anyone* up on that ridge, watching through binoculars—

'I think I should go back now,' she said firmly. 'I can cycle from here, it's not very far.' She was suddenly anxious not to let him know where she was living – if, indeed, he did not already know.

The little coppice of trees seemed, all of a sudden, to be stifling, the branches crowding in on her. She wanted to get away.

*   *   *

114

'You've lost a lot of weight, haven't you?' Lucas said.

They lay, not touching, on his bed. She opened her eyes, astonished that he should speak to her; he so seldom did. What did he think of her? She often wondered. As to what she felt about him, that she could not decide. Perhaps in the colder weather of autumn, at university, she would look back on these days and feel shame, even loathing. And astonishment at her own behaviour – certainly astonishment.

'I suppose I have,' she said.

In the semi-darkness of his room, his eyes gleamed under the heavy lids. A slice of sunshine, sharp as a carving knife, glittered between the long shutters pulled across the open windows. She could hear the child murmuring on the terrace below, and hoped it had not heard the sounds of a few moments before.

Getting up, she walked to the windows. Outside, the garden stretched away from her, white in the afternoon heat. Below, the child sat cross-legged, hugging the puppy, kissing the top of its head. As Hannah watched, the puppy broke free of the fierce embrace and scampered down the terrace steps, the child running after it. The two of them, child and puppy, crossed the grass, the puppy trailing its yellow leash.

'Who does that child belong to?' Hannah asked.

Lying on his stomach, Lucas murmured into the pillow. His long back still shone with sweat; she could see each knob of his spine and the elegant curve of his shoulder blades. Only a short while ago, she had kissed them, held him fiercely to her; now she felt nothing but repugnance, both for him and for herself. Why did she allow herself to be used like this? Why was it so shameful and yet at the same time, so magical? So . . . *liberating*.

'What did you say?' she asked.

He spoke again, into the pillow, then turned slowly on to his side. 'God knows,' he said.

'You must have some idea.' Hannah tried hard to keep the asperity out of her voice. 'People don't have stray children around without knowing where they come from.'

'I expect it belongs to – to the housekeeper,' Lucas said, and his indifference chilled her.

'But you don't know for sure?'

'For God's sake, Hannah,' he said. 'Don't be a nag.'

She wanted to reach him and knew she could not. 'Ask me for something,' she begged.

'What?'

'Something. Anything.' The need to be needed . . . 'Not sex, I don't mean.'

'There's nothing you can give me,' he said, leaning on the personal pronouns. His voice was edged with coldness and she was tempted to tell him to go to hell. Without answering, she left him. On the landing she found furniture set out on the gallery floor; bending, she recognised the black-banded wardrobe of burr maple, the headboard, the miniature painting of a water-carrier, but the child who must have removed them from the doll's house was not there, and as she hurried down the stairs, she wondered why it had so carefully removed the furniture from the room which corresponded to Lucas's own. As always, as she went through the *salone* and out on to the terrace, she had the impression of disturbed air, as though someone had just passed through, of a door closing softly in the distance.

Walking down into the woods, she stood at the edge of the pool. It lay absolutely still, the weed a flat carpet of bright green, the turbulence at its centre no more than a faint bulge on the surface. With the dead-hair clumps of dried weed hanging down the sides, it did not invite. Rather, it seemed sinister, poisonous. The stone faun leered, his expression sly. Listening, she could hear nothing, not even a stir from the dry bamboo leaves, or the skitter of lizard-feet on the marble pillars. The dragon-flies had gone. Above, the enemy sun spied on her through the leaf dazzle.

Quickly, she walked up to the house. Standing under a cold shower, she scrubbed herself hard with soap and flannel, and fiercely wished that whatever spell bound her to Lucas, she could break it.

She *must* break it.

As the heat intensified, as physical movement became ever more of an effort, Hannah's existence grew increasingly surreal. She knew that somewhere, in another world, ordinary things were happening, though for her they were not; she moved through the syrupy days as though her limbs were weighted.

She discovered a refuge from the heat, a small room below the kitchen, lined with stone shelves, where even the sun of late July did not penetrate and a kind of mushroom dampness lay tenderly on sweating skin. A game larder, perhaps – Italians were great hunters. Or a disused wine cellar. There was no indication of its function. It was empty now, and dark, full of swinging spiders; she could never stay down there long, and then only with the heavy door propped open, which allowed in the snarling sun and so partly defeated the purpose.

She stood there now in the gloom, reliving the afternoon, and wondered what would happen if the door swung shut and she could not get it open. If she no longer obeyed his summons, would Lucas come looking for her? Would Susie, getting no answer when she telephoned, call the police?

She doubted it. She was not a prisoner here. Both of them would assume she had gone off somewhere, or was simply out of reach of the telephone. The thought of banging fruitlessly at that solid door, scrabbling at the walls, trying to find a way out, knowing there was no one to hear her cries while the spiders busily span and munched, terrified her. Buried alive. As she grew weaker, would they cocoon her as they did the living bodies of their insect prey? Would she lie there in the darkness, immobilised, wrapped in a shroud of white silk, while her life ebbed away? She ran out into the sharp, white light.

The garden sweltered. Trying not to imagine Faustino up on his hill, watching her sport and play with Lucas, she hurried through the leafy walks to the ruined chapel. Even though she no longer worked here with the little fork, the floor was at least half-uncovered now, and orgiastic. She wondered whether the twin chapel in the Villa Diana – there must be one – was in better shape, whether the roof had been preserved and the floor kept swept.

She slipped through the boundary fence between the two properties and pushed her way through tall hedges of *leylandii* and plumbago to where the building should be. And there it was. Not a chapel at all but a gazebo, a folly, a fancy of arched windows and delicate stone tracery. A tiny terrace lay in front of the door, looking out over a shallow fountain of white marble. The basin was empty now, but a puddle of clean water lying at the bottom suggested that the fountain might sometimes play here. Pushing at the wooden door, she wondered who had so recently set the water dancing: Lucas?

Inside, the single room was intimate. And still, it seemed, in use. Light slanted from the delicate high-set windows; she could see a table of some black wood, two chairs, and, at the far end, a kind of built-in Roman couch on which lay a sheet-covered mattress.

Not just in use, but used recently; there were crumbs of bread on the table, glasses, candles set in a branching candelabra of tarnished silver and a half-full bottle of wine.

Did the child come here? Sit at the table, eat make-believe meals, sleep on the mattress? Of course not: where would a child find wine, glasses, candles? Was it something altogether more sinister? It was easy to imagine hooded, half-glimpsed faces lit from below, a voice intoning satanical gibberish, and on the couch a sacrificial virgin, bound and waiting for the kiss of the knife. A strip of oriental carpet lay beside the bed: the mosaic floor depicted a lapidary scene of debauchery. Semi-clothed women arched backwards from the embraces of lascivious almond-eyed men, others lay in attitudes of expectancy, still others fondled and kissed. She determined to persevere with her labours in the ruined folly on the other side of the fence, if this magnificence was to be the result.

And then he called her. She tried to defy him, to blank him out, but it was impossible.

'*Hannah.*'

Clenching her fists, determined to resist him, she thought of other things, but the sound of her name filled her mind; he wanted her and, enslaved, she had to go.

Where was he?

Powerless, she pulled the door to behind her and walked into the woods. Was he waiting for her at the pool? Heat hovered between the tree stems, clung to the shiny leaves; she lifted the hem of her skirt and wiped her neck and forehead. She heard a thin, screaming sound; disorientated, she thought at first it was a car braking suddenly some distance away, someone sawing wood. Then, as the scream rose higher, she realised that it was a living thing – an animal – in pain. The horrific sound rose and fell; the back of her neck was cold with distress as she hurried towards it, all thought of Lucas forgotten.

Bursting between the bamboo stems into the clearing round the pool, she saw the child's puppy.

It lay flat on its stomach with a barbed hoop of steel across its back and paws. There was blood around its soft mouth as it tore and chewed at itself. The sight of the bloodied paw dizzied her. Blackness swirled in her brain and she dropped to her knees, sickened, unable to go any nearer. Blood . . . she raised a hand to her mouth, head drooping, heart pounding with fear and self-disgust.

Lucas came crashing through the bushes.

'Good God,' he said. He knelt beside the puppy and pulled apart the stiff steel jaws, his muscles straining with the effort. The little body lay limp in his hands, the hindquarters jerking and quivering; the puppy whimpered, quieter now. Hannah could hardly bear to look at it, but as she did so, Lucas took the puppy's head and twisted it violently to one side. There was an audible crack and with a final convulsion, the puppy was still.

She could scarcely believe what she had just witnessed. 'You . . . *killed* it,' she said.

'I know.'

'But why . . . what did you— ? That's horrible. *Horrible!*' Tears were suddenly in Hannah's eyes and she brushed them away. The single brutal action had more of violence in it than anything she had ever seen before. 'How *could* you?'

'Don't be so sentimental,' Lucas said. 'Couldn't you see its back was broken in two?'

'But—' Hannah could not find the words to explain that it was the swiftness which she found repellent, as much as the action itself. One second the puppy was alive; the next it was not.

'It was the best thing,' Lucas said. 'The only thing.' He knelt beside the pool and rinsed his hands. 'At home on the estate, you often come across wounded animals. It's best to put them out of their misery.'

'I can't . . . believe I saw you do that.' There was sweat on Hannah's brow and she wiped it away.

'It couldn't have survived,' Lucas said. 'It couldn't have walked. For God's sake, Hannah, pull yourself together.'

'It's just—'

'What worries me much more is what the hell that bloody thing's doing there.' Lucas bent over the trap. 'It's brand-new, too.'

There was a movement nearby, a flutter. Hannah lifted her head. 'Oh my God,' she said.

'What?' On one knee, Lucas swivelled round. The child was standing there, among the bushes on the other side of the pool, watching them, angelic, androgynous. Pale hair haloed its face as it stared intently at Lucas and the thing he held. It was impossible to decide to which sex it belonged; perhaps, like an angel, it belonged to neither. It opened its mouth as though to scream, staring at the dead puppy, at the big domed head too big for the rest of the small furry body, then turned and pushed noiselessly back in among the covering leaves.

'How long has he been there?' Hannah said quietly.

'No idea.'

'Oh, God, Lucas. He – she – must have been watching when . . . when you'

'I'll get another,' Lucas said carelessly. 'What worries me much more is *this*. How did it get here?' He straightened up and stared round the clearing. 'Why would it be here?'

'I've no idea.' Hannah walked away from him; anger and repulsion made it easier to ignore the call he sent after her.

She walked through the evening shadows of the Villa Giulia. Even with the shutters folded back and the windows wide open, the hot air hung round her like a shawl. Deep within the looking-glasses, her reflection moved like a moth as she drifted on bare feet across the parquet floor of the ballroom, leaving ghostly footprints in the fallen plaster from the ceiling. He had told her she was too thin: as though hypnotised by the thought of him, she stood in front of the big mirrors and pulled off her clothes. Twenty Hannahs stared back at her from the webbed glass, a hundred, one behind the other, receding, growing ever fainter. When she opened her mouth, so did they, when she lifted a hand to her throat, they did the same. The glass showed little detail; she saw her reflection reduced to a face, legs, dark eyes, a pale mouth, two nipples, a triangle of black hair. Was that all she was now? A body?

Dressed again, she wrestled with the catches on the french windows and walked out on to the terrace. The night was absolutely still, except for the cicadas beating out their contrapuntal rhythms. From the direction of the Villa Diana came the faint sound of people talking; she could make out Lucas's deep voice and a woman's answering laugh. There was a clink of glasses, a bead of sound in the darkness. Although she listened with urgency, she could hear no one else, no other voices. Just the two of them.

Below her, leaves rustled as though the garden itself had shivered. A warm breeze stroked her forehead. Just out of her line of vision there was a flitter of movement but when she turned her head, there was nothing to be seen.

He would be sitting under the grapevine arbour, she thought, his handsome head thrown back, his uncaring eyes on the face of a woman who laughed. There would be wine, glasses, white cheeses, a bowl of fruit. Moths would wreath the candles; perhaps, hidden, the child would be watching, candles reflected in those enigmatic, uninnocent eyes.

Would he take the woman to bed, later? Would he touch and kiss and rouse her as he so skilfully, so dispassionately, roused Hannah? And if he did, would it matter? She had not considered until now that Lucas might have other women, though rationally she knew that skills such as his were not learned overnight. Would she be jealous to discover him with someone else? She thought not. Grieved, yes. But how could she be jealous when he was something to which she had never had any right?

Somewhere near her heart, there was sorrow. What was she like, this other woman. Would he be the same with her as he was with Hannah? Curiosity impelled her. Before she had fully considered what she was doing, she was walking across the terrace and descending the brick stairs to the garden. Under her bare feet, the stone was cool; small cushions of moss pushed against her skin. She walked around the side of the house and across the grass, past the statue of Pan which glimmered in its shelter of laurel, into the green tunnels between the bushes. Despite the overhanging trees, there was enough light from the high moon for her to see her way as she walked the silent pathways, flitting ghostlike down tumbled steps, past crumbling balustrades, brushing beneath umbrella-like ferns towards the depths of the overgrown garden.

She ducked between the broken railings which marked the boundary line between the two estates; frogs were clamorous as she skirted the edge of the pool and started up the steep slope which led to Lucas's house. The darkness throbbed with the sound of cicadas as she broke through the screening leaves and found herself directly in front of the folly. The wooden door stood wide open, spilling yellow light; the small fountain threw arcs of moonlit water into the air.

It was like watching a scene from a play, the darkness focusing attention on the lighted square of the stage. There was the set, there within it, the characters. A man: Lucas. A woman: black-haired, broad-faced. She sat at the table, formal in a low-cut dress of lemon silk. The shifting flames of the candles caught sparks from the diamonds round her neck and at her ears; her skin was tawny, unimaginably rich against the gorgeous material of her dress. There were rings on her hands; the glinting gold made it clear that she was married and she wore another, a big yellow diamond which shone like a sun.

Lucas wore a dinner jacket. As Hannah watched, he eased out of it. The starched white shirt and black braces emphasised the melancholic lines of his face; though the woman laughed, he did not. He reached quickly across the table and seized her hand, crushing it to his mouth, turning it over and pressing his lips against the palm.

'You are killing me,' he said.

The woman watched him. Her dark eyes were sad. She made a movement, as though to caress the bent blond head, but drew back. She laughed again. Her white teeth gleamed against the ardent tones of her skin. Only Hannah could see the pain on her face.

'We agreed, Lucas,' she said, pulling back her hand. 'We said we would not be serious this evening.' She spoke in English, though Hannah could hear from her accent that it was not her native tongue.

Lucas lifted his head. 'I cannot help myself.'

'We agreed, when we started, we agreed that we would enjoy what we had, that we would live for the moment.' She turned her head to stare through the open door into the darkness outside; her earrings shone like tears.

'But we have so few moments.' There was a heartbreaking catch in Lucas's voice. 'How could we have known?'

'A summer fling,' she said. 'Isn't that what you wanted?'

'I wanted *you*. That's all I've ever wanted, ever since we were children.'

'And now you have me, Lucas.'

'For an hour here or there, when you can get away. It's not enough. You know it is not nearly enough.'

The woman leaned forward. 'Every time we meet, you talk of this. But talking will not change our circumstances, Lucas. Talking will not alter the fact that I am forbidden fruit, and that you have responsibilities you cannot avoid.'

'You know how gladly I would share those responsibilities with you, if you would only allow me to.'

'Oh, Lucas, *caro mio*. What about our shared responsibilities? You are such a boy still. You think that if you only wish hard enough, things will be as you want them to be. Life is not like that.'

'You love me, don't you?'

'Always, Lucas. Always. This you must believe. But I cannot have you – except this way, briefly, sadly.' Her eyes seemed to grow larger and Hannah saw that they were suddenly full of tears. She pressed the back of her hand against her face, as though to stop them welling over. 'Oh, *God*,' she said, and her voice broke on the syllable.

'How long is this to go on?' Lucas demanded.

'My husband is a good man,' the woman said.

'Good? *Good?* But you're terrified of him.'

'Only occasionally. Only when he has drunk too much or is enraged.'

'Only—'

'And he has good cause to be angry, Lucas. He knows that it is you I love – oh, so passionately! – and not him.'

'He hits you,' Lucas said. 'I've seen the bruises. Leave him, my darling. Come to me.'

'Every time I think of you, I sin against him,' the woman said sadly. 'Can it not be enough for you that despite this, I continue to see you? And to suffer?'

'I suffer too, God knows.' Lucas banged his fist softly against the tablecloth. '*Why* do we have to suffer? Couldn't we at least—'

'There is nothing we can do, Lucas. *Nothing*. Do you understand?' When he unwillingly nodded, she went on: 'I would prefer that we did not discuss it again. We have so short a time together as it is. Let us not waste it on futile conversations.'

'Sometimes,' Lucas said quietly, 'I feel that I shall die for love of you.'

The woman pressed her hand hard against her heart. With an effort she did not try to conceal, she laughed again. 'Oh, Lucas,' she said gaily. 'Instead of dying, why do you not tell me how much you love me?'

'I cannot live without you. You know I—'

'Tell me how beautiful I am, how much you desire me,' the woman said feverishly, colour standing in her face, She reached towards the green bottle of wine between the candles and filled her glass; her hand was not quite steady.

'There are no words—' Lucas pushed back his chair and got up. He walked round to stand behind the woman; gently he touched her hair. When she raised her face to his, he bent and rested his mouth on hers, while his hand slipped down to caress her breast.

She closed her eyes. 'Oh, Lucas,' she said. The passion in her voice was unmistakable.

He pulled her to her feet and turned her into his arms. He began to kiss her, gently at first, then with increasing desperation while she moaned in his arms, pressing herself against him. Bright and beautiful, the two of them stood together in the soft light.

As they began to move towards the couch at the end of the folly, already pulling at each other's clothes, Hannah stepped back into the shadows outside. The scene would be imprinted on her mind for the rest of her life: light filtered through green glass, whiteness of candles, glitter of silver on the table, dullness of stone. She had no right to be spying on them like this. She felt ashamed at her intrusion; a kind of anguish seized her. However sorrowful, they had something she did not – might not ever – possess.

Blinded by tears, she took the orderly paths of the Villa Diana's garden up towards the house. Although it was longer to walk back to the Villa Giulia by road, she could not have passed the folly again. Some large animal crashed ahead of her, unaware of her presence; a fox, perhaps, unless there were deer in these woods.

Parked behind the house, beside the back entrance, was a black car with a Rome licence plate; she walked round it and up the long drive to the gates. She tugged at the rusty chain and padlock, as Lucas had shown her, and with some difficulty was able to prise them apart and slip out through the gate. Before her, the bone-white road glimmered; black hills edged the silvery sky. Distantly, there were lights.

The tarmac was still warm from the day's heat. She walked for a while, wincing as stones bit into her feet. Tears began to fall down her face and on to her dress. Unhappiness possessed her. She had thought she knew at last what love was; now she knew that she did not have the vaguest idea. She could not help wondering what the two of them had meant by 'forbidden fruit', by responsibilities, by having so little time together. She felt no sense of betrayal, only a sense of space, of imminent collapse, as though some supportive structure had been removed, leaving her temporarily destructible. That Lucas found her attractive she had no doubt; never for a moment had she thought he loved her. Yet she had thought she loved him, needed him as he did not, could not need her.

She knew that she was finally free of Lucas, that the spell had been broken. Curiously, she felt desolated.

Somewhere in the darkness behind her, she heard the sound of a car. In a moment, it had rounded the bend in the road, its headlights throwing her shadow ahead of her. She stepped to the side to let it pass, then continued to walk in the middle of the road.

Two hundred yards ahead, the car came to a stop. Until then, Hannah had not considered that it might be dangerous for a woman to be alone in this deserted countryside late at night. Now, as fear dried her throat, she began to regret the impulse which had led her to return to the Villa Giulia by road. Someone – a man – got out of the car and leaned against it. She saw the glow of a cigarette and tobacco smoke drifted towards her.

A man's voice said: 'You must be English.'

Hannah did not answer.

'Only an English girl would be so foolish as to wander around alone so late at night. And without shoes.'

'And only an Italian man would try to scare the shit out of any barefooted English girl he came across so late at night.'

'I can give you a lift, Anna, if you wish.'

'Thank you, Faustino. I prefer to walk.'

'If you do that, I shall feel it my duty to drive slowly behind you, nipping at your heels to make sure you arrive safely at your destination. It would be easier if you did as I say.'

'All right, then.' Hannah got into Faustino's car. 'Honestly, I hope you realise how you scared me. I thought you were a rapist.'

'I might easily have been. You should be more careful.' He started the car again. 'Where to?'

'It's only about half a mile down the road,' Hannah said. 'I'll show you where.'

'And have you simply been admiring the moonlight?' Faustino said.

'Uh—'

'Or visiting your lover?'

Hannah was embarrassed. 'Don't be ridiculous,' she said.

'Or maybe,' Faustino said lightly, 'you have been having dinner with the English milord.'

'Which milord would that be?'

'Wyndham, of course. Do you see much of him?'

'I don't see anything of him,' Hannah said. 'I've never met him.'

'I think you must have done.'

'Who is he?'

'He is English, like yourself. Lucas Wyndham: you have not met him?'

'Oh, *Lucas*.' Hannah had never heard his surname, certainly been unaware that he was titled. 'Is he a milord?' She tried to assess whether the fact that he had a title made any difference, and decided that, in some deeply painful way, it did. Susie had never mentioned it, though now Hannah recalled her speaking of bloodlines, saying that Lucas's branch of the family was very grand. 'Yes, I see him from time to time.'

'He is not always here, I believe.'

'Perhaps not.' Though as far as Hannah knew, Lucas had been around all summer long.

'He is a difficult man to get hold off.' Faustino said.

'I suppose he is. But I – I know he's around at the moment.'

'How?'

'What do you mean?'

'How do you know he is here?'

'Because I often . . . see him.'

'Do you?' Faustino stared at her and she could feel herself flushing, as though he could see the naked images of herself and Lucas.

'Yes. And as far as I know, he's planning to stay here all summer.'

'Oh, yes?'

Something disbelieving, disdainful in Faustino's expression made Hannah rush on, attempting to dissociate herself from his assumptions about her and Lucas, even though she could not deny that they were true. 'He's expecting a good friend to arrive from Rome any minute,' she said. 'If she hasn't already got here.'

'She?'

'That's what he said.'

'I see. I wonder why he keeps his gates chained together like that. Is he afraid of us Italians, or what?'

Hannah tried to remember what Susie had said about her cousin: he'd been burgled, been attacked, something like that. 'They're not really locked,' she said. 'You just have to twist the chains about. It's to keep people like – like double glazing salesmen out, I think.' She leaned forward, peering through the dark windscreen. 'It's the next turn. You can drive right up to the house.'

'The Villa Giulia?' He slowed down.

'Yes.'

'You are staying there?'

'Yes, Faustino. What's so odd about that?'

'But why have you never told me this before?'

'You've never asked. And it's never come up before.' Hannah frowned at him. 'Why should it matter?'

'I thought the place was empty. Has Susanna not hired a car and driven down to Rome?'

It had not occurred to Hannah that Faustino knew Susie or her family, though if he were a regular visitor down here, it was obvious that he must do. 'Yes,' she said. 'Though what business it is of—'

'So you are here alone?'

'Yes.'

'With no more visitors to come?'

'Not for the moment.'

He put a hand on her knee. 'Is this wise, Anna?'

'*Han*nah. Why shouldn't it be?' He had turned in between the gateposts and was driving slowly towards the house. His headlights caught the dark shrubs on either side and slid over them like yellow polish.

'There are always men who are willing to take advantage of a defenceless girl,' he said.

Hannah could not help smiling. 'Who says I am defenceless?'

'I think that you are.' He looked along the drive to where the house waited, glowing faintly. 'I wish—'

She could smell him beside her in the dark car, a sensual male smell. Reaching out, she touched the inside of his elbow. 'What do you wish?'

'Perhaps I wish that I were a different kind of man.' He pulled up below the terrace. 'I will say goodnight to you, Anna.'

Hannah did not wish to go into the house. She did not want to be alone with her thoughts, to see again the pictures which waited to be endlessly re-run through her mind's projector. She had tried to persuade herself that she did not mind about Lucas loving another woman, but she did. She wanted to love like that, to share that kind of overwhelming passion and feared, in that moment, that she never would.

'Why don't you come in for a coffee,' she said lightly, not wanting him to sense her need. 'Or a nightcap. Or something.' Or *any*thing, she should have added. Anything which would keep the thoughts at bay.

'Are you sure it is not too late?'

'Positive.'

Fireflies danced around them, green flecks in the darkness. Faustino put an arm around her shoulder and together, companionable, they climbed the steps up to the terrace. At the top, he walked over to the balustrade and looked down, though he could not have been able to see anything.

'And the milord,' he said.

'Lucas? What about him?'

'He lives over there?' He pointed.

'More or less.'

'And you can reach his house through the grounds of this one?'

'Yes. I often go that way myself.'

'I see. There is much visiting between the Villa Giulia and the Villa Diana, then.'

Hannah stood next to him at the balustrade. 'Faustino,' she said wearily. 'Would you please stop all this nonsense about Lucas and me. For a start, he's not interested in me.'

'Then he is not a man.'

Despite her inner turmoil, Hannah laughed.

'It is lovely to see you laugh,' Faustino said softly. He bent his head into her neck. The feel of his hair against her throat was – she tried to push him away but he seized her hands and held them close to his heart. 'Anna,' he murmured. 'I have desired you since the first day I saw you.'

'I know.' She felt a swooning pleasure as his hand cupped her breast; old voices in her head asked her how she could do this, cheapen herself, let a man she knew to be married make love to her. And over them, suddenly, she heard another voice, a wordless, soundless cry. Was it her name he called, or another's?

She pulled back. Frowned. The voice was faint, but unmistakable.

Faustino's hands were at her clothes. 'If you are not making love with the milord,' he said softly, 'will you make love this evening with me?'

'No,' she said, and knew it was exactly the kind of no which meant the opposite. '*No,*' she said, more firmly.

'Anna,' he murmured. Drink had softened the contours of his voice.

'It's not what either of us really wants,' she said. 'We aren't that kind of person, Faustino. We're friends. Aren't we?' She pushed him away and saw him realise that she meant it.

'Forgive me,' he said, pulling back from her, bending his head, smiling. 'Of course we are friends. And shall, I hope, always be. Now,' he looked about the room, turning away, but not before she had seen the hurt look of his mouth. 'Did you speak of coffee? I should love a cup before I drive on home.'

THE DIARY

. . . 'It's good,' he says.

'Good?' I try to act nonchalant. What the fuck does he mean: good?

'But is it true?' he says.

'In what sense?'

'It reads like a novel,' he says. He puts on his Wise Witch Doctor look. 'I'm assuming that most of it is fiction.'

I sit forward, about to get out of my chair. Rage is powerful within me. But I can't let him see it. I can't give him that satisfaction. I have to pretend that I am restless or excited or something as I wait for his opinion.

'I like it,' he says.

I don't know why this annoys me. Perhaps it's the condescending way he says it – 'I like your fucking diary' – as if I've been on tenterhooks ever since I gave it to him, as if I can't assess my own view of it until I have his. It's my life we're talking about here, not some popular novel.

'Some interesting symbolism in there,' he continues.

'Like what?' I say.

'For instance, the way the heroine has her right hand cut off before she's killed.'

That time I did leap out of my chair. I stood over him, both fists clenched. I was glad to see him back away from me. I enjoyed that, watching Mr God Almighty actually cower in his chair. 'She is not the heroine,' I say through gritted teeth. 'I am.'

He turns the pages, looks up at me. 'You are? That's very interesting. So it is autobiographical, then. Not fiction. But when we've talked about it, you've always said you couldn't remember.'

Fuck fuck fuck.

. . . Today he had that shit-eating smile on his face, the one I hate, the one which says he's scored a point even though I didn't know we were fighting each other.

'So you don't see Anna as the heroine of your—' he sketches inverted commas in the air, 'book?'

'One usually identifies with the central character,' I say, 'and for me, that's the Child, not Anna.'

He stares at me through his glasses (the new ones, which I still haven't got used to). I can see red veins in his eyeballs. I can see a patch of dry skin by his nose. Nobody would call him an attractive man, although his voice rivets me – almost literally. He has only to say my name and I am still, pinned down, attentive to whatever he has to say. 'I see,' he says.

'What do you see?' I ask. I can feel the anger building up inside me. I breathe deeply, in . . . out, in . . . out. Control, I tell myself. Control.

'That you seem to have blurred the parameters between illusion and reality. That you seem unsure whether any of this really happened.' Tap tap with his pointy fingernails on the cover of my book.

Go with the flow . . . 'Yeah,' I say.

'I'm also interested in why you have the murderer cut the woman's hand off,' the Dr says. 'What do you think?'

I think you're a pretentious little shit, I want to say. I hate the way, over the months we've been together, he has entered my mind, delved around in there, opened my cupboards, looked under my beds, fingered my privacy, sucked out my thoughts, without giving away one tiny speck of himself. I mean, he knows everything about me – almost everything – and I know fuck-all about him.

'I don't see the symbolism, myself,' I say. I look at him kinda cute. 'Symbolism's tricky stuff, Doc,' I say. 'When you get right down to it.'

. . . *He was still on about Anna today. 'If you cut the right hand off a musician, for instance, or an artist – or an author, for that matter – they would find it very difficult to practise their chosen professions, would they not? But since Anna is not a musician, it must have some other symbolism for you.'*

'She is a musician, she plays the cello,' I say. Then stop. Had I put that in my diary? How did I know that? Is it something I remember hearing somewhere, all those years ago? I was starting to sweat.

Why had I had cut the woman's hand off? I couldn't quite remember. I could feel my memory grinding, cranking up like a flat battery trying to start a car. When I'd been writing the scene, I'd been so certain that this was the right, the only way to go. But where had that certainty come from? And why did I now think that there was something which rang not quite true about it?

'The cello?' the Dr says, wrinkling his brow, looking down at the pages drifting through his hands. 'I don't remember that.'

'What are you trying to say?' I ask. I'm falling apart, not certain what is and what is not.

'I don't know. What do you think?' he says again. Standard psychiatric trick, make the patient do the work.

I could so easily kill him. Put my hands round his neck and squeeze until his eyes popped out of his head, the way I used to squeeze those blue butterflies. It wouldn't take much, he's not a big man.

I'd take his glasses off first, though!

Kill him. It's a sobering thought.

Sobering? But I am not drunk.

I wonder how I would manage if he wasn't there. If I knew that he would never be there again, that henceforward I had to stand on my own two feet.

Would T help me?

NOW

10

'Mrs Barlow?' the woman asks, and with the words, Hannah's careful life cracks in two.

The woman is uniformed, silver-buttoned. She carries a cap with a black-and-white checked band; in the road, beyond the privet hedge, sits a white car with an unlit blue lamp on its roof. Behind her stands a man.

'Mrs Barlow?' the woman asks again. She is not smiling. Hannah cannot answer. Standing at the open door, one hand clutching at the jamb for support, she nods. The movement causes her immense effort, as though her neck had been welded into a brace. Lucinda, Adam: something not tolerable has happened to one of them.

Behind the woman's words, her children curvet and tumble across the years which start to roll through the shadows of her mind, fast-forwarding from babyhood to adolescence to near-adulthood. Sweet baby breath, starfish fingers, the lovely limbs of childhood, holidays, picnics, Christmases—

And now one of them . . . one of them is—

No, she wants to scream, this isn't happening. It is early in the morning, the street not yet alive. In the park across the road, a pair of mallards waddle importantly among the corporation daffodils. The river glistens at the end of the road, lined with yellow-furred willows which are wild in the winds of early March. Not yet dressed, she pulls her robe tight around her neck as though to block out the policewoman's words which she now realises are being repeated for the third time:

'Is it all right if we come in, Mrs Barlow?'

'No,' Hannah says loudly. 'It is *not* all right.'

She starts to shut the door, to shut out the information – no news is good news, isn't that right? – which this woman is bringing her. In her heart, she knows this will change nothing, will offer no comfort, will only defer what she does not want to know, so stands aside and allows the bad news to enter.

'I don't believe it.' She sits bolt upright in her darkened bedroom, feeling the words cascade from her, over and over again, magician's ribbons endlessly flowing from her almost-screaming mouth. 'I don't believe it. I don't believe.'

Then Adam is there in the darkness, the strong male body which used to be so helpless and she feels the tears on his face and knows that he too is weeping for the lost daughter, the lost sister, that he is helpless once again.

'Mum,' he says. 'Mummie—' He puts his arms around her and burrows as he used to, blindly, like a mole-baby, wanting her to do what she has always done and chase away the nightmares.

She cannot. She holds him against her breasts and rocks, back and forth, his hair rough under her chin. He is a man now, not a child and she understands, with a sense of loss she has not experienced before, that he has to bear his own burdens, she can no longer bear them for him.

'Mum,' Adam says, whispering against her skin. 'She didn't. I know she didn't.'

Agonised, Hannah presses her lips together, but cannot repress a groan . . .

'Not that way,' Adam whispers. 'Not like that.'

Clearly, Hannah sees the figure of her beloved daughter crashing through the air, leaping from lichened stones, steadying herself on the broken-down parapet before she takes the final step into oblivious eternity.

'No,' Adam says. He sobs; his tears are wet against her nightdress. 'She couldn't have.'

'The police say that—'

'No,' he says strongly. 'Not Lucinda.'

He is right. Lucinda might have killed herself, but not that way, not, as the police maintain she did, jumping from a tumbledown tower in a northern field to shatter on the mossed rocks below. It is inconceivable that she would take her own life, yet there are always internal stresses, always problems which seem insurmountable, and it is possible, Hannah must concede that it is possible.

But not like that. Adam is right.

She rocks, griefstricken, in the darkness, holding her only child to her bosom, and her tears fall without cease into the thickets of his hair.

'I want,' she said firmly, 'to speak to whoever's in charge of the Lucinda Barlow case.' Yesterday, grief and shock had numbed her; today she was fiery, determined.

There was a wait. A man's voice came on to the line. 'Inspector Mayfield,' he said guardedly, as though by admitting too much, he might somehow make himself vulnerable.

'This is Hannah Carrington – Barlow, I mean,' said Hannah.

She waited while he made the connection between her name and that of Lucinda.

'Ah, yes,' he said after a moment.

'In the matter of my daughter's death—' Hannah wondered how

she could speak so calmly, so efficiently of something so terrible.

'Yes?'

'I believe you're treating it as a – as suicide,' said Hannah. She could feel the tears hovering.

'That's right.'

'It's impossible.' Hannah was firm.

'We've talked to her friends,' Inspector Mayfield said, and she heard the gentleness of the north in his speech. 'There was a considerable amount of stress, I believe. Examinations coming up, a lot of work to cover. Sometimes it only takes the smallest amount of pressure to push someone over the edge.'

He paused, and Hannah felt him wishing he had chosen some other form of words. 'Boyfriend trouble, for instance,' he added. 'And of course, this drug thing won't have helped.'

'Drug thing? What are you talking about? My daughter didn't have anything to do with—'

'Perhaps you hadn't realised,' the mild voice said. 'The university authorities had been investigating all the students sharing your daughter's house.'

Hannah had *not* realised. Was this what Lucinda had meant when she spoke of '*things*'? 'But Lucinda didn't—'

'As far as I am aware, your daughter and her friends have all been cleared. But the stress might have added to any . . .' Delicately, Mayfield let the sentence trail.

Had Lucinda spoken to her housemates about the hidden watcher, the doctored tape, the spoilt dress? Hannah wondered. Mayfield did not mention them; perhaps Lucinda's friends were unaware of these extra stresses. Even so—

'I'm prepared to accept that Lucinda might, under certain circumstances, have been tempted to – to take her own life,' said Hannah. 'I find it difficult to believe – she was a sensible girl, she had a strong sense of priorities – but I can just about accept that she *might* have – have done it. But there is absolutely no way she would have jumped off that tower.'

'Mrs Barlow, however hard it is to accept, I'm afraid all the evidence points to the fact that she did.'

'You're not listening,' Hannah said. 'If she did kill herself – and I say *if* – she would never have chosen that method.'

'Why not?'

'Because she was terrified of heights. *Terrified*.' As she spoke, Hannah saw Lucinda again, ten years old, riding the escalator in John Lewis's with her eyes shut tight, Lucinda refusing to go on the top deck of a London bus, Lucinda backing away from high windows. She bit down hard on her lower lip. 'She couldn't possibly have gone up that tower – you said it didn't even have a proper balustrade. She would have been far too frightened.'

'Mrs Barlow,' Mayfield said. 'I appreciate your position. No one wants to think that their daughter might have—' Leaving the sentence, he initiated a new one. 'The more frightened she was by heights, the more suitable that tower must have been for – for her purposes.'

'Pills,' said Hannah. 'Or slitting her wrists in a bath. Or drowning – she wasn't a good swimmer.' It seemed bizarre, unacceptable, to be listing the ways in which her daughter could have taken her own life. 'But not that way. Not. Not. Not.'

She repeated the word, feeling its knock against her brain, and with each repetition, knew more certainly that she was right.

'Mrs Barlow, if—'

'If it wasn't suicide, it must be murder,' Hannah said loudly. 'Someone killed her. Someone carried or dragged her up those steps and threw her off. I've been thinking about it.' No need to say that she had been thinking of nothing else ever since it happened; Mayfield knew that. 'Don't you see, there's no other explanation, because it certainly wasn't an accident. She must have been knocked out first, or drugged – did they find drugs at the autopsy?'

'Only traces of Diazepam, which could have been accounted for by the prescription sleeping pills which were found by the bed.'

'Sleeping pills,' repeated Hannah. Lucinda must really have been worried if she had resorted to such things. Like so many of her generation, she hated to contaminate her body with chemicals. 'But nothing else?'

'Nothing.'

'You're not going to suggest that she took an overdose, either by accident or design, and climbed those steps, are you?'

'Not at all. For one thing, the traces were too slight to suggest such a thing.'

'What does her boyfriend say about it? Surely he must know what she was doing.'

'She was there with someone?'

'Yes, of course she was.' Alarm pricked at Hannah's underarms. 'Haven't you spoken to him?'

'Not yet.'

Possibilities leaped. 'You don't think they might have quarrelled and he – he—' She could not finish the sentence. 'Or that someone else came in and – and murdered her, hit her or something, then threw her from the steps to disguise what had happened?'

'At the moment, I think nothing, Mrs Barlow. All avenues are open. For the moment, I must advise you not to get your hopes up.'

'Hope is hardly the word, Inspector. Hope is gone.'

'Of course.' He soothed her. 'Of course. But it is more acceptable, in a case like this, a young person dead, to feel that it was not a voluntary thing.'

He was right. She knew he was right.

'The point is, the simplest solution is usually the right one,' Mayfield said. 'The scenario you suggest is complicated and – I have to say – unlikely. Why should anyone wish to murder your daughter?'

'I don't know.' Hannah paused. Should she tell him about Lucinda's fear that she was being watched? Or would that simply reinforce his theory that Lucinda was under severe strain? For the moment, she decided to keep it to herself.

And suddenly she was hit with the memory of a vine-covered arbour, blue hills fading into darkness, the taste of wine in her mouth, and a man calling, her head sounding, pounding with the weight of her own name as it bounced between the bony canyons of her brain. Another girl; another death: why did she feel, with absolute dread, for no logical reason whatsoever, that the two were connected?

And that there was worse – far worse – to come?

Twice she has telephoned Susie in Rome; twice received only the pre-recorded message saying that Susie is not available. The first time, she leaves only her name, the second, replaces the receiver without speaking. What is there to say?

'I'm sorry to disturb you,' Inspector Mayfield said. Today he sounded preoccupied; Hannah imagined his tie askew, buff folders piled up on the desk in front of him. 'You said when we spoke before that she was in Swaledale with a boyfriend.'

'That's right.'

'Are you sure about this?'

'Yes. She told me so herself. At least, she said she was going up there with him. At least—'

'It's just that although we have a couple of witnesses who saw her arrive at the cottage, they both state that she was alone.'

'How strange.' Thinking about it, is that what Lucinda had told her? Or was it the previous weekend there that she spent with the boyfriend?

'And, in fact, we ourselves have been unable to trace him. I wonder, could you give us any more details about him? We need to eliminate him from our inquiries?'

'I – uh – I can't—' Hannah tried to remember. 'I don't think my daughter ever told me his name.'

'I see.'

Because he sounded faintly censorious, she rushed to explain. 'You know how it is, Inspector. Children – daughters especially – can be so private. I didn't like to sound like an interfering mother.'

'Mmm.'

'I knew that when Lucinda was ready to introduce him to us, she would have brought him home.'

'You're absolutely sure this man existed?'

'Of course I am.'

'It couldn't be that she didn't want to admit that she hadn't got a boyfriend? You know how girls behave sometimes. Peer pressure, and all that.'

'Inspector, my daughter wasn't in the habit of lying to me. Nor did she have any problem attracting the opposite sex.'

'It's just that we can't seem to find any trace of this man you say she went to the Dales with.'

'It's not what I *say* – it's what she *told* me.'

'But you don't know his name?'

Hannah trawled again through her memory, but could come up with nothing else. 'No. I—'

'How old he is? Where he comes from?'

'Yes. He's American. Living in London.'

'Was he a fellow student of hers at the university?'

'I – I don't think so. She said he was a freelance journalist.' With a sinking heart, Hannah remembered Lucinda talking about going to the cottage in Swaledale: she had spoken of 'I', not 'we'. It was not until Hannah asked the question directly that she had mentioned the boyfriend, and that had been in connection with her earlier visit.

The information did not impress Mayfield. 'The thing is, Mrs Barlow, your daughter's friends all say that they hadn't met anyone Lucinda said was special for a while.'

'I don't understand it. She distinctly said—'

'Odd she didn't introduce him to her house-mates,' Mayfield said heavily. 'And that she apparently told the boy – Tom Morgan – whose parents own this cottage – or *implied*, that she was going up there on her own, to do some revising for her examinations and, so he told the officer who interviewed him: "to try to get her head together".'

'Why would she tell me something different?'

'That's not for me to say, Mrs Barlow.'

'Why should she invent a man? It's absolutely ridiculous – I don't believe she'd do such a thing.'

'She seems to have been lying to someone, that much is clear. Or at the very least, not being entirely truthful.'

'Not to me,' Hannah said firmly. 'She never lied to me.' But even as she said it, she wondered how she could be so sure, whether she really knew her daughter. It was perfectly possible that Lucinda was, in fact, an habitual liar.

It was another certainty that her daughter's killer had destroyed.

'Which one is her boyfriend?' asks Hannah. She looks round the churchyard. There are trees around the edge, not yet in full leaf and daffodils stand bright against the uneven stone wall which surrounds the ground. She tries not to think of spring and new beginnings and promise.

At her side, Sarah, Lucinda's closest friend at university, stares vaguely at the scattered groups of mourners. Earlier she had helped Hannah with the sad business of packing Lucinda's possessions up and moving them out of the shared house; the two of them had wept together as they did it. 'I don't think he's here.'

'He must be, surely.'

One of the other girls who had shared the house with Lucinda and Sarah, shakes her head. 'I don't think so. Between us we know all the others and she wasn't going out with any of them. And that one over there is Jim, who shares the house with us.'

Hannah tries to remain calm. Whatever Mayfield said, she is certain the man who had been in the Dales with Lucinda existed. But if he did, wouldn't he be here? At this point she cannot bear to accept that Lucinda might have lied to her, nor the re-evaluations this would entail. She begins to shake, feels her teeth rattle against each other, huge sobs rising at the back of her throat.

Susie, wrapped in furs, puts an arm around her. 'Hannie, don't,' she says softly. 'They'll find him somehow.'

'Yes,' she murmurs. The strong body of her friend is a comfort.

'The thing is,' says Sarah, 'we never met him.'

'I didn't think there *was* anyone at the moment,' one of the other girls says. 'That's what we told the police.'

She and Sarah look uncertainly at Hannah.

She knows they feel uneasy. All of them had given evidence at the inquest, reluctantly agreeing that Lucinda had definitely been upset in the past few weeks, that she had complained about her work-load, the importance of doing well in her finals, the drug investigation, the difficulties of getting a job in the current economic climate. Sarah had added that she did not think Lucinda could possibly have killed herself. Hannah had waited to hear that the autopsy showed Lucinda had been pregnant but that was not so. Predictably, the verdict was suicide.

'Perhaps she didn't want to talk about him until she was sure,' says Sarah. 'Hubris, or something.'

'If a relationship looks like it might be important, you don't want to risk it by talking about it too soon,' says the other girl. She spreads her hands, not looking at Lucinda's mother. 'You know how it is.'

Hannah does know. She also knows they are trying to comfort her and the realisation that she no longer has a daughter of her own who might, in her turn, some day offer comfort to a middle-aged stranger in need, only underlines her sense of loss.

A burly man in a tweed coat approaches. 'Mrs Barlow?' he says, and though her eyes are full of tears, she recognises the northern lilt in his voice.

'Inspector Mayfield.' Hannah touches a gloved finger to her eyes and holds out her hand.

He takes it in both of his. 'I don't need to say how sorry I am,' he tells her.

She bows her head. 'No.'

Mayfield stares about him. 'We still haven't caught up with this young man who's supposed to have been in the Dales with her. Even though we were fairly sure of the outcome of the inquest, it seems strange that if he's around somewhere, he didn't approach the police.'

'Perhaps he doesn't know about – about Lucinda,' suggests Hannah. She feels a need to exculpate this unknown man, even though Mayfield clearly does not believe in his existence.

'That could be.' His expression indicates scepticism. He has a blue woollen scarf wrapped round his neck and he adjusts it, shivering slightly as the wind whips across the graveyard and bows the daffodils to the ground.

'I mean, he could have left before the weekend was over, perhaps he had to be somewhere important, an interview to do or something, and left Lucinda there,' offers Hannah.

Bleakly, she sees her daughter in an isolated cottage, green hills rising to the sky all round, darkness falling, the night-time coughs of sheep, the crackle of a log fire. Had Lucinda grown so depressed on her own, in those lonely surroundings, that she had gone out and climbed up the inside of the disused tower in order to cast herself down? Surely not. Surely it was impossible.

Mayfield looks doubtful. 'As you say, perhaps he had to leave early – go abroad or something – and still doesn't know what happened.' He turns to the two girls. 'I know you've been asked this before, but neither of you knew anything about him at all, is that right?'

They shake their heads. Tears spill from Sarah's eyes and roll slowly down her cheek.

'Presumably he'll make himself known to you, Mrs Barlow, if – when – he finally shows up,' Mayfield says. 'Or even to one of you two ladies. Perhaps, if he does, you'll ask him to get in touch with me.' He gives a card to each of the girls; Sarah tucks hers away in her bag, the other girl stuffs it into the pocket of her coat.

Hannah can tell Mayfield is already certain that the young man only ever existed in Lucinda's imagination, and that for him, her daughter's death is, as the inquest returned, the cut-and-dried suicide of a young person under considerable stress.

The label on Mayfield's scarf, a small rectangle of woven threads incorporating one which glitters slightly, is coming loose. It reminds her of the nametapes she used to sew on to Lucinda's school clothes at the beginning of term. The need for the gentle tasks of motherhood is overwhelming; the knowledge that Lucinda will never undertake them in her turn is unbearable. She feels herself beginning to disintegrate, to splinter.

Again Susie's arm goes round her. 'I know,' she murmurs into Hannah's ear. 'Be brave, darling, just a bit longer, for their sakes as much as your own.'

Susie is right, of course. These young people have already faced too much in losing their friend; she should not subject them to the full impact of her grief.

'I never thought,' Susie said, 'that – that—' She turns to Hannah. 'I was going to come and see her next week, a flying visit, before she finished—'

'I know,' Hannah says gently. Susie has told her this several times, as though by repeating it, she can somehow bring back the possibility of it still taking place.

As the two women start to turn away, a young man comes up and takes Hannah's hand. She had seen him vaguely, elsewhere; at the inquest, perhaps? 'I'm Tom Morgan,' he says. 'It all happened at – at my parents' cottage. I can't tell you how devastated they – we *all* – are.' His face contorts. 'She was such a lovely person, you know. We all really . . . *loved* her.'

'Yes,' Hannah says gently. She touches his shoulder. As well as having lost a friend, for these young people, this is probably the first death of their own generation, their first brush with their own mortality.

Mayfield frowns again. 'Do *you* know anything about this mysterious boyfriend?' he asks.

'No,' answers Tom. 'I already told the police: Lucy didn't mention anyone else going with her, just asked if it would be all right for her to go up to the cottage – we sometimes used to go up as a group in the vacation, as Mrs Barlow knows, so she was quite familiar with the place – and I asked my parents and they said yes.'

Would it have been different if they had said no? Would Lucinda still be there with them? Hannah sees the same question darken behind Tom's eyes; his mouth quivers. Who could say? Whatever had happened, it could not be laid at this nice young man's door, though she suspects that for years to come, he and his parents will feel somehow to blame.

She sees Anthony, tall against a yew tree, and wishes sharply that she had, after all, allowed Marcus to be here today, as he had so urgently asked to be. She had refused his offer, thinking it somehow unfitting for her lover to attend the funeral of her former husband's daughter. Now Anthony catches her eye and nods, bleakly. He is talking to a younger woman in a fur hat whom Hannah takes to be his new partner. Adam is at his side, and she sees how alike they are, the kind of grown man Adam may become. Anthony seems calmer now than he had been when she first contacted him to break the news. He has been strong in this crisis, handling the details, sparing her what he could but knowing him so well, she can see, as he comes over to her, walking between the grey headstones, the imminence of breakdown, the fragile hold he has on himself. She says nothing; what is there to say? The two of them stand together, arms round each other, silently sharing their grief.

She and Adam travel home in silence. They have lingered, offering sandwiches and tea, whisky for those who need it. Standing with her son and her former husband, greeting people, friends, distant relatives, acquaintances who have journeyed here for her sake, she feels as though she is attending some bizarre party. Susie has already left, with a flight to catch at Heathrow.

'I'll call you, Hannie,' she says, huskily. 'I can't believe any of this. Lucinda was so— She was the nearest thing I'll ever have to a child of my own.' Her voice breaks, and Hannah is devastated at the sight. Susie is strong. Susie has always been there, invincible, unswerving – except for that single night, when Lucas died. Now another death has broken her: for Lucinda is Susie's god-daughter as well as Hannah's child.

Adam drives; she is glad to let him. Once or twice, seeking comfort, she puts her hand on his thigh and he covers it with his own. As they are turning into their own road, he says: 'She was murdered.'

Hannah does not respond.

'I know she was. For a start, who the hell is this mysterious boyfriend? Where is he? Why wasn't he there? Why hasn't he spoken to the police?' Furiously Adam grinds the gears.

'You heard what the Inspector said.'

'It was him,' Adam says savagely. 'I know it was. This boyfriend of hers. He's the one who killed her.'

'No one seems to think there was a boyfriend,' Hannah says, feeling weary. 'She didn't mention him to any of her other friends.'

'But she did to you. Why would she say something which wasn't true?'

'The Inspector thinks she might have made him up so as not to look as though no one wanted to go out with her.'

'Balls,' says Adam. 'In that case, she'd have lied to her friends, not to you. Besides, have you ever known Lucy without a horde of men after her?' He eases the car up against the kerb, into the space between the cars of their neighbours. 'I bet what happened was they had a quarrel or something and he bashed her on the head and killed her, then lugged her up that tower in a panic and threw her down to make it look like suicide, and then buggered off somewhere.'

What he says only reflects what Hannah herself has been thinking. 'Maybe,' she says cautiously, too exhausted to react as he wants her to.

'It's obvious.' Adam parks in front of their house, turns off the ignition and takes out the keys. He turns to his mother. 'Think about it.'

'I am. I have been.'

'And because he didn't know Lucy all that well, he didn't realise about her head for heights, it didn't occur to him.' Adam takes his mother's hands in his. 'That's how we'll get him. That's his fatal mistake.' Already his hair is greying; he runs his hand through it and Hannah realises with a catch of the heart how much she loves him, how much more he will mean, now that he is all she has.

'Maybe,' she says again.

At the end of the road, the river is ruffled, pale, reflecting the thin blue of a spring sky.

Hannah went heavily up the stairs to her bedroom. She was exhausted. Grief lay unswallowed inside her; she felt as though her heart had been concreted over, that she would never again feel anything but the weight of her loss, she would carry it with her for the rest of her life. In the mirror on her dressing-table, her mother's face looked uncertainly back at her. Taking off her skirt, she pulled back the bed-covers and lay down. Below, in the sitting-room, she could hear Adam playing a Chopin nocturne on the piano; it had been one Lucinda used to play. Tears came into her eyes and rolled down her face. She wanted to sleep but dared not close her eyes, knowing that if she did so, she would see Lucinda again, Lucinda, darling daughter, beloved child.

She turned over, pulling the pillows round her head and her fingers felt something lying under one of them. Assuming it was the book she had fallen asleep over the night before, she pulled at it. It was the wrong weight, the wrong size. She held it in front of her eyes.

A postcard. On one side, a picture of the countryside around the cottage belonging to Tom's parents, taken from some high place. A scatter of white cottages set against the wide bare moors, and, if she looked closely, the ruined tower, almost invisible, where Lucinda had died.

Slowly she turned it over. Words were written on the blank space in bold black capitals.

WHO IS NEXT, ANNA?

What did they mean? For a moment, they made no sense. The letters were there, recognisably their familiar shapes, but the words they formed had no meaning. How had the card come to be under her pillow? Raising herself on her elbow, she read the message again. WHO IS NEXT, ANNA?

She felt very cold. As though it were some poisonous spider, she flung the card away from her. Leaping out of bed, breath coming in sobbing gasps, she began to tear frantically at the sheets as though they had been contaminated, as though they were covered in powdered glass.

'Oh God, oh God,' she said under her breath, pulling at the pillows, throwing them away from her, flinging them to the floor. And then, lifting the last one, she stopped.

Whimpering, she pressed both her hands against her breast.

'No,' she whispered. 'Please, no.' She shook her head.

Lying there on the white sheet was a brooch. The design was old-fashioned, a basket holding three blooms; the heart of each was a fine fire opal. Once, it had belonged to her mother. It had seemed magical to Hannah, as a child, that fire could exist in the heart of a stone. It had the same mysteriousness as the pebbles found on a shingle beach which, when held up to the sun, glowed with a yellow light. Dying, Hannah's mother had given the brooch to Lucinda on her thirteenth birthday. Now, through the blood-rush of her pounding nerves, Hannah recalled Lucinda's voice telling her that the brooch had been stolen. Yet here it lay in her own bed, mocking, poisoned. For a single second, she had a vision of something dark, winged, monstrous. Eyes glowed in the blackness. Then she was running clumsily from the room, her face smeared with terrified tears, calling her son, hysterically shrieking his name.

'It's obvious, isn't it?' she said. Standing in the hall with the telephone in her hand, exhaustion clouded her brain. She could see the carpet, the wallpaper, the vase of fresh flowers, the pictures on the wall but they had taken on an unreal quality, as though viewed through a pane of flawed glass. It was difficult to concentrate; her mind darted restlessly from one topic to another. 'Someone must have broken in while we were at the funeral and put the brooch under my pillow.'

'You're absolutely certain that it's your daughter's brooch?'

'Inspector, it was designed by my grandfather and made up specially for my mother on her thirteenth birthday. Which is why she gave it to Lucinda on hers.'

'Not you?'

'It was given to me on *my* thirteenth birthday, but it's not the kind of thing I wear,' Hannah said coolly. Why did he ask such a question? Did he have some vague notion that she had killed her daughter in order to get the brooch back? 'I gave it back to my mother and it was she who suggested giving it to Lucinda before she—'

Another memory she had wanted to erase, her mother waxy against the pillows of her empty double bed, painfully dying. Holding the gaunt hand, Hannah had thought back to her critical youth, her disdain for her unattractive parents. Why didn't you love me? she wanted to ask, but her mother's eyes seldom opened now as she wandered through morphia-dreams, and anyway, she knew that such a question could only surprise and wound. According to their lights, they had loved her; it was unfortunate that they had loved each other more.

'And there's no possibility of a mistake being made – your daughter leaving it there for you, perhaps, last time she was home, something like that?'

'This is ridiculous.' Hannah held the phone away from her and breathed deeply, trying to fill herself with some semblance of calm. 'I've changed the bed linen several times since Lucinda last came home. The brooch was never there before. Nor was the card. It's obvious that the same person broke into my daughter's house at university and into mine.'

'Mmm,' said Mayfield, the sound somewhere between a groan and a sigh.

'Doesn't it make it much more likely that the same person . . . *killed* her?' Hannah started telling Mayfield about Lucinda's last telephone call, her suspicion that she was being watched, spied on.

'Why didn't you give me this information earlier?' he asked.

'Would it have made any difference?'

He was silent.

'And there was a cassette,' she continued. 'Someone put it into my car.' She explained further.

'It certainly changes things,' Mayfield said carefully. 'I'll have to put one of my men on to the case, get him to go through the evidence again, see if he can find something new which might give us a lead.'

'What about my son?' Hannah shouted. 'What about Adam?'

'There's not a great deal we can—'

'This madman is obviously going to go after him next,' Hannah said, and wondered how she could utter such words without breaking down.

'Has he reported any incidents? Anything alarming, or suspicious?'

'No. I asked him just now, before I called you. He said there hadn't been anything.'

'Leave it with me, Mrs Barlow. Let me give it some thought.'

'Don't think too long, Inspector. I don't think I could bear it if—'

If they took Adam too . . .

When she put the phone down, it rang again almost immediately. She snatched it up to hear Susie's voice.

'Oh, Hannie,' she said, 'I just got home. I've been thinking about you ever since I left you.'

'Susie, my dear,' Hannah said quietly. She closed her eyes, standing in the dark hall, aware that, if she could, Susie would take this burden from her, and strengthened by the knowledge. She wondered whether to tell Susie about the card under her pillow, the brooch, and decided against it. Susie would ask questions, demand Hannah's theories, and inevitably that would lead into the past. Where did rationalisation begin? She could not now say to Susie: if only you had come back, instead of lingering in Rome, then Lucinda might still be alive, and Lucas. We might both of us be happy instead of . . . what we are.

147

'There's nothing to be said, so I'm not going to try. I just wanted to tell you that my – my heart is with you, and how much, how very much I wish—' Susie's voice fluttered to a stop.

'I know,' Hannah said. 'I know.'

'The last time I visited her at the university, she was so . . . so joyful,' Susie said, with a gasping intake of breath which Hannah recognised as the prelude to weeping. 'And her friends . . . so like her . . . so kind and – and loving . . . such lovely young people.'

'Yes.' Which would have made it all the more poignant for Susie, who had no young people of her own.

'Oh, Hannah—'

'Susie.'

Much later that night, she stands at the window and stares out at the river. The glass panes are chill under her palm; a bitter wind throws rain coldly against the glass. She shivers; the central heating has gone off and the room's warmth is long since dissipated.

She had sat up with Adam, discussing what to do next. It has been agreed that he shall go first to his father and then, secretly, with the utmost circumspection, to stay with friends in the States. The university authorities will be asked to agree to a term's absence without penalty; he can continue to study, keep up his grades. If anyone is watching him, they must not realise that he is going; she considers it unlikely that phones have been tapped, cars bugged. If he is careful, it will be simple for him to disappear for a time.

At the end of the road, the river waits, higher than it has been for some time, water rocking slowly against the edge of the grass along the embankment. She is seized with rage at this sudden snatching away of her daughter. A clawing hatred of the person responsible for Lucinda's death hooks itself on to her heart, like a cancer. It is a long time since she has felt such raw emotion and she savours it. Remembering the past, she knows that she has done her best to endure, to deceive, to forget. It has never been easy; sometimes it has been more than painful. Walking parallel with her, as though behind a glass wall, in step with her but separate, has always been the reflection of her younger self, and behind that, the image of the death she caused. It has been impossible to forget and yet she has tried to do so . . .

Now, she thinks, with a sense of relief, perhaps the time has come when remembering will be less painful than forgetting. And remembering, might she not somehow be able to reinterpret, look again with some measure of hindsight at what had seemed merely linear but which now, older, she knows must have been surrounded by a scatter of other resonances of which she could not have been aware.

Like the day of the picnic, for instance . . .

THEN

11

Under her bare feet the marble tiles were warm and solid. Hannah placed her hands on the balustrade, intensely aware of pitted stone, lichen rough against her palms. Increasingly, the hot days were made up of sensation rather than emotion. Occasionally she wondered if these were the first stages of starvation, this lightness of bone, this sense of a body not quite joined together. For the past few days she had eaten nothing but some ripe pears and a melon; it was too hot to concentrate on the techniques involved in the finding and consuming of food.

Recently, if she moved her head too fast, she would find herself falling to one side, things dipping and lurching about her. Sometimes, opening her eyes she would find the world beyond her eyelids had taken on a whitened aspect, as though an arc light had been switched on. Often there was a chemical taste at the back of her throat.

The summons from Lucas had ceased. Was it because he somehow sensed that she had broken free of him? Or was it because he was preoccupied with the woman in the lemon-yellow dress? Or had the heat so enervated her that she could no longer pick up his signals? Whatever the answer, none of it seemed to matter very much. The summer, she knew, was nearly over. After the peaks of her affair with Lucas, there was only the imminence of her return to England and the flatness her life had hitherto been. Would she ever again experience such a sense of being consumed? Would she ever give herself again so willingly, so wholeheartedly?

In the dimness of the house, the telephone rang. She turned slowly towards the sound, drifting across the terrace and in through the open french windows. As she walked through the long ballroom, her reflection kept pace with her; the glass image seemed to have almost more solidity than she did.

'Yes?' she said into the telephone.

'Susie?' The voice was English.

'She's not here. She's in Rome.'

'This is Tristan Carrick. And you are?'

'Her friend, Hannah Carrington.'

'Sounds familiar. We've met, haven't we?'

'In Cornwall,' agreed Hannah. 'Years ago.'

'I remember you,' said Tristan. His deep voice lapped round her like warm water as she stood barefooted in the dim house. 'Dark, pretty, clever: a cello player, yes?'

Hannah said nothing. She glanced down the hall towards the rectangular slab of white heat outside, framed by the open doorway, the straight lines of the threshold fuzzed, as though the light was leaching into the darkness.

'The thing is,' Tristan said, 'I was hoping to come and stay for a couple of days next week.'

Hannah frowned into the receiver. 'I'm sure Susie would have been delighted to have you stay here if she was around. But since she isn't, I'm not sure whether I—'

'I can't imagine that anyone would object,' Tristan interrupted. 'Certainly not Edward or Giulia.'

It was an effort for Hannah to remember that these were Susie's parents. 'Uh—'

'*You* might mind, of course . . . your reputation or whatever, if people still care about such things—' Tristan paused, waiting for her to deny it. When she did not, he went on, 'But I'd so much rather stay at the villa than with the Trevelyans, good friends though they are. Those children are a bit too lively for a confirmed old bachelor like me.'

'Well . . . I suppose it's all right.'

'So I'll see you then,' said Tristan.

'Are you coming alone?' Hannah asked, belatedly realising that she would have to lay in supplies, check sheets, tidy up. Susie's family and Tristan's were close friends, and they would consider it impolite if she was not properly hospitable to him.

'I'm driving up from Rome with a couple of friends but you needn't worry about them, they're pushing on, they've got bookings on the cross-Channel ferry and don't want to miss them.'

'I see.'

Over the intervening days she tried several times to contact Susie in order to let her know about Tristan's arrival, but without success. Although she let the number Susie had given her in Rome ring and ring, thirty, forty times, no one ever answered.

Today the landscape lay unmoving, as though at the bottom of a mortar, waiting to be crushed by the pestle of the heat. In the distance the little hill crowned with its campanile hung against the sky, absolutely still.

Hannah, too, waited. She felt brittle, light-headed. Any minute, cars would come up the drive, people would wave, laugh, speak to her, expect a reply. The thought of so much time in the company of others seemed an effort not worth the making, but it was too late now for her to stop the unfolding of the day. She thought of pleading illness: she knew they would believe her for even she herself had been shocked by the reflection in the clouded bathroom mirror that morning.

She wished that she had more forcefully declined Nancy's invitation to a picnic. A week ago, she had been standing trapped in the black shadows directly beneath the ramparts of the little town, summoning up the resolve to leave the shade and venture out into the bite of the noonday sun. Across the piazza was the *trattoria*; she had intended to gain the shade and perhaps have a coffee there, summon up some strength before cycling back to the Villa Giulia. She heard her name being called but in the white light could see nothing. When she finally reached the tables, she found Nancy Trevelyan sitting there with a beaded glass of transparent wine in front of her.

'What on earth were you doing?' Nancy asked.

'When?'

'Just now? On the other side of the square. You looked as though you were psyching yourself up to jump off the top diving board.' Nancy scrutinised Hannah through sunglasses which hid the nuances of her expression, then went on without waiting for an answer: 'I'm glad to see you, actually, saves me a phone call. I've only just realised you were still around: didn't you and Susie go to Rome?'

'Only Susie.'

'You should have let us know. I should think you were bored out of your mind, all alone in that big house.'

'Not really,' said Hannah. 'I—'

But Nancy was racing on. 'We're organising the End of Summer picnic,' she said. 'We have it every year, the last get-together before everyone starts drifting home. You have to come.'

'I'm not sure I—'

'We're going down to that little lake – have you been there? – about twenty miles south of here. I'll organise someone to give you a lift – the Halls, maybe. Or the Lambourns.'

'Sounds like fun,' Hannah said feebly.

'Oh, it always is. Such a pity Susie is away. Especially since that's the day Tristan will be arriving.'

'Is it?' She realised that until then, she had not known when he would appear at the Villa Giulia.

'So he said when he called us a couple of days ago.' Nancy looked at her watch. 'Where on earth has Lew got to? Look, don't bother to bring anything to the picnic, there's always masses of food.'

'I'm not really sure if I—'

'I'll give you a call,' Nancy said, getting up as a dusty car swept into the piazza and arms waved from the windows in greeting. As she climbed into the front passenger seat of the car, she turned: 'Oh, and bring your swimsuit. The water's lovely down there.'

The lake was roughly rectangular, its shores of reddish earth, bounded on three sides by coarse waterside grasses and pine trees, on the fourth by low hills. A finger of land protruded into the lake from the right-hand side, thus creating a narrow strip of water between itself and the southern shoreline. By the time Hannah and the Lambourns – two adults and three polite teenagers – arrived, a large contingent of noisy picnickers had already begun staking out their territory, marking it with portable barbecues, picnic baskets, plaid blankets, even folding chairs.

Hannah quailed. The effort of exchanging conversational nothings with people who did not have any idea who she was made her feel literally faint. Staring round, beleaguered, she saw that in the middle of the lake was a square wooden raft; if she swam out to it, would anybody miss her – or even realise she had gone? She thought not.

Around her, people strenuously spread table-cloths, unpacked hampers, popped corks. Talk rushed and eddied round her: about departure times, about school terms and the purchase of uniform for offspring who had outgrown last year's, about new jobs or changes in old ones. Voices spoke with regret of summer's end, although here there was little sign of it; melancholy hovered. Down by the lake's edge, a group of adolescent youths stood huddled together, smoking in a defiant, furtive way, aloof from their parents or younger siblings, relishing their last chance to be individuals, rather than part of the school herd again.

Despite all the jollity, Hannah found the atmosphere faintly menacing, as though they gathered to partake in some ritual which would end in a blood sacrifice. Adopting a general smile, she scanned them quickly and saw only a few faces she recognised: the Trevelyans, the red-faced novelist, a man who had been at most of the gatherings whose name she had never discovered and who seemed as out of it as she did herself. She could not see Tristan, or, rather, anyone who looked as if he was someone Tristan might have turned into, though she could not be sure since it was, after all, some years since she had last seen him. Moving away, she changed out of her cotton dress under a towel, then made her way into the water. Her body moved about inside the looseness of her bathing suit; her bones protruded unbecomingly from the cover of her flesh and she felt unattractive, even freakish. Quickly she stepped further into the water. Under her feet the sandy pebbled bottom moved, slipping away from her. Did she hear someone – Nancy – call her name? If so, she ignored the cry, running on into the water, sending up a cascade round herself then flinging forward to propel herself away from the land.

When she turned on to her back, the shore seemed unexpectedly far away. Under the pines, the picnickers appeared reduced, static, as though they were figures in some bucolic landscape. Nobody was looking in her direction.

She swam round to the back of the raft and climbed on to it. Despite the lack of shade, the sun was less obtrusive here, perhaps because of the water's cool. There was no one else around as she stretched out, the boards uncomfortable beneath her thin shoulder blades. Italian syllables drifted towards her; isolating the sounds which reached her from the shore, she could hear voices, subdued by distance, the small plash of water against the wooden pilings below her, a bird calling harshly beyond the land-spit, the muted screaming of a child.

The sun touched her like a lover. Like – she could not screen out the thought – Lucas. She wondered where he was, whether he would come to the picnic. Why did she feel nothing at the ending of their . . . whatever it had been? No pain, no longing. Nothing. Was that because, although she had believed herself to love him, she had in fact felt as little as he? And if so, what did that make her? She knew that she was not, nor ever would be, the kind of woman for whom the sexual act was just that: an act. So why this neutrality, this total lack of emotion? She turned over and lay on her stomach, resting her head on her folded arms, feeling heat against her eyelids, the smell of sunbaked wood almost tangible. There was no point in endlessly rehashing what had happened. It was over.

Under her, the raft rocked as someone climbed up out of the water on to the boards. She did not move.

'Hannah?'

Surprised, she turned on to her side and squinted up at the man who stood above her, colossal against the sky.

'It *is* Hannah, isn't it?'

She nodded, shading her eyes against the sky's glare.

'They said you were over here.' He leaned down towards her. 'It's Tristan. Tristan Carrick.'

'Oh, yes.' Hannah half-sat, pulling away towards the edge of the raft as he squatted down beside her.

'So how are you, Hannah?'

'Fine, thank you.'

'They said you were not feeling well,' Tristan said. He nodded towards the shore. 'They said you looked sick.'

'And do I?'

'You do indeed,' said Tristan. 'If you were mine, I would be wanting to do something about it.'

'So it's just as well I'm not.' She smiled at him. 'Yours, I mean.'

His hair was as thick as she remembered it, but somehow, although white, less *old*. Or was it that she herself had advanced towards him, and saw him now from a nearer perspective?

'I don't know that I'd go along with that,' said Tristan. He grinned. 'I'd be a poor sort of man if I didn't feel a pang to hear you say it.' He leaned down suddenly and kissed the side of her face. 'It's been a long time since last we met.'

'Six or seven years, I think.'

'And now we meet in Italy.' Tristan looked shorewards again. 'Tell me: I was wondering, is Susie's cousin coming today?'

'Lucas?'

'That's the man.'

'I'm not sure. Why?'

Tristan shrugged. 'There are things we want to discuss with him.'

'We?'

'Friends of mine.'

'I thought your friends were driving on.'

'They are, but they'd hoped to have a word with Wyndham.' Tristan stared shorewards. 'We heard he was staying here for the summer.'

'He is.'

'But he's not coming to the picnic?'

Wondering at his insistence, Hannah said: 'I think Mrs Trevelyan told me he might show up later, for the barbecue.'

'There's to be a barbecue, is there?'

'So I've been told. But that's this evening. Nancy's organised a picnic lunch. Not that I brought a contribution to it.'

'Neither did I.' Tristan leaned down closer towards her, so that she could see the strong lines on either side of his mouth, and the blackness of his lower eyelashes, incongruously girlish. 'I've got a car. Why don't we go, you and me, and find a restaurant somewhere? I've never been a man for picnics, I have to say. I could bring you back in time for the barbecue.'

Swiftly Hannah weighed up the disadvantages of lunching alone with Tristan or spending the rest of the afternoon isolated from the others. Before she could come to any conclusion, he had reached down and was pulling her to her feet.

'Won't they mind, if we sneak off?' she asked.

'We'll invent an urgent need for a *farmacia*, if they ask. But I guarantee they won't.'

'What about the friends you came with?'

'They'll be OK.'

'All right,' Hannah said. Standing with toes curled over the edge of the warm wood, she looked over her shoulder at him and grinned. 'Race you back.'

Behind her, as she dived, low and swift, into the lake, she heard Tristan hit the water, felt his hand slide past her ankle, but by the time she reached the shore, she was several feet ahead.

'What have you done to yourself?' he said. 'You used to be so . . . not pretty, exactly—'

'You said pretty on the phone,' Hannah pointed out, flirtatiously.

He paused, searching for the word, his wine glass tilting at his mouth. 'Striking is more like it.'

'And now?'

'You've become someone . . . different from what I might have anticipated.'

'Perhaps I've grown up.' Hannah spoke lightly, knowing that it was more than that; this summer she had learned to swallow life whole rather than merely nibble at its edges. The restaurant they had found was dark, full of heat and the good smell of food. Outside, bright light dazzled in the empty street.

'But you look ill. Or are you in love?' Tristan's dark, almost black eyes, watched her thoughtfully as she slowly shook her head. 'I've seen love do that to a woman, eat away at the heart of her until she's no more than skin and bone.'

As with everything Tristan said, this remark appeared to have a further significance than the mere words which formed it, so that Hannah was forced to interpret it as she might a foreign language, searching first for something vaguely recognisable and then matching it up to whatever little knowledge she might possess. She cut at the edge of the veal on her plate and lifted a small piece to her mouth, considering the matter.

'Not love, just the heat,' she said. She raised a hand to brush hair from her forehead and was aware of the bones beneath her suntanned skin, brittle as the skeleton of a fallen leaf.

A fly buzzed against the small, plant-obscured window. Above their heads an old-fashioned ceiling fan wheezed, faintly stirring the torpid air.

'Did you meet up with Susie while you were in Rome?' Hannah asked.

'We had a drink together,' said Tristan.

'I didn't realise she was going to go for so long.'

'Lonely, are you?'

'Not at all. It's just, I wondered what . . . what exactly she's doing down there all this time.'

'I saw her a couple of other times,' Tristan said. 'By chance. She didn't see me.'

'Was she . . . *with* anyone?'

'A man, of course.' Tristan smiled. 'As her friend, you must know how much Susie likes men.'

Hannah thought of Susie's avowed intention to marry Lucas some day. Did she merely see her cousin as a good catch, someone to give her the children and the money she was always talking about? It seemed less than admirable – or was the fact that she went out – slept – with other men a way of getting back at Lucas for his indifference to her? 'Did he look nice?' she asked, rather wistfully.

'He had no obvious physical defects,' Tristan said. 'I'm afraid I wasn't in a position to judge the niceness of his character.'

They ate in silence for a while, then Tristan frowned, looking full at her, though she could tell that he did not really see her, that although he was with her, he was somewhere else at the same time. 'Have you had much to do with our aristocratic friend?' he asked.

'Do you mean Lucas?'

'How many other arrogant, two-faced, treacherous lordlings are there around here?' asked Tristan. His voice sliced contemptuously at the shadows of the dim room, his lips stretching back from his teeth in an unamused smile. Hannah was chilled by the glimpse of steel she detected beneath his words. Arrogant? Lucas was certainly that. But two-faced? Treacherous? Did Tristan mean because of the woman who had died – for she remembered the story now, the faithless wife, the adulterous lover, a wet road in the night, screech of brakes, clash of steel, slow drip of petrol before the deadly eruption of flame. But surely, whatever the moral implications, it had been an accident, had it not? And the wife must have been a grown woman, able to make decisions for herself. That she was there at all with Lucas on the night of the accident had been – had it not? – her own choice. But perhaps not. Hannah knew herself how Lucas could call, could force her to his side.

She stared down into the glass of red wine which Tristan had poured for her.

'So?' he said.

She looked up. 'What?'

'Have you seen much of Wyndham this summer? Or is he too busy chasing other men's wives to waste time on a girl like yourself?'

'I haven't been keeping tabs on him,' she said, cold in her turn. Anger flared. 'Besides, since Lucas is nothing to do with me, nor do I know anything about what he may or may not have done, I don't think we should be discussing him like this.' The broad wooden paddles of the fan whirred slowly, lifting the ends of her hair. Despite the momentary cool, an undefined anxiety brought sweat out on her forehead.

For a moment, he stared bleakly through her. Then he said: 'I'm sorry.' He finished his wine, holding the empty glass for a moment. 'Now tell me, Hannah: how have you spent your summer in Italy?'

What would he say if she told him? Or if she said it was no business of his? It was obvious that Tristan Carrick was not used to being held accountable either for what he said or for what he did. She remembered his beautiful, shabby house set on the Cornish cliffs, the chipped, gold-painted dishes and wax-encrusted silver candlesticks on the table, the yellow room full of sunshine.

'Pottering, mostly,' she said, non-committal. She shrugged. 'Swimming. Walking. Mostly lying about: it's been so hot. And you? You've been in Morocco or somewhere, haven't you?'

'Somewhere,' he agreed. 'But only for a week. I've been working on an important project in Rome, and on top of that, since my parents died, I have to keep dashing home to supervise their farm. You can't leave land too long, even where there are competent folk to care for it in your absence.'

'Why not?' Was he aware of parallels between himself and the man he spoke of with such dislike, both of them come young into their inheritances, both, somehow, strayed from the true?

'Land is like a woman, Hannah. It needs attention, the knowledge that it matters. It needs . . . caressing.'

In another man, such words might have sounded pretentious or affected. Her mind produced a glimpse of him on some bleakly windswept moor, under storm clouds, looking down at his acres, loving them. A child of the suburbs, she had no concept of land-pride, no tradition of generation succeeding generation in the house where each was born. In many ways, she envied him.

'And do you have a woman to whom you pay attention?' she asked. 'Whom you caress?'

'No one permanent,' he said lightly.

'Aren't landowners supposed to get married and establish their heirs as soon as they can?' Hannah did not know why she was asking such personal questions.

'I'm an architect first, and only secondly a landowner. It was my parents' farm, not mine. I ought to sell the place, but I keep thinking of my children – if I ever have any.'

'So you're still looking for Miss Right.'

'At my advanced age, it's more likely to be the Widow Right,' said Tristan, laughing. 'Or the Divorcée Right.' He drank the wine in his glass and refilled both hers and his. 'Good thing my parents aren't still alive – they'd be horrified at the mere idea of a divorced woman sitting at their table.' He touched her arm across the table. 'Are you ready to go back to the lake?'

'Not just yet.'

'Then let's have coffee at one of the outside tables: it won't be too hot in the shade.' He sighed, breathing her name so gently that the aspirate went almost unheard. 'I do believe you've filled out already, Hannah.'

'Good.'

Later, much later, they walked around the little town. Hannah thought she had probably drunk too much wine: the earth did not seem quite steady beneath her feet. Passing a dried-up fountain streaked with rust, the dusty cobbles suddenly gave way beneath her and she clutched at Tristan's arm to prevent herself falling. He tucked her hand into the crook of his elbow and held it there, smiling briefly down at her. They stopped at the ramparts and looked down at the vines, which spread thick and leafy across the plains. In the distance smoke columns rose to the hot sky, where farmers burned off the stubble left from already-harvested corn. At the horizon, just above the land, white cloud was gathering, high-piled like a row of elaborate perruques. Every now and then lightning needles darted between the heavy masses.

'Looks as though there might be a storm tonight,' Tristan said.

'Let's hope it doesn't ruin the barbecue,' said Hannah. 'Poor Nancy's spent so much time organising everything.'

'I like the rain.'

'Me too.'

'And I'm sure she's thought of ways to keep the barbecue dry.' He stopped. 'I'll take you home when it's over, if you like.'

'Fine.'

'We might even sneak off early, if it looks like dragging on.'

'Will your friends still be there when we get back?' Hannah asked.

'That depends.'

'On what?'

As though abruptly reminded of something he had managed to forget for a whiie, Tristan turned away from the view. 'I think we'd better go,' he said. Any rapport which had developed between them during the afternoon seemed suddenly to have evaporated, as though he had more important things to consider.

By the time they returned to the lake, thunder was mumbling in the distance. Under the pines, the resiny air was hot; the tree-trunks had already begun to blur into the twilight. More people had arrived, Lucas among them. He was talking to a woman Hannah did not know, apparently trying to reassure her about something. He seemed relaxed, a plastic beaker of red wine in his hand, yet the set of his shoulders made it obvious that he was less at ease than he appeared.

Nancy and her minions had been busy. Close to the shore, a large pit had been dug in the sandy soil and a long makeshift spit erected above the glowing coals, on which were skewered several roasting carcasses. Smaller portable grills had also begun to glow and a smell of cooking meat pervaded the air. A series of boards spread across orange plastic milk crates and then draped with checked cloths acted as tables. There were huge bowls of potato salad, lettuce, tomatoes, dishes of ratatouille and pasta, crusty rounds of bread, risottos, platters piled with sausages, artichoke hearts soaked in olive oil.

Hannah could hardly bear to look at so much food. Separated from Tristan by Nancy, who had given them a narrow-eyed glance, she wandered down to the edge of the lake. Taking off her sandals, she waded in until she was calf-deep in the milk-coloured water. She felt disturbed and uneasy. Was it the coming storm? Or because of something heard or seen earlier that day? Something to do with Lucas?

She tried to pierce through the wine haze which obscured her remembrance of the afternoon but could not do so.

Behind her in the gathering dark, shadows moved between the glowing coals. Someone had started a fire on the beach using wood thrown up on shore by winter storms; in the fading light, as thunder stalked the hills, the scene took on a lurid aspect, like a scene from Hieronymous Bosch.

To one side, a little away from the crowd, she could see Tristan, indistinct across the fires. With him was a smaller, stockier man. The two of them were staring intently at Lucas; there was something disturbing about the furtiveness of their attention and the fact that they clearly did not wish Lucas to notice them. Did he know that Tristan was watching him? Did he sense harm waiting for him among the trees?

She found herself drawn into several meaningless conversations with a series of people only half-known to her. Someone – a German, a Swede? – pulled her over to the tables and filled a plate with food for her; although she was not in the least hungry, she accepted it, smiled and murmured, yet all the time she was acutely aware of both Lucas and Tristan. At some point in the evening, she thought she saw the child from the Villa Diana, hair almost white in the fading light, down by the shoreline, standing with the man Tristan had talked to earlier. Who had brought it here – Lucas? It seemed improbable.

Much later, when she was at last able to wander away, she could not at first see either Tristan or Lucas. The stocky man, whom she took to be one of Tristan's friends, was talking to the same woman who had earlier been with Lucas – was it the housekeeper? She was shaking her head vehemently, her face screwed up with fear. Again Hannah was aware of danger moving below the surface of the evening. She wondered whether to join the couple; the woman was obviously in distress. Was the man demanding to know where Lucas was?

'Hannah, my dear Hannah.' It was the man whose name she had never learned. He was obviously suffering from the effects of too much sun and cheap red wine.

'Hello,' she said.

'We've never spoken before.' He staggered a little. 'My name's Jim Dixon. Lucky Jim, indeed, to find you like this, alone and palely loitering. Surprised you're not with the rest of your little chums.'

'What?' He seemed an irrelevance; she was too well brought up, or perhaps too repressed, to tell him to go away.

'The *jeunesse dorée*,' he said, gesturing largely with the beaker of wine in his hand. 'The gilded youth. All those Mungos and Hugos and bloody Charlottes. Your . . . *crowd*.' He swayed with the effort of pronouncing the word, leaning towards the ground as though about to vomit.

'I don't have a crowd. I'm as out of it here as you are,' Hannah said, thinking to be kind.

'I've been out of it all my life,' Dixon said sadly.

'That makes two of us, then.'

She walked away from him along the lake's edge, wondering where Tristan had got to, trying to still the flutter of alarm in her chest. He had been so contemptuous about Lucas at lunchtime, his questions so insistent. At the edge of her vision something moved and she turned to see them – Lucas, Tristan, a couple of other men – among the trees on the jutting finger of land, separated by a stretch of water from where she stood. Instinctively, she took cover behind one of the trees which marched almost into the lake. Under her feet the pine needles were soft and slippery; she moved without sound. Could they see her? She doubted it, with the darkness of the land behind her, but none the less she kept in close to the trees, at the same time edging forward. Almost at the lake's edge, she stopped. Across the strip of water, no more than thirty feet away, they were talking – or some were. One – Lucas – said nothing.

She strained to see more clearly through the almost-dark. Then gasped, biting at her lower lip to keep from calling out. From here, it looked as though Lucas was tied to one of the trees, his arms pulled back behind him, like someone facing a firing squad. But why had he not called out? She stared over her shoulder at the barbecue fires. He could not possibly be in any danger: there were people, lights, help only yards away.

'I told you I'd come for you, Wyndham,' one of them whispered fiercely, the sound carrying clearly to Hannah under the pines.

'Sooner or later,' said another.

'You can't run for ever.'

'People like me don't run,' Lucas said quietly.

'Someone's got to put a stop to you,' one of the men said, Hannah could not tell which. 'You've hurt too many people, it can't go on.'

There was a silence, during which Hannah scarcely dared breathe. How could these people be threatening Lucas, why had he allowed them to tie him up, when all he had to do was shout for help? It didn't make sense.

One of the men stepped closer to him. She saw, to her horror, the greasy shine of a blade. 'I'd do it here and now if I thought I could get away with it,' he said violently. Hannah could not be sure but it looked as though it was the stocky man who'd been with Tristan earlier.

'A knife, Mark,' Lucas said. 'Tut tut. I thought you'd put away childish things when you left that Boy Scout patrol you were with.'

'You fucking piece of scum—' began the one called Mark, starting forward, but Tristan stopped him.

'We could hold your head under water until you drowned,' said the third. 'They'd think it was an accident.'

'Or break your bloody neck,' said Mark, still holding the knife.

'*Much* more difficult to explain,' Lucas said coolly.

'Don't think we'd hesitate.'

'I'm quite sure you wouldn't. Not when there's three of you and only one of me. And I'm tied up.' The contempt in Lucas's tone was unmistakable.

One of the men hit Lucas hard across the mouth. 'Shut up,' he whispered angrily, 'shut *up*!' then stared across the water at the barbecue fires.

Was it Tristan? Hannah began to tremble. The heavy lunch she had eaten, the wine she had drunk, the palpable menace exuded by the shadowy scene being enacted in front of her, all combined to make her feel as though she might faint.

'Besides, you don't deserve to go on living,' one of the men said, his voice only a fraction above inaudible.

'Then why don't you get on with it?' Lucas said evenly. 'Go on. Kill me now. You know how much you want to.'

There was another pause.

'I wouldn't mind,' Lucas added, when no one said anything. 'In fact you'd be doing me a favour.'

One of them said: 'So you're not scared, Wyndham?'

Lucas did not answer.

'Nothing to say?' sneered someone. 'I'd should think—'

'Only this.' Lucas did not whisper, his voice carrying easily to where Hannah stood. 'If you seriously think I'm scared by a bunch of psychopaths like you, you're even more full of shit than I realised. You're simply trying to blame me for your own pathetic inadequacies.' He jerked his head at one of them. 'You, for instance. Don't blame me for what happened. Or you—' He indicated another of the men. 'If you were more of a man and less of a—'

The second man – the stocky one? – lunged forward and punched him hard in the stomach then, as Lucas involuntarily doubled over as far as his bonds would allow, snapped his head viciously backwards. Blood spurted, black against the white of his shirt. He groaned, and Hannah guessed he despised himself for that small weakness.

She was shaking so hard that she thought she would fall. She had never seen naked aggression before, never seen violence done. What action should she take? If she rushed forward, splashed across the thin divide of water, might they not overpower her too, even kill her? Would she be able to help Lucas if she did? She could start screaming, but even as she thought this, she knew that it was the very last thing Lucas would want. If they touched him again, she would have to – but one of the men said urgently: 'Let's go.'

Who were they?

Part of the horror for her lay in the fact that Tristan must be one of them. How could the man whose company she had enjoyed that afternoon have been party to such ferocity? Even though he had referred so contemptuously to Lucas, he could not have really meant it. And who were the others?

At one level, what she had overheard was little more than playground bullying. On the other hand, grown men did not whisper threats if those threats were idle. Bile rose in her throat. At the same time she became aware that someone else was nearby. She could hear the faint rustle as limbs moved inside clothing, and the almost imperceptible sound of someone breathing. Was the other person aware of her own presence?

She stood rigid against the tree trunk while, across the narrow strip of lake, Lucas's attackers conferred in low voices, then abruptly one of them moved close to Lucas and raised his arm. Although one of the others tried to restrain him, grabbing his arm, whispering, 'For Chris*sake*—' at the same time looking, or so it seemed, directly at her, there was a swift movement, a gasp from Lucas. Then the man with the knife was gone, followed by a second man, both of them running off into the night.

The third – *was* it Tristan? – hesitated, indecisive, looking at Lucas, then he too moved swiftly away, hurrying along the shoreline, round the edge of the spit to be lost in the darkness. The person behind Hannah moved too, following the line Tristan must have taken as he angled towards the barbecue fires.

In the distance a car door slammed. An engine revved up and then came the long, slow noise of tyres turning and heading away into the night. Immediately afterwards, a tremendous clap of thunder reverberated, sending ripples of sound rolling across the lake, causing night-birds to rise screeching out of the reeds and producing exclamations of dismay from the gathered picknickers.

Through the gloom, Hannah saw Lucas sag against the ropes which bound him. Oh God: was he dying? Or dead? 'Lucas,' she called urgently, keeping her voice down. '*Lucas!*'

He lifted his head, peering into the darkness. The movement caused him obvious pain. 'Who's that?' he asked, peering into the darkness.

'Hannah.'

'What the fuck are you doing?' he said weakly.

'I – I—'

'How long have you been listening? How much did you hear?' He sounded angry rather than relieved that she was there.

'N-nothing,' Hannah said. She could not see the expression on his face, but she could guess at its cold distaste.

Above her rain began to patter against the tree branches. There was another roll of thunder and over the drumming of water on the lake's surface, she could hear the faint sound of Nancy rallying her friends, assuring them that everything was under control.

She ran into the water. It was warm, not sandy here but rough underfoot with fallen pine twigs; it came no higher than her waist. She pushed onwards, rain plastering her hair to her skull, until she could stumble out on to the land spit; closer to Lucas, she could see a spreading stain on his shirt, just above the waist. Blood. She pressed her hand to her mouth. Even in the dark she could barely face it. 'Lucas. Are you all right?'

'That's a stupid question,' he said cuttingly. 'Obviously I'm not.'

She fluttered round him. 'What shall I—'

'You could start by untying me.'

'But you're covered in blood.'

'I know that, woman.'

'I – I can't, I—'

'Don't be so bloody *stupid*.'

'You don't understand, I—'

'You *must*, Hannah.'

She gritted her teeth, shuddering, trying to keep her fingers away from the seeping wet of his shirt as she fumbled with the knots which kept him tight. As the ropes loosened, he staggered against her then fell on one knee.

'Lucas—' She closed her eyes. Was he dead? 'Lucas, are you—'

'Help me over to the water,' he said. Then, impatiently, 'For God's sake, Hannah. I'm not going to die.'

She breathed harshly through her mouth as he put an arm round her shoulders and together they made for the water's edge. 'Who were those men? What did they want?' she said. Was there blood on her clothes? On her *skin*? She could feel hysteria welling. A series of long shudders shook her.

'Nothing. They were nobody.'

'But I saw—'

He gripped her wrist hard. 'What did you see?'

She tried to pull away. No longer under the trees, she could see him more clearly: one side of his face was swelling, and there was dried blood under his nose. 'Men,' she said. 'Threatening you. Hitting you.'

He walked into the water, holding his side, and immersed himself, while she watched, nauseous, from the edge. 'Recognise any of them?'

'Not really. Lucas, do you—'

'Are you sure?'

'Tristan Carrick, maybe. But I—'

'You know Tristan?'

'Not very well. But I— Who *were* they, Lucas? Why did they want to kill you?'

He did not answer.

'Was it because of . . . of her?' she said.

He lifted his head and stared at her and even in the darkness, she felt the coldness coming from him so that without realising it, she took a step back. 'Her?' he said.

'You know who I mean.'

'Tell me.' The whispered command was heavy with menace.

'The – uh—' With difficulty, she swallowed. 'The woman who was in the car with you, the one who died.'

She heard him take a deep breath. He began to undo the buttons of his shirt. 'Don't meddle, Hannah, in things which don't concern you.' He sounded so inimical that tears came into her eyes. At the same time, she detected the very faintest edge of relief in his voice. Taking off his shirt, he dunked it several times in the water, then held his face, eyes closed, up to the rain until the blood had washed away.

'Why didn't you call out?' Hannah demanded. 'People would have heard you and come.'

Lucas gave a strange smile and shook his head.

'Why, Lucas?'

'Perhaps, in a way, I agreed with . . . with what they said. Perhaps I *don't* deserve to go on living.'

'You can't mean that.'

'You know nothing about me; you can't possibly judge.'

'Lucas, I only want to help,' said Hannah, and heard her voice tremble.

'I don't need or want your help,' he said, holding one hand to his side, so she turned and walked away from him through the rain, back along the edge of the lake towards the red light of the fires.

THE DIARY

. . . Looks like the Dr's idea is working. Is bringing back my memory. Because today, I caught sight of them. The beast with two backs. Him and her. I'd forgotten about it, but this morning, in the shower, a sudden flash of light cut my mind into two jagged-edged parts. I could see them again, all lit up, as though the sun had come out, the two of them in that big bed, the shutters half-closed, the dark bands on the furniture, the colours of the pictures on the walls.

I saw them, sweating, holding on to each other, shouting things.

The beast with two backs. I know what it means. Someone said that about them. Who was it?

Where was it?

The Dr asked me once about – gulp! – sex. (I have a real problem with that word, don't know why.) Not generalised sex, but my own sexuality.

Asked me if I'd ever – not to put too fine a point on it – had sexual intercourse. Jesus, the very thought makes me want to vomit. I remember once, when I was at college— It's all blood and sweat and screaming. Beast. Beasts. No thank you very much. Not that I said so to the Dr. Didn't actually say anything, just kind of implied that I was pretty swinging, pretty loose, hanging in there, hey, Doc, know what I mean, huh, huh?

I'll bet he doesn't *know* what I mean. He leads a thoroughly normal life, no hang-ups at all, far as I can tell. On his desk there are pictures of his family in square silver frames: wife and three children. The kids all have braces on their teeth. They're all laughing.

I don't remember laughing when I was a child.

Not once.

. . . *Sex.*

It's been haunting me since my last session with the Dr.
Sex with T.
What it would be like. Whether I would be able to 'perform'.

In spite of what I said to the Dr, I do want to make love with someone
– with T. When we're together, I'm aware of all sorts of . . . feelings.
I long to reach out and touch, stroke.

Which makes it all the more urgent that I sort out the mess of
my past.

. . . *He's looking at me in the way I know means he's going to suggest something which he's not sure I'll go along with. He's got my diary on his knee again; he's tapping it with those beasty fingernails of his. He paints them with clear nail varnish, I don't know why.*

'*What?*' *I say.*

'*Listen to me before you respond,*' *he says.*

'*OK,*' *I go.*

'*Have you ever thought of publishing this as a book?*' *he says. For once he doesn't sound entirely sure of himself.*

'*A book?*' *I say, mouth hanging open. A book? Words mean so much to me, other people's words. I've often dreamed of writing, but never seemed to have the concentration, never been able to hang on to my thoughts for long enough.* '*A book?*'

'*Yes.*'

'*Publishing?*'

'*Yes.*'

'*You mean, like a novel or something?*'

'*Exactly.*'

'*But it's my diary,*' *I say.* '*It's my private thoughts. It's my . . . therapeutic tool.*'

'*It also makes fascinating reading,*' *he says. Does he see himself as involved in this process, like that Dr who wrote about the woman with all those multiple personalities?* '*It would only require a little tidying up.*' *He gives me a smile, the one which makes him look like a skull.* '*A little shaping of the narrative, a certain depersonalisation of the tale-teller. Do that, and I really think it's quite saleable as a straightforward story.*'

'*I – uh – I don't know.*' *I make out I'm hesitant, but my mind is revving like the engine of a sports car. My journalism instructor at college told me I was talented: I've never forgotten that. A novel! Published!*

'*Think about it,*' *he says.*

Yeah. I'll do that.

. . . I thought about it. A lot.
I like the idea. Yeah.
I really like it.

I'll talk to F about it.

I can still remember the actual physical jolt it gave me – thirteen?
fourteen? months ago – to dial the numbers, hear the ringing tone,
the receiver being lifted and then – F's voice. The first time for years.
Amazing. Why didn't I do it sooner, years and years ago?
  When I told him who I was, he sounded as if it had been no more
than a couple of months since we last met. So warm. Instant friends.
I'd resented him all these years, hated him, if the truth be told. I could
feel the block of hate melting under the sound of his voice.
  'I looked for you,' he said. 'But there was a lot of stuff going on
then, a lot of terrible emotional stuff.'
  I could understand that. I know about emotional stuff.
  'I still can't talk about it, even now,' he said.
  I could understand that, as well.

When I told him about the Dr's idea, he was enthusiastic. 'I'll give you
the name of an agent,' he said. 'When you've finished rewriting it.'
  At the time, I didn't think I ever would finish. 'And I'll send you
a copy of it, when it's published,' I said.
  I doubt if either of us thought that would ever happen. Not really.
Not in our hearts.

Gives me a thrill to think that the same blood pumps through our
separate hearts, his heart and mine.

NOW

12

Hannah walks beside the river, head on into the wet and freezing wind. The water meadows are flooded again, bounded by willows which stand root-deep in the brown water. This is a walk she has taken a thousand times before: taking it now, she remembers other days, former years, the children small, hanging from her hands, the old dog – dead now – plodding beside them, Lucinda and Adam playing Poohsticks, watching the new ducklings, finding blackberries in the bramble thickets alongside the banks where the river winds away from the town and into the open countryside. She remembers Lucinda weeping down the phone at the news that Badger had died, saying that he was part of her childhood and with his death, she realised she had finally grown up.

Grown up . . . Hannah bows her head and lets the cold tears flow. Lucinda will never know how infinitely prolonged is the process known as 'growing up', will never learn that part of her would always have remained a child.

The trees snap in the bitter wind as Hannah stands with both hands on the balustrade of the wooden bridge. She had been brought up to repress her emotions. To mourn like this, to weep, to scream out loud, as she now does, beating her hands on the rail like a madwoman as tears pour down her contorted face, shrieking at the unfairness of that young life snatched away, is, she understands, part of her own growing up, for by behaving thus, she is sloughing off years of accumulated behaviour.

The patterns were set by her parents. But in thinking of them, of what she perceives as their damp, mushroomy lives, she finds herself wondering. Even as a child, embarrassed by them, bored, ignored, she had felt the strong links between the two of them. She is of the generation for whom the cinema offered paradigms of the great experiences life has to offer. What she knew of 'love' was taken from the screen. That her parents might have experienced those same unbridled lusts for each other, despite their unfilmstar-like looks, has never crossed her mind.

Huge screen kisses, moist mouths, naked bodies filmically turning, dissolving into each other . . . It should have occurred to her long before that the passions which informed her own experience, during that long-gone summer of dalliance and death, did not spring randomly. *Why didn't they tell me?* She raises her gloved hands to her face and smears away the tears. It was there all along, waiting to be ignited – and who had laid the fire, who *could* have, except those two, her parents? Walking on, boots sinking into the muddy path along the water's edge, she thinks about them with a kind of wondering enlightenment. It was difficult to believe that two such unprepossessing people had enjoyed the same sexual pleasures she had briefly known with Lucas. But perhaps they had; perhaps that was why they had always kept her on the outside. Not deliberately, but because they were so connected, each to the other, that it did not occur to them to expand their charmed circle of two to accommodate a third.

Perhaps she was already programmed, long before that summer, to realise that the need to be loved was always going to bring deprivation. Always suing for affection and never being successful – it was bound to affect her attitudes.

Standing under a bleak winter sky in a place where she has never felt at home, it seems incredible yet reasonable that this might be so.

Her boots slide in the wet, between tussocks of dead grass. Here and there, the path is under water which is solid with debris: uprooted reeds, plastic bottles, leaves. Beside her, the river flows strongly as mallards struggle against the current, and on its surface bobs something amorphous, wrapped in black plastic. What does it contain: severed limbs, a dead cat, garbage . . .?

As she walks, she continues to reappraise her academic parents. Mother: long-toothed, flat-chested, musty somehow, as if she had never bathed enough. Mother, in her dreadful sweaters, her drooping skirts, with her large hands and careless hair. Could she possibly have inspired lust in Hannah's father? And he, psoriatic, dishevelled, fingers stained with nicotine, nose beaky and veined, could he . . . surely not. And yet, there, under the rain which has begun to slant across the fields and beat at the surface of the water, Hannah remembers other things: secret laughter, afternoons when her parents were home but not around, crumpled sheets, the little smile her mother sometimes wore as she prepared yet another execrable meal. Ugliness, Hannah now sees, does not have to preclude desire; lack of grace need not imply lack of ardour. Had she, too keenly aware of the ugliness, missed out on the passion?

As for herself, since those few summer weeks, she has never experienced anything like that pleasure. Nor, until now, has she seen this as anything but her due, her punishment.

The inexorable years, the change in her from girlhood to motherhood, from youth towards middle-age, have sometimes terrified her. *Is this all there is?* she would wonder, when the children were gone, the house was quiet, the chores all done. Other women with unsatisfactory relationships either take lovers or provide themselves with the pleasures their husbands do not. Hannah has never felt either course was open to her, the first because she did not have the right, the second because she scarcely knew where or how to start.

Once, she tentatively suggested to Anthony that he vary his sexual routine, that he perhaps touch her *there* instead of – but he grew sulky at the implication that her lack of enjoyment was somehow his fault. In the darkness, she cowered while he pushed himself into her dry body, then came and grunted and rolled away from her. There were tears, afterwards, as she watched the moon roll across the sky beyond the drawn curtains. *Is this all there is?* If so, it was no more than she deserved. Using Anthony as an escape from the consequences of what had happened in Italy was cowardly and unfair: based on such a flimsy premise, it was no wonder their marriage had crumbled. Because she knew herself to be at fault, she had borne her increasing misery with what she hoped was fortitude.

Clumping back home through sodden fields, Hannah hopes fervently that Lucinda's sexual encounters were happier and more rounded than her own.

That evening the telephone rang. 'I'd like to come and see you,' Anthony said. He sounded humble, nothing like the self-assured man she knew. None the less, she did not wish to encourage him.

'When?'

'Tomorrow?' His voice was almost apologetic. 'I'll be driving up the A1: it's not much out of my way.'

Instead of agreeing, she said: 'Why?'

The question seemed to astonish him. 'Why?'

'Yes, Anthony. Why do you want to see me? What have we got to say to each other, especially now.'

There was a long silence, She could hear the uneven gasp of his breathing, as though he sought to control hysteria. Then he said violently: 'I need to see you, Hannah. I need to—' His voice broke and then more quietly he said: 'She can't possibly understand.' There was no need to ask who he meant. 'She's never had children of her own, never even met Lucinda—'

'No.'

'The truth is, I just can't seem to make sense of any of this.'

Once, Hannah would have rushed in, warming, comforting. Now she said harshly: 'And you think I might be able to help?'

'I – I don't know. But I have to talk to someone.'

'And I'll do?'

'Not *do*, Hannah. You're the only person in the world who would understand.'

'I can understand my own grief,' she said. 'I can see my own pain. I'm not sure I can do the same for yours. Or that I want to.'

'Hannah, please.' In the silence she left, he added: '*Please.*'

She grudged him the time he would take. 'All right,' she said, nonetheless, and let him see her reluctance.

'Tomorrow. Around six.'

She put down the telephone without replying.

'I can't understand why the police don't know who he is,' Anthony said. His fair hair was brushed back from his high forehead. He paced across the sitting-room carpets, a glass in his hand, his eyes rimmed with red, though whether from sleeplessness or recent tears Hannah was not disposed to ask. She had been shocked by his appearance: there was an air of frenzy about him, of things falling apart, like a man in a hurricane trying to hold on to his possessions without enough hands to do so.

'She didn't introduce him to any of her friends,' she said.

'It doesn't make any sense,' said Anthony for the tenth or twentieth time.

'The police think maybe he doesn't exist at all,' Hannah said patiently, as she might have spoken to a child.

'How do you mean?'

'They have this theory that she didn't introduce him to her friends because she didn't actually have a boyfriend.'

'That's preposterous. Lucinda wouldn't—'

'What's preposterous: the idea that she didn't have a boyfriend, or the possibility that she lied about having one?'

'Both. A beautiful girl like – like—' his voice wavered. He stared across the room at a silver-framed photograph of his children.

Hannah rescued him. 'If she was lying, then it means that she went up to that place in the Dales on her own. Which – or so the police think – means that she intended to kill herself.'

'No!' The word exploded from Anthony with the force of a thunder-clap. 'Not Lucinda. Not my – my little girl.'

Hannah was not in a mood to accommodate sentimentality. 'Lucy was a woman,' she said. 'Capable of rational thought, quite capable of deciding to commit suicide. What I'm trying to make the police see is that however despairing she might have been, it would have been so unlikely as to be impossible that she would choose such a method.'

'That's right,' said Anthony, nodding. 'She couldn't stand heights, could she?'

'It couldn't have been an accident, either,' Hannah said. 'She would never have got herself into a position where she could have slipped and fallen. The police think I'm clutching at straws when I say this.' She looked up at the man who had been her husband for nearly twenty-five years and wondered that she could feel so little for him. 'Incredible as it may seem, I think that she was . . . murdered.'

In the old days Anthony would have raised derisive eyebrows, stared at her with silent contempt, made disparaging remarks about menopausal women. Instead, he said quietly: 'If you're right, do you have any idea why?'

'None at all. But someone obviously means us harm. Me. Lucinda. Adam.' She explained her reasons for thinking this: the brooch, the postcard, Lucinda's break-ins, the cassette in her own car. She heard out his exclamations of horror and disbelief, then added: 'I've made arrangements for Adam to go abroad, but for the moment, I'm not going to tell even you.'

She was relieved that he didn't try to argue with her. 'Fair enough,' he said. 'Do you have any inkling of who's behind this?'

Hannah shook her head. She had never clarified her precipitate return from Italy, nor did she intend to do so now. It was thus impossible to explain her growing conviction that all this was intricately connected to the past.

'What are we going to do, then?' Anthony began feeling in his pockets for paper and pen: he had always felt safer making lists, itemising things, giving them numbers which could in due course be ticked off.

'We?' For a moment Hannah considered a sharp retort. But Lucinda was Anthony's daughter too; if anyone did, he had a right at least to discuss what further action might be taken. 'The main thing is to try and think why anyone would wish her – or us, through her – harm.'

But as she watched Anthony uncap his gold fountain pen, she knew that he was nothing to do with any of this, that he was redundant, even though he – and Susie, of course – had been the other significant adults in Lucinda's life. Thinking this, she remembered something.

'Lucinda stayed with Susie on the way through Rome this summer,' she said, starting up from her chair towards the telephone, picking up the receiver, dialling. 'Why on earth didn't I think of it before?'

'Even if she did, how can it help?'

'Lucinda *and* her boyfriend,' said Hannah. 'So maybe we *do* have a description of him, after all.' She could hear Susie's telephone ringing. 'If we can convince the police that he exists, they might start to believe that he could have killed her. At the moment, they're not really looking for him because they don't think he's real.'

But Susie did not answer her ringing phone. 'I'll try again later and let you know,' Hannah told Anthony.

At the front door, she kissed him with an unaccustomed feeling of warmth. His hands lingered on her back. 'I'll keep in touch,' he said.

When he had gone, she sat staring into the fire. Lucinda's death had not precipitated the feelings she had about her former husband: those had already been in place. But her manner of dealing with them had changed. She could be irritated with him and show it; she had the right to disagree with him and tell him so: his anger could no longer wound her. She could even allow herself to like him.

Later in the evening, she rang Rome again. Susie picked up on the third ring. *'Pronto?'*

'Susie. It's me – Hannah.'

'My dear. How are you feeling?'

'Bad.'

'Silly question: what else could you feel?'

'I'm ringing because I've just remembered that Lucinda called in to see you in the New Year, didn't she?'

'That's right.'

'She and the man she was with.'

'Man?' Susie's voice was guarded.

'Yes. Her boyfriend.'

There was a silence. Hannah said: 'Susie?'

'I'm still here.'

'So what about this chap of hers? She apparently didn't introduce him to any of her friends, so none of us knows what he was like, or anything. Could you tell me about him? Or his name: we don't even know that. The police here seem to think—'

'What did she say to you?'

'That she was travelling round Italy, that they'd stopped in to see you, that they'd had a fabulous time in Rome.'

'I'm sure they did,' said Susie. 'I took them to my favourite dress shop. Since Carlo died, I've got more money than I know what to do with.' She laughed. 'Remember how I always said I wanted lots of money?'

'I do indeed.' Between them hung the rest of Susie's oft-repeated wish: *and lots of children. And Lucas.*

'Anyway . . . I bought them each a new dress.'

For a long moment, Susie's words didn't make sense. 'What?'

'A dress each, Hannah.'

'I don't understand.' But she did. Or thought she did.

Susie went on: 'Lucinda's friend – or the one she brought to my apartment, at any rate – was a girl. A bit older than she was, kind of butch, if I'm not being politically incorrect to say that. Pleasant, well-spoken. Definitely not male.'

'But— But what? Hannah could think of nothing else to say. Had Lucinda said she was travelling to Italy with a man? Or had Hannah just assumed it – or been allowed to assume it? The evidence was pointing to a deviousness on Lucinda's part which she would never have thought her daughter capable of. Was it also pointing to something else: to the fact that Lucinda was not heterosexual, that she fancied women rather than men? And if so, that she had not felt able to tell her mother?

Even as she entertained the thought, Hannah knew it was absurd. The evidence of Lucinda's attraction to and for the opposite sex was far too strong. Besides, in view of the closeness between them, she would certainly have told her brother and in the light of Lucinda's death, Adam would never have kept such information to himself.

'Why did you think it was a man?' Susie said now. 'Oh dear: I hope I haven't betrayed some secret or other.'

'If you have, it can hardly matter to Lucinda now,' said Hannah. 'It's obviously a misunderstanding. I just assumed that she was travelling with her boyfriend.' There was another silence. Hannah said: 'Susie, the most awful thing.'

'What, darling.'

'We – me, at any rate – I'm beginning to think she was murdered.'

'Hannah!'

'Seriously.'

'You don't think you're being just the teeniest bit – you know – paranoid?' Susie said cautiously.

'No.'

'But why would anyone want to murder Lucinda?'

'There's absolutely no way she could have climbed the steps in that tower where she was found.'

'Why not? I mean, if she wanted to kill herself—'

'She was terrified of heights, Susie. Surely you knew that.'

Susie said: 'No, actually I didn't – it never came up. But if that's the case— What do the police think?'

'Naturally they think I'm just a hysterical bereaved parent, desperate for evidence to prove that my daughter couldn't have been so despairing that she committed suicide and I didn't even notice that she was unhappy,' Hannah said bitterly.

Susie said: 'Would you like me to come over and be with you, Hannie? I've got some vacation due: I was going to go to the flat in New York, but I can easily—'

'No thanks,' Hannah said. 'Really, I—'

'Or you could come here. It might help just to get away.'

'That's sweet of you, Susie, but at the moment—' Saying this, Hannah knew that her refusal was no more than a reflex. She was going back. She *had* to go back, if not immediately, then soon.

'If you change your mind—' Susie said.

'Actually, what might be helpful,' Hannah said carefully, thinking as she spoke, 'is if I could go and stay in the Villa Giulia for a few days.'

'The Villa?'

'You still own it, don't you?'

'Yes.' Susie sounded distant, thoughtful, as though she had moved away from the telephone receiver and was staring into space, turning over Hannah's request in her mind. 'God,' she said suddenly. 'It's all so long ago now. Poor Lucas. Poor Tristan.'

'Until this happened, it was the worst thing in my life,' Hannah said.

'Poor you, too. You know, I really hated you for what happened, even though I realised it wasn't anything to do with you.'

'I never blamed you for the things you said.'

'It took me ages to realise that it was jealousy, as much as anything else. Envy, because you were there and I wasn't. You saw him at the last and I—'

'It wasn't anything to be envious of, believe me.' Hannah felt the memories ripple like a veil and saw again the watery blood-trails, the white torn flesh, dead eyes staring at the moon. Blood . . . she had run, retching, terrified, and when she forced herself to go back—

'God knows what kind of state the Villa's in,' Susie said. 'I haven't been up there for years and years. In fact, since Carlo died, nobody has much, although someone comes in once or twice a month to dust and check the mice aren't chewing the furniture to pieces. It was let for a while but when the tenants moved out, I didn't bother to find anyone else.'

'That's all right,' said Hannah. 'I'm not looking for four-star hotel accommodation. In fact, the nearer the Villa is to how I remember it, the better.'

'Why do you say that?'

'Because it was so . . . perfect then. So peaceful.' Until that night, she meant. 'So separate from everything else going on in the rest of the world.'

'I think we're talking Sleeping Beauty here,' Susie said, with a laugh. 'You'll probably have to hack your way through the thorns to find the front door.'

'That's OK. As long as, if I stumble across someone who's been asleep for a hundred years, I don't have to kiss them awake.'

'I can't promise any Prince Charmings, either.'

'That's all right. I wouldn't recognise one if I saw one.'

'Some of the old crowd are still living there,' said Susie. 'The Trevelyans, quite a lot of the time. And one of their girls married a local chap. That woman novelist – a bit doddery now, and pretty ga-ga – she's still around.'

'What about Faustino?'

'Faustino Castelli?'

'Yes.'

'I didn't know you'd met him.' Susie sounded almost annoyed.

'It was while you were down in Rome,' Hannah said apologetically. 'Getting acquainted with Carlo.'

'I see.' The pause Susie left was somehow chill. 'Yes, Faustino's still around, though he lives in Florence most of the time.'

'I thought he lived in Rome.'

'He did. But – perhaps you didn't know – his wife ran off, God knows where. He moved so he wouldn't be reminded of her – or so he told my mother, some years ago.'

'So,' Hannah said, 'can I go?'

'Of course. Just let me know and I'll make arrangements of some kind about the keys.'

'Oh, Susie, I'm so—'

'You don't have to say anything,' said Susie. 'I know.'

'Can you cope on your own?' Hannah asked. 'You haven't been here that long.'

'Of course I can,' Zoe's hand caressed the roof of the Edwardian villa.

'For a whole fortnight?'

'Yes, Hannah. Yes. Yes. In fact, if you won't take offence, I can't wait for you to leave so I have the place to myself.' Zoe stared round the shop, her eyes bright. Hannah guessed she was thinking of flow-charts, efficiency studies, overhauling the accounting system.

'I hate to ask you to do so much extra when you only agreed to work here part-time,' she said. 'I'll give you a bonus to make it worthwhile.'

'No problem. It'll be good practice for when I finally make it as president of my own international conglomerate.'

Hannah raised her eyebrows. 'Start as you mean to go on, eh?'

'You bet.' Zoe's face shone. 'No, honestly, Hannah. You can feel absolutely safe: I'll look after the business as though it really were my own.'

'I'll keep in touch by telephone, of course, in case any problems come up.'

'I'm sure they won't.'

'And give you a number where you could reach me if there's an emergency.'

'There won't be.' One of Zoe's stubby, childlike fingers rubbed at the edge of one of the roof-tiles.

'And you'd better give me your phone number at home too. Just in case.'

'Will do.'

'How will you manage about your little boy? Does your mother live near by?' Asking this, Hannah was ashamed to realise how little she really knew about Zoe.

'She lives abroad.' There was a finality about this sentence which told Hannah that this was all Zoe was prepared to say about her mother; sensitive, she did not pursue it. 'But my mother-in-law can come and stay. She's always banging on about not seeing enough of her little boy. It'll remind her what being a mum's like these days, even with microwaves and washing-machines. The way she tells it, she was scrubbing nappies on flat stones at the river's brim every morning before sun up, and that was before a full day's work down the mines!'

'Do you get on with her?' Hannah asked, tearing the plastic wrap off a catalogue which had arrived that morning.

'She's OK.' Zoe looked away, fiddling with some papers on the desk. 'Do you mind my asking: is this trip you're taking anything to do with the – the death of your daughter?'

Anything?

*Every*thing.

Hannah nodded.

'You know how sorry I am—' Zoe said awkwardly, as though ashamed of her excitement at being left in charge.

'Yes, of course.' Hannah covered the younger woman's hand with her own. 'And thank you so much for the flowers. White roses: they were Lucinda's favourite.'

'I know. You told me. That's why I chose them.'

Zoe had recently had her hair cut very close to her head, emphasising the lines of her skull and the frailness of the neck which supported it. She seemed waiflike, scarcely old enough to have left school, let alone be the mother of a child. Looking at her now, Hannah felt her own loss well up again. Although Zoe had little in common with Lucinda, she was, nonetheless, another vulnerable female creature. She wanted to ask whether she loved her child as Hannah had loved Lucinda. For a moment, she was tempted to reach out and stroke the short pale stubble of Zoe's hair.

'Anyway,' she said, 'it'll do me good to get away. I feel it's time I resolved some of my own . . . conflicts. Something happened to me in the past which I've never really properly come to terms with.' She would have said more but it seemed unfair to burden Zoe with personal details.

Shrugging, she looked at her watch. 'I must go or I'll miss my train up to London. I'll see you tomorrow and we can run through everything again. Check it all out.'

'Quit worrying,' Zoe said. 'If you decide to leave before the weekend, I can manage perfectly well on my own.'

'Your mother-in-law won't be coming until Monday.'

'My husband can help out until she gets here – if you want to take off early, I mean.'

'You sound as though you really can't wait for me to go.'

'No, honestly, I didn't mean—'

'That's all right.' Hannah had not yet met Zoe's husband, but he sounded the dependable type, and lucky to be in a job which allowed him a certain amount of flexibility. It was this, according to Zoe, which had prompted her original impetuous suggestion that she work part-time for Hannah. 'By the way, I've been meaning to ask you.'

'Yeah?'

'That book—' Elaborately casual though she tried to be, Hannah could feel herself blushing, her body overheating as though she had been set on fire . . . 'It was on your desk about a month ago.'

'Which one?'

'There was a picture on the front of – of someone drowning, I think.'

'What about it?' Zoe seemed defensive. Perhaps she thought Hannah was about to tell her off for reading during her working hours.

'Nothing really. I noticed it was an American imprint and wondered where you'd got it. I – er – I just glanced through but it seemed rather interesting.'

'My husband brought it back,' Zoe said. 'When he was in the States on business. I told you.'

'Did you?' Hannah felt guilty. Sometimes she simply tuned Zoe's chatter out.

'Apparently it's big over there. He picked it up at the airport in San Francisco to read on the flight home.'

'Ah.'

'The heroine's called Anna,' Zoe said. 'I thought of you when I was reading it, since you told me you spent time in Italy.'

'Did you?'

'Though she's much younger than you are – I mean, she's just a girl,' said Zoe hastily, clearly not wanting to offend.

'Weren't we all, once?'

'Were we?' Zoe grimaced comically. 'Can't say I remember. I'll lend you the book, if you like.'

'Actually, I've already looked through it. A friend of mine is a book reviewer and he had a copy.'

'You look dreadful,' Marcus said.

'Thanks.'

'As if you haven't slept for several years.'

'I feel like it.' Hannah was not going to tell him how many nights she spent propped up against her pillows instead of sleeping, her bedroom curtains open so that she could see the shine of the street lamps on the creeping water at the end of the road. She was not going to describe how every groan of the settling house set her heart racing, nor the times she started up, adrenalin hammering at her nerve ends, certain she heard a footstep on the stairs, the stealthy turn of the door handle, the creak of a betraying floorboard. The thought of Adam threatened made her sweat like an athlete, even though she kept the upstairs windows wide to let in the icy winter air: was he safe, had he been tracked down, was he even then in danger? With Lucinda for ever gone, her claim to the central love of her life was staked in her son.

This was what her invisible opponent wanted, had counted on, this dislocation of a life. Only by resolutely pretending each dawn that the night hours had not happened could Hannah feel she still had some control.

Every move you make, every claim you stake . . .

Involuntarily, she stared around the Soho restaurant. Was someone, even then, watching her, spying, noting her movements, learning every detail about her? She caught the eye of a young man three tables away who frowned as she stared at him then leaned across the table to speak to his companion, jerking his head in her direction. The two of them stared back at her. What did they see: their victim, their prey? Or simply another anonymous almost-invisible older woman?

Marcus's voice dropped into the middle of her thoughts. 'I'm glad we were able to meet for dinner. I'll miss you while you're gone,' he said, folding Hannah's hand inside his. 'Are you sure you wouldn't like me to come with you?'

Hannah shook her head. 'It's something I've got to do on my own.'

'I know Cornwall quite well: I used to spend a lot of time there once. In fact, I met my wife there.' His mouth moved painfully.

Hannah made no response. I have enough burdens of my own, she thought. I do not wish to carry his as well.

Marcus went on: 'I've got a good friend who'd be glad to—'

'Thanks, but I'd prefer to go on my own.'

Without knowing quite why, Hannah had said nothing to him of her suspicions with regard to Lucinda, whom he had never met, nothing beyond the bare fact of her death. He believed she was going away to be alone, to try and come to terms with her grief; what would he say if he knew she hoped to flush out a killer?

'I can understand that.'

'I may also come to your part of the world before I go to Italy,' Hannah said.

'Italy—' The edges of Marcus's eyes turned red, as though the thought of the place angered him. He drank from his water glass. 'You say you're going to try to clarify something which happened to you in the past: is it something you want to talk about?'

'No.' Hannah smiled at him, to soften her refusal.

'The past can be uncomfortable territory to explore, Hannah. Are you sure you're doing the right thing?'

'I've no idea.'

'Like they say, you can't go home again.'

'I've never really known where home was.'

'How terribly sad.'

'Yes.' Hannah smiled at him. 'If I do come up north, I'll contact you.'

'Darling, I'll be on tenterhooks.'

She stands at the edge of the river. Under the tangerine glow of the street lamps, the town is quiet. Lights in the houses have been extinguished; people are in bed. At her feet, mallards sleep one-legged, heads tucked backwards under their wings. Above her head there is a rush of wings as an owl makes for the safe darkness of the park. The water has crept higher than she remembers it ever being, stretching across the pavement and on to the road. Brown scum marks the water's limit, along with straw and twigs; an empty plastic bleach bottle knocks gently against the tarmac. Wet, ridged footprints lead off along the pathway into the dark, companioned by the paw marks of a dog.

Will the river rise even more while she is away? Should she make use of the corporation sandbags again? She can scarcely be bothered to register concern.

Tomorrow, she will drive down to Cornwall.

Tomorrow, she will see Tristan again.

THE DIARY

. . . An Agent rang me from New York today. A friend of a friend of F's. He's got a name which sounds like Cesarewitch (isn't that a horse race?) – something deeply middle-European, anyway. He said one of the top publishing houses liked the book, was offering, bottom line – are you ready for this? he said – a sum which seemed to me so huge that I literally staggered. Jesus.

I've never had more than a few dollars in my hand in my entire life, and those were mostly given to me by someone else, as though I were still a child.

'I know it's not a lot,' this Agent says. 'But I'll ask for more, of course. I always ask for more, on principle.'

'Only person I know who asked for more was Oliver Twist,' I said. 'Didn't get him very far.'

'Say what?' he said. Lots of street-cred there, I could tell.

'How much more?' I said.

'Dunno,' he says. 'See how far they'll go. Gotta warn you, first book and all, it won't be much more.'

Didn't want to give away the fact that I was totally damned ignorant about all this. Nor that the sum he'd mentioned seemed like a fortune. 'Oh, well,' I say.

'They'll probably go a couple of thousand more,' he says.

I go: 'Yo, baby!' just to show that I may live in the sticks but I have some of that street-cred myself.

He got the extra too. I can see it's not a huge sum, but it's more than I ever dreamed of. Not that money figures much in my dreams.

When I told F, he said, you have to be cautious. Agents are always enthusiastic, it goes with the territory. You have to listen to the 'buts', he said, rather than the hype. He was right, I knew that.

I've tried to be cautious, as the months have gone by, but it's hard.

. . . Today I held in my hand a Book, a Book which I wrote, which came out of my head, my memory. My heart. Amazing!

I never thought it'd happen. I've never stuck at anything before. Sitting down, day after day, producing words, making a whole book – I can't believe I did it!

I don't think the Dr can, either, although he pretends he always knew I would.

For me, the most exciting thing about it all is that at last I have status, something I've lacked all my life. I have an occupation: the bits of me which never seemed to add up to anything much now add up to Author.

It's a strange feeling, after so many years of wondering who I am, where I came from, where I'm going, to have this label to tie round my neck.

AUTHOR!

. . . Now the Book is finished, I miss the discipline of writing things down every day. It was therapeutic, too. Calming. I need that calm – which is why I'm going to go on keeping this diary, see where it goes. And maybe the missing bits will come back to me if I don't think about them too hard. Maybe I'll be able to hold on to myself. I find that difficult, sometimes.

NOW

13

The house was much as she remembered it, distinguished, solitary, set at the end of a lane. It stood alone, neighbourless, looking out over the sea towards a jutting headland, with other further headlands beyond. The same – but not the same. Things recalled are always more spacious than reality: now it seemed smaller, shabbier, less imposing than Hannah had pictured it on the long drive down to Cornwall. The garden, which she recalled as open and unshaded, had matured. Trees which had been young more than thirty years ago now towered on all sides, crowding up against the windows, overhanging the lawns, tangling with the tall beech hedge which surrounded the entire garden. She did not even remember the magnificent copper beech at the side of the house. Last time she had seen it, the house had been unadorned. Now the rendering added by some early Victorian improver was criss-crossed with bare creeper, of which a few brilliantly scarlet leaves still clung to the straggling stems.

About to open the latch of the garden gate set into the hedge, Hannah stepped back and looked up at the house again. A pleasant place, she thought, where pleasant things have occurred. Behind her, the sun was sinking into the horizon, casting a thick gold dazzle on to the long windows, painting the slate tiles with honeyed light.

The front door – green, panelled, with brass knocker and letter-box – opened. The man who came out and stood for a moment on the step was, despite all the years which had passed, immediately familiar.

'Hannah.' He held both hands out as he came down the flagged path to meet her.

Seeing that stern and lonely face, the lines drawn deep on either side of the mouth, the thick white hair, Hannah felt her throat constrict.

'Tristan,' she said. 'You haven't changed in the slightest.'

'You have,' he said. 'You've still got those wounded eyes, but you're even more beautiful than I remember, now that life has added some character to your face.' Reaching her, he bent and kissed her cheek and she remembered a far-off afternoon in another country when he had done the same.

'Goodness,' she said. 'It's been a long time.'

'Twenty-five years.' He hugged her, pulling her towards the rough fawn jersey he wore over faded green corduroys. 'I've been thinking about them ever since your telephone call, trying to remember it all.' He laughed down at her. 'So many memories.'

'Not all of them good,' she said.

'Not all of them, no.' He led her into the house, and settled her in the drawing-room on a large, comfortable sofa set at right-angles to the fire which blazed in a stone hearth. The walls of the room were painted yellow; the windows faced the brilliance of the setting sun so that the whole room shimmered with golden light.

Hannah said: 'I'm so glad you've still got the same colour in here. I was only fourteen but I've never forgotten walking through the door.' Tristan offered her whisky in a heavy tumbler of cut glass. 'It was like stepping into a room full of buttercups.'

'Exactly. That's why I've never changed it,' Tristan said.

'You told me on the telephone that you live alone.'

'Yes.'

'Did you – if I'm not being too personal – ever have a wife?'

He shook his head slowly, a wry expression on his face.

'So you never found Miss Right, after all?'

'Not even the Divorcee Right,' he said solemnly. They both laughed but behind the laughter was Hannah's memory of the picnic and, beyond that, of the last time she had seen him. Blood on his hands, blood staining the front of his torn shirt, blood dark in his white hair as he looked back at her through the grilled windows of the police van. The dawn air had smelt of death and violence, as the sun came up over the trembling poplars. In the depths of the house Susie had screamed Lucas's name over and over again, until someone came and took her away, gave her sedatives, calmed her, but Hannah had stayed there on the terrace, long after the van was out of sight, fearful, knowing that her life had taken an irreversible direction.

Tristan stretched his long legs in front of the fire. 'I expect you're tired,' he said. 'We won't eat too late, so you can have a bath and get to bed.'

The words were no more than the banalities of hospitality, but they seemed to convey certainties which Hannah had never known, and for which all her life she had longed.

She nodded, embarrassingly close to tears. 'Thank you,' she said.

'Meanwhile, do you want to tell me now why you came, or would you prefer to wait?'

'I'd better tell you some of it now.' Hannah sat up straighter. 'But after I've told you, I don't want you to feel you have to express concern or grief.'

'What can you be going to tell me? Look, if you'd rather—'

'The first thing you have to know,' Hannah said quietly, 'is that a few weeks ago, my daughter, Lucinda, was murdered.'

He stared at her, his eyes almost hidden in the shadows round them.

'My dear Hannah,' he said after a moment. 'How – how completely desolating for you.'

'It's all right,' Hannah said. 'There's no need—'

'How could I *not* be concerned, at hearing something so terrible?'

'Yes, well.' Hannah stared into the fire. 'I don't want it to overshadow the rest of the evening.'

'Why are you so defensive?' Tristan said slowly. 'It's going to overshadow the rest of your life – there's no point pretending it won't.'

'What I was trying to say was, it needn't overshadow *you*. I mean, you didn't know her or anything, and—'

'I know you, Hannah.' He got up and came to squat down in front of her, taking her hand in his. 'You should not try to divest me of humanity by implying that I would feel nothing at hearing your sad news.'

'I'm sorry.'

'So,' he prompted. 'You came to see me because—'

'Because I believe,' Hannah said, feeling her voice begin to waver out of control, 'for various not very clear-cut reasons, that her death is directly connected to what happened that night in Italy.'

'When Lucas was killed? How can that be possible?'

'I don't know. I may be wrong. It's just that a – a number of small things have added up to convince me that I'm right. So I wanted to ask you to tell me exactly what *you* think happened, exactly what *you* saw or didn't see.'

Still holding her hand, he sat beside her on the sofa. 'Hannah,' he said gently. 'You aren't still blaming yourself for Lucas's death, are you?'

'And for what happened to you?' She could not meet his eyes. 'Of course I am. I was responsible.'

'No more than anyone else.'

'I betrayed him. All the way along the line, I betrayed him.'

Tristan sat back. 'What did he do to you? Ask yourself that. Didn't he betray you, too?'

'Maybe,' she said unwillingly. 'But I didn't end up *dead*.' Even as she said it, she wondered just how true that was. Hadn't she been no more than half-alive for years, hadn't she been living a kind of death, imprisoned in an underworld of lies and shadows?

'Tell me about Lucinda,' Tristan said gently, so gently that, doing so, she did not bother to hide her tears when they came. At some point, he moved to hold her close, murmuring softly as she bent her head and wept. 'She was so beautiful,' she said, 'so full of life, so . . . so *eager*.'

'Isn't that part of being young?' said Tristan. 'And isn't that why it's so much more wicked to destroy the young?'

'It was just as wicked to destroy Lucas.'

'Lucas—' He got up and poured more whisky into his glass. 'I truly believe that Lucas was an exceptional case.' Behind him, a ship came into view, inching across the wide space of sea. The sky flamed, its fiery colours dyeing the rocking waters of the bay.

'You can't mean that you think he deserved to die, can you?'

'Lucas had a death-wish.'

'Did he?'

'His life had gone wrong and he wasn't prepared to change it. Dying was what he wanted.'

Was Tristan right? Hannah remembered that evening by the lake, and Lucas's scornful voice as he faced his persecutors.

'I can never forgive myself for what happened to him,' she said.

'But Hannah, you must. You have to let it go, let it float away. To some extent, we – and others – were to blame, but—'

'To some extent? Between us, we *killed* him, Tristan.'

He drew away from her, bewilderment and the beginnings of anger creasing his face. 'You can't really believe that.'

'I do. I do.' I have to, she thought, otherwise my life for the past twenty-five years and more has been meaningless.

'He killed himself,' Tristan said.

She stared. '*Suicide?*'

'I mean he was responsible for his own death. Just as he was responsible for his own life. And above everything else, Lucas wanted to die.'

Why don't you get on with it, he had said. *Kill me now,* and there had been no fear in his voice, only a kind of longing.

'. . . ever since we were at school together,' Tristan was saying. 'He was always a rebel, so much so that as I grew older, I couldn't help wondering if by deliberately insisting on his difference from the rest of us, he hoped to hide from himself, as much as from everyone else, the fact that he actually was not one of us, that he didn't belong.'

'Didn't he?'

'On one level, of course, he looked as if it all hung together. Handsome, rich, clever, good family, future mapped out for him. But inside—'

'That mother of his didn't help,' Tristan said. He sat opposite her in the warm country kitchen, elbows on the table, drinking coffee from a mug he held with both hands.

Composed now, Hannah was beginning to feel sleepy. Tristan had fed her on a substantial beef casserole and baked potatoes, looking quizzically at her when she said something about making a salad, informing her that he was a farmer, thanks very much, not a Hampstead foodie, and in any case, didn't hold with lettuce.

'Wicked Aunt Diana,' she murmured drowsily.

'All those husbands of hers – I don't think one of them lasted longer than five years. No wonder Lucas was screwed up. Naturally, when he fell in love, he was determined that it would be for ever. And, of course, in a way, it was.'

'Mmm,' Hannah said. She forced her closing eyes to open again.

'I was there when it happened,' said Tristan thoughtfully. 'When he fell in love, I mean. We were down at that marvellous classical pool they had in the woods. Well, you know—' He looked awkward. 'Where they found him, of course.'

Like a flash of light, she recalled the tree-shaded pool in the Italian garden, the heat, yellow flowers rocking on black water, and a naked man, lovely as a statue, pagan against green leaves. She had thought: I shall remember this moment for ever; yet, until now, had not done so.

'Yes.' Hannah hoped he would continue without expecting any further conversational contribution from her. What he said was fascinating but any moment now she was going to drop her coffee-cup unless she concentrated on keeping awake.

'Marina,' Tristan said. 'The old Contessa's granddaughter. God, she was beautiful, even as a girl. I'll never forget her coming for the afternoon to swim. I swear I actually *heard* Lucas fall in love with her, like a clapper-board snapping shut. Fifteen, she must have been, maybe sixteen. He was only fourteen or so himself. She was wearing a black one-piece bathing suit and was terribly shy, she'd never been allowed to join in anything at the Villas before, because of the feud between Susie's grandfather and her own grandmother. Black hair, black eyes, and that amazing, moist skin that young Italian girls have—'

'Was it mutual?'

'Absolutely. Even though they were only children, really. They went on seeing each other when they could, which wasn't often, until they left school.'

'But she wouldn't marry him?' Hannah said, hoping he hadn't noticed the way she slurred the words.

'Not wouldn't – wasn't allowed to. Letting her go swimming at the Villa Giulia was one thing – almost like scoring off the *inglesi* – though, come to think of it, the Dragon Lady might not even have known about it. But countenancing marriage to the old boy's grandson was quite another. They packed her off to Rome and she eventually did as she was told and married some respectable piece of minor aristocracy.'

Marina . . . It was a beautiful name. In Hannah's mind, the past began to thicken, to fill out. 'Was she happy with him?' she asked.

'How could she be? I really believe that she and Lucas were made for each other,' said Tristan. Pouring more wine into a glass, he had not seemed to be aware that Hannah was drooping, nor did she wish to bring the evening to an end by asking if she could go to bed. 'Light and dark,' he said, almost to himself. 'Sun and shadow. Two halves of a whole. It was tragic, really.'

'Tragic?'

'After he—' Tristan looked up from his glass at Hannah. 'Didn't you know this?'

'Know what?'

'After Lucas's death, she disappeared. Completely vanished. Last time I spoke to the Trevelyans – they still live out there, you know – Lew actually mentioned it for the first time in years.'

'Vanished? Hannah thought about this. Susie had never mentioned it.

'I wondered if she'd taken the standard mediæval cure for blighted love and gone into a nunnery, or something similar. Neither hide nor hair of her's ever been seen from that day to this.'

'Did Susie know about Lucas being in love with Marina? She said he'd been keen on the Contessa's granddaughter but she didn't say he was *that* keen.'

'Everyone knew.'

'But she was always saying that she was going to marry him herself.'

Tristan smiled. 'I've heard her! But she only started that after we heard that Marina was hitched up with this other man.'

'But . . . if Lucas was in love with Marina, why did he have . . . all those other women?' Hannah asked. Did Tristan know that she herself had been one of them?

Tristan shrugged, holding his glass up to the light and squinting through it. The bottle – the second – was already half-empty and Hannah knew she had not drunk that much of it. 'What else was he supposed to do? He was a man, after all. He couldn't have the one woman he wanted so he had a lot of women he didn't want.'

Heat rose from Hannah's chest. She felt as though she were on fire with embarrassment and, even after all these years, with pain. Tristan's words were brutal: she was sure that he would not have spoken in quite the same way if he had known that she— She took a deep breath, trying to calm herself. Twenty-five years, and she still did not know whether what she had felt for Lucas was love or not.

'. . . which was fine,' Tristan said, '. . . until he started going after other men's wives.'

'As a policy, do you mean?'

'He deliberately went after the wife of one of my friends. Jane. She was perfectly happily married until Lucas took it into his head to seduce her.'

'Seduce? What an amazingly old-fashioned word.'

'That's what it was. Deliberate seduction.' Tristan's face was cold.

Hannah was beginning now to find her second wind. 'You make it sound as though this Jane had no will of her own, as though she was no more than a kind of – of Sleeping Beauty waiting for Lucas to kiss

202

her awake.' She'd heard about this before, she remembered, sitting at the Trevelyans' table. Jane and – Mark, was it?

'That's more or less what she was.'

'In that case, don't tell me that she was happily married. It should have been her husband kissing her awake, and if he didn't, then you can't blame her if she looked around a bit.'

'It was as if Lucas was determined to wreck things. He made a dead set at her, wouldn't leave her alone. Sent her flowers, took her out to the theatre, wrote letters, telephoned—'

'She probably loved it. I bet your friend never sent her flowers or letters. I bet he always forgot their wedding anniversary, or her birthday or something.'

'Be that as it may, Jane was—'

'Be that as it may,' mocked Hannah. 'When someone says that, it's a sure sign that they know they've lost the argument.'

Tristan ignored this. 'In the end, she left. Just walked out, took their child with her.' Tristan stared across the table at Hannah. 'He only ever saw them again once. Until recently, that is.'

'What happened to her?'

'She shacked up with Lucas for a while, I believe. Then he dropped her, picked up with some other girl. Flaunted her in front of poor Jane until she married someone else and went off to America. But it was Marina he wanted.'

'What about your friend: did he remarry?'

'He did get into a long-term relationship, a woman who had two kids, but he's never remarried.'

'What I want to know is . . .' Hannah said, holding her head between her hands as she leaned her elbows on the table, 'does he now admit that he wouldn't have lost his wife – Jane – if he'd treated her better?'

'Absolutely not,' Tristan said. 'He still insists they were terribly happy, that for some reason, Lucas deliberately went after Jane.'

'Why would he do that?'

'The two men knew each other,' Tristan said, sounding uncomfortable. 'They disagreed about a number of things. He's often said to me since that he'd have killed Lucas himself if someone hadn't done it for him.'

'You sound as if you think he meant it.'

'He did,' Tristan said soberly.

Hannah was taken aback. 'A violent man, then.'

'Not so much violent as primitive. Believing in simple things. Marriage is for ever. Men should protect women. An eye for an eye.' Tristan stood up. 'Hannah, I've kept you up talking when you look as if you should be in bed. Come on, I'll show you where things are.'

As she followed him up the graceful staircase which curved up from the centre of the hall, Hannah said: 'Lucas had another woman, didn't he? Who died—?'

Tristan stopped and turned to look down at her as she stood a couple of steps below him on the stairs. 'She didn't die, she was killed. By Lucas.'

'I thought it was in a car accident.'

'It was. Lucas was driving.'

'That doesn't necessarily make it his fault.'

'It does if he was drunk at the time. So drunk that when the lorry came round the bend on the wrong side of the road, his reflexes simply didn't respond.'

'You can't be sure of that.'

'He admitted it, at the inquest.' Tristan frowned at her. 'He got a slap on the wrist and his licence endorsed. At least that wouldn't happen now.' He continued up the stairs. 'Lavatory,' he said, tapping a door. 'Bathroom. There's a basin in your room for teeth and things. Otherwise, if you want a bath, the Aga sees to it that there's always hot water.'

He stopped further down the galleried landing. 'I've put you in here. I'm a couple of rooms further down, in case you need anything in the night.'

'Thank you.'

'Another marriage Lucas wrecked,' he said, abruptly. 'The woman who burned to death in his car was married to someone I knew quite well.'

They stood together in the centre of the room. Hannah could think of nothing to say. In the end, she reached for her bag, which he was still holding. 'You're very kind.'

He hefted the bag on to a long stool at the foot of the bed. 'Not really. I wanted very much to see you again.' He put his hands on her shoulders. 'Look, I may sound harsh about Lucas, but that's not to say that I too don't wonder about what happened that night.'

Hannah looked up at him.

'You should have come before,' he said quietly. 'I searched for you, Hannah, afterwards. I tried to find you. But I never knew your married name, and I couldn't remember your maiden name. I asked Susie but she wasn't exactly cooperative.'

'She didn't tell me,' Hannah said.

'Why would she? She was very bitter. Off her rocker for a while, if you ask me.'

'I know. It was years before we made it up.'

'Tomorrow we'll talk about the things you came for, right?'

'Yes.'

He kissed her forehead, as though she were a child. 'Forgive me if

I'm being either patronising or presumptuous, but you look as if you've been neglected for some time. Uncherished.'

'Do I?'

He hesitated. 'Don't take this the wrong way, but if you want someone to – just to hold you, remember that I'm here.' He stared over her head at their reflection in the mahogany-framed mirror which hung above the empty fireplace. 'Sometimes, I could do with being held myself.'

Hannah bit her lip. *Why are we still paying?* she wanted to demand. 'I'll remember,' she said, watching him leave the room and close the door behind him, afraid that even a lifetime's atonement was not going to be enough.

In the night, she wakes suddenly. About her, the unfamiliar room is dark yet full of a grey light which she realises must be from the sea below the windows. For a moment she contemplates going to him, imagines the strength, the warm male smell of him, the pleasure of folding herself into his arms, not for sex but for comfort. She reminds herself that he is, after all, a stranger, and, despite the secret that they share, will remain one.

She sighs, pulls the covers closer round her ears, remembers the pool among the leaves, the lascivious smile of the stone faun, the dragon-flies. What would Lucas be like if he were alive today? Would he still be beautiful or would he have grown fat and balding? Would he be the father of palely golden daughters and sons as handsome as he was then? Sons, she thinks, who would look something like that young man seen through the glass of the Festival Hall. She wonders whether he would eventually have forgotten the unobtainable Marina.

The curtains at the open window are sucked outwards by a cold breeze. She hears the moaning sea, the hiss of breaking waves.

'He never learned that you can't possess someone,' Tristan said. He stood on the very edge of the cliffs, looking down at the sea. 'He never learned the first lesson about love: that what you can't have will always seem more desirable than what you can.'

'I'm not sure that's true,' Hannah said. They had been tramping along the cliff path for more than two hours and she was looking forward to some lunch at the pub which Tristan assured her was only a few minutes away.

'Why not?'

'I know the grass is supposed to be greener on the other side and all that, but love isn't the same as grass. I believe you *can* have the person you love, and go on finding them infinitely desirable.'

'You sound as if you've been reading too many Mills & Boons,' Tristan said.

'And you sound bloody patronising.'

'The whole thing wrong with getting what you want – the man or woman you love—' Tristan jumped down into a hollow cut into the cliff path and held a hand up to help her; the edge of the cliff seemed alarmingly near, 'is that familiarity breeds contempt.'

'Con*tent*,' said Hannah.

'Do you really think so?' He was still holding her gloved hand. The end of his nose was red and the wind was whipping tears from the edges of his eyes.

'I'd like to.'

'You're divorced, aren't you?'

'Yes.'

'Isn't that what happened? Love turned to familiarity, which in turn became divorce.'

'No.' Sorrow, regret, welled up inside Hannah. 'It wasn't like that. I married Anthony without really loving him, without even knowing what love is. The divorce is my own fault.'

He took hold of her other hand. 'Hannah, for God's sake stop trying to take all the responsibility for the bad things which have happened to you.'

'All right,' she said, looking up at his height, wondering if her own nose was red, if the lines on her face, her less than perfect body, seemed unappealing to him. 'I'll stop, if you promise to get me out of this horrible hole before we both fall over and are dashed to pieces on the rocks.'

'Just follow me.'

'Marina,' Hannah said, when they were seated at a table in the pub. After the whipping wind outside, the warmth was almost soporific.

'What about her?'

'Was she married to someone called Faustino?'

'I can't remember his name – if I ever knew it. I never met him.'

'Yes, you did. Didn't the two of you discover . . . the body?'

'Was that Marina's husband? It's all so long ago.'

'Did they own a pink house, with trees at each corner, on a hill?'

Tristan shook his head. 'I don't know. Maybe. Lew Trevelyan's the one to ask. I believe the old Contessa gave her a house in the area after she married. She owned half the real estate round there.' He bit generously into a homemade pasty, so that crumbs of pastry showered his sweater. 'I didn't spend that much time in Italy, once I'd graduated and started working for Smythson Blair. Marina was still at school, the last time I saw her. I stayed with Susie's family occasionally, but when I came to the Villa Giulia that year, it was the first time for ages. I only really knew the Trevelyans, and that was because Jennifer – one of Lew's cousins here – is a friend.'

'Would it help if I talked to her?'

'To Jennifer? What can she possibly know?'

'I don't know. Perhaps nothing. But before I go back to Italy, I feel I need to have as much information as I can possibly get hold of.'

'Makes sense, I suppose.'

'I was blinkered that summer. I saw absolutely nothing except what was happening to myself. If I'd been a bit more aware, more in touch with what was actually going on, maybe I could have . . .'

'What? Saved Lucas? Is that what you're trying to say?

Hannah shrugged.

'Look, I keep telling you that what happened wasn't your fault. However much you learn about the people who were there, nothing's going to alter that fact.'

'He called me,' Hannah said stubbornly, 'but I wouldn't help him.'

'Called you?' Tristan was staring at her. 'We were together that night, Hannah. The only time the phone rang was when Susie telephoned from Rome.'

'He didn't use the phone.'

'I see.' Tristan stared at her intently.

'He had a way of – of tapping into my brain,' Hannah said. 'It sounds ridiculous, I know. But he did. He could call me, make me go to him.' She smiled at Tristan. 'I know it sounds far-fetched but it's true.'

'It doesn't, actually. I remember Jane telling me the exact same thing: she knew he was dangerous, that he might break up her marriage, but she couldn't resist him. She had to go. In the end, of course, she went for good – or until he died.'

'Tristan! Fancy seeing you here!' Two burly men in heather-knit sweaters and waxed coats appeared in front of the tiny round table at which Hannah and Tristan were sitting. Their eyes took in Hannah and immediately began to conjecture.

'Brian. Geoffrey.' Tristan introduced them to Hannah and they sat down, one on either side of her, their cold-weather clothes taking up too much of the narrow bench.

'Skiving off, eh?' Brian said.

'Hardly,' said Tristan. 'It's Sunday.'

'I thought you were supposed to plough the fields and scatter at this time of year,' said Geoffrey. 'I'm sure that's what they're doing on *The Archers*.'

'Bumper edition,' said Brian. 'We listened to it in the car on the way here.'

'Brian, despite the impression of total inanity which he conveys, is a barrister in the Inner Temple,' Tristan told Hannah.

'Down for the weekend.' Brian raised interrogative eyebrows. 'Like yourself?'

She nodded.

'And Geoff is a local solicitor,' said Tristan. 'We're friends from way back.'

Hannah was happy to sit there in the fug, wedged in between the two large men and pay no attention as they ignored the token woman and began to discuss rugby and England's chances against the All Blacks. Male bonding. She didn't mind. They made her feel very secure.

'Known Tristan for long?' one of them – Brian – suddenly said quietly in her ear, obviously not wanting the other two to hear.

'Yes,' she said, then realised that the question was prompted by a desire on Brian's part to discover whether she and Tristan were romantically linked. 'Thirty years or so—' she added, 'but this is the first time we've met for years.'

'An old flame, is he?'

'Not at all. My closest friend's parents had a house down here once. They were very friendly with Tristan's parents.'

'I see.' Brian's clever eyes rested on her, not quite smiling, despite the amused lines which surrounded them. 'That wouldn't have been the Wiltons, would it?'

'Yes. Did you know them?'

'Edward and Giulia. And stark raving Susie, as we used to call her. Yes, I knew them. Knew the cousin too. The one who died. It's a small community down here, you know. We grew up together, us local lads. All went away to school, so the occasional people – like the Wiltons and whatever the cousin's mother was called then – were assimilated during the holidays when they appeared and not really missed when they didn't.'

'I came to visit once,' said Hannah. 'That's when I met Tristan.'

'So there's nothing between you two?'

'*No*,' Hannah said, over-sharply. 'At least, not in the way you mean. Nothing – I mean, we're not in love or anything. Or even—'

'Shame,' Brian said. 'We'd like to see the old boy settled. He needs a nice woman.'

Hannah remembered something temporarily forgotten. Men like this might well offer a kind of security, but only if you accepted the whole patronising masculine package. 'The question is,' she said tartly, 'does a nice woman need him?'

'Until he meets one, we're never going to know the answer to that, are we?' said Brian.

'I'm amazed he hasn't.'

'So are we. Carrying a torch, Geoffrey says. But if he is, he doesn't talk about it. Says he likes things the way they are. Says no woman would have him, anyway. Says he's never found the right one. Says a lot of things. Load of nonsense really – they're not the real reason he's still on his own when the rest of us are already shaping up to be grandparents.'

'Perhaps not.'

'Do *you* have any idea what the reason might be?'

'I told you,' Hannah said. 'I haven't seen him for twenty-five years. And even if I did know, how would it change things?'

'Probably wouldn't. But he's a friend, and he's lonely and we worry about him.'

'There's a woman called Jennifer,' said Hannah.

'Jennifer Gilbert? She's married to Geoff's partner. Nothing to do with old Tristan.'

'I didn't mean that. Just that I'd like to have talked to her about – about something.'

'They're away in the Seychelles at the moment.'

Hannah made a regretful face. So much for questioning Jennifer, though she probably wouldn't have been any help. 'I'm afraid I can't really be of much use to you.'

She half-expected Brian to propose that she herself took on the job of making Tristan less lonely, but he leaned across her and started talking about the Baa-baas and the Quins, names which meant nothing to Hannah.

She had time to think, however, about what Brian had said. *Carrying a torch*: who for? Surely not Susie. The woman called Jane? He'd brought her into the conversation several times. Or this Marina: was it possible that he too had fallen for her, all those years ago? He seemed to have very vivid memories of meeting her for the first time.

Ultimately, did it matter? She had one or two more questions to ask him and then she would leave tomorrow morning and almost certainly never see him again in her life.

'You don't have to leave,' Tristan said diffidently. 'You could stay on if it's any help. It's calm down here. I wouldn't be around most of the time. You could walk, read, whatever.'

'You're very kind,' Hannah said. 'And thank you. But no. I've got places to go and questions to ask.'

'I hope you get the answers you want.'

'I don't know what answers I'm looking for,' Hannah said. They stood together in the window-bay of the drawing-room, looking out over the sea. Tristan put an arm around her shoulders.

'Will you come and visit me again when you've found them?'

'If I ever do,' said Hannah. 'I don't want revenge on whoever is behind my daughter's death, but I do want some kind of justice for her. And I want my son to be able to live without looking over his shoulder all the time for some madman.'

'Is finding out who killed Lucas going to achieve that?'

'I hope so.'

'You don't think the same person is responsible for your daughter's death too, do you?'

'I don't know.' Hannah looked up at him. The hooded eyes were

209

staring down at her and she was suddenly uncomfortable, remembering how often she had suspected, despite his denials, that Tristan had been the one who had smashed Lucas's skull with an iron bar before pushing him into the pool. His obvious loneliness, his lack of family, his solitary way of life: were they the result of some even more explicit guilt than her own? Was his need for atonement even deeper-rooted?

He had told her what he had seen, the night of Lucas's death, how he had reacted, all those years ago; his version of events was more or less the same as he had given at the time, both to her and to the police. Yet, although she now felt that she knew a little more about the players in that dark drama, she still knew almost nothing about the play.

As he took her hand and led her into the kitchen, she wondered whether he knew what she thought, that she believed him capable of murder. It all seemed so far away from the present, yet she was certain she would have to unravel what she thought was the past and reknit it if she was ever going to get at the truth.

'Sit down,' Tristan said. 'Have a glass of wine and talk to me while I organise dinner for us.'

For a while she watched him being domestic, feeling no compulsion to offer help. She turned the wineglass slowly between her fingers, wondering if she dared bring up the topic and at the same time knowing she would have to.

'Do you remember the night of the barbecue?' she said reluctantly.

'Of course. What about it?'

'You – you—'

'What did I do?' Tristan was pounding green peppercorns into a piece of olive-oiled fillet steak.

'Some people – three men – attacked Lucas. One of them hit him, punched him in the face.'

Tristan turned. 'From the way you say that,' he said quietly, 'you know very well it was me.'

'Yes.' Hannah could not look at him.

'I'm not proud of it.'

'He was tied up,' Hannah said. 'Who did that?'

'Not me. But I . . . stood by while others did it.'

'Why did he let you?'

'He didn't have much option.'

'But he wasn't gagged. Why didn't he call out? Was it because one of you had a knife?'

Tristan stood very still. 'You know that too?'

'I was watching.'

'I knew someone was.' He made a gesture both regretful and angry. 'It certainly wasn't me with the knife. But then I had less cause to want to hurt him than either of the others did.'

'A *knife*,' Hannah whispered, struck afresh by the horror of it. Lucas had dared them to kill him, but perhaps all along he was terrified that they would call his bluff.

'We'd all been friends for years,' Tristan said. 'The chap with the knife was a professional soldier, he went to Sandhurst direct from school, and then into the SAS. Knives – it was the sort of thing he was used to. It was the sort of thing he *did*.'

'You almost sound as if you admired him for it.'

'No,' Tristan shook his head. 'Absolutely not. But we were much younger then, more pitiless. More, I suppose, primitive.'

'That's the same word you used to describe the friend who was married to Jane.'

'He was the one with the knife.'

'Who was the other?'

'He was the one – it was his wife who – died in the car crash. He still has nightmares about it.'

'Perhaps Lucas did too.'

Tristan turned back to the steaks. 'Perhaps he did. I hope so.'

It was obvious that however much time had passed, for Tristan and his friends, the old wounds had never healed.

'Tristan.'

'Yes?'

'It wasn't you who killed Lucas, was it?'

'No, Hannah. It was not.'

Did she believe him? And if not, what relevance did any of it have now? 'Look,' she said, 'for the rest of my stay here, let's not mention Italy or Lucas or the past, all right?'

'I'll drink to that,' Tristan said.

At some point in the evening she found herself in Tristan's arms, slowly moving between the buttercup walls of the drawing-room. Sound issued from an old-fashioned wind-up gramophone which had belonged to his parents. Languidly the two of them swayed together to the mellow tones of some forgotten big-time band – Victor Sylvester, was it? Henry Hall? – and the voices of once-famous crooners, *Love is a tender trap*, the scratchy 78 rpm records revolving on the turntable, *Catch a falling star* . . . Hannah and Tristan, both lost, both alone.

The music reminded him of his youth, Tristan said. And me, Hannah told him, of mine. Their reflections lingered on the uncurtained windows, lit by the fire from the hearth. A tall, white-haired man; a woman no longer young, both of them, surely, past the accepted age of love or romance. Yet the possibility of both was palpably there.

She remembered again how, twenty-five years ago, they had stood together while lust leapt like a flame between them. Did he remember too?

She knew that were she even tentatively to respond to Tristan's unspoken invitation, he would gladly, even gratefully, make love to her. She did nothing, aware that this was neither the place nor the time, and that Tristan was almost certainly not the man.

None the less, he held her close, his cheek against her hair, while the needle hissed and ash fell softly in the hearth. *Goodnight, sweetheart . . . Goodnight . . .*

14

Frost covers the fields as she drives northwards through the dawn. Black hedges, wet wooden fences, shine in the pale sun. There are congregations of gulls scavenging the long lines of plough which stretch across the contours of the land. Here and there, among trees, are roofs clustered round church spires. Occasional country houses stand magnificent in parkland. Idyllic England. And yet, behind closed doors in places just like these, people will have died violently during the night, women been raped, children screamed as they were abused by adults they should have been able to trust.

As the sun comes up, the fields thaw and the white coating of frost gradually melts and disappears. Traffic is light, it is still early, and when she slits open the car window, the freezing air solidifies on the windscreen. She drives without thinking about it, under foot-bridges, across roundabouts, past garish symbols indicating Happy Eaters and Little Chefs, past filling stations and roadhouses and signs inviting her to visit places she has no wish to go. She is temporarily suspended in time, like a foetus in the womb, animate yet without reason or regret.

Turning eventually off the motorway, taking the empty roads towards the moors, she reflects that despite the cold streams, the lovely hills, the spacious beauty of sky and grass all around her, idylls no longer exist. Then thinks further that perhaps they never had, that those who thought they did, who wrote about them in the past, chose to ignore reality.

Today we are overloaded with bitter knowledge, she tells herself. For us, creatures who stand on the brink of the twenty-first century, every breathtaking view, every combination of sky and distance and hill is tainted with brutal facts about man's inhumanity; it is no longer possible to see them without remembering that, elsewhere, people are suffering, dying.

Crossing the dale head beyond Reeth, she drops down into Teesdale while the bare moors spread all around her. Although they have become familiar to her in the year or so since she first met Marcus, they never fail to fill her with a pleasure so intense that it is almost sexual.

Clouds chase across the wide skies. She stops the car and listens: she can hear sheep, wind, curlews, water dashing against stone. The slopes which rise on the other side of the dale are crowned with a long line of snow and more snow lies piled against the dry-stone walls which intersect the fields. A lonely place, she thinks. A lonely place to die.

Nearing Barnard Castle, she pushes a tape into the car-player and hears again that sinister androgynous voice: '*Listen closely, Anna.*' It has to be someone she knows: someone who knows her. It has to be the person who killed Lucinda. But try as she might, pressing, re-pressing the buttons to play the three words again and again – '*Listen closely, Anna*' – she cannot recognise the voice. Is it young or old? Male or female? Nor can she tell for certain whether her name is in fact properly pronounced, the aspirate there but almost inaudible, or not. Does it make a difference?

It does; it has to. How many people who know her use the name Anna instead of Hannah? After a while, the menace which the message projects grows muted; is it because she is better armed now? Has the worst it could have promised been fulfilled? After Lucinda's death there is nothing which can now hurt her, except Adam's. Certainly not her own.

Beyond the little market town she pushes on up into the dale, pausing in lay-bys to consult the map. Behind the snowy hills the sky is sombre; the only colour comes from the dead bracken which covers the lower slopes.

At a motorway stop near Bristol, she had telephoned Carringtons.

'How's it going?' she asked, knowing already that she need not have bothered to ask, that Zoe, as always, had everything under control.

'Cool,' Zoe said. 'Real cool.'

'Good. Uh – no problems? No enquiries?'

'Not a thing, Hannah. How about you? Did you find out anything in Cornwall? Was Mr Carrick able to help?'

Hannah frowned. She did not at first recall telling Zoe why she was going to Cornwall, nor even where. But Zoe asked so many questions that she probably had. And she had, of course, given her Tristan's number. 'Not really,' she said.

'That's why you went, isn't it? Because of Lucinda?'

'Yes.'

'Maybe something more will come out of your trip to Italy.'

'Maybe,' said Hannah.

'You all right?'

'I was just thinking that your memory for—' Hannah had been going to say 'other people's business' but pulled back, 'detail is phenomenal.'

'I told you: I remember everything.' There was a pause, and Zoe added softly, '*Nearly* everything.'

'It's one of the curses of getting older, that you forget even the simplest things,' Hannah said.

'Is that right?' Zoe sounded as though Hannah had just offered a blinding revelation. 'Where's Adam?'

'What?'

'I just wondered where your son was.'

'Staying with friends.' Why did Hannah find the question faintly disturbing?

'It's just that one of his mates from university rang up, wondering where he was.'

'Are you sure it was a university friend?'

'Yes. Why would he say he was if he wasn't?'

'All sorts of reasons.' Hannah had found her knees were suddenly weak. She leaned heavily against the side of the phone cubicle. Oh God: was this Lucinda's killer? Was he on the trail of Adam now?

'Anyway, I told him to call back, that I'd ask you when you rang in.'

'I don't have the number on me,' lied Hannah.

'Oh well. If he really wants Adam, he'll keep calling,' Zoe had said cheerfully.

'Quite.'

Trembling, Hannah cut the conversation short. With unsteady fingers, she had then telephoned Tom's parents, listened with sympathy to their self-reproaches, tried to convince them that they were blameless, though knowing they would not believe her.

'Of course,' his father had said, sensible and concerned. 'You must go if you want – but is it wise? In the circumstances, is it the best thing?'

'I don't know,' admitted Hannah. 'But I feel I must see where it – where Lucinda died.'

Tom's mother had taken the telephone from her husband. 'Of course you must,' she said warmly. 'I understand. I'd want to do the same if it were one of mine.'

The richness implicit in the words was painful: *one of mine* conveyed a bounty of children to which Hannah no longer had access. The two women exchanged words but it was the messages unspoken which comforted Hannah. She felt culpable, knowing that Tom's family would never enjoy their get-away-from-it-all cottage again.

Crossing a humped stone bridge above a tumbling stream, driving through a village which is no more than a street of stone houses, she realises that she has been here before, with Marcus. It was springtime then but such bleak landscapes do not greatly vary through the seasons; it had looked substantially the same then as it does now. They had stayed the night at a guest-house near by though she could not recall the name of the little town. Perhaps if she telephones Marcus . . . but she does not wish to do that. He will suggest they meet, that he drives over and joins her. He will express concern, want to offer support. But she prefers to make this pilgrimage alone – except perhaps for the pale ghost of her dead daughter.

The cottage lay halfway up the dale, looking down on a small hamlet set beside a frothing stream. A patch of rough grass in front of the house was enclosed by a wall with a gate let into it; behind, the garden was mostly terraced against the hill, planted with shrubs. Inspector Mayfield had spoken of eye-witnesses who said Lucinda had come here alone. Who could they have been? Hikers? Farmers or shepherds or gamekeepers? It was hard to see who else might have been watching.

But if she had arrived alone, it did not necessarily mean that she had remained alone. A second person could have driven here under the cover of darkness. Would Lucinda have been expecting him – or her – or had his appearance been a surprise? And if so, was it a welcome one?

The little house was warm. Tom's mother had urged Hannah to make herself at home so she filled the electric kettle with peat-coloured water from the tap and plugged it in. Waiting for the water to boil, she climbed the stairs to the first floor. Here, there were three wooden-floored bedrooms and an icy little bathroom. She stood in the middle of the largest bedroom and closed her eyes, willing her daughter into her mind. Had Lucinda sat on the deep window-seat in the hours before she died? Had she slept in this bed alone or shared it with another? Had she leafed through one of the books which lay on the table by the bed: P. G. Wodehouse, Joanna Trollope, Dick Francis?

The kettle screamed in the kitchen and she went down the steep steps gingerly, hands on the plastered walls, knowing but not caring that she was moving as her mother used to, like any old lady, careful about falling.

Making a mug of tea, she went into the small living-room. There were bookshelves here, a radio, a big inglenook fire with cast-iron accoutrements, pieces of old china. The stone windows offered a magnificent view across the valley which was already beginning to darken, the sky formidably grey, heavy with further snow.

Hannah concentrated, probing the room, senses sharp as antennae, and caught traces, she was sure, of Lucinda's presence. Tatters, like the ectoplasm produced by a medium, as though her daughter had just that second turned at the window, risen from the lumpy sofa, paused in the doorway. That chair, that table, those books—

Hannah put her mug down on the round table in the centre of the room and went over to the armchair beside the empty fireplace. Lucinda had sat here, facing the window. She had stared out at the sky, she had fiddled through the stations on the radio which stood on the floor beside the chair, had flipped through the magazines in the wickerwork holder, had searched the books, looking for something to read.

Hannah did the same. Holiday reading, lightweight paperbacks for the most part, designed to be untaxing. Spy stories, crime fiction, a few inflated women's novels from the States. Two or three hard backs.

She tensed. One of them she recognised. Flat across the tops of the other books in the shelf lay *Hurled by Dreams* by Max Marsden.

216

Why was it here? Marcus told her that it was only published in the US. Zoe had said that her husband had bought it in the States. So how could it be here? For Hannah, the presence of the book was the determining factor she had been looking for, the confirmation that her past and her present had fatally mingled.

The telephone rang, a sharp, penetrative buzz which made Hannah jump. She snatched it up.

Tom's mother: 'Is everything all right, Mrs Barlow? I asked a neighbour to turn on the heating so that you wouldn't freeze to death.' She broke off abruptly, conscious of her inept phraseology.

Hannah was touched. 'It's fine, thank you. I'm fine. But I wanted to ask—'

'If you'd like to stay for the night, there are sheets in the airing cupboard. And things in the freezer, out in the shed. Do please feel free to help yourself to anything you—'

'Mrs—' What was her name: Price? Morgan? Something Welsh. 'uh, there's a book here, called *Hurled by Dreams*. Do you happen to know where it came from?'

'A book?' Hannah could feel the dismay in Tom's mother's voice, a kind woman wondering whether Hannah, this stranger, had been mentally affected by the tragedy of her child's death. 'I'm not sure what we've got there.'

'Would Tom know? Or your husband?'

'I could ask.' The voice is hesitant, anxious.

Hannah gulps air, striving to sound calm. 'It must seem a little odd, asking about a book,' she said, laughing a little. 'But it could be important.'

'What was it called again?'

Hannah told her. 'By someone called Max Marsden.'

'Just a moment.' A hand was placed over the receiver; there was muffled conversation. Hannah could imagine the raised eyebrows, the expression of dismay as she spoke to her husband and son, trying to convey her concern without Hannah hearing. Then Tom himself came on the line.

'Mrs Barlow.'

Hannah explained. 'It's a book that I happen to know is only published in the States. I wondered how it got into your cottage, whether Lucinda could have left it there. Because if she did—'

'Yes?' Tom said gently.

'It could have a bearing on her death.'

There was a silence during which Hannah could feel him trying to hide his puzzlement as to how she could possibly imagine such a thing. Then he said: '*I* certainly didn't take it up there, I've never heard of it, nor have my parents. I should think it must have been left there by Lucinda – we were just saying that she was the last person to use the cottage.' He coughed, awkward at using a dead girl's name.

'So it looks as though she might have brought it with her – or was given it by someone while she was here.'

'It does, rather.'

'Thank you, Tom. And please tell your parents how very grateful I am for all their kindness. I shan't stay here tonight; but I'll be driving back south in the morning. They've been most kind.'

In her hand, the book burns like a heated iron.

She puts it down on the table. The weather outside has turned colder, bleak clouds scurrying across a white sky. The wind whips down the side of the moor and across the valley, slamming the door against the wall of the hall as she opens it. There is a thick scarf of bright pink wool hanging on a hook, along with others, with coats and jackets and a hat-stand studded with walking sticks. She wraps the scarf round her neck and walks out to see where Lucinda died.

If she had had doubts before, they were laid to rest the moment she found the tower. A disused dovecote, in reality, attached to a few ruined lines of stones which lay sunk in the sheep-cropped green turf and testified to the remains of a monastery or abbey.

She looked up at the bulk of the structure. Circular, maybe thirty feet high, built of stone. It was amazing that it still stood, that the local people had not carried away the dressed stones for their own purposes. One portion of wall had subsided into a tumbledown heap; the top was open to the sky. The façade was punctuated by arched apertures to enable the birds to fly in and out. She scrambled up on to the fallen stones and peered inside. A narrow stair climbed up round the interior of the tower, reaching a kind of platform about two-thirds of the way up. Even the most agile of the religious brethren who had formerly used it might have found it a vertiginous experience to climb up there. It was difficult to imagine dragging a body up those precipitous steps, but easier than believing that Lucinda had climbed them herself. Even with a gun at her back. Or a knife. Or had she forced herself to overcome her terror in the desperate hope of gaining a few more minutes of life?

A cold wind howled through the gaps in the walls; the long grass moaned. Normally a place like this would have had some evidence of passing humanity: crumpled cigarette packets, the ubiquitous plastic bag, condoms, maybe, if it were a place where local lovers came. But the floor was clean, unnaturally so. Hannah guessed that Inspector Mayfield's officers had combed the interior for any clue which might be helpful, had cleared the rubbish into bags to be gone through later by forensic scientists. None the less, she found herself searching, kicking at the weeds with her foot.

Had Lucinda's blood soaked into that hard-packed earth? And – other things? Had she survived for a while, cheek pressed against the bird-limed soil, eyes staring at the rank grass, the rubbish, and seeing only death? Hannah forced herself to look up at the platform, to imagine her child falling through the cold air, faced the terror as questions she should not ask if she was to hold on to sanity tried to crowd into her mind. Was Lucinda conscious as she fell? Had she known what was going to happen to her? How long was she afraid? Hannah's fists were clenched, her face contorted with hatred. Murder is the most arrogant of crimes but she, too, could kill, should the need arise.

Her heart had begun to beat so rapidly that she felt dizzy. Rage consumed her. Rage was a more constructive emotion than despair and she let it spread like fog through her body. She felt as though her blood had turned to anger: she could feel it in nerve and muscle, urging her onwards, demanding action. Had her daughter's murderer appeared, she would have torn him apart without compunction or mercy.

Breathing heavily, she went outside again. She could hear nothing except the wind, which pulled at the ends of her scarf and brought cold tears to her eyes. At the edge of the field, a group of brightly-dressed walkers passed in single file along the path, staring curiously at the dovecote. What did they make of her, a wild-eyed woman wrapped in an incongruous pink scarf? Did they know a girl had died here? Did they see her as some ghoulish thrill-seeker? Did they see her at all? They were of the same age as Lucinda: she wanted to scream, to curse.

This was not a good place to be. Following the young people at a distance down the muddy stone-jagged pathway, she knew she would not come to this place again. Lucinda's memorial was somewhere else, not here.

She wondered suddenly what Tristan would say, were he with her. Certainly, he could not accuse her of trying to assume responsibility for what had happened to Lucinda. Whatever the tortuous reasons which had led to it, and however far back they stretched, she knew that of this death, at least, she was innocent.

Back at the Morgans' cottage, she went upstairs. The police had already searched the place but none the less, she too searched, hoping for some last trace of Lucinda. There was nothing. The drawers of the chest were empty; there was nothing under the bed, the corners hid no secrets. She pulled back the edges of the carpets, though there was no reason at all why Lucy should have hidden something – unless she had realised she was in danger. Down in the living-room, she felt down the back of the armchairs and found a single earring but it could have belonged to anyone, nothing about it spoke of her daughter and she left it where she had found it. Before leaving, she turned off the heating, checked that lights had not been left on, closed doors. In her bag was the book by Max Marsden.

* * *

She found the guest-house where she had stopped for the night with Marcus. There was one other couple staying there, elderly Americans, touring the north of England. Over a drink in the cramped little communal sitting-room, they told her that they preferred England in the winter, the roads were emptier and since they came from California, they were always excited by the possibility of snow. This trip was to celebrate their forty-fifth wedding anniversary, they explained. They held hands, touched each other frequently, made their mutual love clear. Hannah envied them. It was too late for her to celebrate such milestones: six months ago, such a thought might have depressed her but she was surprised to find that in fact she found it liberating. At her age, there was no longer time to lay down the foundations for long-term relationships; all the more reason to enjoy, for however long they lasted, the ones which came along.

Like Tristan. Like Marcus, who was, in effect, her 'relationship'. Yet she felt curiously separate from him, even up here, in what she thought of as his territory.

They moved into a whitewashed dining-room, and were served with a pâté so execrable that she blushed with embarrassment, unable to eat it, hoping they did not think this was representative of English cuisine.

The husband of the couple who owned the guest-house shuffled into the dining-room, wearing braces and checked slippers, carrying plates of grey beef slices, mashed potato from a packet, tinned peas. He placed one in front of each of them.

'Everything all right?' he enquired.

English Hannah murmured that it was fine, thank you. The Americans, at the next table, nodded. When the man had gone the American wife remarked mildly that the food wasn't too great here, was it?

'It's awful,' her husband observed. 'But what the heck? You win a few, lose a few. That place we were in last night was terrific. And a lot more expensive.' He looked at Hannah and winked.

You win a few, lose a few. How very true, Hannah thought, pushing the tinned peas to one side, cutting an edge off the beef. Maybe it's time I started to win, for a change. She smiled across at the Americans.

'I've always wanted to visit California,' she said. 'What's it like living out there?'

The evening passed pleasantly while they told her. She bought them a whisky later; they bought her another. They did not ask personal questions and Hannah was grateful for their company.

Lying in the huge bed which took up most of the room, Hannah thought about the last time she had been here. Marcus had brought her, saying she needed cheering up, saying it would do her good to get away from the house she used to share with Anthony. By then, she felt she knew Marcus, and could trust him. If she was honest, she would admit that she was flattered by his attention, and was fairly sure that he would make love to her if she accepted his invitation to visit him. Knew, too, that she would not refuse him.

Their original meeting had been purely accidental. Nearly two years before, Hannah had been invited by a friend to play once a week with an amateur string quartet in London. She had wanted to refuse – it was years since she last played her cello – but her friend had been insistent. Every Thursday evening, therefore, Hannah travelled up to Hornsey to make music, despite Anthony's scoffing, and though at first she was out of practice she had persevered until some of her old skill returned.

One night a man had flung himself into the carriage and in trying to sink into the empty seat beside hers just as the north-bound Inter-city train lurched away from St Pancras, had fallen heavily on top of her. Apologising profusely, he had removed some papers taken from his briefcase and they had not spoken until she reached her station, when they had nodded, murmured goodbye.

She'd seen him again a couple of weeks later. They'd smiled vaguely at each other, got into different carriages. One night they found themselves hurrying together along the platform; it had seemed natural to sit together. When the train stopped outside Luton and showed no likelihood of ever starting again, they had begun to talk to each other. They exchanged names, he asked why she came to London every Thursday; she explained. He asked where her instrument was: she told him she played on a borrowed one, practised on her own at home. He spoke of Elgar's Cello Concerto; she mentioned Jacqueline du Pré. After that, it became an understood thing that they would sit together, save each other places. One night he suggested that they might catch a later train, meet beforehand for a drink.

Despite the unsatisfactory nature of her relationship with Anthony, this had seemed a bold step to Hannah. She knew that, by accepting his invitation, she would be taking the first step on to a slippery bridge she was not sure she wished to cross. He had seen her hesitation, seemed instantly to grasp the reasons behind it. 'Don't worry,' he had said, 'I'm not trying to compromise you!' and they had both laughed lightly, both aware that in fact he was. But she had not agreed to meet him.

An hour's delay was announced one evening as she came hurrying into the station. She went into the bar, ordered herself a whisky; he appeared five minutes later. 'So,' he said, 'we're having that drink after all.'

'Yes,' Hannah said. 'But this way, I feel Fate had a hand in it.'

He understood exactly what she was trying to say, that she need not feel that she had connived at betrayal of her husband, nor he, if he had one – something she still did not know – his wife. That it was therefore all right for her to step on to the bridge, despite the chasms which yawned beneath it.

Later in the year, when Anthony left, Marcus was there to comfort her. She gave him her telephone number: he took to ringing every week and then, gradually, every evening. Eventually he had invited her up for a weekend in the Dales and they had stayed at this guest-house.

She turned on her side, the horsehair mattress rustling under her as she did so. It was a sound she had not heard for years, since she had last spent the night at her grandmother's house as a child. On the covers was the copy of the book which she had taken from the Morgans' cottage. She opened it and flipped through the pages. Doing so made her shudder again. However hard she tried not to read the text, words leaped out at her. Particularly the name of the woman who committed the violence at the book's heart.

Anna. It must be more than coincidence. What could Lucinda have thought, reading this – if she had? It couldn't have driven her to suicide, could it? Given her the perverse courage to climb that steep little stair and cast herself down? No. Hannah shook her head. She had never told Lucinda about Italy or the events of that summer: there was no reason why she should connect the fictional woman called Anna with her mother. Whoever had given her the book must have been aware of this: had there then been some means of bringing it to Lucinda's attention? An inserted card, a message scrawled on the fly-leaf, words written in the margins? She found nothing.

Instead of driving directly south the next day, she went eastwards, towards Marcus. When she got to Crickgarth, she would telephone: if he was free, she would drop in, if not, she was only a few miles from the motorway and the road south.

Despite the light cover of snow which had fallen during the night (the Americans had been delighted), the sky was blue today, the air mild, though still edged with the acid bite of winter. Ahead of her rose the great barren bulk of the fells, the land folding and refolding into itself like pleated fabric. To one side a stream full of snow-melt leaped between flat green banks, every now and then catching the sunlight in a spray of brighter drops. It was so tranquil: she needed a measure of tranquillity. She stopped the car, got out and stood at the edge of the stream. It was colder here than in the south, the spring much less advanced. The air caught at the back of her throat. At the edge of the snow-heavy sky, a deeper shade of white lay along the hills. To her consternation, she felt something very close to happiness.

At Crickgarth, a village consisting of a single wide street flanked by stone houses, she parked. There were a few shops, nothing much, a bakery, a newsagent, a couple of antique shops, a chemist. An alleyway led between high stone walls to a parking area serving the tiny supermarket which lay behind the main street. There was a telephone kiosk here: she crammed into it and dialled Marcus's number. As she waited for it to ring, someone stepped into the slice of sunshine where the alleyway met the High Street, looked up towards her, and passed on. She stared through the glass at the gap just vacated.

It was him.

Again, fleetingly, she feels the burden of guilt fall from her. If he is somehow, miraculously, alive, then . . . but it is not him. She knows that. She slams the receiver back on its rest, leans against the weighted door of the phone booth to open it, runs down the narrow alley and into the main street. Although only seconds have passed, she cannot see him. She walks, half-runs, in the direction he was headed, peering into shops as she goes, pushing past people, head turning to cover the wide roadway. She cannot see him. People are staring. She understands why when she catches sight of herself in a shop window; there is a wildness about her, as though any moment she will fly apart. It is a wildness not unfamiliar: from time to time she has observed them herself, middle-aged women with who knows what private griefs, too turned in on themselves to be aware of the chaos which leaks out of their own lives and touches, briefly, the lives of unknowns who shy away, not wanting that intimate brush with a stranger. Women on trains, on buses, on park benches, women whom some crisis has temporarily unmoored from their habitual anchorages.

If he had a name, she would shout it aloud, regardless of the passers-by, or what they might think. But for her, he has no name, no handle by which she can catch him and pull him to herself. She had almost persuaded herself that the encounters at the Festival Hall, outside her shop, were no more than wild fancy, a slight resemblance encouraged into full-blown likeness by her own imagination. Now she knows that this was not so. She knows, too, that his presence here – she will not try to persuade herself that she was mistaken in what she saw – has to do with Lucinda. With herself. With the unresolved past.

At the end of the street is a monument, some kind of war memorial, and behind that, as the road slopes downwards to a river, moors rise. She walks in the other direction, unnerved by so much space. She needs to be hemmed in by ordinariness, for what is happening, what has recently happened, to her is far from ordinary. There is a bus stop, people waiting. A pub. A butcher's shop, the window vehement with animal carcasses, raw, bleeding meat wrapped in cream-coloured fat. A hardware store displaying galvanised buckets and mops dandelioned with heads of white string. At the end of the terrace is a second-hand bookshop.

She steps inside. The shelves are crowded, for the most part, with dog-eared paperbacks of popular authors, plus a few shelves of local history, gilded and leathered, bound sets of Tennyson, some detective stories. Anxious to regain control of herself, she feigns an interest in a tattered Ed McBain, a grubby Catherine Cookson. Her eye falls on a shelf of Georgette Heyers: she picks up a copy of *Faro's Daughter* and, eyes closed, flips the pages, her back turned to the uninterested woman who sits knitting behind a table piled with old copies of *National Geographic*.

How could he – the question bangs in her brain – in the three or four seconds between her first glimpse of him and her arrival in the main street, have so completely disappeared? He is tall, striking. She tries to remember what he wore. A waxed jacket, corduroys, country clothes: she can come up with nothing more than that.

Did she simply miss him, pass him without realising? Did he, aware somehow of her presence, deliberately conceal himself? Or – and this is the question which sets her heart hammering for it opens the doorway to insanity – was he, however corporeal he seemed, only a conjuration, the product of her need and grief?

She puts down *Faro's Daughter*, picks up *Sprig Muslin*, glancing over her shoulder at the shopkeeper. The woman is counting stitches, lips pursed, too absorbed in her knitting to pay attention to a strange women thumbing the softbacks.

Hannah reminds herself that the first time she saw him, Lucinda was still alive, she had not yet seen a copy of *Hurled by Dreams*, the furniture of her life was still in place. The second encounter might have been self-induced, but the first surely was not. Therefore he exists. Therefore he is findable.

She buys both the paperbacks and walks back down the street. There is a café halfway along: gingham curtains, polished copper, bowls of demerara sugar on the table. She finds a table by the window and orders a pot of tea. She keeps watch.

If he appears again, she will see him. Yet, as she sips the strong gingery tea which is brought to her, she still fears that even were she to take him by the arm, he would dissolve in front of her eyes, evanesce, vanish back into the limbo from which someone – herself? – has called him.

She glanced along the street with its backdrop of empty moor, her gaze sweeping along and up towards the bus stop and the pub. Her attention was suddenly caught by a familiar back. A man was walking briskly away from her, a backpack slung over one shoulder. Surely that was – she rose, adding a pound coin to the money she had already put on the table in case she needed to leave in a hurry. She ran out through the café door and into the wide street. Where had he gone? She craned her neck: ah yes, there he was.

'Marcus!'

He turned, eyes narrowing as he tried to see who had called his name. She waved, arm high in the air. 'Marcus!'

He saw her. For a moment, an expression of bewilderment crossed his face, as though he had expected someone else. Then he smiled, hurrying towards her. 'Hannah, my dear. What are you doing here?' And then, as he remembered, as he realised what she must have been doing, his smile drooped and disappeared. 'Of course,' he said softly. 'Of course.'

'How odd to see you here,' Hannah said.

'Not really. They have a sports shop here where you can buy superb fishing flies. The chap who owns it ties them himself.' He reached into his backpack and pulled out a small square box. 'Look here, if you don't believe me.'

'Of course I believe you,' Hannah said, thinking him absurd. 'Why shouldn't I? You don't have to show me proof.' At the same time, she was curious. The mere fact that he was so anxious to have her believe him automatically set up a presumption of guilt: about what, though?

A mistress was the most likely answer. What could be more natural, given that she herself lived so far away from him, and he was a vigorous, lusty man. Even though he had told her he loved her, he might well need more than the distance between them allowed her to provide.

'My darling Hannah,' Marcus said warmly, as though guessing her thoughts. 'Let me cosset you. Let me buy you lunch, or a drink, or take you home with me and make love to you. Or all three. Not necessarily in that order.'

Hannah could feel the fly-away pieces of herself reassemble under the influence of his steady presence. 'I was going to ring you,' she said. 'I thought I'd drop in on you before I headed south again.'

'Will you stay the night? Or merely the afternoon?'

'I can't really spare more than an hour or so,' she said.

'Plenty of time.' Marcus's expression made it clear what he intended. But Hannah did not want to undress, get into his big bed, make love with him. She felt closed and private, unwilling to open either body or emotion to him just at present.

'I really have to get going,' she said quickly. 'Since we've met up, why don't we have lunch here?'

'But I want to—'

'It's not a good time for me,' she said gently. She put her hand on his arm. 'I really don't feel like—'

'That's never bothered me,' he said and she realised he thought she was referring to her period.

She started to say that that was not what she meant then stopped. 'I don't feel like it,' she repeated.

He shrugged, holding her gloved hand in his, keeping her close to him. 'Fair enough,' he said. His eyes swept the street behind her. 'Come on: lunchtime.' He kissed the tip of her nose as though she were a child again. 'But we won't have it here: remember that little pub I took you to once? Over in Tunby?'

'How far is it?' Hannah said, as he took her arm rather roughly and

225

more or less marched her across the road to where his Range Rover was parked.

'Ten, fifteen minutes.'

'I'm short of time, Marcus.' She tried to free herself from his insistent hold. 'I'd much prefer just to have a quick sandwich in the pub than go traipsing off in search of gourmet meals.'

'Come on, darling. Don't argue,' Marcus said. He opened the passenger door and helped her to climb in, then came round to the driver's side. He gunned the motor and they were away, roaring up the road almost before the gears had engaged.

Hannah, ruffled, pulled down the sunshield and looked at herself in the mirror. The surface of her face seemed blotched and pitted. Under her eyes the skin was wrinkled like a crone's. She looked every one of her years, with a few added on. In front of them, a woman in a padded green jacket slowly backed a horsebox into the road, carefully manoeuvring herself into a position to take the same direction as they themselves were headed.

'Christ on a bicycle!' Marcus banged impatiently on the steering wheel. 'Why can't the bloody woman get a move on?'

'Marcus, what on earth is the matter?' Hannah could not understand him. This was a different Marcus from the one whom, over the past year, she had grown, she believed, to love. Had he always been so quick to anger? 'If you're worried about lunch, it really—'

'Bloody hell!' Marcus yelled. 'What the fucking—' He smashed his hand down on the wheel again. 'What the *hell* is that moronic female doing?'

'For goodness' sake,' Hannah protested. 'She's only trying to—'

'Sorry,' Marcus put his hand on her leg, stroking the cloth of her jeans in an effort, she decided, to shut her up. 'I'm sorry. I'm a bit uptight at the moment.'

'That's all right,' she said stiffly, brushing his hand away, annoyed with him. She glanced away from him, out of the passenger window and there, on the other side of a row of parked cars as Marcus suddenly shot out into the road in order to overtake the horsebox, *he* was. Watching them.

His glance caught Hannah's and it seemed that something akin to the beginnings of a smile fractionally altered the otherwise unreadable expression on his face. She was close enough to see the distinctive almost-opal eyes, the way his hair fell over his forehead, the particular set of his shoulders.

Lucas. Oh God . . .

But not Lucas.

The likeness was uncanny.

'Stop!' she cried. 'Stop, Marcus, I want to get out!'

But Marcus, hunched over the wheel, his teeth gritted, appeared oblivious to her words. She contemplated opening the door and leaping out, even at the risk of an undignified landing on hands and knees. She remembered with what longing she wished to meet the man who stood now at the side of the wide street, how much she wanted to touch, like Doubting Thomas, to reassure herself that the flesh was solid and the heart still beat.

Marcus, however, pressed his foot hard down on the accelerator and before she could do anything further they were leaving Crickgarth, racing towards the open moors, while floating after her came the voice in her head, like a thread of mist: '*Hann. . . ah . . .*'

She had been thinking, putting things together, not sure what they added up to, but certain that the equation was there.

'Where did you get that book?' she asked him, as they sat in front of a wood-burning stove in the pub he had driven to.

'Which book?'

'*Hurled by Dreams*. The one you had in your study when I came up in the New Year.'

'I told you. I was sent a couple of copies to review.'

'Why?'

He made a face indicative of amused puzzlement. 'Because I'm known as a book reviewer. You know that.'

'Why,' persisted Hannah, 'would they send you a book from the States? It's not normal practice, is it?'

He lifted his mug and drank concentratedly from it, the beer rippling past his Adam's apple. When he put it down, he wiped his upper lip with his sleeve. 'They probably wanted a quote for the paperback,' he said offhandedly.

'Have you read it?'

'Of course. I'm not one of those critics who make do with the blurb, the first page and the last paragraph.'

'What did you think of it?'

He shrugged. 'It was a book. Quite nicely written, if slightly hysterical as to style.'

'What about content?'

His face took on a wary expression. 'What's this inquisition for, Hannah? Am I going to have to sit an exam paper in Eng. Lit. before the end of the day?'

She refused to be diverted. 'What did you think of the story?'

There was a long silence. 'Interesting,' he said. Under his jaw the muscles bunched momentarily.

'Was anything about it familiar to you?'

'Familiar?' He shook his head from side to side. 'Hannah, what in the world is all this about?'

227

She changed tack. 'Did you notice that boy, Marcus? That young man, in Crickgarth?'

'What sort of question is that? The town was awash with boys *and* with young men.'

'The one standing outside the bank, watching us as we drove away.'

'I can't say I did.'

'Did you ever know someone called Lucas Wyndham?'

He pulled out his pipe and began to pack it with loose tobacco. Shreds fell from the bowl and he tapped them back into his waxed pouch, before patting his various pockets and producing a box of matches. As he lit the pipe, not looking at her, he spoke around the stem. 'Never heard of him.'

He is lying. Every instinct tells her so. But to which of her questions has he given a false answer: all of them, or only some? And why?

She remembers again how they met. Was it as random a meeting as she had previously thought? Or had he lain in wait for her, Thursday after Thursday? Driving down the A1, she tells herself this is nonsense. He could not have known she would be on that train, for she had not known herself. She reminds herself of his kind voice, the steadiness of him, the love he has brought back into her life.

How would he have known she caught that train, that she went to London each week? How *could* he have known? She tries not to remember that he is – or was – a journalist, that he is trained in the skill of finding things out.

Marcus has many secrets. She has always known that. She has always accepted that. Just as she herself is not what she seems, so neither is he. But for the first time, she begins to wonder what his secrets might be, and whether, in some mysterious way, they are related to hers.

THE DIARY

. . . The Dr was asking about F today. Wanted to know how I felt about him, what I remembered. Told him I couldn't remember anything before O was born, that my memory of things before then was a complete blank – or had been until I started to write it down.

Said that the events which took place in the Book could be fact or fiction, that I was not really sure which, that scenes had come to me, that events had surfaced and I had written them down, told a story, but couldn't be certain which was truth and which was embroidery.

He looked as if he didn't quite believe me. How does he know? He can be a real smug bastard sometimes, sitting on that swivel chair of his, with his fingers arched under his chin. Hey, look at me, man, I'm real, I'm a Dr.

At least he doesn't have a bust of Freud on a plinth, or a signed letter on the wall from Jung or Adler or someone. I wondered, this morning, walking by the river, whether I like him. Couldn't answer the question. I'm involved with him. I'm closer to him than to anyone else in my life except O. Sometimes I hate him. But do I like him?

And why do I conceal things from him? Like my relationship with F? The other day the Dr was talking about the Agent, where I'd got hold of him, how I'd known who to call. I just stopped myself in time from saying that F had recommended him.

. . . The main thing about the money is that it would give me freedom to travel. I haven't been anywhere but here for years. Now I can afford to buy a plane ticket and search out some of those places which I remember from time to time (selective amnesia?) when I'm caught between sleeping and waking, or in the middle of a smoke. I know that if I could go back, the thing at the centre of my mind, the lump that's obstructing me, preventing me from getting on with my life, would be cleared.

What would the Dr say if I told him I was leaving? He can't stop me, I know that, but he could advise against it, could undermine my determination, sow the subtle seeds of failure in my skull.
   What would T say?
   I'll talk to F about it.

What would happen if I was travelling and I needed the Dr?
   The Dr is my drug. My morphia. Perhaps I should do some cold turkey. Start preparing myself for when I go away from here – if I ever decide to.

. . . *Had to do an interview this morning. Because of the Book. We did it over the phone. Down the line, they call it.*

This reporter came on. Her first question was: 'Where does it all come from?'

I did one of those Margaret Attwood numbers. 'Where does it come from?' I repeated slowly, sat back in my chair, closed my eyes for a moment. God: I should have checked beforehand to see what kind of things she was going to ask me.

'It comes from my heart,' I said. Opened my eyes again. 'From my soul.'

'So it's a work of imagination, rather than experience?' the bitch asked. Even though I couldn't see her I knew I didn't like her. She had an idiosyncratic voice, her tone was held-back, as though any minute she was going to burst out with insulting opinions about my intellect or mannerisms or character. Or the Book.

'Isn't fiction usually a combination of the two?' I said, cool as shit.

'Of course. But—'

'It's Ivo's story,' I said. This woman was making me feel very edgy.

'Who exactly is Ivo?' She spoke right into the phone, as if she was trying to look at my face. I hate that, hate someone crowding my personal space like that. I was glad she wasn't in the room with me: I don't know how I'd have coped with that. 'Tell me about Ivo,' she said.

Wanted to say: Read the Book, bitch. But it wouldn't look too good in the journal or whatever it is she was writing for. And I had agreed that I would do limited publicity when I signed the contract, though no face-to-face contact, no press conferences or bookshop signings. Nothing which involved being close to people, I'm not too good with people.

'He died years ago,' I say. 'But I grew up knowing him. My mother told me over and over again what he did, what happened to him. He became my personal icon. The book is a mythic re-creation, if you like, of a life outside my own experience.' God, I'm thinking, is any of this stuff real?

Sounded as if she was wondering the same. 'Is that just authorial crap?' she asked. 'Or do you really mean it?'

I turned on some charm. Laughed disarmingly. 'I really hate that kind of phoney writer's talk. Truth is, this was a story waiting to be told and when I was ready, I told it.'

233

She says: 'Twenty-five years is a long time to wait before writing a book like this.'

'I know.' I gave a big, chummy chuckle. 'But I needed to digest what had happened, to filter it, if you like, through the creative process. After all, the man at the book's centre might really have existed.' He did, of course, but I certainly wasn't going to go into all the bad stuff with her. It's hard enough telling the Dr. I could feel my stomach churn. I felt as though I'd fallen into a swollen torrent and was being swept helplessly along, tumbling over rocks, battered by waves, towards destruction. For twenty-five years I've laboured to build my fortress. Now the whole edifice was crumbling about me and I didn't even know why.

Was it just because of a few intrusive questions?

Was it the mention of Ivo?

That scene in the Book, where Ivo is lying there, his face covered in blood. I could feel it inside me, swelling like a balloon, moving closer and closer to the front of my head as though it would burst out through my eyes any moment.

I wanted my wolf suit. I wanted the Dr.

'We'll have to stop now,' I said.

'What?'

'I can't go on with this,' I said. My voice was kind of rising, the way it does when I start losing control. The Dr taught me relaxation techniques to handle it but I couldn't remember them. 'I have to stop.'

She didn't like it. She did a heavy number, tapping her teeth with a pen – over the phone, it sounded like corn popping – and sighing. 'This is really uncooperative of you, you know. And very unprofessional. I don't have enough material to write anything substantial. And there's my own reputation to—'

I said I was sick. Food poisoning, I said. Told her to maybe call again another time, set it up with the Agent. Made myself sound kind of wan. There wasn't much she could say to that. She had to go along with it, of course, but she was pretty nasty about it.

No doubt she'll write a hostile review of me and/or the Book. F says any publicity is good publicity when you're in the writing biz.

Don't think I'll do an interview again, not on my own. The more people who question me, the more chance there is of someone breaking through my pseudonym. Maybe I could write my own questions and come up with some good answers, just mail them off when people ask for interviews. Or ask them to send in written questions. That way, I wouldn't have to speak to anyone. I'd avoid people like that woman today.

. . . *The Cesarewitch man rang up today. The Agent. Two-book contract, he kept saying. Two-book contract.*

It was one of my Bad Days and I was having difficulty hearing him. Was it the phone or was it me? His voice kept retreating as though he was walking backwards down a tunnel and then suddenly whooshing forward, louder and louder, right through my ear and into my head. The phone felt soft in my hand, like one of those Claes Oldenburg sculptures.

Cesarewitch has this terrible New York accent: I could feel those vowels of his staining my brain-cells red and purple and poison-ivy green. 'What? What?' I said.

'Do you have a problem?' he said.

Wanted to say: Only with my life. But I don't have that kind of relationship with him. Nor with anybody, except the Dr. Not even with O. 'No,' I said, lying through my teeth. 'No problem. Just, the phone seems a little distorted.'

'They want two more books,' he said. 'Two more.'

'Who does?' Stupidly, I thought he meant he'd run out of copies of the Book and wanted me to send him some of my complimentaries.

'The publishers,' he said. 'I'll send the contract down to you. Two more: hey, that's really great, isn't it?'

Is it?

It means, doesn't it, that I have to set my feet firmly on the path marked AUTHOR. That from now on, my choices will be removed from me. And I am increasingly uncertain about whether there are any other stories left in me to tell.

He didn't seem to notice my lack of enthusiasm. 'Not a lot of money,' he said. 'Not yet. But that'll come. Meantime, there are reviews. I'll send them to you.'

'Do you wear glasses?' I asked. As soon as I'd said it, I realised it was one of those questions that most people wouldn't understand, that make them look at me out of the corners of their eyes as though I'm a crazy person, even though my reason for asking was perfectly logical. Was he as vulnerable as the Dr, underneath all that energy, that's what I wanted to know. And if he didn't wear glasses, what form of protective covering did he use. Because everybody has something they hide behind. Everybody.

'You what?' he said.

'Doesn't matter,' I said. 'I was thinking of something else. 'Yeah, send me the reviews.'

NOW

15

What had she expected? That nothing would have changed? That the town would have remained as it was twenty-five years ago, encysted in the past?

Yes.

This was what she had anticipated: the same café fronting the square, the same elderly men in straw hats reading newspapers on benches, the same businessmen in light suits sitting over a *grappa*, the same cat slowly crossing the square, tail held high. Looking from side to side as she took the road up the hill to the centre of the little town, slowly bumping over the cobbles (they, at least, had not changed) she realised she was still watching out for the padre in his flapping cassock, the old woman with the five poodles on a lead, the hare-lipped boy who sat all day on a hard chair outside his parents' house, endlessly twisting pieces of coloured wool.

Instead, there was modern development at one end of the town, concrete blocks of apartments, raw ground being snatched from the edges of the vineyards for houses, a football stadium, a tyre factory, long rows of factory sheds containing various light industries.

There were bright shops, some selling furniture, some fashions; there was a brash new hotel with neon signs above the entrance. The grocery store had expanded into a mini-supermarket, one side devoted to lit freezer chests; alongside the peppers and the pasta, it sold English teas, popping-corn from the States, bamboo shoots packed in Korea, pâtés from France, smoked salmon.

And yet the town had not, in essence, changed. Hannah parked her hired car and walked up to the piazza. To one side the terrace still looked out over the roofs of the ugly municipal housing to vineyard and mountain; at the top of a crooked side street, the square-roofed campanile still stood against the sky, birds curvetting between the bells. And just as she crossed the square, a cat – a different cat, certainly, but none the less identical in its felinity – stalked from a narrow passage between the houses and stepped a delicate path to the other side. There was even an elderly gentleman in the window of the café, a folded copy of *Il Correo* on the table in front of him.

She found herself scrutinising faces as she passed, attempting to add twenty-five years and see if she recognised them. Entering the café, she nodded at the man in the window and sat down at a table topped with marble-imitating formica. She ordered a *cappuccino*. So many of her memories seemed bound up in this place, yet it had been no more than eight or nine weeks of a far-off summer that she had spent here. And most of the time she had been at the Villa Giulia, not in this town, in this café. Yet the seminal fact remained, that she had sat here with Susie, with Lucas, with Faustino; she had felt and suffered here, she had lived as she had not lived since. Raising the thick white cup to her mouth, Hannah felt the ghost of her younger self do the same, as though the two bodies, the corporeal and the insubstantial, had blended; for a moment, time missed a beat and woman and girl were one.

A car circled the square and went down one of the side streets, but not before the driver had waved anonymously from the window. Nancy Trevelyan? Probably, since Hannah had earlier telephoned her, arranged to meet her here in order to pick up the keys to the Villa Giulia. In a few seconds Nancy, unmistakably, appeared on foot. She was a dozen years older than Hannah, boyishly thin, wearing a leather jacket over a silk blouse and jeans. The years had been kind, Hannah thought, as Nancy approached, though her skin was thickened by too much sun.

'Nancy.'

'Hannah!'

The two women kissed, fluttered, settled. 'I won't say I'd have recognised you anywhere,' Nancy said, when she too had a coffee in front of her. 'But you've changed very little. Still that same mass of dark hair, and that anxious expression. Lew and I always used to say that you looked as if you were wondering whether someone was about to snatch away your ice-cream.'

Hannah laughed. It was weeks since she had last done that. 'I think that's more or less how I usually felt in those days.' For ice-cream, read love.

'So how are you? What brings you back here?' Nancy said briskly.

Hannah expelled a long breath. 'Where to begin?'

'Is it to do with all the business about Lucas?'

'Mostly.'

'I thought it might be, when Susie rang to say you were coming. There was so much left unsaid, so much unaccounted for. Everyone was shocked out of themselves.'

'That's always the way with sudden, violent death: it's impossible to make sense of it.'

'Is it? I don't know,' Nancy said. 'But even after all this time, it's inexplicable. The town still talks about it, especially since it's linked in our consciousness with all the hue and cry about Marina disappearing almost simultaneously – the Contessa's granddaughter, that is. I don't think you knew her, did you?'

'I know who she was.'

'Faustino – that was her husband – hired detectives to look the length and breadth of the country but they never found her. Interpol, too: never found a trace.'

'Tristan Carrick wondered if she'd joined a religious order,' Hannah said.

'You see Tristan, do you?' Nancy put her head on one side and gave her the same shrewd look as she had when Hannah and Tristan returned to the barbecue, twenty-five years ago.

'Not at all.' Hannah found herself flushing guiltily nonetheless. 'I hadn't seen him since then – not until a couple of weeks ago.'

'What brought the two of you together again?'

Hannah, looking across Nancy's shoulder to the tree-lined square beyond the plate-glass window, explained in as matter-of-fact terms as she could manage about Lucinda.

'Oh, my God,' Nancy said. She pressed Hannah's hand, shaking her head. 'God, how terrible. About ten years ago, my son Jerry was in a car crash back home in the States and for the longest time we didn't think he was going to make it. So I do know something of the horror of losing your child – though I was luckier than you've been.'

'Horror,' Hannah said, 'is what it is.' She did not elaborate on her theories about Lucinda's death, her conviction that her daughter had been murdered. She changed the subject. 'What are your children doing these days?'

Nancy told her: where they lived, what they did, the ages of the grandchildren. She said: 'And what exactly do you hope will happen, now you're back here?'

'I don't know,' said Hannah. 'But those were the most formative weeks of my life – if it's really possible to isolate a single experience like that. Lucas's death has had a direct influence on everything that's happened to me since. I want to try and sort out why.'

'It's lovely to see you again but do you think you're wise to try and stir up the past?' Nancy said. 'Shouldn't you just let things be?'

'I need to free myself from that shadow.' Hannah's expression was rueful. 'If it's possible.'

'You can't go home again,' Nancy said. 'Cliché of the century, I know, but what the hell.'

'I don't want to go home again,' said Hannah. 'I wasn't particularly happy at home. I don't want to rewrite history, either. I just want to . . . to understand the past so I can get on with the future.'

They smiled gently at each other. Hannah had expected encounters with the past to be somehow heightened, extraordinary, faintly rancid, but she and Nancy were no more than women who, a quarter of a century earlier, shared nothing and now, because of the changing years, had an infinite number of common experiences.

Nancy said: 'That's what Faustino Castelli is always saying: I just want to understand.'

'Is he still around?'

'He's often here at weekends. Especially since Marina was officially declared dead. Lew and I didn't really know him back then, that summer when Lucas . . . you know, when it all happened, but we've got to know him quite well since. Look, why don't you come to supper tomorrow? I'll invite him too. It'll be quite like old times.' Nancy looked wistful. 'We were all so happy back then.'

'Were we?'

'I certainly thought so. And now everyone's either dead or divorced or stricken with some terrible disease. Or has lost someone, the way you have.' Nancy bent across the table, closer to Hannah. 'I ought to say, my dear, that there are some here who blame you.'

'Me?'

'Yes.'

'*Me?* But what for? I didn't do anything.' Which, of course, was why things had turned out as they had. She had done nothing, so Lucas had died.

'You spent a lot of time with Faustino Castelli, for instance. Things are different now, but in those days, a young girl, alone with a married man: naturally they assumed the worst.'

'But we didn't—'

'I'm sure you didn't,' Nancy said. 'But this isn't a big place, even now, and attitudes haven't changed much. I don't think you realise just how upset people here were by everything that happened. The murder itself was bad enough, but when the victim was someone who'd been coming here every summer for years, someone everybody knew . . . There were police swarming all over the place for weeks afterwards, which didn't go down too well. Plus Faustino, married to the old Contessa's granddaughter, being flung into jail, not to mention the disappearance of Marina herself, whom the locals had known ever since she was born, and everyone putting two and two together and coming up with all sorts of bizarre theories about what really happened and making connections between Lucas's murder and Marina vanishing into the blue overnight. I mean, there'd been rumours going round about the two of them, especially among us ex-pats who were in a better position to guess what was going on—'

'But I had nothing to do with—'

'For some reason . . .' Nancy shrugged and clucked her tongue, '. . . however unfair it seems, you somehow were cast in the role of villainess, especially since you weren't around to defend yourself.'

'But the police made it absolutely clear that I was completely innocent of *any*thing,' Hannah said. Only she and, apparently – the thought was swift – Max Marsden knew that they were wrong.

'Anyone can be bought.'

'*What?* You're not suggesting that I bribed the police, are you?'

'Calm down, Hannah. Of course I'm not. I'm simply trying to prepare you for the fact that you might encounter a certain amount of hostility, once people realise who you are.'

'Hostility,' Hannah said faintly. It was something which had simply not occurred to her, though she could see now that she should have anticipated it.

'Don't worry about it.' Lightly, Nancy touched her arm. 'Let's change the subject. Tell me: did you form any conclusion as to why a terrific guy like Tristan has never married? It seems such a terrible waste that he should live alone in that beautiful house of his.'

'He told me he'd never met the right woman,' said Hannah, still assimilating what Nancy had said. Through her mind flashed a scene of pitch-soaked rags set alight on the end of staves, bucolic peasantry marching through the dark to storm the gates of the aristocracy, angry fists waving— 'He also said that if you get the woman you love, it's bound to be doomed.'

'Implying it was better to love hopelessly?'

'That's what it sounded like.'

'I wonder who the woman was in his case,' Nancy said thoughtfully.

'There has to be one, doesn't there?' said Hannah. 'I didn't feel I knew him well enough to ask.'

'You know Lew has a cousin who lives quite near him in Cornwall?'

'Jennifer,' Hannah said.

'That's right. Jen says Tristan's the despair of the local women. He takes them out, treats them like royalty, sleeps with some of them, I guess, but won't go further than that.' She rolled her eyes comically. 'Won't com*mit!*'

'And no rumour of a broken heart?' Hannah did not, she discovered, wish to know who Tristan slept with.

'None.'

'As you say,' Hannah said lightly, 'it's a waste.'

She had hoped that the Villa Giulia at least would have remained the same, but here too there was change. The huge, dusty arrangements of dried flowers had gone, there were smart new sofas in the drawing-room, some of the older furniture had been replaced, the kitchen had been completely modernised. Yet here too, as in the town, the spirit of the house was unaltered. Cobweb-grey mirrors in frames of crumbling gilt still lined the ballroom, so that as she walked across the parquet floor her reflection moved as though through mist, a ghost who left footprints in the dust. The beams in the drawing-room were recently stained, darker than formerly, but cobwebs still clung to the corners; the walls were the same dusky rose as she remembered; the room smelt still of woodsmoke from the hearth. Opening the shutters, she found the grey furred corpse of a moth lying on the window-sill, and remembered with sharp clarity how the moths had danced above the candle flames, how, that summer, she too had briefly danced.

The house was damp and cold. In the kitchen Hannah found the controls for the central heating and turned them on. There was bed linen in the airing cupboard, as Susie had said; she hung sheets and pillowcases over the radiators to air. There was little sign of recent habitation, or, indeed, of Susie herself. She had said on the telephone that she had not been to the Villa Giulia since her parents died: that was at least five years ago. In the drawing-room Hannah opened the shutters and stepped out on to the terrace. From here, none of the new development in the town was visible, only the bell-tower on the hill and the tumbling birds to one side, the valley to the other.

When the telephone rang she was startled. It took her a moment to remember where the apparatus was kept. She picked it up. The old phone had been replaced with an up-to-the-minute cordless model. She picked it up. '*Pronto?*'

'Hannah?'

'*Sì.*'

'It's Tristan. Tristan Carrick.'

'Hello,' Hannah said, surprised. 'How did you—'

'Nancy rang me, full of transatlantic energy. You know how she is.'

'Yes.'

'You'd never guess she hasn't lived in her home country for thirty years or more. She said you looked marvellous. I agreed.'

Hannah cleared her throat. 'Why did she call you? Why are you ringing me?'

'She suggested I came over.'

'What for?'

'She's worried about you alone at the Villa. Hannah shouldn't be there alone, she kept saying. Times have changed.'

'I don't suppose you tried to argue her out of that one.'

'You're right.' Tristan laughed. 'But seriously. She said that you might encounter some hostility if you start stirring things up.'

Once, Hannah might have felt grateful that others were concerned about her. Now she recognised that her gratitude was because she saw concern as a facsimile of love. 'Why?' she said harshly.

'Hannah, hasn't it occurred to you that if the only two suspects the police had – me and Dr Castelli – were innocent, then a murderer is still out there somewhere? Maybe even living locally. If you go blundering in, spoiling things for him, he might think it would be easier to get rid of you.'

'That's pretty far-fetched.'

'I don't think so.' Tristan's voice changed. 'How are you, Hannah? Really.'

'Fine, thank you.'

'It was so good to see you. So good . . .'

'And to see you,' Hannah said, slightly awkward.

'Would you like me to do as Nancy suggests? Come over?'

Hannah opened her mouth and then closed it, trying to think of a polite way to say that she would not. There did not seem to be one. 'No,' she said. Only a short while ago, she would not have been able to utter a word so uncompromisingly unveneered by courtesy.

'I see.' Tristan was clearly surprised by her bluntness but she was not going to explain, nor to murmur something apologetic. She had apologised all her life. 'If I came anyway, would you object?'

'I have no jurisdiction over your movements, Tristan,' she said coldly. 'If you want to come, I can't stop you.'

'Right. Meanwhile, will you promise to call me, if you need anything? If you think of any way in which I can help you?'

'If I do, I will.'

Neither of them spoke. Tristan said after a while: 'Well . . . I only wanted to—'

'Tristan.'

'Yes?'

'Thank you,' Hannah said with difficulty, softening her tone. 'I appreciate your call. I really do.'

'I might ring again, one of these days. Just to see that you're all right.'

'I look forward to talking to you then.'

When she had put down the receiver, she stood for a moment, leaning against the wall. How did she feel about his call? Pleased? Yes, she was pleased that he was concerned enough to bother. At the same time, she was relieved that he had not argued about coming out to the Villa. If he arrived to stay with the Trevelyans – and it had been impossible to gauge from his voice whether he planned to or not – it need not impinge on her. She needed to be alone here if she was to come to terms with what had happened, if she was to snatch a new life out of the old before it was all too late.

It was ironic that the last night she had spent here in the Villa Giulia had been in Tristan's company.

Walking out on to the terrace, she surveyed the garden. Twenty-five years had altered its look but not its essential shape. Most of the trees had grown; one or two had disappeared. There was evidence of some horticultural hand: though the shrubbery all along the drive was thicker, the bushes on either side of the grassed patch in front of the house had been pruned and there were new plantings here and there.

Hannah wondered if the unkemptness of the grounds had been

maintained as Susie's mother had liked it; conscious of a fear that it would somehow have been tamed, she decided she would wait until tomorrow to find out.

Later she drove up to the town to stock up on basic supplies. If there was any recognition of her return, she saw no signs of it in the faces at the check-out in the tiny supermarket, no indication of hostility in the café where she drank another *cappuccino* and watched the sun go down. But then she wore the most effective disguise of them all: that of middle-age. She knew that no one noticed women past their forties, too often they were unrevered, lacking both the wisdom of age and the hope of youth, deemed to be past all excitement. Lines from Larkin flashed into her head as she watched the sun go down: '*All that's left to happen is deaths (my own included).*' She smiled wryly. How wrong it was to believe all passion was spent by forty-five. In her own small circle of friends, all roughly the same age as herself, she knew of three tempestuous love affairs, two with men years younger, one with another woman. Careers were suddenly flowering, new roads being followed, risks taken which would have been unthinkable at twenty. Labelled past-their-prime, they were finding their lives were bolstered by a continuous undercurrent of excitement. Even she, despite her attempts to lead a life of anonymity and dullness, had, the past eighteen months, lost a husband, gained a lover, started her own business.

Back at the Villa Giulia, she fixed herself a rudimentary meal, sitting at the kitchen table. Scraps of memory returned: she remembered the hot, dawdling days, peaches in a bowl, damp white cheeses on a blue saucer from which she cut daily slivers, the precise look and feel – the firm roundness, the red plumpness – of fresh-picked tomatoes. She recalled, too, something of the strange dislocations she had suffered, brought on, no doubt, by semi-starvation.

She made up a bed for herself in the bedroom she had occupied then. The same bed, the same chest against the wall, the same chair to one side of the windows. Although it was chilly, she opened them and stepped out on to the balcony. Far away, the lights of a city faintly lit a horizon made undulating by hills. Stars blazed in a cold winter sky. Even as she watched, one of the diamond chips detached itself from its place and whizzed across the heavens in a line of fire, just as she remembered happening years ago. The night-air was fresh and smelt of damp earth.

In the house the telephone started again. Susie, she thought, or Nancy, ringing to see that I'm all right – whatever that means.

But it was neither. Instead, a voice at the other end said, whisperingly, chillingly: 'Listen closely, Anna,' and she heard the music again, the hoarse sound of the singer, *Every step you take, I'll be watching you*. It took two or three bars before she had taken in what she was hearing, before she was banging the receiver down on to its cradle, whirling away from the telephone, heart mad against her ribs. She ran round the house, switching off lights, closing the shutters, barring herself in, keeping out whatever lurked in the alien dark outside, but, as she sat sweating in the darkness, the words she already knew continued to echo in her head: *Every word you say, every game you play, I'll be watching you.*

Who was it? The question haunted her, terrified her. How did they know she was here? What did they want of her?

Who?

And *why*?

The morning was damp. When she threw back the shutters, mist shreds were clinging to leaves and lurking among the laurel bushes. Despite the implicit menace of that androgynous voice she had slept well.

Down in the big kitchen she brewed coffee and drank it black, the bitter taste invigorating. The heat of her bathwater steamed up the glass so that, when she removed her dressing-gown, there was no reflection in the mirrors which ran round the edge of the bath nor in the full-length cheval-glass in a corner. Lying in the tub, she was aware of inner confusion about which Hannah was which: the one she now was or the one she had been. She knew, of course, that she was Hannah-nearly-fifty, soft-bellied, double-chinned, slowing down, with more of her life behind her than in front.

Yet, at the same time, she felt no different from Hannah-twenty-two, for sensations do not change: twenty-two or nearly-fifty, hot water on the skin is just as sensuous now as it was then, the smell of coffee still as promising, hills or music or the sight of a flying bird still moves the soul. Such things continue, timeless; the body grows old, but not the heart. If she did not look down at herself, at the physical sags and swells which the years had brought, she would not *feel* how many years had passed, even though she *knew*.

Dressed, she was glad to see that the sun had taken over the day. Steam was already rising from the wet grass, and though waterdrops still clung to the ends of the laurel leaves, they were otherwise dry, glossy in the bright light.

She sat down at the table with a mug of coffee. Before leaving England, already late for her train, she had grabbed letters from the doormat and stuffed them into a side pocket of her bag. Now, she looked at them. Bills. A couple of letters from friends who had only just heard about Lucinda. A blue airmail form from Adam, saying he was fine, working hard, enjoying the States, wished he was back with her, hoped she was all right.

Another letter was from Mrs Morgan, Tom's mother, owner of the cottage in the Dales. Slowly, Hannah opened it. A short note informed her that if it was of any help at all, here was a copy of the itemised phone bill from the cottage. One was a call which must have been made while Lucinda was there, the number might be of use. She ended with the hope that Hannah was managing, that she understood how things were.

The number was a London one. Unfamiliar to Hannah. The call had lasted ten minutes and thirty-five seconds. She got up and went inside the house. After she had dialled, there were nearly a dozen rings before a sleepy voice answered.

'Hi.'

'Uh—' Hannah had not fully prepared for this. 'Who is that speaking, please?'

'This is Jim Hoffman.'

The voice was young, the accent definitely transatlantic. Might this be the missing boyfriend? 'I'm wondering if – does the name Lucinda Barlow mean anything to you?'

'Lucinda Bar—? No, ma'am, I can't say it does.'

'Are you sure?' Someone at this number had held a conversation with Lucinda for over ten minutes. Unless – could it be? – the person responsible for Lucinda's death had made the call.

'I don't recall anyone of that name,' Jim Hoffman said. 'Unless – hey! you don't mean Lucy, do you?'

'Possibly.' Hannah's pulse quickened. 'We often called her that.'

'You mean, Lucy, Dan's girl?'

'I don't know,' Hannah said. 'Do I? If so, I'm her mother.'

'Is that right?' Hoffman breathed into the phone then said: 'Just one moment, ma'am.' She heard the rattle of the receiver being placed on some hard surface and then, distantly, an excited shout: 'Hey, guys, someone! Get your asses down here, I think we may have a lead here on Dan.'

The words were chilling. A lead . . . what did he mean? Was Dan the mysterious boyfriend in whom nobody believed? She waited while a series of heavy footsteps ran down invisible stairs. She could hear a murmur of voices then Hoffman spoke again. 'Oh, ma'am?'

'Yes,' Hannah said. 'Yes.'

'You're asking about Lucy, right?' Behind Hoffman, someone said; 'Barlow, her name's Barlow.'

'Yes,' Hannah said again. 'My daughter.'

'See, what happened was, Dan – that's Dan Pacino, a friend of ours – went off to see his girl—'

'Lucy?'

'Yeah, right. And we haven't seen hide nor hair of him since. That was – what, guys? – three, maybe four weeks ago.'

'Oh, God,' Hannah said, on the verge of weeping.

'Ma'am?'

She told them what had happened to Lucinda, listened to the outbreak of shocked horror, the questions, the wondering and, finally, the silence.

'I shall have to inform the police,' she said. 'Give them your number.'

Someone took the phone from Hoffman. 'Miz Barlow? My name's Pete Schecter. Lucy – your daughter, I mean, and I'm just so sorry to hear what's happened – she called Dan from some place she was staying, out in the country, and the next day he set off in his car to see her. We've been wondering what could have happened to him because he hasn't been in touch since. We were thinking maybe we should go to the police ourselves, but we figured he might have gone haring off on some story – he's freelancing right now – and just hadn't had a chance to get in touch. But from what you're saying . . . maybe something's happened to him, too.'

'Please,' Hannah said. 'Tell me: he couldn't have . . . could he?'

'Couldn't have – uh – killed her?' Pete said. 'Absolutely not. Dan just isn't that kind of a guy. He's real gentle, real cool. I can't imagine him ever losing his temper, nothing like that. I mean, really *not*.'

One of his friends said, in the background: 'Oh Jesus: I really hope this isn't going to be a bad scene.'

But it was. Hannah knew already that whatever had happened, it was going to be bad.

Once she had put down the receiver on the shocked young Americans in London, she called Inspector Mayfield and passed on their telephone number and the address they had given her.

'We'll look into it,' he said. 'We'll keep in touch.' His voice was heavy. 'I'll keep in touch,' he repeated, and replaced the telephone.

The house seemed to lack air. Although the sky was overcast, Hannah had to get outside. She pulled open the kitchen door and felt a cold breeze in her hair.

She stepped across the damp patch of grass and pushed between the shrubs, suddenly overwhelmed by memory. '*I thought you were a naiad,*' he had said. '*There are wreaths of laurel crowning your hair,*' and so real did it seem that she put up her hand to her hair before remembering that it had all been long, long ago and Lucas had been dead for years.

The tunnels through the undergrowth were still there; she walked beneath them, trying not to think of a young American who had disappeared. That summer, the sun had burned through the leaves, spilling drops of heat which scorched the skin, but today, only a certain quality of the green-filtered light betrayed the fact that the sun was out. She followed familiar paths, renewed acquaintance with the stone flights of stairs, the niches and grots, the huge arching ferns, the verdigrised pots and empty marble basins. Melancholy hung over the garden; if she listened she could hear the sound of water dripping on to leaf and the subdued rustle of rain-soaked greenery.

She reached the ruined gazebo. In the years which had passed, the area she had once cleared had long been covered up again. Yet, she could clearly see where her efforts had stopped. Searching around, she found a fallen branch and for reasons she could not define, she began scraping at the mat of leaves and earth. An eye, purple grapes, a fragment of robe. Over there was the corner where the brass ring was let into the ground; on impulse she scraped at it some more, uncovering the beginnings of an acanthine border and the edge of the ring itself. She squatted back on her heels and for a while, allowed the past to drift over her. Where had the Hannah she had been gone to? Last time she was here, fifty was an impossible, unimaginable age. Now, twenty-three seemed equally incomprehensible. Hannah seldom thought of her childhood or the years leading up to twenty-two, twenty-three; it was as though her entire life up to that point had been subsumed, telescoped into those few Italian weeks.

Lucinda would have been twenty-one on her next birthday.

Dodging beneath dripping evergreens she came to the slope which led down to the boundary fence. From here, she could just see the top of one of the marble pillars, but she found herself reluctant, even unable, to take the steps which would lead her to the bamboo grove and, beyond it, the pool. It was something which would have to wait until later.

Nancy's house seemed to have remained exactly the same. Hannah sat at the black oak table in the dining-room with a sense of familiarity, almost of coming home. Was it because the Trevelyans had children that they had kept everything as it was? There were two other ex-pat couples, pleasant-seeming, unremarkable. She was surprised at how glad she was to see Lew again, a grizzled Lew, still wearing jeans and a striped dress shirt but filling them both out now, his fair hair transmuted to grey curls. Even after so long, she still felt as though she was on the outside, as Nancy and Lew chattered about people she had never known, events she had not shared.

Beside her sat Faustino.

Not the Faustino she remembered but a grey-haired, distinguished man with almost theatrical good looks. Grief and time had changed his face, imbuing it, in repose, with a melancholy, untouchable sadness. As if aware of this, his face was seldom still, his expression constantly changing, even when listening to others.

'Anna,' he had said when she appeared in the Trevelyans' living-room. 'My Anna.' He had raised her hand to his lips, his dark eyes not leaving hers, and Hannah had felt a tremor in the pit of her stomach, like a sigh of regret for what had been begun all those years ago, and never finished.

'*Han*nah,' she said, laughing, shaking her head, and he had swept her into his arms, kissing her boisterously on both cheeks while the Trevelyans looked on with approving smiles.

'So why have you returned?' he asked her now, leaning towards her so that his face almost brushed her own. 'Is it because of—?' He left the sentence unfinished, arching his eyebrows in enquiry, and she nodded.

So did he. 'Because of Lucas Wyndham, yes. This is what I guessed, Ann— *Han*nah. When Nancy told me you had come back, I knew there was a reason, that this was not merely *à la recherche du temps perdu*.'

'I want to talk to you about it,' Hannah said quietly. 'But not here. Not with all these people.'

'Good.' Faustino smiled and she saw him again as she had seen him last, pastel-pink shirt half-in, half-out of his pale chinos, a bruise on his cheek, his mouth swollen, and blood still running from his hairline down inside his collar. He had turned and spoken to her: she could see his lips moving but, trapped behind a glass wall of terror, she had not taken in what he said. Blood, so much of it, black in the moonlight by the pool, the water black, and the echo of screams in her ears.

Though she had relived the moment a thousand times, she had never been able to recall his words. He had been angry, that much she knew. Not merely angry, but burning with rage and horror. His fists had been clenched, the knuckles bloody. His eyes had hated her. She had stood in the ballroom, the lights from the house throwing deep shadows under his eyes; she had watched him stumble away from her between the two escorting policemen, turning his head over his shoulder to shout one last thing at her, but by then she was already falling, fainting on to the dusty ballroom floor and she could only remember his face and the sound of bitter words.

'You could come to the Villa Giulia,' she said.

'No. I think we should meet on . . . neutral ground,' he said, and she guessed that he too remembered that night and her silhouette against the open windows of the drawing-room and the things he had flung at her as he was led away. And perhaps another night, when his hand had touched her breast under thin cotton and the two of them, responsible to others, had let something go.

'Tomorrow, for lunch?' she said.

'I have commitments. Why do you not have dinner with me in the evening? I shall come for you early, since we shall have much to talk about.'

Dinner could be perilous. It led on into the night. She wanted to avoid any repetition of those summer evenings long ago, when tension had hummed between them like a vibrating violin string, but it seemed she had no choice.

'All right,' she said, keeping her voice non-committal. 'Now tell me, what have you been doing since we last met?'

He shrugged, disappointed at her apparent lack of response. 'Making money,' he said. 'For the most part, simply making more money. As one approaches the end of a life, it is not a lot to have achieved, is it?'

'That depends on what you want.'

'I have everything I ever wanted,' he said. 'Everything except—' He broke off. For a moment his mobile face was still, and sad.

'I thought you were a doctor.'

He laughed without mirth. 'A psychiatrist – yes, I was. But apart from an occasional consultation, I gave up all that after—' He did not finish the sentence. 'I was not in a fit enough state of mental health myself to dare try to help others.' He smoothed his napkin on his knee. 'And you, Hannah. What have you done with these twenty-five years since we were parted?' He made it sound as though they had been torn from each other's grasp by a malevolent fate.

Keeping it light, Hannah spoke of her life, making it sound rich, fuller than it had been. Her husband, her children, the year in northern California, the year in Australia, the year in Riyadh. She joked about getting older as though she found it merely comic, while his dark eyes watched her and his face mirrored her expressions. Next time they met, she would tell him more fully how it had been; for the moment, it was easier simply to skim across the surface of the years.

'. . . about the new people at the Villa Diana, Hannah?' Nancy was saying.

'What?' Hannah was glad of the excuse to turn away from Faustino. 'The Villa Diana.'

'What about it?'

'I wondered if Susie had told you anything about the new people.'

'I don't know what you mean.'

'It's let most years,' explained Nancy. 'Through some agency. I was just saying I wonder who the new tenants will be.'

'Who owns it?'

'It's Susie who organises the lettings; I've always assumed it belongs to her,' Lew Trevelyan said. 'Lucas didn't have any children. I think everything went to Susie when old Lady whatever she was called – Lucas's mother – died. Next of kin or something.'

It was something else Hannah had not known. 'What happened to the woman who was working for Lucas that summer?' she said.

Lew frowned. 'That housekeeper? Very mysterious, wasn't she? Nobody ever saw her.'

'We decided she must be one of Lucas's discarded mistresses,' Nancy said cheerfully. 'He had hundreds of them.'

'Screwed his brains out the entire summer,' said one of the other men.

'All year round, way I heard it,' said the other.

'The beast with two backs,' said Lew, throwing back his head to laugh aloud. 'Lucky bastard.'

Hannah smiled. She had heard him use the elaborate phrase before, years earlier, at other long meals when they sat outside under vine arbours and the wine glasses were filled again and again.

'He certainly kept the housekeeper very quiet,' Nancy said, frowning at her husband.

Hannah felt Faustino tense beside her. At the same time, she realised that Nancy would never have spoken about the housekeeper in such terms if she had been aware of the relationship between Faustino's wife and Lucas. How strange that such a thing had been kept secret. Or perhaps not so strange. Marina's disappearance was only linked in people's minds with Lucas's death because of the timing; perhaps no one except Faustino himself – and Hannah – knew of any connection. But that could not be right, could it? Tristan knew. Or did he? Trying to recall their conversation, Hannah realised that he had never suggested that the liaison between Marina and Lucas had continued after the girl's marriage. He had not even suggested there *was* a liaison. Only that Lucas had fallen in love.

'Where did she go?' she asked. 'The housekeeper, I mean.'

Nancy looked at her husband. 'You looked into all that, didn't you, honey?'

'Yeah. We were kind of worried about the place being left empty. There was a lot of valuable antiques and pictures and so forth in the Villa Diana, but every time I called round, the place seemed to be deserted – although a couple of times, I swear that housekeeper was at home.'

'You saw her once, didn't you?' said Nancy.

'That's right. I just happened to look up and caught her peering at me from an upper window, like the first Mrs Rochester or something, though she kept well back from the window. Anyhow, I got in touch with the lawyers handling Lucas's affairs – can't remember where I got their name from—'

'Susie,' murmured Nancy.

'That's right, from Susie. Anyway, they asked the housekeeper lady to stay on, paid her something, and then about three months later, she said she was getting married to some Yank who was renting a place near by, and going back to the States with him.'

'She had a child, didn't she?' Hannah said. Over the years, she had often remembered that sexless, angelic face.

'Did she?'

'You must remember. It was at that picnic, the last summer picnic you organised. By the lake. I presume she brought it. Lucas was there – he must have brought them both.'

Nancy shrugged. 'Doesn't ring any bells.' She passed a wooden bowl of salad. 'It's so long ago. Gaahd, we were young then, Lew, remember? The kids were little. That was the summer you started on the screenplay for *Red Knight* – remember?'

'Sure do.' Lew's laughter rumbled across the table. 'I was still an idealist in those days. Used to turn down work on ethical grounds. What a dope.'

Hannah caught herself staring at him. Could he be the pseudonymous author of *Hurled by Dreams*? He had certainly been on the spot that summer. 'I thought you wrote science fiction,' she said.

'I do, mainly. But I'm easy: I'll write anything. I'm your original literary slut. Wrote the first time for love, the second time because somebody asked me to, since then I only do it for money.'

'Ever written a straight novel?' Hannah tried to sound as if the question was lightly posed but felt that she had loaded it with significance. If he were the author of *Hurled by Dreams* it would mean – would it not? – that he had somehow known of the relationship between Lucas and herself. And if *he* had known, who else had?

'Not yet,' Lew said.

'What?' She was not relating to what he said.

'His Great American Novel is still in the bottom drawer of his file cabinet,' explained Nancy.

'And likely to remain there,' said Lew, sounding as though it were nothing more than the truth. 'Sci-fi's one thing; mainstream literature quite another.'

'What about that woman novelist,' Hannah said. 'The one with the red face. Is she still writing?'

'She means Betsy Spiewak,' Nancy said.

'Oh sure,' Lew said. 'Still churning out those Harlequin romances. Makes a fortune from them, I understand.' He looked across at his wife. 'Maybe I'm in the wrong field, hon.'

Nancy laughed.

'But she's never written anything bigger?' Hannah persisted. 'Under another name, maybe?'

They all looked at each other. 'Not as far as I know,' Lew said. 'And she's such an old gossip, we *would* know. She never keeps anything to herself.'

Nancy reverted to the Villa Diana. 'They've really had some bad experiences, letting the place.' She spoke to the female half of one of the other couples. 'Do you remember, Karen, that German guy who showed up with a harem of young girls?'

Karen, another American, looked across the table at Hannah and giggled. 'He can't have been a day under seventy,' she said, 'and there were at least *four* of these bimbettes.'

'Not one of them over the age of consent, I swear,' sighed her husband reminiscently.

'Jeez,' said Lew. 'I remember it well. They were *gorgeous*. Had to change my shirt every time I saw them.'

'Hal took to wearing a baby's bib,' said the other wife.

'Yeah,' Hal said. 'Couldn't stop drooling.'

'I remember it, too,' said Faustino. 'The people in the village were very excited: they thought they were film-stars.'

'Hamburg professionals,' Nancy said crisply, 'and I don't mean actresses.'

Karen nodded. 'But we have had someone from Hollywood, haven't we?'

'Yeah. Last September.' Lew looked round at his guests. 'Guy named Dave Schellenburg – ever heard of him? – rented the place for six months, came over to write a screenplay with me. And Michael Douglas and his wife stopped by on their way to stay with friends in Greece.'

'This too I remember,' said Faustino. 'It was almost as good as a visit from the Pope. My grandmother-in-law, the old Contessa, was not pleased. She said the people of the town were making idiots of themselves over a man who took his clothes off in public.'

'Yo, baby!' said Hal.

'It was the Schellenburgs who had that weirdo baby-sitter, wasn't it?' his wife said.

'That's right.' Lew looked at Hannah, his eyes shining with laughter. 'Poor old Dave always seems to get himself into these really strange situations.'

'What happened?' Hannah asked.

'They hired this girl two or three months after they got here, some college kid from the States who turned up out of the blue and asked for a job. She was supposed to help out with the kids, keep them out of the way while Dave and I worked on the script and Barbara soaked up the local culture—'

'Not to mention a piece or two of the local action,' Nancy put in.

'Anyway—' Lew paused. 'Did you ever go inside the Villa Diana?'

Hannah began to blush. 'No,' she said, too quickly, too emphatically.

'Well, upstairs, along that gallery place, there's this absolutely fantastic doll's house—'

'You can't call it a doll's house,' protested Nancy, 'it's a work of art, a miniature of the Villa itself, complete in every detail, right down to the saucepans in the kitchen and the sponges in the bathroom. One of Diana Wyndham's husbands commissioned it as a wedding anniversary present.'

'Might as well have flushed his money down the drain,' commented Karen's husband. 'She divorced him a couple of years later.'

'He hired craftsmen from all over the region to make the furniture,' said Nancy.

'What did this girl do to it?' asked Hannah. She remembered the doll's house well.

'Barbara came back one day from . . . whatever she was doing, and found that one of the little rooms had been completely destroyed.

255

Every stick of furniture smashed, the curtains ripped down, the tiny little paintings on the wall all shredded.'

'Heavens.'

'Odd, wasn't it?' said Lew.

'Barbara naturally assumed it was one of her kids who'd done it,' Nancy said. 'But it turns out it was the girl – this au pair or whatever they called her.'

'I have not heard this extraordinary story before,' said Faustino. 'Why should she do such a thing?'

'Nobody quite knows. Naturally they got rid of her – Dave said she was kind of strange, right from the word go, always flying off the handle or sitting about looking homicidal – and Barbara set about trying to find people to put it right. Luckily there was a record of everything in the little house, and who'd made it. She was able to duplicate most of it.'

'At vast expense,' Nancy said.

'Susie was very understanding, I must say. Surprisingly so, really.'

'The girl sounds quite mad,' said Hannah.

'She must have been, to do such a thing. Can you imagine, in someone else's house, for no reason that anyone could see?'

'Which room did she destroy?' Hannah asked idly.

'The main bedroom,' Nancy said. 'At the top of the stairs. It was really weird.'

Lucas's room.

Hannah recalls every detail of it. The beautiful treacle-coloured wardrobe of burr-maple banded in ebony, the matching chests-of-drawers, and headboard, the two bedside pieces, elegant sets of four narrow drawers with ebony handles. There were a couple of elaborate Venetian mirrors, and paintings: a man holding a water-pot on his shoulder, a curious St George and the Dragon, a quiet Madonna.

How many other women had Lucas possessed on those white sheets? Heat fills her as she remembers the two of them, the things he did to her, the things he asked her to do to him. She presses her hot cheeks between her hands and catches Nancy's eye as she does so. The older woman watches with a combination of compassion and satisfaction: for once Hannah is glad to be at the age when sudden flushes can be accounted for.

But why, she asks herself, should this unknown girl have decided one afternoon systematically to remove the furniture from the miniature house, from that particular room, and smash it? What motivation could she possibly have? Hannah remembers how she would sometimes find pieces of furniture taken from that same house, years and years ago, and know that it was the child who set them there, on the polished side flaps, that the child carefully replaced them in the miniature rooms when danger – when Hannah – had gone.

*　　*　　*

Faustino insisted on driving behind her car to the Villa Giulia, just as he used to. 'I really can take care of myself,' she had said, laughing.

'You shouldn't have to,' he told her. 'Besides, a beautiful woman like you is not safe on her own.'

'Rubbish.' She had started to protest more vehemently, but then remembered Nancy's words. If there really was a feeling among the people of the little town that she was somehow involved in what had happened to Lucas, then the more she was seen with Faustino, the more she would allay their fears.

'And we shall meet the day after tomorrow,' he said. He held her hand against his heart. 'I am already impatient, Anna.'

'Me too,' she said, but knew that her impatience was based on something quite other than his.

She cannot sleep. For a while she dozes, only to start awake, sweating, consumed by a huge and throbbing terror. Unlocated, intangible, it hovers just beyond her reach, so that she cannot snatch it from the darkness and analyse it into manageability. Why does she remember, suddenly, the room below the kitchen – wine cellar? game larder? ice store? – and shudder at the thought of the woven cobwebs, the twisting skeins above, below, around her, silently enmeshing her in a lattice of conspiracy until she can no longer move? She had stood there, hiding from the heat, and imagined herself captured, cocooned, struggling in vain against the steely delicate strands.

THE DIARY

. . . The reviews. There was one thing I hadn't anticipated: they all went on about the character called Anna. So rounded, so vulnerable, how could Max Marsden, a man, have burrowed so vividly, so wholly, under the skin of a woman? Lots of stuff like that. I wanted to scream at them.

Assholes.

Couldn't they see that Anna was not the main character, even though so much of the action is mediated through her? Couldn't they see that it is the child who matters? That it's the child's story we are supposed to experience?

Anna.

Her again. I tore them up, every one. Every single review. Those who can, do. Those who can't, criticise, get hold of the wrong end of the stick, stupid, stupid assholes.

Spoke to F. It was about two thirty in the morning. He said: 'What's happened? Why are you ringing at this hour?'

'Anna,' I said.

'What?'

I explained.

He said the name meant nothing at all to him, how could it? Find her, I said. I could hear myself whining.

'You'd have to go back to the beginning,' he said. 'Back where it all started.'

'On my own?' I said. Shocked.

'Why not?'

I couldn't explain about the Dr. Just as I've concealed F from the Dr, so I've kept the Dr from F. Anxiety was churning my stomach. Alone – could I do it? I said: 'Sure. Back to the beginning. Great idea.'

'When you've set it up, I'll give you a couple of names,' he said. 'People who live there. They might be able to help you.'

How does he know? He wasn't there himself, was he?

. . . I told O I might go travelling. He wanted to know why, his voice sharp and suspicious, like a wasp's voice would be if wasps could talk. Wanted to know where to.

Said Italy might be good. I could get some kind of job, maybe. He didn't like it, I could tell. Asked how I'd cope without the Dr. I said I thought I'd be OK. Said I'd gained confidence, got things under control.

He said what about what happened three weeks ago?

I was beginning to get angry. He asked what the Dr thought about me going off.

'The Dr's not God,' I shouted. I wanted to hit him, even though I love him. I had that tight feeling inside, as though my interior organs had been grabbed in a huge fist.

He told me to calm down. I think he's frightened of me sometimes. It's not good when the people you love are frightened of you. The more I felt this, the angrier I got. Of all people, why should O be scared? I'd never hurt him. Never. I think of him sometimes as my child, not M's.

'You can't stop me, anyway,' I said. I did some deep breathing, thought of the Dr and imagined his calm voice in my head.

'I'm not trying to stop you,' he said. 'I just want to be sure you can cope on your own.'

'Of course I can,' I told him.

'What sort of a job would you get?' I could see him trying to be kind. 'I mean, what can you do?'

I shrugged. 'I don't need to work,' I said.

Thing is, I haven't told O (or M, naturally) about the book, or the money I'm being paid for it. And don't want to, either. So far it's been quite easy to conceal it from him. Don't know why I'm anxious for him not to know, but I am.

'What are you going to live on, then?' he said.

It's a natural question, I suppose. 'I told you. I'll get a job. Wait tables, or serve up hamburgers and fries in a McDonald's,' I said.

He shook his head. He's so good-looking that sometimes it gives me a pain inside. A cutting pain, like a knife slicing through my memories. He reminds me of something I don't want to remember.

Does anyone think I'm good-looking?

T, for instance?

'Remember what happened last year?' O said. He gave this kind of sigh. It always pisses me off when he does that. I mean,

I really don't need this kind of shit. And anyway, I'm older than he is.

'Look,' I said, *and I really was trying to keep things reasonable.* 'It wasn't my fault. I already told you that. Told the man at the burger place, too. It was the customer's fault, not mine. Griping like that, holding up the line when all the other people wanted was to pick up the stuff they'd paid for and get out of there.'

'So, to speed things up, you try to flick this guy's face with a knife?' *O says, all sarcastic.*

'No,' I said. 'All I did was wave the bloody spatula at him. It's not my fault if some paranoid thinks I'm trying to take his eye out.'

'Well,' says O, *like he's my father or something,* 'that really speeded things up, didn't it? By the time the cops had come, I'll bet all the hamburgers were stone cold.' *He gave me that cold look he sometimes gets.*

'I didn't hurt the man,' I said.

Didn't add that I wanted to. Wonder what he'd have looked like with his cheek sliced off so his teeth showed through, his eye hanging out on a bloody string.

NOW

16

'Did I not tell you once, years ago,' Faustino said, 'that you were beautiful?'

'Was that before or after you criticised my clothes and my size and the way I rode a bicycle?' Hannah said tartly.

'Ah, Anna. *Han*nah. You are teasing me again. So much time has passed and still you are making fun of me.'

It was as if all the years between had never happened. 'It's so good to see you again,' she said warmly.

'For me, too, it is good.'

They sat smiling across the table at each other, unremarkable, middle-aged, seeing not themselves, but the people they once were, just as parents will look at their grown children and, superimposed on the newly-fledged adult, see the baby, the toddler, the adolescent now left behind. Time, Hannah thought, is so elastic, so accommodating.

Faustino's face was suddenly still. 'You have heard about my wife?' he said quietly.

'That she disappeared? Yes. I'm so sorry. Tristan Carrick – do you remember him? – told me.'

'I have spent years trying to find her,' Faustino said. In his voice she could hear the weariness of all the hopeless days. He spread his hands in a gesture of resignation and incomprehension. 'No one has ever found her – alive or dead.'

'And you have no idea why she went? Or where?'

Fleetingly, an expression which hovered close to uneasiness swept across his face. 'None at all. In the end it was necessary, for various reasons, to have her declared dead. I had to accept it, even though I could not – and still cannot – believe it.'

'She was very beautiful,' Hannah said.

'You met her?'

'No. But I knew what she looked like.'

Blood rushed into Hannah's face as the two of them simultaneously remembered the afternoon of the day on which Lucas died, and realised the circumstances under which Hannah must have gained this information. She had stood astride her bicycle in the breathless afternoon heat, telling this same man that Lucas had a lover, describing the colour of her hair, her jewels, her earrings, the huge yellow diamond on her hand, so that there could be no mistake. But how could she have known at the time that the beautiful woman in the golden dress was Faustino's own wife?

They spoke together.

'Why are you—'

'Did you—'

Faustino gestured at Hannah to continue.

'Did you . . . remarry?' she asked.

'After Marina, there was nobody I wanted. I have not been a hermit, of course. I am a man like any other, but I live alone.' His face reflected the shadow of long nights when he had lain awake, wondering whether Marina still lived, whether she suffered before she died, whether she was happy somewhere with another man, heedless of his pain.

Hannah nodded. She understood.

He leaned closer to her, his breath catching the candle flames and making them flicker. The hollows beneath his eyes were the colour of earth. 'But there is another thing which haunts me,' he said.

'Which is what?'

'The thought that I myself was responsible for her disappearance.'

Guilt was familiar territory. 'Why do you think that?'

'I was angry with her that night. Furious. I admit it now, though at the time I did not. She was leaving our house as I came in: she wore jewels I had given her, but she was going – it was obvious – to see her lover. I called her terrible names, I . . . I even hit her. She was frightened. She ran from the house. I only saw her again once.'

'A harsh punishment, Faustino, for raising your fist. It may not be pretty, but it's not the worst crime in the world.'

'That was not the first time. I was often angry with her. She tried so hard to be a good wife, but I could never forgive her for loving Lucas, rather than me, who was her husband. Even as we stood at the altar, I knew that however much I loved her, nothing I could ever do or say or be was going to change that.'

'Why did she marry you if she was in love with Lucas? Or, for that matter, why did you marry her?'

He laughed bitterly. 'In those days, Italian society was far more repressive than it is now. There was something almost oriental about the way the young obeyed their parents, let them choose their friends, professions, marriage partners. Looking back, I can see that I should never have agreed to marry Marina, in spite of the pressures her family put on us both.'

'Did you love her?'

'Everyone loved her. Everyone. I adored her. And yet I hurt her. Not just emotionally, but physically as well. I was so violent, Hannah . . . yet I am not a violent man. She was frightened of me. Sometimes she would hide and I would roar around the place until I had found her.

Looking back, it does not seem as if it was me – the Faustino I am – at all.'

'You can't blame yourself because your marriage failed. Young people don't have enough experience to take a wide view of life, or to weigh up the results of their actions.'

'I can blame myself for the way I treated her. The most degrading thing of all is that I got a feeling of satisfaction when my fists thudded into her body, when I saw the terror in her eyes. Sometimes it was as though I beat them both – her *and* her lover.' He drank wine, swallowing the contents of his glass as though hoping to wash away the words which had been in his throat. 'And all,' he said bitterly, 'for love. Ah, God, Hannah.' Again the mobile face ground to a halt. 'I have lived that last night over and over again: you and her, Wyndham, Carrick, my rage and its fearful consequences. What I would give to have those few hours back again.'

'What were you going to ask me just now?' Hannah said.

'What I asked before. Why have you come back? I know it is because of Wyndham, but what exactly do you hope to achieve by digging into this again?'

'Perhaps, like you, I'm trying to get back those few hours, and this time make sense of them.'

'You have set yourself an impossible task, my dear.'

Hannah put down her knife and fork. She stared at him, watching his face settle. She said: 'Faustino.'

'Yes?'

'Did you kill Lucas?'

Had he been expecting the question? Certainly he showed no surprise, nothing more than a muted anger. Tiny images of the candle flames flickered in his eyes. 'Would you believe me if I said I had?' he demanded brusquely.

She had thought he might ask whether she would believe him if he *denied* it. Posed this way round, her enquiry took on a new aspect. Would she believe him? Did she really think he had been the person responsible for the body at the edge of the pool, the yellow hair spread flowerlike on the water amid a widening circle of blood, the pulpy mess of the crushed head? Before she could draw her defensive curtain, his hand rushed into her mind – that bloodied hand – and she felt faint, overpowered by nausea, just as she had been—

'Hannah! Are you all right?' Faustino's voice was sharp, cutting across her sickening thoughts.

'Thank you, yes.' She put a hand across her mouth. 'Oh, God.'

'What is it?'

'Memories.' She shook her head. 'Perhaps it was not a good idea to come back.'

'You have not yet responded to my question,' he said. 'If I told you I *had* killed Wyndham, what would you say?'

'I don't know the answer to that. I would find it difficult to believe that you could callously beat another man to death, after God knows what kind of . . . On the other hand, you were there, you were around, you admit you were in a rage, you had . . . you had good cause to hate him, maybe to wish him dead.'

'All that you say is true.'

'Well?' She looked at his hands, at the long, olive-skinned fingers with the gold band of marriage still on his left hand. Could they have wielded the iron rod with which Lucas was murdered?

'Well what?'

'Did you, Faustino? Did you kill him?'

He shook his head, smiling slightly. 'Why should you believe me, whether I say yes or I say no?'

'After all these years, I just want the simple truth. I just want—'

'My dear,' he said gently. 'Truth is rarely simple. Which is why I ask whether you would believe me if I said I *had* killed Lucas Wyndham. Mine is, I think, a very much more important question than yours.'

'What you mean is that I have to work it out for myself.'

'Is it? Is that what I am saying?' He took her hands in his. 'When you have been through the trauma of losing someone much loved, as I did, such questions begin to seem almost irrelevant.'

'I have.'

'*You* have? Tell me.'

He listened without comment as she repeated what she had told Nancy about Lucinda. And suddenly, as his thumb absently caressed the back of her hand, she felt herself falling apart. 'Which is why,' she tried to finish, her voice wobbling as the huge grief poured from her heart, 'I can't believe I'm really here, eating, drinking wine, *living*—' Tears were spilling down her cheeks, '. . . that I'm alive, while she is dead. She's *dead*, Faustino. My child. My daughter. While I sit here, *enjoying* myself with you.' She tore her hands from his grasp. Around them other diners watched with open curiosity. 'What kind of person am I? What right have I to be happy when she can't be? Why is it me who's alive while she – she—' The images she could not escape came back to her: the wintry churchyard, the yews shaking in the bitter wind, the grey hills, the coffin. The coffin . . . by now, Lucy's body would be rotting, putrefying, the flesh turning to jelly, the eyes liquefying, the pretty face larded with maggots—

Her tears burned like fire. She reached towards him. 'Help me,' she said.

He shared her bed. Gently he undressed her and then himself, and she found that the infelicities of middle-age did not seem to matter, as though they had grown used to each other's bodies over a number of years. Under the cold sheets, he held her against his chest, not speaking, as she wrapped herself around him and cried, a stream of tears which had been waiting a long time for this release. Some of the time, he, too, wept.

It was scarcely dawn when she awoke to find him standing fully-dressed by the bed. 'I will go now,' he said quietly.

'No.' She reached out a hand. 'Faustino, stay with me.'

'It is better that I leave now,' he said. 'Sleep some more, Hannah.' His hand touched her hair. 'I will telephone you later.'

'Faustino—' She struggled upright to sit against the headboard, a sheet wrapped round her. The room was chilly; soon it would be lonely again. She wished, without desire, that he was still in her bed.

'If it is of any use to you,' he said gravely, 'I will tell you what happened. I fought with Wyndham, that night. It is another truth I denied. I knew she was with him. I went into the cellar of my house and found a tool we used for the outside watercocks – I don't know what it is called in English – and I went after them. They were in that little place – what do you call such a place? a folly? – and I burst in. They were drinking wine by candlelight – I cannot, even after so long, tell you how much it hurt me. I ran at them, I turned over the table with the wine and the fruit and candles. I hit him. She ran from me, into the darkness. He and I fought, down by the pool. I hit him with the – the iron bar which I still had in my hand. I hit him across the body many times – I could have killed him. I wanted to. But I did not. To take another life: it would have been against everything for which I stand, for which I have worked all my life. Instead I swung it at his legs. I think one of them must have smashed a bone, for he staggered backwards and collapsed among the bushes. I heard him fall on to something and give a sudden cry and I thought, the hell with him, I knew what I was getting when I married Marina. I searched for my wife but did not find her and so I went home. It was later when I came back. Much later.'

'There was a trap,' Hannah said. 'A metal thing with the most terrible jagged teeth. Lucas fell on to it and I think his hand was caught so that the only way he could escape—' She could not finish the sentence.

'I know. It is one of the reasons I no longer practise as a psychiatrist. I put it there.'

'You?' And now she remembered an afternoon when he had lifted her bicycle into the back of his car, and she had seen a curve of stainless steel, flat metal plates, and taken it to be nothing more than tools, the kind of thing men carry around with them.

'I think I was sometimes mad, in those days,' Faustino said. 'Mad with love, with jealousy.' He ran his hand over the lower half of his face. 'I put it there, outside that place where they met, in the hope that one of them—' Hannah did not need to be told who he meant, 'would be

271

caught in it. When I saw later what it had done to Lucas—' He broke off and stood silently looking down at her, before adding, 'You do not have to believe me, Hannah, but this is the truth. A less than simple truth, perhaps, but a truth none the less.'

She telephoned England. There was still no answer from the shop and she frowned, checking her watch. Zoe had obviously forgotten to switch on the answering machine before she left the night before, making it impossible to leave a message, but she should in any case be there by now. Hannah hoped that there had not been some domestic upheaval: the baby-sitting mother taken ill, or the little boy going through one of childhood's many crises.

Several times she dialled the number Zoe had given her, but on each occasion got only an unobtainable signal. Finally she called International Directory Enquiries, to check that she had the correct number.

'Name and street?' the operator asked.

She gave both.

'There's no one of that name,' the operator said, his strong Scottish accent making him almost incomprehensible.

'There is,' she said impatiently. 'She works for me.'

'Sorry, madam, but we have no record of anyone with that name living at that address.'

'What address *are* they living at, then?'

'We have no record of anyone of that name, madam.'

Telephone companies had done this to her before, denying the existence of people who had lived at a particular address for years, whose number she had dialled a hundred times, but temporarily forgotten. She tried to keep the frustration out of her voice. 'Could you please look again,' she said. 'The surname is Griffin.'

But there was, the operator repeated, no record of anyone of that name at that address.

'But there is an address?'

'Yes.'

'Can't you give me that number?'

'I'm afraid not, madam, not without a name.'

Dammit. Hannah banged down the receiver. There had to be an explanation. Did Zoe still use her maiden name at work? Lots of girls did, these days. If so, how was Hannah going to find out where she was? She rang *Carringtons* again; there was still no answer. In half an hour she would call Enquiries once more and hope she got a different operator.

In the kitchen she sat over a coffee, while around her the central heating pipes gushed and sobbed. Looking back, she wondered if half of the enchantment of those green-and-gold days had resulted from the fact that she had been truly alone, in a way she had never been before or since. As though it were a photograph, she saw herself refracted through greengage light, caught for ever half-turned in a doorway with the sun behind her and a wild tangle of garden glimpsed beyond. Alone.

She had walked the rooms of this house and not been afraid; she had basked like a salamander in the heat; solitary, she had flowered.

Pushing back from the table, she went to the drawing-room. With the shutters closed, it was dark; she switched on one of the lamps so that the room was full again of medieval colours. For a second, as though impressed on time, they were there once more, ghostly, caught in the web of the past which she had tried so hard to subdue: Helena leaning against Dorian, Mungo with Charlotte, Kim, Susie, Hannah.

Where were they now? If she sought them out, would their memories help her retrieve the past? No. None of them had been here that time-stopping night. Only Tristan and Faustino, Hannah and Lucas himself. Susie had not shown up until later, along with the police, the ambulance, the local newspaper. Only the vanished Marina and – surely? – someone else.

Was it the same person who had stood behind her at the lake on the night of the barbecue? The person who had watched without a sound as Tristan's friend, the wronged husband, stabbed Lucas with a knife?

Startlingly, the telephone shrilled. It was Susie.

'How long are you planning to stay at the Villa?' she said.

'I hadn't really thought.'

'I imagine you mostly want to be there alone.'

'Oh Susie—' As always, Hannah was moved by her friend's quick understanding.

'The thing is, I wonder if it would disturb you if I came up next weekend. Otherwise I'm afraid you'll just go back home and I'll miss you.'

'You don't think I'd go back to England without visiting you, do you?'

'Of course not, darling. But if I come up to you, it will kill several birds with a single stone. And quite apart from seeing you, I ought to cast an eye over the house – I'm thinking of letting it this summer.' She sighed theatrically. 'Ah me: the responsibilities of being rich.'

'You always wanted lots of money,' Hannah said.

After a moment Susie said, as if Hannah had not spoken: 'Also, I'm desperate to get away from the city. Even in winter, the pollution here . . . sometimes I swear I'm turning into a combustion engine myself. Smell like it, sound like it – *look* like it, on a bad day.'

'Ridiculous woman,' Hannah said, laughing.

'What I'll do is, since I've got something on on Friday night, I'll drive up on Saturday morning, yes? Be with you by lunchtime?'

'Sounds fine.' Hannah hesitated. 'Susie—'

'What?'

'Are you sure – I mean, will it be – can we *cope*, the two of us?'

'What with, for heaven's sake? If you mean cooking, we can eat out or just—'

'No. I mean being back here, together, where it all—'

There was a silence broken only by the faint blare down the line of car horns in the street outside Susie's flat. Then Susie said softly: 'Annie, dear. It was all a long time ago. Besides, it wasn't your fault – it wasn't really anybody's fault.'

'Except whoever killed him,' Hannah said.

'After all this time, we're never going to know who that was, are we?'

'There's this book,' Hannah blurted.

'What book?'

'It's written by some American called Max Marsden, though I don't know if that's really his name. It's uncanny, Sooz. It's all about what happened that summer, while you were gone, in the most incredibly accurate detail. More or less everything—'

Too late Hannah realised that if Susie read *Hurled by Dreams*, she would realise something which, despite Susie's bitter accusations at the time, Hannah had repeatedly denied: the fact that she and Lucas had slept together. It would not take the genius of an Einstein to realise who Anna and Ivo, the two main characters, were based on.

'You mean, about Lucas's death?' Susie asked.

'That's the only bit which isn't accurate.' Hannah did not enlarge on the chilling fictional denouement, the chase through the garden, Anna's hand being cut off before she is stabbed to death with a kitchen knife beside the pool.

'I'll look out for it,' said Susie.

'It's not published in Europe yet,' Hannah said.

'That's OK. I'm going to be in New York next month.' But Susie did not seem greatly interested and Hannah was glad to let it drop.

'So are you all right?' Susie said. 'As all right as can be expected, I mean?'

'Yes.' Hannah hesitated. 'Except—'

'What?'

'Nancy Trevelyan—'

'She's looking good, isn't she?'

'Yes. Nancy suggested that the people here could be hostile to me being here. She said they would resent all that business being stirred up again.'

Susie laughed derisively. 'They're going to march on the Villa like the peasant mobs storming the Bastille, is that it?'

As always, Hannah was moved at the way their two minds turned towards the same images. 'Sounds ridiculous, doesn't it?'

'Certainly does.'

'And you, Susie? Are you all right?'

A pause. 'Without Carlo, do you mean?'

'Yes. It's not very long since he died.'

'I know. Of course I miss him, but, because we didn't have children, in one way we led very separate lives: his business, my career at the university. In some ways, I'd got used to being on my own, and now he's no longer around, nothing much has changed.'

When they finished talking, Hannah stood for a moment with her hand on the receiver. How could she have been so tactless? As though she stood on one side of an abyss she heard Susie's young voice call from the past: *'All I want is lots of children and lots of money. And Lucas, of course.'* She had ended up with the least important of the three, for without the other two, the money meant nothing.

She rang Marcus, needing suddenly his strength and reassurance, but there was no answer and as she replaced the receiver, she reflected that she was here in order to face things on her own, that she must find her own strength, rather than rely on someone else's. She rang *Carringtons* again, but there was still no reply. Replacing the telephone receiver, she wondered what she ought to do. Probably nothing. Having entrusted the shop to Zoe, she should leave her to get on with things. Zoe had already proved herself to be almost shamingly efficient and she had Susie's number in Rome, if for any reason she needed to get in touch.

Briefly, she contemplated ringing Inspector Mayfield. But if he had anything new to tell her, he knew where she was.

Hannah can no longer avoid the pool. She walks the green tunnels again, footsteps quiet on the thick carpet of dead leaves. Every now and then she runs into spider's webs slung across the path and feels the thin silk on her face. There is a smell of wet earth and decay; the stone balustrades are thick with moss. Tiny fir cones lie embedded in the mulch; under her shoes they crunch like bones.

Stepping gingerly down steps covered with wet leaves and water-logged moss, she slips and almost falls, hands grasping at empty air. She wrenches her knee but, wistful for the suppleness of youth, manages to remain upright. At the foot of the slope, which she has reached by grabbing hold of branches as she inched her ungainly way down, she steps carefully over the boundary fence into what had once been Lucas's property. The dripping trees do not stir. She follows the pathway, down to the tangle of bamboo, which is taller than she remembers it, and wilder.

As she pushes past the demanding leaves, remembered terror makes her heart drum in her chest. God: how it comes back to her, the night, the screaming, the blood. And the heat, that almost tactile heat, obsessive, oppressive. The pool waits for her, just as it had the very first time she saw it, the surface opaque with waterweed. This time there are no dragon-flies, no half-open water-lilies. The marble columns are greened with winter damp and the slabs around the edge of the water are almost hidden by drifting leaves.

He was lying there, *there*, almost at the edge. A black trail of blood led back towards the crowding leaves. He had called her, his voice dying in his throat; she ran towards him, saw the blood, backed away, dizzy and nauseous. Her mouth had moved round his name but no sound emerged.

'Help me, Hannah,' he said. 'For God's sake, help me.'
But she did not.
'I need you,' he said, as she had always wanted him to.
But she had seen his hand.
She *could* not.

'*Beware*,' he had said. '*Beware, Hannah Carrington.*'
She stands alone, Hannah Carrington once more, a middle-aged woman confronting the unresolved past. She remembers the first time they met, his voice echoes in her mind again: '*If I were to pursue you, would you try to escape?*' and she thinks sadly, You *did* pursue me, Lucas, and I tried, yes, I tried so hard to escape you, but I have never done so, nor, I truly believe, ever will.

THE DIARY

. . . *rang F today.*

'Do you know what time it is?' he said.

I'd forgotten. I must watch it. Don't want to give him the impression that I'm some kind of screwball – even if I am! That's another thing I haven't told him, though maybe M has.

'Sorry,' I said. I hate saying sorry. But don't want him to ring M, which I know he sometimes does because I've heard her talking to him, and he just might do so if I don't keep myself and my impulses under control.

'What is it you want?' he said. He didn't sound what I'd call friendly.

'Anna,' I said.

'For heaven's sake,' he said.

'No,' I told him. 'I remembered some more. She was there. She was at a table under some leaves, with a lot of others, she had this cloud of black hair and sad eyes. She was there.'

'Where,' he said. 'What are you talking about?'

Stupid man. Stupid—

'At the beginning,' I said. 'That summer. Anna. I wrote about it, I sent you the Book.'

'I don't know what you're talking about,' he said.

I could tell he hadn't bothered to read the fucking thing. Probably hasn't even lifted the cover. 'She was there,' I say again, though I kind of sensed I'd lost my audience. 'You must be able to find her for me.'

'I'll see what I can do,' he said, and rang off without saying goodbye.

Uh-oh.

. . . *My mind is like the surface of a frozen pool. Not thawing, but cracking. A sense of the water underneath the ice.*

Last night I dreamed I was holding a serpent covered with blood. It writhed and rippled in my hand until I dropped it and it slithered away among the leaves. Doesn't take much Freudian analysis to work that out, I suppose. I mean, we all know what a snake symbolises, don't we?

The beast. I can hear the voice saying it, saying the beast with two backs, and laughing. Whose voice? Ivo's?

There was another woman. She wore a yellow dress. Her hands sparkled.

I've got to go back. I've got to straighten things out, see where memory and reality meet. Otherwise I might just as well slit my throat now, rather than go on living this half-life.

I want to be happy.

. . . F met me off the plane.

I'd imagined him to be different. Tall and handsome and, well, young.

He's old. Not actually ancient but certainly middle-aged. Rough grey hair, blue eyes like mine, a used sort of face.

Told me it was good to see me. I told him the same. Told me he thought I'd have more of an accent. Said, once a Brit, always a Brit. Clichés. Stilted words. Verbal mortar patching the holes in our relationship. He stayed with me until it was time for me to get on another plane. 'Will you be all right?' he said as we waited at the barrier.

I said I would.

He looked worried. 'Are you sure?'

I could feel myself getting angry. Of course I was fucking sure. Breathed: in . . . out, in . . . out. Control, control. I could feel that old wolfsuit.

'Why do you ask?' I said, sweet as treacle.

'It's just that, from what I've heard, you—'

'You what?'

'Have a slight problem relating to other people,' he said rapidly. 'To strangers.'

I couldn't hear him too well, his voice kept coming and going, and then there were all the people in the terminal, thousands and thousands of them milling around, their mouths opening and shutting and literally millions of words spewing out, filling the air so thickly with words – hellos and goodbyes and have a good vacation and don't forget to feed the cat, stuff like that – that I could hardly breathe.

'What?' I said. 'What?' and realised I must have spoken too loudly because people were turning round to look at us and F had his hand on my sleeve, which I absolutely hate.

'It's all right,' F said.

'A problem?' I said. 'You think I have a slight problem?'

He backed off, the way they always do. 'No, no,' he said.

'Who told you that, anyway?' I asked. Silly question, really. M, I suppose. Or O.

Didn't say anything. Just turned at the ticket desk and waved, caught him in the middle of a huge frown, biting his lip.

Stupid man. Of course I'll be all right.

. . . I'm here. I made it. Never thought I would. Never thought I'd get away from the Dr and O and M. 'How can I reach you?' O said, when I told him I was going.

'I'll be in touch,' I said, kind of airy, like, get out of my face, man. Like I was some hot shot executive talking to the man who takes out the garbage.

'What are you going to do?' he said.

'You gotta go with the flow,' I told him. I reached out to touch him on the shoulder – I, who never touch people – and he flinched away from me. He actually flinched, as though he thought I was going to stab him or break his neck or something.

'I don't think you should go,' he said. He looked anxious. 'You won't be able to cope. You'll—'

'I'll what?' I said.

He shrugged. 'I don't know. But you do lose your temper so easily and when that happens—'

'I've got it under control,' I said.

I hope I'm right. If I'm wrong, I'm going to be a helluva long way from the Dr.

At least I'll have my therapeutic tool with me.

T was upset when I said I was going. Took my hand. Said we were just getting to know each other.

I said I'd be back soon. Things would be different then, I said.

Oh God: I hope I'm right.

. . . Rang O, to let him know where I was.

'Isn't that where—?' he started.

'Yeah,' I said.

'Why did you choose there, of all places?' he goes, all worried.

'Destiny,' I said.

He says: 'What?'

'We all got to follow our star,' I said.

Heard him breathe in exasperatedly through his nose. God, I hate it when he does that, like I'm just a little kid and he's this oh-so-responsible Mr Do-Right.

'Did you find a job yet?' he wanted to know.

Told him, not yet.

Rang T who sounded pleased to hear from me. Said 'I miss you.' Oh, that felt good. Don't think anyone's ever missed me before. 'I miss you, too,' I said. It felt wonderful, saying that. The age difference doesn't matter. Does it?

Rang F. Had an almost identical conversation to the one I'd had with O, but at least he seemed more sympathetic. 'I can understand you wanting to go back,' he says. 'Did you get a job yet?'

'More or less,' I said. 'Met this man who's looking for kind of odd chores about the place.'

'What's he called?' F says. 'Maybe I know him.'

I could see through that one. Like, and maybe I could also ring up and warn the guy that he's got a person who has 'a slight problem relating to other people' on his hands.

'Can't remember,' I said. 'But he's very respectable. Wife and two point four kids, all that stuff.'

'Kids?' F goes.

'Yeah.'

'Remember how easy it is to hurt kids,' F says.

'What?' I say, in my wolf voice.

'They're fragile, that's all I'm saying,' says F.

I threw my head back and opened my mouth and out came this enormous laugh. I wanted to say, tell me about it. I mean, fucking tell me about it, I know how easy it is to hurt little children, I've been there, you fucker, and where were you, when I was being hurt?

Stupid man. As if I'd hurt a child.

NOW

17

Time passes. Hannah drifts with it, directionless, not quite sure why she has come here but finding some kind of satisfaction in being back at the heart of her internal landscape, some easing of her grief at the death of her daughter, though it is a pain from which she knows she will never recover. Getting up each morning, she is always aware of the hours moving imperturbably, unstoppably, towards the day's close. One day, she too will reach her end and then none of this will have mattered, not Lucas, not Lucinda, none of it. She no longer expects to be happy.

She climbs the hill to the centre of the little town. Although there are people about, shopping, chatting, sitting in the *trattoria*, no one speaks to her. In the church, she breathes deeply of the cold, scented air which fills its gilded, pillared spaces. At the back stands an iron rack of lit candles, their flames moving erratically in unfelt draughts; next to them are trayfuls of new candles. Dropping money into a box, she takes two of the longest, lights their wicks from those already burning and thrusts them into empty sockets. One for Lucinda, one for Lucas. The flame bends, wavers, gives off a tallowy smoke; after a second or two it burns straight, trembling slightly.

Hannah sits down in one of the pews. She is immensely weary yet at the same time grateful that such a serious, peaceful place exists amongst the clamour of modern life.

Hands thrust deep into the pockets of her raincoat, she walks the roads as she used to cycle them, that summer. The white soil is sodden under her feet, rutted with tyre tracks, the furrows greened in places with mould. The fields look sullen and dark; close-pruned vines wait for the return of the sun. Ditches once rampant with poppies and high grass are water-logged, lined with clumps of withered straw.

Much of the land which used to stretch unbroken towards the hills is now covered with new developments. Half-finished structures of sloppily-mortared cement blocks start from the earth, each one surrounded by yellow lifting gear, concrete mixers, banded stacks of new brick. Behind, like a spoor, lies a trail of red-roofed villas in ice-cream colours, each with its regulation balcony of bulging ironwork, its new brown shutters, its heraldic front door.

She sees no one on these walks. Even the building sites are deserted.

Occasionally a youth on a moped rushes past in a burst of blue exhaust fumes and ear-splitting noise, otherwise the countryside seems entirely uninhabited. Late one afternoon, she turns down a track which leads between pines to the edge of a low escarpment. Across the shallow valley lies a promontory; on it stands a pink-washed house with cypresses at each corner. She recognises it as Faustino's house – and Marina's. The plaster is faded and peeling; the shutters are closed except for those at an upper window, which swing half open, as though someone is watching secretly from within.

It must have been through that door Marina came, Hannah thinks. What had been her state of mind as she stepped through it for the last time? Had she known she would never return? Battered by her husband, locked in a loveless marriage, had she decided at last to end it? Was she going to her lover, as Lucas had so desired her to do?

Was that why Lucas had died?

Faustino has told her that he and Lucas had fought because of Marina: did he come rushing after her, shouting? Did he kill Lucas, beside himself with rage and hurt pride? How could Marina have vanished so completely unless she had planned her disappearance? There is so much Hannah wants to know, but Faustino's tragedy is not hers, nor does she feel she has the right to question him.

Behind the open window she sees movement. Quickly she steps back among the screening trees. Is it Faustino? Has he seen and recognised her? If so, she hopes he will not think she has been spying on him. Walking slowly back to the Villa Giulia, she passes the Villa Diana and, on impulse, pushes at the tall wrought-iron gates. Though stiff, they open wide enough for her to get through and she finds herself once more walking down the sandy yellow drive to the terrace steps.

She slowly climbs up to the terrace and stands looking out between the urns to where bushes – laurel, box, plumbago – take over from the grass. Where does 'now' end and 'then' begin? Which has more substance in the caverns of memory? Vividly she remembers an afternoon of heat when she had stood on this very spot, watching the child run across the grass, the puppy skittering along behind, tumbling sometimes on its fat legs. The child had stopped, had held up its hands like a crucible, had closed them gently round one of the chalky blue butterflies which used to hang in clouds above the lawn.

Descending from the terrace, Hannah steps across the wet grass and pushes her way into the bushes to where the tunnels begin. She takes the path which leads to the little folly which she had once thought was a chapel. Dirty water, browned pine needles, a few rotting leaves now lie in the bowl of the fountain in front of it. The door is closed, but she does not need to look inside to recall the scene she had witnessed there: the fair-haired man, the amber glow cast by the candles, the woman's yellow dress, the golden sparkle from her jewels. There were grapes, green grapes in a dish, and wine in greenish glasses.

Passion had filled the space, pressing against the walls, pushing up at the roof. She herself had been too ignorant, too innocent, to recognise grief or she might have seen that Lucas was a man crammed and overflowing with sadness. Instead, she had hoped he would love her. How blinkered she had been, how unaware of what was going on around her.

Has she changed?

She walks on, avoiding the path which leads to the bamboo grove and the pool.

She was drinking coffee in the kitchen when Tristan telephoned. He sounded unfriendly, grimmer than she remembered. 'I'm booked on a morning flight to Italy the day after tomorrow,' he said, without preamble.

It seemed like an invasion, particularly since she had specifically told him she would prefer him not to come. Angered, Hannah started to point out that what he did was not her concern, that he was under no obligation whatsoever to let her know of his arrival. He cut her off in mid sentence. 'I'm not going to go into it now,' he said, 'but my reason for coming is because I may have some information which could be of help to you.'

'Information? What sort of—'

'We should be at the airport by ten o'clock. By the time we've hired a car and so on, I reckon we should be with you around lunchtime. We'll go to the Trevelyans': I know you don't want us to come to the Villa Giulia.'

'I didn't mean—'

'We'll ring you from Nancy's house.'

'We? Who's we?'

'I'm bringing my friend Mark with me.'

'Mark? Isn't he the one who—'

'—se wife ran off with Lucas? Yes, he is.'

It was not what Hannah had intended to say. Under her breast her heart jumped. 'He's the one who—' she began again, but remembering the cruel shine of the knife blade by the lake and the blood on Lucas's shirt, could not finish the sentence.

'I telephoned him yesterday,' Tristan said. 'From things which came out in our conversation, it seemed best if we both came over and talked a few things through with you.'

'About Lucas?'

'Yes.'

'But I don't know him. What can it have to do with Mark? He wasn't even here when Lucas was killed. Anyway, why can't it wait until I get back?'

'There are . . . other more urgent factors.'

'Such as what?'

'We'll talk when I get there.' Tristan was brusque. 'There's a lot to do before we leave.'

He rang off without saying goodbye.

As she replaced the receiver Hannah could feel the heavy beat of her blood.

Mark was coming. Mysterious ex-soldier Mark, who was violent enough not only to carry a knife but also to use it, who had lost his wife to another man, who was still raging over that loss, all these years later. Tristan had information to pass on to her, information so serious that he felt it necessary to fly over to see her. It was logical to assume that it had to do with the matter which had originally propelled her back here: Lucas's death. Obviously it concerned Mark: the only possible conclusion was that Mark had been in some way involved.

Was she finally going to discover what had happened?

Stumbling a little, Hannah made her way to the living-room and swung open the doors of the big painted cupboard where drinks were kept. Drinking alone was bad enough; drinking alone at breakfast time was probably the final fatal step before the onset of delirium tremens and cirrhosis of the liver. None the less she poured herself a large slug of the local *grappa* and drank it in two gulps.

As the strong spirit found its way into her bloodstream she reflected that more than anything in the world, she wanted things cleared up. None the less, now that it appeared as if she might be on the brink of knowing, she was, oddly, afraid.

She went into the ballroom. From the fireplaces at either end, a fan of soot had fallen on to the polished floor. Above the mirrors, opaque as pearls, hung faded gilt sconces, still bearing tears of wax. Hannah could barely see her own reflection as she moved carefully across the parquet towards the shutters, only a kind of ghost in the glass which moved at the same speed as herself, shadowing her.

As she unfastened the shutters, she saw the Trevelyans' Fiat come down the drive and pull up at the foot of the terrace steps. Nancy got out and marched up them to the front door. She seemed in combative mood.

When Hannah opened the door, Nancy stalked past her into the hall. 'What the hell's going on?' she said curtly.

'How do you mean?' Hannah was taken aback.

'We've just had a visit from the mayor – and believe me, it's pretty damn serious when Signor Famiglietti gets off his fat butt and goes visiting.' Nancy took a deep breath. 'He spent the entire time hinting that unless we control our friend, Signora Anna Barlow, we might find ourselves in difficulty when it's time to renew our visitors' permits.

Not only that, who knows what might happen about our water rights? God!' Nancy raised her hands and raked them theatrically through her hair. 'Have you any idea what it would be like trying to get through the summer here without a reliable water supply?'

Hannah said: 'I don't know what on earth you're talking about.'

Nancy stamped across the hallway towards the back of the house. 'Any coffee going?'

'Of course, but—'

'I warned you,' said Nancy. 'I told you the natives might get restless, I said so when you first arrived, didn't I? Well, it appears they have. Someone's telephoned Signor Famiglietti and made a helluva stink, said you were causing trouble, raising hackles, annoying people when everyone had done their best to forget what happened all those—'

'Nancy!' Hannah said sharply. She put her hand on the older woman's shoulder to stop her precipitate march into the kitchen. 'I've done nothing.'

'Doing isn't necessary. Just *talking* to people is enough to cause problems.' Nancy stopped and turned to face Hannah. 'Look, there's quite a lot of anti-American feeling about in Europe, believe it or not. Lew and I have always kept our heads down, tried to blend in, not make any display of conspicuous transatlantic-style consumption.' She snorted derisively. 'Why else do you think we'd be driving that crappy old Fiat? If you go on like this, you could really make things awkward for us.'

'Didn't you hear me?' Hannah said loudly. 'I haven't done anything, I haven't spoken to anybody except the people in the supermarket – and then it was only to ask if they had any garlic olives or something equally domestic.'

'Are you sure?' Nancy plonked herself down in one of the chairs pulled up to the kitchen table.

'Absolutely. I've spent most of my time here just walking, not seeing a soul, let alone questioning anyone about Lucas.'

'Signor Famiglietti said it had been "brought to his attention" that you were annoying people.'

'Who by?' Reaching down the old-fashioned wooden grinder, Hannah poured greasy black coffee beans in under the lid.

'I didn't ask.'

'I wish you had.' Hannah turned the handle and listened to the crunch of beans; she savoured the strong, delicious smell for a moment before pouring boiling water over the ground coffee. 'I can't think who could have contacted the mayor, but I assure you I have done absolutely nothing controversial. Unless someone saw me having dinner with Faustino Castelli and took exception to it.'

'Odd,' said Nancy. She had calmed down now.

'Isn't it?'

'It must have been someone important, to make him come to our house.'

'Someone with a grudge.'

'Or someone trying to make trouble.' Nancy stretched her mouth about and stared up at the ceiling. 'Look, I'm sorry I barged in here and started beating up on you. But people like the mayor can make life very difficult, if they want to.'

'That's OK.'

They sat on either side of the table, each with a mug of coffee in their hands. 'Did you know that Tristan's coming the day after tomorrow?' Nancy said. 'With his friend Mark.'

'He told me.'

'I'm going to put them in the Villa Diana.'

'Oh?'

'We've got the keys, and Susie's always said we could use it if we need to. My daughter's coming this evening, with husband and children, and our house is going to be packed out. And I gather you didn't want Tristan staying here.'

'That was only because—' but it was too difficult to explain and Hannah let it go.

Nancy laughed. 'Talking of the Diana, Lew came home yesterday from grocery shopping and said he saw that girl we told you about, the one who wrecked the doll's house.'

'Girls all look the same these days.'

'That's what I told him. But he swears it was her.'

'She's hardly likely to come back, is she?'

'Quite.' Nancy sipped some more. 'Mark's the one who was married to Jane, isn't he?'

'I think so.'

'Did you ever meet him?'

'No. But I know just what he can do.'

'That sounds very significant,' Nancy said, smiling.

'I saw him attack Lucas with a knife once.'

'What?' Nancy put down her mug. '*Mark?*'

'It's true.'

'Where was this?'

'At the barbecue you organised that year. Down by the lake.'

'But he wasn't there,' said Nancy, looking bewildered.

'He was.'

'I didn't see him. And I certainly didn't see anyone with a *knife*.'

'They all took good care that you shouldn't.'

'Who did?'

'All of them: Lucas, Tristan, Mark, someone else who was with them.'

'A knife—' Nancy widened her eyes and slowly shook her head from side to side. 'I can't believe what I'm hearing.'

The two women stared at each other. Nancy said: 'Do you think Mark was the one who—?'

Hannah shrugged. 'He was supposed to be long gone by the time Lucas was killed, but that could have been lies, there was nothing to stop him sneaking back if he wanted to.'

'Do you think he's coming over with Tristan in order to confess?'

'I honestly don't know. We'd best wait until they get here.' Changing the subject, Hannah said: 'If you've got family coming, why don't I make up the beds over at the Villa Diana, and save you the trouble?'

'That's kind of you but I'd have to go down there anyway. I'm not sure, without checking it, which rooms it would be best to use.'

'Lucas's old room, presumably,' Hannah said. 'And the one next to it. That way the two of them can share the bathroom.'

Nancy put her head on one side. 'I thought you said you'd never been in the Villa Diana.'

Hannah faltered. 'I – uh – I suppose I must have. I can certainly remember the layout of the rooms – maybe that's because it's exactly the same as here.'

'I see,' Nancy said slowly. Eyes on Hannah, she raised her coffee mug to her mouth and drank from it. Putting it down, glancing away, she said: 'I never realised it until now, but you must have been Lucas's—' She coughed. 'We knew there was someone else, but we never guessed it was you.'

Hannah said nothing.

'Beside the housekeeper woman, I mean,' said Nancy. 'And Marina, of course, when she could get away from Faustino. Susie, too, I shouldn't wonder – she was always dead keen on him.'

I deserve no less than this, Hannah thought. *It is part of my punishment.* Which did not stop Nancy's words from hurting. She had not known about Marina until the end. She had never once guessed that the housekeeper, the woman who had always just disappeared through a doorway a second before, the presence who watched from the shadows, was also – to be absolutely clear about it – was also fucking Lucas. Though that had to be speculation: there was no way anyone could have been sure of that, was there?

Nancy was shaking her head. 'My goodness. I simply never had the faintest notion it was you.'

'I didn't try to hide it,' Hannah said. She shook her head. 'I didn't know how to.'

In the garden, something is screaming, on and on, like the whistle of a kettle. Getting out of bed, Hannah runs across the room and flings open the shutters. The floor is cold under her feet. As she lets in the damp night air, the screaming grows louder, and is terribly familiar.

She shivers. Once she ran through the green tunnels of leaves towards such screaming – not just once, but twice, for now she remembers the puppy with its back broken and blood on its smooth fur. Lucas had killed it with a sudden movement of his hands; there had been a sound like a stick snapping and she had looked up to see the child watching them, expressionless.

Horrible. *Horrible.*

She listens again. The screaming stops abuptly, a kettle removed from the heat, a puppy suddenly dead.

She tells herself it was probably nothing more than an ambushed night creature, a dog howling in the distance, a car alarm. Perhaps she even imagined it. And then she hears something in the bushes below, footsteps thudding among the leaves like the beat of an anxious heart. Her mouth dries. Although it is cold, she is sweating, her nightdress damp where it touches her skin. She remembers Nancy's warnings of local hostility to long-buried troubles being exhumed. But a mob would not move like that. And even a single troublemaker would use the drive, not creep through the bushes. Resolutely, she closes the windows and bolts the shutters. She lifts the telephone and listens to the reassurance of the dialling tone. If she needs to, she can summon help before anyone could get close enough to attack her.

But once back in bed, she cannot sleep and though she tries to read, she is unable to prevent the images of torn hands, broken backs, bloodied fur, returning.

The next morning she dialled *Carringtons* again. There was still no answer. Fear for Zoe began to chill the edges of her brain. What could have happened to her. She remembered the boy – young man – standing across the road from her shop: had he been looking for an opportunity to harm Hannah herself, and encountered Zoe instead? Seeing him outside the doll's house shop, she had been willing to suspend disbelief, fancy him different from the man she had seen at the South Bank, even persuade herself that he was no more than a potential burglar checking the place out, wondering if it was worth breaking into.

She dismissed the thought. She had seen him in Crickgarth, as well. And he had seen her. He had smiled at her.

Against her will, her mind began to fill with pictures of Zoe on the floor, limbs sprawled among the little houses, blood splattering the walls of Tudor cottages, Georgian mansions, Queen Anne residences, her pudgy child's hand perhaps clasping one last piece of miniature furniture: the chess table, perhaps, or Major Perowne's spinet.

And then the truth came to her. She wondered how it could have taken her so long to realise that the young man glimpsed through glass on the South Bank, so like Lucas as to stop the heart, could be no one else but Lucas's son. If that fact was accepted, it would explain so much. He wanted revenge for the wrong he perceived her – Hannah – to have done in leaving his father to die. Which would explain Lucinda's death. If he possessed even half Lucas's charisma, he would have had no difficulty at all in getting close to Lucinda. Perhaps he even possessed his father's gift for entering the mind and once he had Lucinda in his power, it would have been easy for him to wait for the right moment and then kill her.

A new thought came. Could he be the American boyfriend Lucinda had spoken of? Was that why he had been in Crickgarth? His friends thought he had vanished but perhaps he had merely wanted to return to the scene of his crime, to gloat, to remember how Lucinda had felt in his hands, how her dying eyes had pleaded for mercy and he had refused, just as his own father had been refused. Had he—

Resolutely, Hannah cleared Lucinda from her mind and picked up the telephone again. This time, she ended up being put through to her local police station in England.

'I'm worried,' she said. 'Something's wrong. Could someone go round to the shop and take a look? I can call you back this evening.'

'That won't be necessary, Mrs Barlow.' The stolid unemotional voice was as soothing as a massage. 'Give me the telephone number where you are now, and if there's anything we feel you need to know about, we'll give you a ring ourselves.'

'It's probably nothing,' Hannah gabbled. 'I'm probably making a stupid fuss—' But she knew that she was not.

Oh, God. If Zoe had been harmed as a consequence of working at *Carringtons* . . . Hannah wondered how she would manage if she had to shoulder this additional load of guilt. There was the child, the husband . . . she told herself there was probably some perfectly rational explanation, but did not find her own arguments persuasive.

The police did not ring her back that afternoon although she stayed in the house in order not to miss the call if it came. The fact that it did not should have reassured her but she found it sinister rather than comforting.

She telephoned Nancy. 'Does the name Marsden mean anything to you?' she asked.

Nancy thought about it. 'No. Should it?'

'I wondered whether there'd been people around that summer – you know – who were called Marsden.'

'There was a family called Buckden, I seem to remember.' Nancy said. 'Brits. Came from Manchester, or somewhere. But no Marsdens that I recall.'

'None of those young people hitch-hiking around Europe?'

'Don't think so. Sorry.'

'Just a long shot,' Hannah said. If Nancy did not remember the name, it was fairly certain that no such people had been around at the time. Which only confirmed the fact that the name was a pseudonym, covering some other name which those involved might otherwise have recognised.

She was restless. The weather was worsening: all day huge clouds had surged across the sky, scattering cold rain, and wind tugged fiercely at the evergreens. She had considered ringing Faustino and asking him to come over but eventually decided against it. When darkness fell, she went round the house carefully closing windows, fastening the shutters, locking the doors. She sat in the living-room, trying to read, but was unable to concentrate, conscious of every noise the house made as it settled for the night. Someone had been sufficiently alarmed by her presence in the area to complain to the mayor, someone with enough clout to stir him into action. She told herself that it was only natural, therefore, for her to feel a certain apprehension.

The shutters rattled in their sockets; soot tumbled into the hearth as wind roared above the chimney. She shivered, although it was not particularly cold. Were it not for the arrival tomorrow of Tristan and her desire to see Susie, she would be making plans to return home, particularly in the light of Zoe's absence from the shop. Some, at least, of what she had come to do had been achieved – perspective, resolution, a definite easing of the heart – and she knew that she had never seriously believed she would solve the long mystery of Lucas's death.

There was another gust of wind and she got up, intending to go to the kitchen and heat some coffee. As she rose from her chair, she heard someone run across the terrace outside. The footsteps were light; had she not already been on the alert, she might have mistaken them for nothing more than a handful of dry leaves blowing across the flagstones.

She stood with one hand on her chest as the pulses on either side of her throat began to drum. Already her senses were assessing the information they had received: quick light footsteps indicated someone who could easily outrun her if she tried to escape. Were they to break into the house, she would not stand much of a chance.

Before she could do anything further, one of the windows shattered as a stone crashed through the glass. The noise seemed overwhelming. Hannah stared stupidly at the shutters, for a moment not making the proper connections between the deed and its presumed intention.

Then she screamed, diving for the telephone, fear making her clumsy so that she tripped over a table beside one of the sofas and fell awkwardly on to one knee, at the same time trying fruitlessly to catch the expensive crystal bowl and the framed photograph of Susie's parents which stood on its polished top, along with a silver cigarette box. She grunted with effort, her knees giving way as she tried to stand, as though they could not support her weight, while splinters of glass shot across the floor.

Scrabbling for it, aware of how undignified she looked, she got hold of the phone. She realised she had no idea what the emergency codes in Italy were but pressed the redial button on the phone to get Nancy Trevelyan's number. This time there was no answer. She stared at the closed door of the sitting-room, unable to open it and face what might be on the other side. Suppose whoever had thrown the stone had been only one of several intruders. Suppose that even now they had gained entry to the back of the house and were coming up the passage.

Faustino's number was what she wanted, if she couldn't get the police . . . and then some degree of sanity returned and she found herself dialling the operator. When a voice answered, she asked for the police station, explaining that it was an emergency and that speed was essential. A matter of life or death, she wanted to say, but her knowledge of the language had dried up, and she could only repeat, *'Polizia, emergencia, pronto, pronto,'* all the time staring at the door of the room, half-expecting at any moment to see it burst open and a screaming horde of vengeful citizens to pour into the room.

But nothing further happened. The wind sucked at the gap between the shutters, but no more stones were thrown and by the time the police arrived, racing up the drive to pull to a surely unnecessary screeching halt at the foot of the terrace, Hannah was seriously beginning to wonder whether the window could have been smashed by a falling tile, a freak hailstone, a blown branch.

The carabinieri searched all round the house but found nothing except, immediately beneath the broken pane of glass, a rock the size of an orange. The senior officer handed it to Hannah, looking away as though embarrassed. 'Boys,' he said, lifting his shoulders and then dropping them. 'Children, making mischief.'

Both of them knew this was unlikely to have been the case. She wondered whether he knew of the mayor's visit to the Trevelyans, whether it had also been brought to his attention that the Englishwoman at the Villa Giulia was causing trouble.

As if he knew what she was thinking, he said: 'You will be quite safe, signora. I shall let someone know about the window and he will come in the morning to mend it.'

'Thank you.' Hannah said humbly.

As she was closing and bolting the front door behind them, the telephone rang.

'How's things?' Susie said. 'I'm just going to bed but thought I'd see how you were.'

'You must be telepathic!' Hannah found she was smiling. In spite of her fear, she felt invigorated. She had deliberately manufactured for herself a life without extremes. Now, for the first time in twenty-five years, although threatened at every turn, she was once again aware of being alive.

'What do you mean?' Susie demanded. In the Rome apartment, a clock chimed. One stroke. One o'clock. Hannah had not realised how late it was.

She told Susie about the footsteps on the terrace, the broken window and the arrival of the police.

'Oh, Hannah,' Susie said worriedly. 'Nancy was obviously right when she said the town was hostile – hadn't you better move in with the Trevelyans? I'm sure they'd have you.'

'Even if I wanted to, I couldn't,' said Hannah. 'One of their daughters is arriving tonight, along with the grandchildren. There won't be any room at all. Which is why Tristan and Mark will be staying at the Villa Diana tomorrow instead of there.'

'Tristan Carrick?'

'I forgot: you can't have heard that he's arriving here tomorrow, with his friend Mark.'

There was a long pause, then Susie said lightly: 'He hasn't been over here for years and years. Why's he coming now? He hasn't got the hots for you, has he?'

'That's absolutely ridiculous.' Hannah laughed. 'My dear, don't tell me you're jealous.'

'Of you? Why on earth *would* I be?' There was a coldness in Susie's voice which Hannah had not heard for years.

'Anyway, I've only met Tristan three times in my life,' she said, not adding that the most recent encounter had lasted for three days.

'And Mark's coming too?'

'Apparently.'

'Is that the Mark we used to know, years ago?'

'You may have done; I've never met him.' Again Hannah did not add further detail.

'And why aren't they staying at the Giulia with you?'

'It's just—' Hannah was not sure how to explain, but once more Susie's mind rushed to meet hers.

'You wanted to be alone, didn't you?'

'I did. But after tonight, I'm not so sure.'

'Hang in there, baby,' Susie said. 'I'll be down there with you myself in a couple of days, and then just let them try chucking stones at the window.'

'They'd never dare.'

'You'll hang on to Tristan until I get there, won't you?' Susie said.

'If I can.'

'I'd simply love to see him again after all this time.'

'I'll do my best.'

'You always do,' said Susie.

Except once, Hannah thought. The one time it mattered, I failed to do what I ought to have done, and I've spent the rest of my life paying for it.

'Ciao, Anna,' Susie said. 'And don't worry, OK?'

'OK.'

How can she not worry? Once again the past shifts and settles in the house, oozing between the doorways like a mist, floating in at the windows, drifting above the garden. Past and present blend and become the same, become interchangeable.

Without knowing why, as though she has plucked the fact from the air, she perceives danger.

THE DIARY

. . . I made myself go down there today.
  Horrible.
  Horrible.

I stood there among the leaves and all of it, all of it, came back. It was as though I had swallowed a strong laxative for suddenly there I was with diarrhoea of the memory, suffering from the reminiscent runs. The bowels of my mind moved and I voided at last, my amnesic constipation finally purged.

Everything came out of me in that defecatory flood of remembering. I was shitting names, excreting places, crapping the past. Hannah, Marina, Susie and Lucas. Tristan and Hugo, Mark and Jane, Helena, Damian, Chloe . . . on and on, places, and people, vines along the pergola, dragon-flies and flowers, breasts and buttocks white against the green, painted porcelain, knives slicing, spoons stirring, the beast, the two-backed beast, butterflies, sun falling across a terrace, screams and blood.

I soiled myself with memories.

Even so, there was still some shit left in my recollective gut, hard balls of impacted memory which were too terrible to let go of. Pale and shaking, I looked at myself in the mirror which hangs on the wall of the cold white bathroom and wondered who it was who stared back at me. Certainly not the familiar face I had grown up with. This was a gaunt, hollow-eyed wreck whose mouth opened but produced no words, whose hands fluttered like trapped butterflies, whose body writhed like a bloodied snake with the pain of that hideous evacuation.

No wonder. For though I was not yet completely emptied, there was one fact which I could not deny. Something I can't escape.

I begin – and I tremble as I write this – I begin to suspect at last what it is I do not know.

Do not want to know.

THEN

18

Although it was only seven o'clock in the morning, the day's heat had already begun to fill her room. Too restless to stay in bed any longer, Hannah pulled on a cotton shirt and went down to the kitchen, hoping that Tristan was still asleep. But there were signs that he was already up: the vivid skins of oranges lay beside the sink and there was a flat circle of bread on the table, raggedly cut, under a lingering smell of fresh-brewed coffee. The door to the outside stood open, letting in a tranche of brilliant light.

A lizard skittered up the whitewashed wall as she poured herself a lukewarm cup from the coffee pot on the stove. She took it outside and sat on a carved wooden bench set against the house, below the veranda. The scent of bay drifted from the laurel bush which grew profusely along the wall. Under the guttering, wasps fussed around their gourd-shaped nest, occasionally swooping down to pulsate briefly above her hands.

Last night, she had opted to come home from the picnic, as she had arrived, in the Lambourns' car, in spite of her lunchtime acceptance of Tristan's offer to drive her back to the Villa Giulia. At some point in the evening he had sought her out and repeated it, saying they could leave whenever she was ready to go, but this time she had declined, moving away from him as she did so, not meeting his puzzled gaze. The thought of sharing a car with someone who had viciously punched a defenceless man in the face, who, even if he had not wielded a knife himself, had stood by while another did so, was intolerable. He had seemed annoyed at her refusal.

Small stones in the sanded ground between house and lawn cut into her bare feet as she winced across to where the grass began. To appease her burgeoning sense of guilt – how could she have watched violence done to him last night, without running for help? – she needed to find out how Lucas was even though she knew he would hate her for asking.

Under the trees it was still cool. The smell of damp earth rose from the silent paths between the bushes; lurking among the leaves, the pipe-playing Pan gleamed momentarily, white under its shawl of ivy. The best way, she decided, was boldness; she would go to the kitchen door of the Villa Diana and ask the elusive housekeeper straight out whether Lucas was all right.

Resolution began to falter as she drew nearer. Suppose she found, not the woman, but Lucas himself, up early just as Tristan was. Or suppose that she found the housekeeper but, by asking after Lucas, gave away information which he had hoped to conceal. Suppose the woman herself would not talk to her, refusing to open the door.

She tried to persuade herself that her errand was pointless; despite his knife wound he had seemed all right when she left him the night before. Besides, it was no business of hers. Furthermore, given the way he had spoken to her by the lake after his attackers had gone, he was unlikely to treat kindly any further enquiries from her as to his condition.

Coming to the boundary fence between the two houses, she stepped across and walked up through the trees to the foot of the slope in front of the Villa Diana. Despite last night's downpour, heat had drained the savour from the laurel leaves and the mulch underfoot. The lichen-roughened stone of half-concealed balustrades was hot under her hand; dead leaves rustled as she made her way down flights of steps almost hidden beneath the giant hands of overhanging ferns. Reaching the point where the bushes ended and the Villa Diana's lawns began, she stopped. Ahead and above her, the house shone in the citrine light of early morning. Although no one was about, all the windows had been thrown open and the outside shutters fastened flat against the wall. She was just about to make her unobtrusive way towards the back entrance when, as though he knew she was there, Lucas stepped out onto the balcony. As far as she could see, he seemed none the worse for the violence inflicted on him yesterday, apart from some puffiness above one eye and around his jaw. He stared down across the sloping lawn to where she stood concealed among the leaves; could he see her? Hastily, Hannah shrank back, wishing she had worn something which blended in better with the surrounding green. He stood with eyes narrowed; in the pale light, his fair hair seemed almost transparent. He put one hand against his ribs, where the knife had gone in, as though they hurt, then went back in through the windows to his bedroom.

One question at least was answered: Lucas was all right, despite the way he had held the place where the knife had entered. But there were other questions. Had the housekeeper tended the wound for him? Had he seen a doctor? Hannah guessed the former rather than the latter. If so, she must live close at hand. For a moment Hannah toyed with the notion that the housekeeper and the woman she had seen only days before, the woman with the yellow diamond ring and the passionate eyes, were one and the same person, before dismissing the possibility. If that was the case, Lucas would hardly be declaring his passion to her and, at the same time, making love to Hannah, under the very roof they shared.

About to plunge back into the undergrowth, Hannah suddenly saw the child appear on the terrace, fragile as a petal, mothlike against the bulk of the house. It looked up at Lucas's window. From where Hannah stood, the tiny figure had an oddly menacing air; she had the strangest impression of desired violence, as though the child – but the notion was absurd – wanted to inflict damage. And then, before she had fully registered this effect, the child was gone again, running through the windows in answer, perhaps, to some call from inside the house.

Hannah turned and pushed her way through the trees towards the pool. At least she need not worry about Lucas; what she had to do now was to sort out her attitude towards Tristan. She wondered how long he intended to stay; on the telephone he had spoken of a couple of nights. She hoped he did not expect her to spend time with him. Planning activities which would keep her out of his way – a long bicycle ride, a trip into the town, perhaps a visit to the cinema, even though her Italian was not good enough for her to be able to follow more than a quarter of the action – she reached the stand of bamboo.

An aeroplane droned languidly above her head, and she looked up to see it tiny and far away, pasted against the blue sky like a silver cross. Pushing through the stems, she shrugged away the tickle of the pointed leaves, and emerged at the side of the pool. She had her hands crossed, holding the hem of her shirt, about to pull it off and leap in among the yellow water-lilies, when she saw Tristan. He stood almost opposite her, on the other side of the pool. His white hair flared against the dark leaves which crowded the banks behind him. His hands hung loosely at his sides. He was naked.

Hannah's first thought was how dark his body was, compared to the lunar beauty of Lucas's. He seemed entirely elemental against the green backdrop; his reflection reached across the black water of the pool towards her. Had he raised a pipe to his lips and played some wild pagan melody, she would scarcely have been surprised.

I shall remember this for ever, Hannah thought: whatever happens to me in the future, I shall always have this particular moment, this sky, this man, the black water, the incandescent dragon-flies hanging above the water-lilies. She was surprised by the flame of disinterested lust which leaped momentarily inside her.

'Going in?' Tristan said. 'It's wonderful.'

'I – uh – was—'

'I won't look,' Tristan said mockingly. Making no attempt to conceal himself, he paced slowly along the marble tiles towards the stone bench where his towel had been flung. A hot stillness lay between them as he wrapped it round his waist.

'Go on, Hannah,' he said. 'Don't mind me. That *is* why you came down here, isn't it? To cool off?'

'Uh—' In spite of her complete lack of shyness with Lucas, despite the weeks spent with Susie's uninhibited friends, Hannah still did not find it easy to appear unclothed in front of an almost total stranger. Neither upbringing nor inclination had prepared her for it. She longed to be more blasé, more worldly-wise, as the Charlottes and Helenas were. Yet at the back of her mind was the memory of the time she had stepped naked from the pool and been rejected by Lucas. Recalling that humiliation, she said: 'Yes, it is,' and jumped in.

The water thundered and chuckled in her ears as she went under. She pushed against the silt at the bottom, felt the hardness of the floor beneath, and emerged, blowing water, into the warm green air. Tristan spoke but she could not hear what he said. She turned over on her back to kick at the water, taking in the dancing, iridescent insects just above her head, and beyond them, the patch of blue sky between the trees, the vapour trail left by the plane.

Out of the corner of her eye, she saw him come into her line of vision, saw his mouth open as he stood on the edge of the pool and leaned towards her, speaking. She splashed harder, water cascading above her head and catching rainbows in the air. He shook his head, smiling slightly, and knelt on one knee, waiting.

'Why didn't you want to come home with me last night?' he said, as soon as she stopped.

'I arrived with the Lambourns. It seemed more polite to go back with them.' Although he seemed to lack inhibition, Hannah was embarrassed. She tried to keep from staring at him and the dark space beneath his towel where thigh met thigh.

'That's not what you said at lunchtime.'

'It's a woman's prerogative to change her mind.'

'Don't be stupid. Something happened.'

'Did it?'

'I want to know what.'

Hannah closed her eyes and floated. Her shirt clung to her body, wet and heavy, dragging at her upright nipples. She could feel the faint pulse from the feeding spring under her back; she could hear the last echoes as the plane trailed southwards towards Rome.

'What, Hannah?' His voice bounced off the water, sharp, even anxious. Good, she thought. Maybe he suspects that I saw him. Maybe he's even afraid I'll tell someone.

The pool reverberated; she opened her eyes to find him in the pool beside her. Before she could move he had grabbed her wrist and pulled her towards him.

'What, Hannah?' he said again, through gritted teeth, looking down into her eyes while water dripped from his face onto hers. 'What made you change your mind?'

'You're hurting me,' she said, coolly. 'Would you please let go?'

'Not until you answer my question.'

'Why are you so worried?'

'Because—' He paused. 'Because I thought we were friends.'

'Friends? We hardly know each other.'

'None the less, you were perfectly happy to come back with me at lunchtime but by the evening you'd changed your mind. And when I finally did get back, you'd gone to bed with the door locked, incommunicado.'

'How do you know it was locked?'

'Because I tried the bloody handle.'

As she again attempted to pull away, Tristan splayed his hand on her back, under her shirt. At the same time, the towel round his waist came loose. Hannah twisted in his grip but could not get free; with one hand at the back of her head, he pulled her closer. As they stood together, his body hardened suddenly and she saw how his eyes dilated in the second before his mouth came down on hers. For a single taut moment his lips were warm, for a single moment she was aware of a desire to respond – then she was struggling to escape again, twisting then ducking, pulling downwards when he had expected resistance backwards. Free, she swam strongly for the steps. The stone faun leered as she pulled herself out and began to run among the trees, into the green tunnels she knew so well. As she darted between the leaves, she could already hear the thud of his feet on the dense-packed leafy floor behind her. 'Hannah!' he called. 'Come back! Don't be such an idiot!'

Pursuit and escape, a latter-day nymph fleeing from her pagan ravisher – she would have smiled were it not for the expression on his face as she looked back over her shoulder. She did not seriously think she was in any danger: the potential kiss had resulted from proximity rather than any desire to force her into intimacy. Nonetheless, she was glad when she reached the shelter of the house and could lock the door of her bedroom behind her. So he had tried the handle last night, had he? Just as well she had taken the precaution of turning the key: had he confronted her, she would have found it difficult to conceal her knowledge of the way he had treated Lucas and her disgust. This morning she had had time to adopt a mask, but, as she heard him run up the stairs and knock peremptorily at her door, she realised she was going to have to find some excuse for her change of attitude.

'Hannah!' he said loudly. 'What's the matter with you?'

'I could ask you the same question,' she said.

'Look. I'm sorry about – about what happened in the pool. It's just that you're a beautiful girl and—'

'Shut up, Tristan,' she said. And to her surprise, he did. She continued, 'I'm going out in a minute and shan't be back until this evening.'

'I see.' There was a pause. 'Are you trying to avoid me? Is it something I've said?'

'Not in the least,' lied Hannah. 'I simply happen to enjoy my own company.'

'Why don't we eat together this evening?'

'Maybe.' Hannah had no intention of spending any more time with him than she could help. Yet she had to concede that, had she not stumbled across the encounter between Lucas and Tristan's friends last night, she would probably have enjoyed being with him.

'I wish you'd explain what it is you think I've done,' Tristan said plaintively.

For a moment she contemplated telling him exactly what she had seen the night before. But she was alone here with him, a man who had already proved himself to be violent. She forced lightness into her voice: 'I already said: you've done nothing.'

Behind the wooden panels of the door there was silence. Then Tristan said: 'You can come out now, my dear. I'm not going to hurt you.'

'Good.'

His footsteps retreated down the passage and then, slowly, returned. He knocked again. 'Hannah?'

'Yes?'

'I meant it, you know.'

'Meant what?'

'That you're beautiful.'

She did not bother to reply. Then down in the hall, the telephone began to ring. She heard him clatter down the stairs to answer it, heard his laughter. Conversation followed but she could not hear what was said. After a while, he came back up the stairs, taking them two at a time.

He knocked at her door.

Hannah hesitated. But it seemed idiotic to keep her door locked, as though he presented some kind of danger. She opened it. 'Yes?'

'That was Susie. She's coming back tomorrow.'

Hannah's throat constricted. 'I – uh— Good.'

'You don't seem very pleased at the thought.'

'Of course I'm pleased. Susie's my best friend.' And all summer long, she thought, I have betrayed her. Behind the thought was another: she knows me, she will see, she will find out and hate me for it. If she were to lose Susie's affection, she would be desolate indeed.

White dust rose in clouds as Hannah cycled away from the Villa Giulia. There were butterflies today, multicoloured: peacock-blue, brown and black, red. Poppies burned in the roadside ditches. The sun was insistent, weighty, pressing down on tree and roof and field. All moisture seemed to have been sucked from the brittle earth.

Some miles from the town, she rounded a bend and found herself facing a landscape which looked like a sea of blood. Poppies again, but exuberant, unchecked, spread like jam over the ripe corn as far as the eye could see. Small birds darted here and there; they were never plentiful in Italy and she watched for a moment, standing with the bicycle between her legs, as they wagged and chittered among the corn stalks.

Behind her a car sounded its horn, two short yips of greeting rather than the long honk which impatient Italians favoured. She turned to see Faustino leaning from the driver's seat. He laughed.

'You look like a – what is it? – a miller,' he said. 'You are completely white with dust.'

'Are you spying on me, Faustino?' she demanded, brushing at her face and hair.

'Why do you say that?'

'Because wherever I go, you come creeping up behind me.'

'Creeping?'

'Driving, then. What are you trying to find out about me?'

He did not know whether she was serious. 'Me? I am not—'

'Are you still hoping to catch me with my lover?' she interrupted sarcastically. There was sweat on her neck, and more of it trickling down the centre of her back. 'Me and Lord Wyndham together – is that what you're after?'

His face reddened under his tan. He seemed confused, guiltily shaking his head. 'Of *course* not.'

'Then why are you always where I am?' Still astride her bike, her faded cotton skirt drooping on either side of the frame, she raised her voice a little. From here, she could see how the land was shaped, the way slopes rose out of the earth and fell back again, contours flowing as smoothly as a heaving sea. To her right the road wound between trees and fields back towards the foot of the hill on which the town perched; to her left the land tumbled down towards the narrowing valley which led eventually back to the shared grounds of the Villas Diana and Giulia, and the other houses near by.

'Coincidence. Nothing more.' Faustino shrugged casually, but she knew he was not telling the entire truth. 'Why do you accuse me in this – this strident fashion, Anna? Are you, in fact, off to see Lord Wyndham?'

'For God's sake,' Hannah said impatiently. 'I've already told you he has a lover, a much more beautiful woman than I am.'

'This I do not believe.'

'She is,' Hannah insisted. 'With the kind of body that I know you admire, not all scrawny like me.'

'Scrawny? What is this word?'

'And she's rich,' Hannah said. 'You can tell from her clothes – and her jewels.'

'Her jewels,' said Faustino, his voice lazy. His arm hung out of the window, the fingers drumming slowly against the door of his car. Biceps bulged under the arm of his short-sleeved shirt. 'So she is rich, this lover of Wyndham's?'

'Earrings,' Hannah said quickly. 'Diamond earrings. And a ring. A huge yellow diamond on her hand. A necklace.' Why did it matter so much whether Faustino believed her?

'And this lady who is Milord Wyndham's lover: is she blonde, as he is? Or is she dark, like you?'

'She's dark, but not in the least like me. I *told* you,' Hannah said. Sweat rolled slowly down the inner side of her thighs. The cool black water of the pool commandeered her thoughts: she would go swimming when she got back, provided Tristan Carrick was not around.

'Does she have a name, this beautiful, bejewelled, black-haired lady?' Faustino asked. He too was sweating in the heat of his car; his cheeks shone as though they had been painted with treacle and his shirt was wet along the line of his shoulders.

'Obviously she does, but I don't know it.' The countryside shimmered; cicadas ticked among the high grasses; heavy as a blanket, the heat bore down on them both. Hannah swayed suddenly, head and body momentarily disengaged, as so often these days. Was she going to faint? She thought again of the pool. 'I must go,' she said.

'One moment.' Faustino held up his hand. 'This woman, was she – where did you see her, the two of them?'

'In a kind of chapel,' Hannah said.

'Chapel?'

'Though they weren't exactly saying their prayers.' Laughing, she stepped down hard on her pedals and scooted past his car, back along the rutted white road. As she sped off, her skirt caught in the chain of the bicycle and she tugged it free, heard it tear as, behind her, Faustino crashed his gears as he tried to put the car into reverse. It would take him a while to turn in so restricted a space, by which time she would have turned on to a track which led between pines to another road.

By the time she was in the pool, she had begun to regret the information she had given Faustino. Lying on the surface of the water like a drowning Ophelia, it occurred to her for the first time that there had been method behind his questions. What secret had she revealed? Who had she betrayed?

Another betrayal. Another disloyalty. First Susie. Now Lucas. Once she had thought herself someone to be trusted, someone honourable. Now she saw that this was not so. Trepidation gnawed at her as she began to contemplate the possibility that the woman she had described in such detail to Faustino was his wife.

That afternoon she cycled over to see the Trevelyans. They were sitting on the patio at the back of the house, watching as their children and assorted friends leaped in and out of the swimming pool.

'Hannah! Good to see you.' Lew ensconced her in a padded chaise and poured her a glass of juice.

'How've you been doing, all alone in that big house?' Nancy asked.

'Enjoying it,' Hannah said.

'Bet you're glad of Tristan's company. It's kind of isolated over there, in spite of the neighbours all round.' Unselfconsciously, Nancy wore a bikini bottom but no top, revealing flat, large-nippled breasts. Hannah tried to imagine her own mother in similar costume but the image defeated her. As so often on this visit, she was struck by the realisation that, for other people, such things were commonplace, that not everyone chose to live in ugly austerity. Lying back on the cushions, with ice-cubes clunking at the brim of her glass, she wondered whether she would have been a different kind of person had she been born to different parents.

'I like being alone,' she said.

'When does Susie get back from Rome?'

'She just rang the house this morning to say she'd be back tomorrow.'

'Did Tristan say whether he was going to come up and visit with us?' Lew asked.

'I've scarcely seen him,' said Hannah. 'He had a dip in the pool this morning, but otherwise—'

'Why don't the two of you come for dinner?' said Nancy.

'Hey! That's a great idea!' Lew began to heave himself from his chair.

'I've really no idea what Tristan might be doing.'

'Why don't we find out?' Lew was already walking towards the patio doors. 'I'll go give him a call right now.'

Hannah took a breath. 'I'm not sure if I can actually—'

'It's no trouble,' said Nancy. 'There's a whole bunch of stuff left over from the barbecue. You could help us eat it.'

Hannah subsided. When Lew emerged from the house a few moments later to say that Tristan had accepted their invitation, it seemed a reasonable solution to the problem of getting through the evening. She would be able to hide her feelings about Tristan behind a façade of sociability. No one would notice if she didn't say much – they were used to that.

But she was here for confirmation of her suspicions, not for social reasons.

'I bumped into Faustino Castelli this morning,' she said. It was more or less true.

'How was he?' Nancy said.

'He seemed a bit concerned about his wife.' Hannah cast this upon the conversational waters, fairly confident that no one would examine it too closely.

'I'm not surprised,' said Lew. 'I would be too, if I were her husband.'

'Come on, Lew. You don't *know*,' his wife said. 'You're only guessing.'

315

Hannah assumed a bright look of enquiry. 'Know what?'

'The word is,' said Lew, leaning towards her as though anxious not to be overheard, 'that Mrs Faustino Castelli is doing a number with—' He paused, sat up, tapped the side of his nose.

'With?' said Hannah, looking from husband to wife.

'None other than Lucas Wyndham.' Lew nodded, waiting for Hannah's reaction, but she had none beyond a sudden sense of disaster. And, beyond that, of distaste. Gossip had never been part of her parents' ethos, partly because their circle of acquaintance was confined mostly to colleagues like themselves who did nothing gossip-worthy, partly from a natural fastidiousness which forbade the discussion of others or of their private affairs. Here, now, under the brittle sun, this seemed a wholly admirable trait. But although Hannah felt shoddy, the search for information overrode her instincts.

'Oh?' she said. 'Have I met her?'

Lew looked over at Nancy, who shook her head. 'I shouldn't think so. She doesn't mix with us ex-pats.'

'Except for Lucas,' added Lew, with a gross wink.

'I met someone last week,' lied Hannah, 'who I thought might be her.' All bright enquiry, she looked at Lew, despising herself for her duplicity.

'A gorgeous brunette, was she?' the American said. 'Very womanly?' He sketched curves in the air.

Oh God. Although the description could have matched nearly every Italian woman she had ever met, Hannah was somehow sure that the woman she had described to Faustino was indeed his own wife. 'Does Faustino know about this?' she asked, her voice cracking halfway through the question.

'He's always sneaking round, hoping to catch them on the job,' Lew said robustly, 'but I don't think he knows for absolutely sure.'

Not until now, Hannah thought. Not until I spelt it out for him so he could not possibly be mistaken. She had believed that Faustino followed her in order to catch her with Lucas; she had not realised he must be spying on his own wife. She felt as though she had stumbled into the middle of a Greek tragedy, as though doom was even now rolling down on them all, growing larger and more destructive, gathering danger as it gathered speed on its rush towards them. Apprehension bloomed in her chest. What would Faustino do, if his suspicions were confirmed? Was Lucas under threat?

'They knew each other when they were young,' Nancy explained. 'Faustino's your typical Italian male: jealous of anything in long pants. Especially if it glances at his wife.'

'And not averse to using his fists,' Lew said. 'Ever wondered why that poor woman so often wears sunglasses in the evening?'

'Now then, Lew. You're guessing again,' Nancy said reprovingly.

Struggling to her feet, Hannah said: 'Look, thanks for the drink. I'd better go now.'

'But you'll come to supper?'

'Thanks. Yes, I will.'

'You and Tristan can come up together.'

'Yes,' Hannah said. If they did, they would also have to go home together. But she could handle that. She could plead tiredness, illness, she could say she wished to go to bed early. And then tomorrow evening, Susie would be here and everything would be all right again.

Wouldn't it?

THE DIARY

. . . *My puppy. It had a yellow lead. I remember running across the grass with it. Cuddling its funny, round, bumpy head, so much too big for its body.*

She told me that a dog was a man's best friend. Certainly it was mine. Not just the best, but the only.

I heard it screaming, a thin, attenuated scream like one of those whistling kettles, I followed it through the bushes, already knowing something terrible had happened.

My puppy. He was holding it in his hands. The two of them were there: I could see their reflections in the pool and my puppy in his hands, still screaming. Its back's broken in two, he said.

And the crack as he twisted its neck. The crack.

God.

And she said that's horrible, horrible, *and he told her not to be sentimental.*

I didn't know what the word meant at the time but I didn't care. I hated him. The beast with two backs.

They saw me. I remember opening my mouth to scream but nothing came out. It was as though I had been struck dumb.

That was the first time I heard the beast run, its big feet hitting the ground as it kept pace with me when I ran away through the bushes, the leaves hitting my face, and all I could see was blood, all I could hear was that screaming noise and the thud of the beast beside me.

My best friend.

. . . They want me to leave.

That doesn't matter – I too want to go. I wish to find Anna, I wish to sort it all out at last, go through it one final time and then put it behind me. I have suffered enough, now it's someone else's turn.

With memory returned, I recognise that M suffered too, but she deserves to, just as Anna does. Whereas I, I, I was done to, not doing.

NOW

19

Asleep, it took Hannah a moment to realise that the shrill, half-heard insistence was the telephone. She pushed back the covers and, stumbling, ran downstairs, hoping she would get there before the ringing stopped.

'*Si?*' she said breathlessly.

'Is that Mrs Carrington?' The voice was English, half-remembered.

'Yes.'

'With reference to your telephone call yesterday, Mrs Carrington. One of my officers went round to your shop—' It was Sergeant Bowen, from her local police station.

'Yes?' she said quickly, glancing at her watch. Nearly ten o'clock; she had overslept.

'We did not effect entry, because the damage seemed too slight to warrant forcing the lock. However—'

'Damage?'

'A small amount of disturbance was discernible through the front entrance but, as I say, not enough to—'

'You must,' Hannah said urgently. 'You have my full permission to get in whichever way you wish, even if it means breaking down the door. You must make sure that my assistant isn't in there somewhere. I'm really worried about her.'

'We checked around the back, Mrs Carrington. It was possible to have sight of most of the premises and as far as we could see, they were empty.'

'What about this damage you mentioned? Surely that would indicate that something's wrong.' Something was *terribly* wrong. Where was Zoe? Why was she not at the shop?

'It seemed to my officer more as though someone might have stumbled against one of those toy houses you sell.'

'Why wouldn't my assistant have cleared it up, then? And, in any case, why should she fall, unless she—?'

'Perhaps she was in a hurry, knocked something over on her way out, and intended to clear up as soon as she returned.'

'But what reason could there be for her to—?'

'There could be any number. Things happen which you can't predict. Didn't you tell me this young woman had a child? Maybe he's been taken ill, maybe her husband's in hospital, anything. And in rushing out of the shop, she knocks over something but doesn't have time to clear it up.'

'I really can't bel—'

'Have you had any success in contacting your assistant since we last spoke, Mrs Carrington?'

'I told you before: I don't know her home number. Or her address.'

'That's right: you did mention that. Don't know her surname either, if I remember corrrectly.' A heavy pall of suspended belief hung over the sergeant's voice.

'I've never had occasion to telephone her at home, you see. And the address I have seems to be wrong,' Hannah said, trying to justify her ignorance.

'How long has she been working for you?'

'Just a few weeks.'

'Funny, wouldn't you say, not to be sure of her last name?'

'What I meant to say was, I didn't know what name her telephone is registered under. I mean, her name's Griffin, but I'm not sure if that's her maiden name, whether she kept her maiden name for work, and her husband's, her *married* name, is something different.'

It all sounded so implausible. So thin. Hannah could hardly blame Sergeant Bowen for not believing her. Or, at least, for not perceiving any need for urgent action. None the less, she was certain that wherever Zoe was, she was in danger.

'At the moment, Mrs Carrington, we really don't have enough evidence to issue a Missing Person notice,' the sergeant said, soothing. 'Even if she has gone missing, it may well be for reasons of her own. Like I said, could be domestic reasons, a sick child or a fight with her husband, something like that.'

'But she could be—'

'However, our patrolling officers will be informed of the circumstances you have described, and will certainly be looking out for the young woman as well as keeping an eye on your business premises. Until we have more facts, I really don't think there's a lot we can do. I'm sorry.'

He was right, of course. Which did absolutely nothing to dispel Hannah's feelings of apprehension.

The telephone rang again almost as soon as she had replaced the receiver.

'Tristan Carrick here,' his cool voice said. 'We're at the airport. We're going to come straight to you, so don't go off anywhere, will you?'

'Uh . . . all right.'

'We should be with you in about an hour. And Hannah—'

'Yes?'

'I don't want to sound alarmist, but there is an element of danger about the proceedings.'

Hannah could not help laughing at his melodramatic words. 'Proceedings? What are you—'

Behind Tristan, distant, another voice said: 'Tell her to keep the windows closed and the doors locked.' Whose voice was it: ex-soldier Mark's? Why did it sound so familiar?

'Did you hear that?' Tristan asked.

'Yes. But who—'

He interrupted her. 'We'll be with you in an hour. Take care, Hannah.' He put down the phone.

Filled with dread, Hannah walked through the house, checking that everything was secure. As she unpeeled the shutters from the salon wall, a dead butterfly fell from some crevice, dusty-blue, the triangle of wing eyed with a black dot set in a circle of white. Summer's eye, Hannah thought, looking down at the weightless, still-bright body which lay on her palm. Questions shot into her mind like comets and fell away again. What did Tristan mean when he spoke of an element of danger? Who should she be afraid of? *Why* should she be afraid? And what had happened to the American boy, Dan, Lucinda's friend? She had no answers; she was limboed there, among the webbed mirrors and dead bouquets, blinkered by ignorance.

Wherever the threat lay, it was impossible for anyone to have been offended, compromised, disturbed by her presence in the Villa Giulia after all these years. She had asked questions of no one but Faustino. This journey into the past was planned in the hope that she might thereby lift some of the guilt that had burdened her through the years, but since her arrival, her perspectives had changed. Lucinda, loss, life and death, coming to terms with herself and the directions she has taken: these were what had preoccupied her. Although she had relived moments from the traumatic past, she had not considered them with the same intensity as she had in contemplating – and dreading – the future.

From an upstairs window Hannah watched as an unfamiliar car came slowly along the drive and pulled up below the terrace. Tristan was at the wheel; he glanced up at the house and, seeing her, smiled, a smile so broad, so giving, that something melted in the frozen parts of her heart. For a long moment, their eyes held, then lifting her hand slightly, smiling too, Hannah went downstairs to open the door.

He was waiting for her. 'Hannah,' he said quietly.

She was unaccountably shy, not having anticipated this rush of warmth. As he brushed his hand lightly across her cheek, then bent to kiss the side of her face, she became aware of someone standing behind him.

'You two already know each other, I believe,' Tristan said.

'No,' she began. 'We've never—' but then he had stepped aside and facing her was a man she recognised all too well.

Marcus?

'Marcus?' she said, not believing what she saw. What was going on? As he came towards her, she stepped back into the hall. 'Why are you—?'

Marcus. Mark. They were one and the same. Why had she not realised? *Could* she have realised? Still gazing at him in bewilderment, she knew there had been nothing to alert her to the possibility that the man who had been her lover for the past months was the same man she had watched twenty-five years ago as he plunged a knife into the body of the man who had been her lover then. Nothing to connect him with any of this, not with Tristan or with Lucas, certainly not with Lucinda.

And yet, he himself must have known, must he not?

'There's some explaining to do,' he said. Apologetically, he took her hand.

'Yes.' Still trying to assimilate Marcus with Mark, she did not withdraw it, although reluctance filled her at having to touch him.

'I haven't behaved well,' Marcus said. 'But when I explain, perhaps you'll understand why I've done what I did.'

'You'd better come in.' Hannah stood aside and the two of them walked into the hall. 'There's coffee in the kitchen.'

The three of them walked in silence down the long passage to the kitchen. She was shivering despite the warmth of the room. While the men sat down on either side of the table, she poured coffee into mugs and then seated herself at the end.

'So,' she said. 'What has been going on?'

'First of all,' Tristan began, 'I had absolutely no idea about any of this – that you knew Marcus, I mean.'

'And I,' said Marcus, 'thought all along that you knew Jane, and what happened to her.'

'I never met her,' Hannah said. It seemed a necessary statement to make, a crystallisation of all that she had not known, a reinforcement of the outsider she had always been during those long, hot weeks.

'You must have met her here . . . that summer.'

'No. She wasn't around.'

'She was,' Marcus said harshly. 'All summer long.'

'You would have surely seen . . . I mean, you were . . .' Tristan was finding it difficult to meet Hannah's eyes. He glanced away from her. 'Weren't you and Lucas . . . I mean, that's what I assumed from what you—'

'That I was sleeping with Lucas, do you mean?' A kind of cold embarrassment dropped over Hannah, as though she were the woman taken in adultery, a latter-day Hester Prynne. I was so innocent, she wanted to say. I knew nothing, I saw nothing, only Lucas and myself

328

and the lovely syncopations of desire that we played on his white sheets. 'What's that got to do with Jane?'

'My wife,' Marcus said, 'was living with Lucas at the time, house-keeping for him.'

'Lucas's housekeeper.' So the woman who had always just disap-peared round a corner, through a door, into the shadows, that was Marcus's wife?

'That's what he called her. The patronising bastard. But she was my wife. And the child with her was my daughter.'

'I often wondered whether it was a girl or a boy,' Hannah said softly.

Marcus cleared his throat roughly. 'One thing you have to understand about all this—'

'Only one?' Hannah said.

'She's – Sophie, my daughter – is . . . she's damaged.'

'In what way?'

'Mentally.' It was difficult for Marcus to admit it. 'I'm not saying she's deranged or anything. But there's some kind of – of abnormality. Some disturbance.' Marcus pounded the table, setting the coffee mugs rattling. 'She was all right until Jane took her to Italy, I know she was.'

Was she? Looking back, Hannah wondered how normal the child could have been who never spoke, who captured smoky-blue butterflies in the sunshine only to crush them and let them fall. She nodded, unwilling to break Marcus's illusions.

'But she was traumatised by something which happened while they were there,' he went on. 'Something dreadful.'

'You and Jane splitting up,' said Tristan. 'Isn't that the obvious explanation?'

'It was more than that. Had to be. Whatever it was, it—' Marcus shrugged, as though he hoped to hide from them how much it mattered.

'Do you have any idea what happened?'

'None at all.' Marcus scowled. He brought out a silver penknife and laid it on the table beside his coffee mug. 'Except that in some way it involved Lucas.'

'You don't mean that you think Lucas might have—' But Hannah could not complete the sentence; such a thing was impossible.

He spread his hands and looked away from her. 'For years after that, she didn't speak. My wife tried everything.' Marcus shook his head as though to clear it. 'Sophie was taken to psychologists and therapists and even hypnotists. Nothing seemed to work. Since they couldn't find out what had affected her, they weren't able to treat her effectively. The result is—' he looked at Hannah with bright sorrowful eyes. 'It's a terrible thing to have to say about one's own child, but she may be disturbed enough to be dangerous.'

'Dangerous?' Hannah frowned enquiringly at Tristan.

Tristan put his hand on hers. 'Until now, she's done nothing particularly serious, thank God.'

'There was an incident a year or so ago. She was accused of threatening someone with a knife,' Marcus said.

'But we now think – Marcus thinks that she's after you,' said Tristan.

'Me? Why?' The two of them seemed to be conversing in a foreign language; though the sounds were perfectly audible, their words made no sense. 'What do I have to do with her?' She stared at Marcus. 'Or do you mean that she is jealous of – of the relationship I had with you? One of those adolescent things girls get about their fathers?'

'Sophie is not a teenager,' Marcus said. 'She's over thirty. Much too old to be dictated to, I'm afraid. And whatever it is that obsesses her about you, it's not your relationship with me.'

'How can you be sure?' asked Hannah.

His mouth tightened. He was obviously unwilling to consider the idea. 'All we can do is keep an eye on her, try to prevent her from harming you,' he said.

'Stop!' Hannah said. She put up her hands so that they cradled her face. 'This is all so bizarre. What reason could your daughter have to be – as you put it – after me?'

Marcus sighed. 'A while ago, she asked me to find someone called Anna.'

'Anna?' The androgynous voice sounded in her inner ear: *Listen carefully, Anna* . . . She saw again the cruel postcard under her pillow: WHO IS NEXT, ANNA? Was all that down to Marcus's daughter?

'That's right. Naturally, I did nothing about it. How was I supposed to locate a woman of whom I only knew the name, even if I wanted to? Then later, she said that she remembered this Anna from that time. She was one of the people who'd been here that summer, she remembered her sitting round a table at the house where she and her mother had spent the summer.'

'Lucas's house?'

'Yes. And since it was the first time she'd remembered anything at all, naturally I encouraged her. I called up Lucas Wyndham's cousin, Susanna – I'd met her several times in the past – and asked about an Anna. No Anna, she said, but my best friend, Hannah Barlow. She gave me your current address, told me something about you.'

'And you passed the information on to your daughter?' Hannah stared at him in angry disbelief. 'Even though you thought she might be dangerous?'

'I would have done, except right around then, she started acting irrationally. Ringing me in the middle of the night, demanding that I find you, threatening me. Obviously, there was no way on earth I was

going to pass on information about a total stranger – as you then were.'
He smiled at her, without really seeing her.

'So you knew about me before we bumped into each other on the train?' Hannah asked, and knew at once by the way his gaze shifted that her suspicions of him had been correct, and their meeting had been contrived rather than accidental.

'I came down south and – and checked up on you.'

'Spied on me, you mean.'

'I found out that you caught that train every Thursday evening. It was easy enough to – to arrange that we met.'

Tears gathered behind Hannah's eyes. 'That's despicable,' she said, her voice shaking. She would have to assess her reaction to this later; for the moment, her predominant emotion was anger rather than distress.

Tristan said matter-of-factly: 'Mark, you're not telling things in their logical order. The point about Sophie is that she is still suffering from amnesia about those weeks, and—'

Marcus interrupted him. 'The most recent psychiatrist my wife consulted—'

Why, Hannah wondered, does he still refer to her as his wife when she's been married to someone else for years? 'I thought Jane remarried,' she said.

'She did.'

'I thought she lived in America.'

'She does, but—'

'Then she can't,' Hannah said clearly, impatient with him now, 'still be your wife. Can she?'

'— suggested that Sophie keep a diary.' He drew another deep breath, his eyes fixed on the terracotta bowl of oranges in the middle of the table. 'It seemed to work. Incidents from the past began to surface at last. He asked her to let him read the diary. He had no means of working out whether what she wrote down had really happened or was the product of her imagination – and Sophie herself seemed unsure. In the end, hoping to force her hand, he suggested she send it to a publisher in New York, and—'

Hannah gasped. 'My God! *Hurled by Dreams*.'

'Yes.'

'But the author's someone called Max Marsden—'

'A pseudonym.'

'I just assumed the author was a man using a false male name. It never occurred to me that it was a woman.' Hannah shook her head again. 'How bizarre that Zoe – my assistant in the shop – should have had a copy, as well as you.'

'Zoe?' Tristan said.

'Oh, my God!' exclaimed Marcus.

'What's wrong?'

'What does this assistant of yours look like?' asked Tristan.

'Small, frail-looking, almost boyish. Blonde hair, a very pale corn-colour.'

'She found you,' said Marcus; the colour had leached out of his face so that his eyes seemed almost black in their sockets.

'Who did?' Hannah looked from one man to another. 'What do you mean?'

'Sophie found you,' Marcus said.

'How can you—' Hannah broke off for a moment. 'You're surely not implying that Zoe – my Zoe, as it were – is your daughter, are you?' She frowned, not really comprehending any of this.

'I think it's more than possible,' Marcus said tiredly. 'When Sophie first began to speak, she could never pronounce her own name: it came out as Zoe and that's what we often called her.'

Hannah raised her hands to her head, forcing herself to speak calmly although her instinct was to shriek aloud. 'Just a minute. You're asking me to believe that my assistant, Zoe, is also your daughter Sophie, who is also Max Marsden, the author of a book called *Hurled by Dreams*?'

'Yes.' Reaching with unsteady hands for an orange from the bowl, Marcus began to carve the skin with his knife. 'Nobody involved with publicising the book in the States realises she isn't a man. She used the pseudonym from the beginning, and if she had to talk to anyone, she – she has this special voice she used, which sounds just like a man's unless you listen really closely. Her wolf voice, she calls it.'

'Wolf voice?' asked Tristan.

'It's from some children's book my wife and I used to read her, years and years ago. About a little boy called Max who—'

'I know it,' said Hannah, suddenly pierced with memories of Lucinda and Adam in their pyjamas, being read to before they went up to bed. The wolfsuit. The wild things. And the final return to the place where someone loved Max best of all— 'Is that why she chose the name Max Marsden to write under?'

'Probably,' Marcus said. He held the peeled sphere of orange in his hand and studied it.

'Marsden was Jane's maiden name,' Tristan said, when it became clear Marcus was not going to elaborate.

Hannah thought about it. Once again she remembered the peeking glimpses between the leaves by the pool, the sound of an almost noiseless footstep, a glint of pale hair. 'Isn't it possible,' she said carefully, picking her words, 'that the most obvious explanation for Zoe's – Sophie's – condition is that she witnessed Lucas's murder? She doesn't go into it in much detail, in the book, but perhaps that's because it's still too traumatic for her to write about.'

'It's possible,' Marcus said. 'But she was – what? Six or seven at the time. She would have been in bed asleep, not out wandering in the woods.'

'She was everywhere that summer,' said Hannah. 'All the time.'

Tristan looked at Marcus. 'Tell her, Mark,' he said. 'Tell her why we came.'

Marcus put the naked orange down on the table and began to fiddle with his knife, opening and closing the blade. He picked up one of the strips of orange peel and began methodically to cut it into the thinnest possible strips. 'She's already been here,' he said eventually. 'She was here two or three months ago.'

'Doing what?'

'She got a job with some American family,' said Marcus.

Hadn't Nancy said—? 'As an au pair?'

'I think so. She did mention something about doing odd jobs but I think au pairing's really what it was.'

'She's come back,' Hannah said. She thought of Lucinda, of the unknown boy called Dan, the tape in her car. Zoe: so many questions asked as they waited for customers wanting a miniature refectory table, a tiny harp, a kitchen dresser. So much knowledge about Hannah's family stored away inside that fragile-looking skull. She knew all about Lucinda; she would have had no difficulty in finding her address, nor in putting the doctored tape into Hannah's own car.

Her sense of betrayal was strong; she had liked Zoe, trusted her. Perhaps even begun to love her. To find herself used by her was deeply upsetting. She remembered the bunch of white roses which Zoe had sent to Lucinda's funeral, and felt sick. But what more did a betrayer deserve than to be, in her turn, betrayed?

Tristan watched the pile of orange-peel parings, each convoluted strip twisted back on itself, doubled up, deformed. 'So she *is* here.'

'Lew Trevelyan saw her in the town yesterday,' explained Hannah, 'although Nancy didn't believe him.'

'I do,' said Marcus. His face was suddenly grey. 'I was afraid of this – that's why we came over here.' He turned to Tristan. 'We'll have to keep a close watch over Hannah until we find her again.'

'But why should Zoe – or Sophie – have any quarrel with me?' Hannah was still not clear what this was all about. 'I've only known her for a few weeks and—'

'She sought you out, Hannah. I'm not sure how she found you, though it certainly wasn't with any help from me.' His expression grew thoughtful. 'At least, not directly. I did have the impression someone had been in the house . . . through my desk—' He shook his head. 'But it's no coincidence that she's been working for you.'

And, thinking back, Hannah remembered how insistent she had been, that waiflike creature with the awkwardly-cut hair who had walked in off the street and asked for a job. She had been so convincing, talking of her wish for part-time work, her child, her husband, her degree in business studies.

'I suppose,' she said, her voice icy, 'that her son, Orlando, doesn't exist, any more than the husband she told me about.'

'Certainly there's no husband. Orlando exists, all right, but he's her brother, not her son. Half-brother, I suppose I should say. The child that Jane – my wife – gave birth to, six months after Lucas died.'

Everything suddenly slotted into place. Pain gripped Hannah's heart, leaving her suddenly breathless.

'Is he your son?'

'No.'

'He looks just like his father used to, doesn't he?' Hannah whispered.

'Exactly like.' The expression on Marcus's face was ugly.

'He's . . . Lucas's son.'

'He is.'

Hannah closed her eyes. For the joy of a summer's dance, she had served a lifetime's sentence; she still did not know whether the dance had been worth the price she paid for it.

'I see.' She felt tired and very near to tears. A lifetime's sentence – and she did not even know for what. Not now. 'All these lies,' she said fiercely.

'Sometimes you can't tell the truth,' Marcus said.

'From the start, everyone has lied.' Including myself, she thought.

'Necessary lies,' Tristan said.

'Perhaps.' Although she did not agree, it was too much effort to argue with him. 'But, Marcus, when I asked you, that morning in Crickgarth, if you knew someone called Lucas Wyndham, why did you lie to me then? What difference could it have made?'

He started to speak, but she held up a hand. 'Or have we all, because of our shared complicity, one way or another, in Lucas's death, become so unaccustomed to the truth that we no longer recognise it?'

'Hannah—' Tristan said, but again she overrode him.

'Orlando is the boy we saw that day, isn't he, Marcus?' It seemed blindingly clear to her now, even though she did not really grasp all the facts. In a way, all this seemed to have started with Orlando, the ghost she had glimpsed through the long windows of the Festival Hall, the ghost who had stepped out of the past and taken over the present.

Marcus hesitated.

'I know you saw him too,' she said quietly.

'Yes,' he said. 'He came over here from the States to find his sister. He didn't know about the book she'd written until after she left and her publishers rang up with some enquiry. He is afraid, just as I am, that she will do something really—' The sentence drifted into silence.

'Where is he now?'

'I don't know.'

'When I told you I was going to Cornwall, why didn't you tell me about Tristan?'

'I – I honestly didn't realise that he was the person you were going to see. Not at the time you told me about it. And later, when I decided that because of what happened to Lucas, perhaps you ought to know that Tristan and I were friends, you'd already—' Marcus lifted his hands from the table and let them fall again.

Hannah stood. 'I don't think I can stand much more of this. All of us, circling round each other, circling round our lives, none of us telling the truth to each other or to ourselves.' Her voice was not steady. 'But there's one question I have to ask.' She stopped, her throat thick with tension. She held her hands together in front of her, as though they might act as some kind of protective barrier against the knowledge she sought. 'If what you say is true – and there's no reason for me to doubt you except that it all sounds like something out of a film – but if it is, then just tell me because I really need to know—' Again she stopped, staring for a moment out of the window, dropping her shoulders, drawing air deeply into her lungs, readying herself. 'Did . . . do you think Zoe killed my daughter? And if so, why?'

Neither of the men said anything, though one gave a scarcely audible cough.

'Well?' she demanded.

'I don't know,' admitted Marcus. 'I can only say that I'm very afraid that she's quite capable of it.'

'None of us really knows what goes on in her mind,' Tristan added.

'She seems to inhabit a world at which I can only guess, which bears no relationship to anything I recognise,' said Marcus.

'But if she did, if it *was* she who is responsible for Lucinda's death,' Hannah said steadily, 'with both of you suspecting that she's – apparently – a walking time-bomb, are you not, in that case, both responsible for my daughter's death?' She stared at the two men in turn, then walked away, out of the room.

In the deserted ballroom she paces up and down the dusty parquet. Within the mirrored glass, the ghost of herself keeps pace with her. She feels nothing but a tumbling confusion: Zoe, Lucinda, lies and mistakes, dreams which hurl the dreamer into nowhere, Lucas dead, wasted years, pain which sucks out feeling and scatters it in emptiness.

Was Lucinda's death preventable? The thought torments her as she treads the herringboned floor. Had Marcus, her lover, allowed it to happen? And can she blame him, if so? He too is the parent of a lost daughter – but she finds that this does not incline her towards either forgiveness or understanding. She knows that what lay between the two of them for a while is now over; on the other hand, she recognises that he has played a part in her liberation.

In the kitchen, the two men were still talking, their deep voices billowing down the passage towards her as she put on a coat and went outside. A cold wind blew as she walked down through the wet trees to the pool. Seen between the marble pillars, the bushes seemed black and sinister, as though the two columns were no longer a triumphal arch but marked the entrance to the yawning pits of hell.

'My daughter,' she said aloud. The words held a particular tenderness, just as they had when Marcus used them. It was impossible to blame him for what he had done, the way he had, as she now saw it, used her. She conceded that she might have done the same. Yet if it were to be discovered that – of all people – Zoe had murdered Lucinda—

She remembered how she had felt standing by the ruined walls where Lucinda had died, and how she had known that she herself could kill without remorse were she to encounter the killer. Easy to say in the abstract; suppose she had Zoe at her mercy and incontrovertible proof that she had been responsible for Lucinda's death – what then?

Hands tucked under her arms for warmth, she stared down into the blackness of the water. Cold leaves lay on the surface, pushed to the edges by the welling movement of the hidden spring. Where is the end and where the beginning, she wondered? If she had been born to different parents, she might not have responded to Lucas in the way that she had, might not have been receptive to his messages, might never have condemned him to die here on the marble paving and thus spent the rest of her life regretting it. But, she told herself, that single act of abandonment could not be attributed to the way she was raised. She, and only she, was the guilty one.

Oh God.

She was seared by the intensity of the feelings she once had for Lucas. Now, as then, her mouth was dry, her body trembled, her mind was blank except for the images of their bodies together.

Sweat – or tears – lay in the sockets beneath her eyes. She covered them with the palms of her hands. Was that true? Here – it had all started here when she had thrown away her inhibitions and stepped naked from the pool and into Lucas's arms. Or had it merely continued? Would the events of that last summer night have taken place in much the same way if she had never come here? Lucas would still have loved Marina; Marina would still have cuckolded Faustino; Faustino would still have fought with Lucas and left him to stumble into the trap hidden in the soft mulch under the bushes. Lucas would still have engendered the hatreds and jealousies which eventually caused his death – and giving shape to this thought reminded Hannah that she still did not know what really happened that night beside the pool.

Perhaps no one ever would.

Did she accept Faustino's version of events? Did she really believe that after swinging at Lucas's leg with an iron bar, he hit his rival on the jaw and left him there among the bushes? And if so, did she further believe that nothing else had taken place between them, as he had told her, or did she think it possible that, maddened by jealousy and drink, he later returned to finish the job he had begun, to kill the only man his beautiful wife would ever love?

Like herself, Faustino was a man riven by his involvement in another's death. Did that imply guilt or innocence? It was difficult to believe that someone other than Faustino could also have been on the spot and have beaten in the back of Lucas's head in the short time it took her to get to the house and back.

On the other hand, she had been very aware that there were other presences in the tunnels that night. And Lucas, though still able to talk and, to an extent, to function – had it not been for the smashed leg, he might even have been able to walk up to the house with her, despite the horror of his hand – had been weakened by loss of blood; he would not have been able to put up any resistance.

Behind her, among the dark bushes, something stirred and she turned. It had been like this that night, twenty-five years ago; she had turned and seen between the leaves, a glimpse of something pale as moonlight, a glitter like a tear.

Had it been the child, the sexless creature she now understood to have been Zoe, Marcus's daughter? Or someone else? She strained to remember. Who else could have been standing there, watching?

She thought of the people involved with Lucas: Faustino, Marina, Jane, Tristan himself. Was the reason she had not found Tristan at the house when she ran back to find help, because he was already down by the pool, crushing Lucas's skull? Certainly, at the time the police thought so, though they had later released him for lack of evidence. They had also taken Faustino and again been forced to let him go. Where did Marina run to?

So many questions, and it seemed that many of the answers remained locked inside the confused landscape of a mind where chaos and confusion lurked.

Hannah looked up at the pewter patch of sky above the taller trees. Unless that mind could be prised open like an oyster, the shattered memories restored, it might be that no one would ever know exactly what had happened that summer night.

Nor why Lucinda had died.

THE DIARY

. . . *From the airport I ring F. I brace myself for his sigh. Anna,
I say. Have you found her?*

He ums and ers.

You have, haven't you? I say. You must tell me where she is.

He doesn't answer.

You must, *I tell him.*

But he will not.

*I can make you, I say, and hear his angry silence. I'm coming,
I say. Look out.*

Beware.

He laughs. Don't be silly, he says.

I'm *not being silly. I want to give myself a chance to live a proper
life. Even if it's not with T, then with someone.*

I'm tired of being sad.

. . . It isn't difficult to find out where F lives, to watch him. Although I see him look about him every time he goes out, he does not see me, because he does not recognise me. Once, I spoke to him directly, lifting my hand. 'Nice day!' I said, and he smiled back at me, nodding, taking me for one of the hikers who infest the area. Not surprising, since I had dressed the part, in walking boots and royal-blue windproof garment, a woollen cap pulled down over my ears. He doesn't know me, that's the point. He's met me but he doesn't know me.

When he drove off, one day, I got into the house. All I wanted was an address and a telephone number. I went through his desk. It didn't take me long to find it.

Not Anna, but Hannah. Hannah Carrington.

I was halfway to the nearest rail-station before he returned, walking across the frozen hills, swinging along with others dressed like myself, fitting like a hare into my form.

. . . I've found her. Hannah. From across the road, I watch her. I follow her home. She is no longer a girl with a lot of black curly hair, the way I remember her, the way I wrote her in the book. But her eyes are still sad. Not that I was really capable of analysing an emotion such as sadness, though looking back I can see how sad I was myself, how bewildered, with M not living with F any more but with Ivo, making the beast with two backs. I remember how she glided through that big house as though she was skating on ice . . .

I remember how easy it was to catch the butterflies and how I crushed them, killed them, as I so much wished to kill the tall fair man we were living with, who never spoke to me, never seemed to understand or care how much I missed F. Never asked.

Killed my best friend.

THEN

20

The night air was heavy and perfumed. Walking back to the Villa Giulia at Tristan's side, Hannah felt no need to make conversation. The evening had passed easily, helped along by the informal group of locals whom Lew and Nancy, always glad of an excuse for an impromptu party, had also invited in. She had been able to avoid too much proximity to the tall man who now took her elbow as she stumbled over some roughness in the ground.

'Careful,' he said. 'I should have had the sense to bring a torch. I hadn't realised how dark it would be, once we got away from the houses.'

'There was a moon a few days ago,' Hannah said.

'Was there?'

They walked on without speaking, Tristan still holding her elbow. All round them was the scent of resin and a faint stir from the cypress trees moving fitfully in a small, hot breeze. Last night, at the lakeside barbecue, it had rained; there would probably be more rain tonight.

'I can't see anything at all,' she said, peering ahead into the darkness.

'Nor me. I haven't the faintest idea where we are.'

'I've never walked back this late. In fact, I've never walked back at all, only cycled,' swooping through the dark, the pale circle of light from her bike lamp sliding along the path in front of her, the warm night rushing past her ears . . .

Tristan looked up. 'No stars tonight,' he said. 'That's why it's so dark.'

'It's frightfully hot, too,' Hannah said. Even though it was past midnight, sweat lay on her forehead and between her breasts.

'Means there's a storm brewing,' Tristan said. 'Or so my father always said. Something to do with a rise in atmospheric pressure.'

'I hope we get home before it breaks.'

Another silence. Their footsteps sounded on the road. Behind them, scattered lights nestled on unseen hills. A dog howled, miles away.

'We turn off somewhere soon,' Hannah said, after a while.

'Hope we don't miss it.'

'There's a white signpost,' Hannah said. She was glad of Tristan's company; the night was impenetrable and frightening. The blackness was more than simply an absence of light; it possessed a palpability of its own, solid and immovable.

And then, as ahead she saw the first glimmer of the narrow board which indicated the track down to the gates of the Villa Giulia, she heard it. Inside her head, Lucas's unmistakable call. She shivered, moving closer to Tristan.

'What's wrong?' he said.

'Nothing.'

Letting go of her elbow he took her hand instead.

'*Hannah. Hannah.*' The words moved into her mind with the weight of birds in flight.

'What?' she said aloud. What did Lucas want? Why was he calling her?

'I said, what's wrong?' Tristan repeated.

She shook her head. 'Nothing at all.'

They turned off the made-up road; before them the chalky track gave off a faint, greasy glow.

'*Hannah.*' The cry came again, as though he called for help.

She bit her lip. With Tristan at her side, there was nothing she could or dared to do. If he found out she was going to Lucas, he might once again try to harm him. She decided that immediately they got back to the villa, she would get hold of a torch and then find out what Lucas wanted. Perhaps the knife wound had reopened, perhaps one of the other men who had attacked him last night had returned.

One day, she asked herself, shall I look back at all this and remember it as a good experience, a learning experience? Or shall I always feel only guilt and shame and bitterness for my own naïvety? Shall I grow old believing that Lucas was anything other than an opportunist who had seen a chance to seduce a virgin and taken it? In that moment, she passionately wanted not to regret these past weeks.

This nearly-ended summer had been entire and whole, she realised. Time out of time. There was no question of her ever seeing Lucas back in England, even if she wanted to. During all the weeks she had never harboured thoughts of a future; she had been more than content to revel in the consuming present.

They were at the open gates now, treading across the gravel drive to the foot of the steps leading up to the terrace. Tristan sprang up them ahead of her and opened the front door, ushering her in.

'Coffee?' he said. 'I'm too spaced out to go to sleep. Lew's always so generous with the vino—'

'Actually, I'm feeling exhausted,' Hannah said, hoping that he would not realise she was telling less than the truth or, worse, sense that she was trying to get away from him. After the morning's experience, she had realised that he did not easily give up when he wanted something.

'A tisane, then,' Tristan said. 'Camomile – I found some in a tin when I was making my breakfast. They're supposed to lull you to sleep, aren't they?'

'I'd rather just go up, if you don't mind.'

'Please, Hannah.' He caught at her hand again. 'Don't leave me on my own. I need company, someone to talk to.'

Used to compliance, she almost gave in to his pleadings. Though she had known him only a short time she had come to realise that whatever had led him to strike Lucas the night before, he was a fundamentally decent man. She was even prepared to concede that there might be a good reason which had made him act in such a way. Whereas Lucas himself . . . she could not help recalling his attitude to her, all through the past summer, the contempt with which he treated her, his reaction when she had tried to help him last night. Seen in the context of Tristan's innate courtesy, she wondered how she could have tolerated such behaviour for so long, how she could have so little sense of her own worth.

But the voice sounded again in her skull, '*Hannah*', fainter this time, as though Lucas was losing strength; whatever his faults, she could not evade her responsibility towards him.

She shook her head. 'Sorry, Tristan. I really want to go to bed. I slept badly last night.' Turning she went away from him, up the broad central stairs and along the gallery. Looking down, she could see him staring up at her, his hair like a flag in the shadows of the hall, his brows pulled together in a frown. She wondered if he believed her.

In her room she closed the door and leaned against it. How long would it be before she dared creep out? Noisily, she closed the long windows out on to the balcony above the terrace, ran water into the basin, made ablutionary noises in case he was listening out for them, pulled back the covers of her bed, switched off the light. Once out of the room, she would be able to lock the door from the outside so that he would not know she was not inside, but she still had to get downstairs and through the front door without attracting his attention. Catching sight of her anxious face in the dressing-table mirror, she pulled back her shoulders. She was a free agent, after all, able to go for an evening stroll if she chose, perfectly entitled to do as she liked without reference to Tristan.

Picking up a flashlight, she stood in the darkened room and started slowly counting to a hundred. Before she had reached twenty, however, her brain was pierced by a clangour so painful that she clapped her hands to her ears.

'*Hannah. Hannah!*'

Lucas! Good God: what could have happened? Another call from him ricocheted like the sound of tumbling barrels round her brain, and she leaped to her feet.

Not waiting any longer, she eased open the door, carefully slid the key into the lock from the outside, pulled the door to and turned the key again. She looked over the edge of the gallery but there was no sign of Tristan, though she heard a clatter of china from the kitchen, and could just catch the edge of the scent of coffee. Swiftly she ran down the stairs and out into the darkness.

The night hung about her shoulders like an overheavy coat. At the edge of the grass where the tunnels began, the marble Pan stood out only just less dark than its surroundings. The breeze was stronger than it had been earlier; the glossy evergreen leaves patted each other, sounding like faint applause. In the curved darkness of the tunnels the beam of her torch picked out the delicate bones of a winter leaf still caught among the branches, highlighted a piece of broken balustrading, the flash of a puddle left from last night's rain. Once, eyes glowed briefly at her, lustrous in the torchlight.

There was another scream, desperate and human. This time it was not inside her head but somewhere at the heart of the garden, deep among the trees. The woods throbbed with the sound.

Was it Lucas? She could not tell. 'Lucas!' she shouted. 'Where are you?'

There was no answering call. High among the trees, the wind was gathering force; thunder rumbled distantly. She listened again but heard nothing from him. She knew, however, where he had to be. Her shoes slipped on leaves still wet from the previous night as she headed for the folly where he met his lover.

Coming to the boundary fence, she ducked beneath it. 'Lucas!' she called again, breath coming in harsh jerks from her chest. Sudden terror filled her.

'Lucas!' cautious this time, aware of her own vulnerability in the silences of the garden. Where was he? Was she herself in danger? The night had become predatory, full of nameless terrors. Switching off her torch, she tried to slow down her breathing as she crept forward, feet silent on the accumulations of leaf and moss.

At what point she became aware that someone else was there, she could not have said. But she distinctly heard an indrawn breath, the slightest of hums in the air as a branch was pulled aside and let go, the brush of a shoe-sole against the ground. Someone kept pace with her as she moved; she dared not call again. Ahead of her, the bamboo rustled feverishly, the leaves clattering against their supporting stems. Weak yellow light filtered through them, from the open door of the little folly. Lightfooted, she ran towards it. Although she knew it must be impossible – that scream, the voice in her head, the inimical night – part of her still hoped she might see Lucas and his lover there, one on either side of the table, red wine glowing in the light from the candelabra, the acid-green of grapes on a dish, passion once again filling the air. But the place was empty. The heavy table had been up-ended: smashed dishes covered the floor and the silver candlesticks lay among shattered glass, the candles guttered and broken. The strip of carpet was rucked up as though someone had kicked it to one side. By the door, a chair lay overturned. It was not difficult to guess what had happened. She could imagine Faustino bursting in on them, threatening violence, the guilty pair scattering into the darkness of the woods.

She turned back into the darkness. The pool: it was the only other place he could be. The night seemed even darker as she pushed aside the bamboo leaves and stepped on to the edge of the pool.

'Lucas,' she whispered.

'Hannah—' It was groaned rather than spoken; she heard something shift on the marble tiles, but could see nothing.

'I'm coming,' she said, cautiously putting one foot in front of the other. There was a sudden gust of wind and, as though it had blown aside a curtain, the cloud layer thinned momentarily; she saw a shape at the water's edge, heard another moan.

'I'm here, Lucas,' she whispered, moving towards him, glancing fearfully at the unrevealing leaves which surrounded the pool.

'Help me.'

'I am, I will.' She took another step, pushed the button on her flashlight, shone it in his direction, tried not to scream. He lay spread across the marble paving, almost in the pool, one arm in the water. A dark trail of blood led back among the leaves towards the dim lights of the folly.

'Hannah,' Lucas said again.

'I'm here.' One more step and she was beside him.

'My . . . hand.'

She shone the torch downwards. He wore a white shirt; the front was stained with splashes of blood, the sleeves rolled above the elbow. Below the elbow – she gagged, turning away, nauseated as he half-lifted his arm from the water and she caught sight of the bloodied lump of flesh which was all that was left of Lucas's hand.

'Help me,' he muttered. 'For God's sake, Hannah, I'm bleeding to death.'

'I – I –' Breathing shallowly through her mouth, she tried to will herself to steadiness but, instead, retched violently again. Blood . . . His hand: what had happened to his hand? There were no fingers, no palm or knuckles, simply a ragged black-jellied stump, as though it had torn off just below the wrist – and thinking of it, she vomited. She was shivering now, her whole body given up to the sensation of shaking. She tried to rip a length from her cotton wrap-around skirt, knowing that if she were to stop the bleeding she must tie a tourniquet around the – around what remained of his arm, but despite its flimsiness, she did not have enough strength in her shaking hands to tear the material.

But even if she had, she would not have been able to help. She stood with her back to him, loathing herself for her weakness, and gulped in

351

air, shaking and terrified, unable to move. *Who would have thought . . . so much blood* . . . He would die unless she helped him – but she could not force herself to turn round; frozen, she could not approach that – that *horror*, much less touch it.

'My arm, Hannah,' Lucas said weakly. 'The bastard's smashed my leg, or I'd—' Again the voice trailed away.

She knew this was really happening yet at the same time she felt herself to be no more than a spectator trapped in a nightmare. It was not Hannah Carrington but some vaguely recognised stranger who stood here beside the blackly stirring water while a man begged her for help she simply did not have the strength to force herself into giving. Clenching her fists, digging her nails into the palms of her hands in an effort to pull herself together, Hannah said: 'Bastard? Who?'

'Faustin—' The sentence petered out.

'Faustino?' At that, Hannah turned around, carefully not thinking about the torn flesh, the blood. 'Is he the one who did this?'

'Some of it.' Lucas's voice was momentarily stronger. 'For God's sake, Hannah, do something.'

Fighting nausea, eyes closed, Hannah took a step towards him.

'I need you,' he said. 'Isn't that what—' It was what she had always wanted him to say. But she had seen where his hand used to be and could not help him.

'Don't leave me here to die,' he said faintly; she could barely hear him over the sound of the wind in the trees.

'Hold on, Lucas,' she said. 'I'll go and find – someone who can help.' She did not want to say Tristan's name, for fear it might make Lucas more anxious. But surely Tristan would not refuse to come to Lucas's aid. Surely he would not allow a man to die, even if she herself was—

She could not finish the thought. Heedless of whipping branches, sprawling roots, steps made slippery by sodden moss and gathered leaves, she ran back through the garden. Somewhere she could hear footsteps, a strangled gasp, but took no notice. She was not the only one abroad in the night but if she was to save Lucas, she must fetch help immediately. Her breath broke around her ears; the thud of her feet on the spongy ground was like the footsteps of some giant beast.

As she burst through the screening shrubbery around the Villa Giulia's small lawn, she began to scream Tristan's name. There were lights on in the house, open windows: surely he would hear and come running.

He did not.

As she climbed the steps on to the terrace, she saw that the entrance door was wide open and though she called his name again, racing frantically between kitchen and salon, up to his bedroom, along the passages, out into the blackness behind the villa, she could not find him.

She ran from the house again, terrorstruck. She had been so sure that Tristan would help her. Now it appeared that if Lucas was to be saved, she would have to conquer the fear which the sight of blood always induced. It seemed as though it took her weeks to reach the pool again, bushes grabbing at her clothes, stones inimical inside her sandals, unseen creeper holding her back, though no more than ten minutes could have passed between her leaving the pool and her return.

Lucas was not where she had left him, however. In the short time she had been gone, he appeared to have slipped or fallen into the water and now lay floating there, his pale hair spread like a fan about his head. Beyond that, a darker stain expanded across the water. Blood streaked his face; the wounded arm floated at his side. The stump made Hannah draw in her breath sharply through her teeth but, determinedly keeping her face away from the sticky trail of blood he had left, she forced herself to kneel at the pool's edge and reach for his shoulder. He slipped from her touch, drifting further towards the centre; she would need something to hook him with. She turned, casting behind her for a stick, a branch, beneath the surrounding bushes. Nothing.

'Lucas,' she said loudly. 'I'm here. I'll help you.'

She shone her torch here and there. A shining hoop of metal sprang out of the darkness into the beam of light; the steel mantrap in which the child's puppy had been caught. And beside it lay – resolutely she emptied her mind of all sensation as hysteria threatened to engulf her. Wasn't that—? Could it possibly be—? It *was*— Oh, Jesus.

Lucas's hand.

How could this have happened?

She untied her cotton skirt and let it fall. Then hesitated. However strong her resolve, she knew she could not get into that bloodstained water. She would have to find something with which to pull him towards her. Frantically searching about, she saw something which gleamed dully in the yellow light from the gazebo, half-hidden by the underbrush. A thin iron rod, one end curved into a circle, the other bent at a right-angle, some kind of tool or implement. It was heavy; grabbing it, she knelt and reached across the pool to hook it under the edge of Lucas's collar. When she pulled him towards her, he came without resistance. His eyes were open; she was not sure he recognised her but she began to murmur to him, words of reassurance and hope.

It was only when she tried to let go of the bar in order to catch hold of his shoulder, that she realised her palm was sticky with blood. Blood – and something else, as was one end of the L-shaped rod itself. She looked down at it, shuddering uncontrollably, near to hysterics, and then at Lucas who floated just below her. Nausea racked her body but she gritted her teeth. Slipping her hands under his shoulders, she tried to heave him on to the edging. Made weightless by the water, at first he came easily towards her, but as more of him emerged, the heavier the resistance his body offered, until she was panting and tugging to get him even half out.

It was not until the upper half of his body lay on the wet marble, that she saw, flashing her torch again, that the back of his head had been fiercely struck over and over again with something heavy. It took her only an instant to realise that the iron rod she had used to drag him to the side must have been the weapon with which he had been beaten.

In the trees above her head, a night bird called insistently. She laid her head on his chest, as she had done so often on their afternoons of love-making, longing for a kind word from him, for affection. There was absolutely no sound at all except for the faint drip of water from his clothes. She shone her torch again, playing the light over his face, but could see no sign of life. Water shone sickeningly on his skin, pale streams of blood flowed from beneath his nose; bruises stood out on the waxy cheeks. His grey eyes stared sightlessly up into the black sky; his limbs were loose, inanimate.

Lucas – it did not seem possible – Lucas was dead.

She backed hastily away on hands and knees, hysteria choking her. Her first and strongest instinct was to run screaming into the trees, anywhere, to get away from the place. Her second was cooler. Had his head been like that when she left him? It could not have been. He had spoken to her, been rational, been his usual callous self, though obviously in pain. Besides, no one could have survived such cruel injuries. Therefore – frightening though it was, the fact must be faced – in the short interval during which she had gone looking for Tristan, someone had killed him.

Murdered him.

Later, she knew, she would be appalled at her own reactions. Later, she would ask how she could have behaved so completely without regard for the ordinary conventions, without compassion or decency. But for now, self-preservation was uppermost in her mind. She had found him, she had pulled him from the water, her fingerprints would be on the iron bar, they would be able to link her with the crime. Calmly, though her heart thundered, she dunked the long piece of metal in the pool, running her hand up and down where she had held it then wiping it with the edge of her skirt. Aware that she was deliberately tampering with evidence, she none the less continued until she was sure that any fingerprints of hers would have disappeared. Was there any other physical evidence to link her with the death? She thought not.

She did not even glance at the shadowed bushes which whispered and murmured. Someone stood there, watching her, watching Lucas, but all she could feel was an overwhelming numbness, through which pulsed the single huge question: who had killed Lucas?

Behind her, something came pushing through the leaves on the shrubby slope which led up through the garden towards the Villa Diana.

Inertia vanished. Instinctively, she whirled, at the same time flashing her torch beam in the direction of the sound. Was it the murderer? Quickly, she switched off the light and moved rapidly round the edge of the pool, but not before she had glimpsed pale hair, the side of a cheek, something which sparkled in the light like tears. But that could not be the same person who was making so little effort to disguise his progress down through the woods.

She heard a voice. Two voices. Men. Calling from different places in the garden. As they came nearer she recognised Tristan's deep tones and the lighter sound of Faustino. Before she was fully aware of what she was doing, she had picked up her discarded skirt and slipped in among the bamboo stems. If they saw her, they might – what? Kill her? Assume she was responsible for Lucas?

Behind her, she could mark the progress of whoever had been among the leaves. A second scenario came to her. Tristan, suspecting that she wished to get away from him, waiting in the shadowed hall until she came downstairs, following her through the tunnels and then, when she rushed back to the villa, seeing Lucas helpless, seizing the opportunity to finish what had been started at the barbecue by the lake.

Or Faustino. Raging at the sight of his wife with her lover, he could have returned to the scene and, finding Lucas, completed what he had begun. Behind her, light spilled from the gazebo. She stopped, peering in, wondering if she could hide there and realising that she had to get back to the Villa Giulia.

Behind her, she heard exclamations, a splash, words of horrified surprise.

'My God!' Tristan said. 'What in the name of—'

Faustino spoke in Italian, his voice harsh and horrified, breaking as he spoke Lucas's name.

'Help me with him,' Tristan said.

Terrified in case they heard her, and not daring to use her torch, Hannah quietly made her way back to the house for the second time. If she showed herself, they would think she had something to do with it; the very thought made her retch as she fled along the paths between the evergreens. Should she call the police? But if she did, they would want to know what she was doing there, what part she had played. And if they discovered she and he had been lovers, they might even suspect her of murdering Lucas herself, motivated by hurt pride and jealousy.

Reaching the safety of the terrace, she turned. Was there movement there among the bushes? Did the box hedges quiver as someone pushed them aside? Though she strained into the darkness, she could see nothing except the faintest glimmer, a lighter patch against the dark leaves, which momentarily hung mothlike in the darkness and then was gone. Was it the statue of Pan, or something else?

She ran into the house. Her first thought was to close the door and bolt it against the menace of the night, but then she remembered that Tristan was out there somewhere and she must leave things as they were if she was to pretend she knew nothing of what had happened.

It was perhaps no more than five minutes later, as she stood watching from her bedroom window for Tristan's return, that a car came up the drive and parked on the gravel below her.

Susie's car.

Apprehension threatened to choke her. Of all the nights for Susie to return . . . Why had she come back a day early? What would she say when she heard about Lucas? With the functioning part of her brain, Hannah realised that, at some point, Susie would have had to know what had happened, but not like this, without preparation, without warning—

Rapidly she undressed. Her blouse was damp; she ran it swiftly under the tap and squeezed out the excess water. As far as she could see – using her torch so as not to attract attention to her window – there was no blood on it, though there was no reason for there to be since she had kept well away from Lucas's wounds. She spread it over the towel rail. She had not been wearing a bra. She did the same with her skirt. The police would come, that much was obvious, but before they did, she would either have an opportunity to destroy it, or hide it, or at least wash it more thoroughly.

But suppose she did not? Suppose they discovered the remains of blood and – and brains on it? She told herself that was impossible: she had only used the skirt when she had thoroughly washed the iron rod in the pool.

She pulled a big shirt on over some underpants. Standing well back from the edge of the balcony, she watched as Susie pulled a bag from the back seat of her car, looked up at the villa, and then was lost to sight as she approached the terrace. Swiftly, Hannah unlocked her bedroom door, and got into bed. Since there were lights still on in the house, Susie might come knocking at the door to see if she was awake but there was no reason for anyone to suppose that she had not been there ever since returning from the Trevelyans'.

Unless they listened to the wild knocking of her heart, or saw the fear in her eyes.

21

'Are you awake?' Susie came into Hannah's room, and walked over to the bed.

'Wha— wh— Susie!' Hannah sat up in bed, hoping she had been convincing enough to persuade Susie that she had been asleep. 'What're you doing here?'

'I've just got back. Susie sat on the edge of the bed. Her face was flushed; she seemed angry, upset.

'Why didn't you say you were coming early? We expected you tomorr—'

'What's going on?' Susie said abruptly. 'Why are all the doors open, and the lights on but there's nobody around? Isn't Tristan Carrick supposed to be here?'

'He is here. We had dinner tonight at the Trevelyans',' said Hannah. Her hands shook; she could not rid herself of the image of Lucas's face, blood-streaked in the dark.

'He's not in the house.' Susie sounded censorious. She stared round the room as though expecting to find the furniture damaged, a cracked mirror, the pictures hanging askew.

'Perhaps he's gone for a walk or something – he said he was really strung out when we got back. He asked me to have a drink and talk to him but I was so tired that I just wanted to get to bed.'

'I see.' Plainly Susie suspected that things were not what they seemed. She got up and walked across the room, her face unfriendly, shoulders rigid under her thin blouse.

A tense drive up from Rome, Hannah guessed. A near-accident, perhaps, a pile-up on the autostrada, bodies . . . 'Are you all right, Susie?'

'No,' Susie snapped. 'I'm not.'

Police sirens sounded outside. Pushing open the windows, she stepped out on to the balcony, saying over her shoulder: 'There are two police vans haring up the drive. What on earth have you been up to?'

'Me? Nothing.' Hannah scrambled out from under the covering sheet. Her legs felt too weak to support her and she sat down at the side of the bed. Deception did not come easily to her. 'Uh— you don't suppose it's Tristan, do you? Perhaps he was knocked down—'

'On this walk of his?' Susie looked at Hannah, suspicion and disbelief – perhaps even dislike – showing in her eyes. 'That wouldn't require two vans – we'd better see what's going on.' She went out of the room and Hannah heard her run down the stairs.

Hannah pulled on some jeans. Her hands were so weak that she had difficulty doing up the buttons at the waist. All her muscles trembled; her legs felt as though they did not have enough strength to support her body. She breathed deeply, trying to calm herself.

By the time she got downstairs, the kitchen was full of people: at least half a dozen police officers, Susie, Tristan and Faustino were crowded round the table. Standing in front of them was a man who introduced himself as the man in charge of the case.

'What case?' Hannah said. She could not meet anyone's eyes.

Tristan came to her, smiling reassuringly but she looked away. It might have been him, she thought. He might be the one who killed Lucas. When he stretched a hand towards her, she backed away from him. He touched her hair. 'It's all right, Hannah,' he said. 'Don't be afraid. Something rather dreadful's happened.'

She ought to ask what, but she could not speak. The muscles of her face tensed as she tried not to cry. At the table, Susie sat with her face in her hands, sobbing hysterically. Hannah would have said: 'I'm not afraid,' but it was not true. She went over to the other side of the kitchen, away from the others, and leaned against the wall. When Tristan followed, she managed to say: 'What is it?'

'Lucas,' Tristan said. He put an arm round her shoulders. 'Lucas is dead.'

Hannah did not know how to react, what behaviour would be most appropriate. In the end, she simply stared at Tristan, biting her lip, shaking her head as though in disbelief. She listened while, between them, Tristan and Faustino described how they had found Lucas dead beside the pool.

Another officer came in and murmured into the Inspector's ear. They all filed after him as he and his men went out on to the terrace and watched as Lucas's covered body was carried up from the pool by two ambulance orderlies. Water dripped from the stretcher. Behind them walked a police doctor carrying a bag, and another man. In the light pouring into the darkness from the Villa's unshuttered windows, it was easy to see that the sheet was stained with dark blood.

Susie ran towards the two men and their sad burden, frantically screaming Lucas's name. Snatching the cover from his face, she stared, horrorstruck, at the wounds on his head, at his hair, darkened now with water. Reaching to touch his face, her hand caught at his sleeve; the arm with its dark-jellied stump was pulled from under the covering shroud to hang over the edge of the stretcher in front of her. She backed away, hands to her mouth, eyes wild.

'My God! Who did this?' she screamed. 'What happened?' She tried to follow as the men stowed the stretcher inside a police-ambulance, but one of the investigating police officers held her back. She shrieked again, hands clawing at her tearstained cheeks as the doors were slammed shut and the two orderlies got into the front and started the engine. 'Come back, come back! Oh, Jesus! Oh, Lucas! I love you.'

'Please, signorina,' pleaded the restraining policeman, 'Please. Calm yourself.'

Susie turned on Hannah. 'This is your fault,' she said. Her voice dropped almost to a whisper; her eyes were wild, white showing all round the irises. 'This is your fault, you murderess, you bitch, you fucking, fucking bitch. I thought we were friends, you scheming two-timing bitch. We were friends, damn you, and you killed him, you killed Lucas, it's your fault—' She would have lunged at Hannah if she had not been held back. Her screams began again.

Through it all, Hannah stood motionless, hands at her sides. After a while, she turned stiffly and went to stand at the other end of the terrace, looking out into the darkness of the garden. Nobody tried to stop her. She would not have been able to argue if they had.

'I should like to speak to everyone of you in turn,' the officer in charge of the case said. 'Please do not think of leaving until I have done so. Dottore Castelli, I will start with you.'

In the pre-dawn darkness, Hannah stood alone on the terrace. Light streamed down from the upper storey as the police searched the villa. For what? She gazed numbly into the thinning night. What did they hope to find? They had the body; they had the murder weapon. They had their witnesses – possibly, by now, their suspect.

At its lower edge, between the poplars, the sky was already tinged with pink. The balustrade felt chilly, clammy with dew; she scratched at gold-edged circles of lichen while the dawn breeze lifted her hair and let it fall.

She felt nothing. Although aware of the sound of birds, the feel of the lichen scales under her fingers, the marble cool to her feet, the fact that it was almost daylight, they were pieces of information she was aware of in the same way that she was aware of the disparate elements of her body – hair, hands, feet – or the place where she now was. They bore no relation to herself, no intimacy; she did not feel them. Disconnected from her, they simply were.

A car appeared down the drive, a black Citroën. She was pleased that she recognised the make, the essential car-ness of it. Perhaps, eventually, feeling would return to her inert brain. The local doctor got out and came hurrying up the steps.

'Where is she?' he said. 'The Signorina Wilton—?'

Hannah did not answer his question, did not even turn her head. After staring at her in puzzlement, he went into the house.

With an effort, Hannah raised her arms and put her hands over her ears. Even so, she could still hear Susie's screams.

She wondered what possible motive she herself could have for denying her part in recent events. An hour ago, she had described her actions during the evening to the investigating officer. She had lied. Although she never lied, would have said she was incapable of it, she had nonetheless offered him a version of how she had spent the previous hours which bore little relation to the truth.

'I had dinner at the house of Signor Trevelyan. Signor Tristan Carrick was with me. Afterwards, around one thirty, we walked home together. It was very dark and we could hardly see where we were going. When we arrived back here, Signor Carrick asked me if I would like something to drink – coffee or something – but I said no, I wished to go to bed because I had slept badly the night before. And that's what I did. Until I was woken up by Signorina Wilton's arrival in her car. Then I came downstairs, and the police came and—'

Here she had faltered. It was one thing to conceal the truth, quite another to implicate others.

'Yes?' The policeman wore a three-piece suit, despite the heat, and a gold watch-chain which stretched across his waistcoated ribs. He spoke very quietly, so that Hannah had to lean forward to hear what he said. 'What then?'

'Then,' Hannah said. She stopped again, twisting her hands, trying desperately to see beyond the words she was going to say, to tease out their implications.

'Yes?'

'Then Tristan – Signor Carrick – came running into the house and said that Lord Wyndham was dead. He had—' She turned her head away. She felt immensely old and, at the same time, as though she had somehow reverted to childhood again. '. . . there was blood on his shirt, and blood on his—' she swallowed: the horror of it, 'blood in his hair, streaks of blood. Then Faustino – Dottore Castelli – also came running. He looked as though he had been in a fight: his shirt was torn, and he seemed to be bleeding.'

The policeman nodded, looking down at his notes. Although horrified at herself, Hannah knew that what she said was obvious to anyone. The skin of Faustino's knuckles was bleeding; his mouth was swollen and there was a cut above his eye. His pink cotton shirt was torn, half in and half out of his trousers: she was not telling the police anything they had not noted for themselves.

'And you saw nothing of this yourself?'

'As I have already said, I was in bed until Signorina Wilton knocked at my door, having just driven up from Rome.'

'I see.' The Inspector studied his notes again. 'Both Signor Carrick and Dottore Castelli state that they heard what sounded like a man's screams coming from the garden, in the – uh—' he faltered a little, searching for the word though his English was surprisingly fluent, 'direction of the pool, and that they both hurried there, meeting each other on the way.'

'Yes,' Hannah said.

'But you yourself heard nothing, although the windows of your room were open and they face towards that part of the garden?'

'I told you, I slept very little the night before. I was really exhausted.'

He had taken her through it all again but she added nothing. Had his questions proved more searching, she might have broken down, but as it was, she was able not so much to deceive as simply to ignore the truth.

'How well did you know Lucas Wyndham?' he said.

'Quite well,' said Hannah.

'And that means—' He arched his brows enquiringly at her.

'It means we—' Hannah tightened her mouth and stared at her hands, clasped on the table in front of her. It was pointless to lie about it; the invisible housekeeper had probably told half the town. 'We were lovers.'

'But this evening, you were not lovers?'

'No,' Hannah said loudly. 'I already told you, I went to have dinner with Signor Trevelyan and his wife.'

'Had you ceased to be lovers?'

'Yes.'

'Recently?'

'Yes.'

'And why, if I may trespass on so delicate a matter, had you ceased to be lovers?'

If she told him that she had seen Lucas with another woman, he would assume that she was angry about it, thus providing a motive on her part to commit a crime of passion. He would never believe that infatuation had died as swiftly as it had begun; that she no longer felt anything for Lucas, and only distaste for herself.

She shrugged. 'You know how it is. We – it was a mutual decision. I'm going back to England any day now . . . there didn't seem much point in continuing it.'

'I see.' From the expression on his face, she could tell that he classed her with all the other English girls who came to Italy looking for a summer fling. Bleakly, she realised that, at last, she had lost her outsider status and, as she once had so much wanted to be, was being classed with the rest of them, with Charlotte and Helena, Damian and Chloe, easy come, easy go.

'How long must I stay here?' she said.

He thought about it. 'If you are prepared to sign a statement that you will return for the trial—'

'Trial?'

'When we find the person responsible for the death of Milord

Wyndham, naturally there will be a trial. If you will come back for that, then I cannot see that there is much reason for you to stay here.' He eyed her narrowly. 'As far as I can tell, you had nothing to do with any of this. I will check your statement with the others and let you know definitely before I leave here.'

'Good.'

Susie's screams had given way to choking sobs and sudden wails of pure grief. After a while, there was silence.

The doctor stepped out of the french windows.

'Signorina Wilton will sleep for some hours,' he said. When Hannah made no response, he added curtly: 'Do you need anything yourself?'

Slowly she shook her head. Need: what did that mean? She needed for this never to have happened. She needed not to have come to Italy, never to have met Lucas. But it was too late. Far too late.

When the doctor had gone, the Citroën vanishing round the bend in the drive though she could still see its lights on the underside of the poplar leaves, she went inside the house. The hall was empty. She went into the ballroom, switching off the lights as she did so. This time, she could not bear to watch her ghost rise to meet her in the cataracted mirrors.

She stood at the window, cocooned in silent horror. What had she done? She had let a man die: it was no more complicated than that. By leaving Lucas, instead of helping him, as she could so easily have done, she had connived at, if not caused his death. It was an act of moral cowardice and she knew that she would be required to pay the price.

On the terrace outside, figures appeared. Faustino, escorted by two officers. He turned his head as he passed the long windows; he saw her. Wrenching himself from the official hands, he spoke to her but she could not hear what he said, only see the way his mouth opened. She felt as though she were imprisoned in a glass tomb; the lights from the rooms above cast deep shadows beneath his angry eyes. There was blood on his face; when she recoiled, he clenched his fist as though he would like to burst through the glass between them. Then the police grabbed his arms again and led him away. At the top of the steps down to the drive, he turned his head and shouted something at her but she could not tell what, only that his face was bitter and his words were full of rage.

Later, zombie-like, she opened the glass doors and stepped out on to the terrace, to stand where she had been earlier. Already she could see the outline of trees against the sky; colour was returning to the landscape: an orange roof here, blue-green cypresses there, the white smudges of villa walls in the hills.

Tristan came through the front door and out into the open air. Like Faustino, he was accompanied by two police officers. He stood still and raised his face to the sky, drawing the freshness of the early morning air into his lungs. If he saw Hannah, he made no sign, nor did he look back as they bundled him down the steps and into the waiting police van. Only when they had slammed shut the doors did he peer out between the grilles. His white hair was darkly streaked. She could hardly breathe as his eye caught hers. Did he mouth her name? She was not sure. He put his hands up to the bars across the cramped pane of glass and watched her as the van bore him swiftly out of sight.

Closer to hand, something moved among the shrubbery at the edge of the grass. The child appeared briefly, white against the green, then slipped back again among the leaves. Why was it up so early? How had it known that there was something happening here, at the Villa Giulia? Or did it come every morning, to stand and gaze at the sleeping house, perhaps to wonder, to wish, to hope? Hannah thought: I should have tried harder.

But there were so many things she should have done, and now the summer was nearly over, and it was all too late. Her life had ended; her life had just begun.

She was in England the following evening. She said goodbye to nobody; Tristan and Faustino were still in police custody, Susie was still under sedation. Nancy Trevelyan, knowing only that Lucas was dead, offered to drive her to the airport but Hannah declined the offer, knowing it would mean two hours of questions and speculation. From Heathrow, she called her parents to say that she had come home. They seemed unmoved by the news, neither surprised nor disappointed nor particularly pleased. When she let herself into the house, an hour later, they were sitting at the kitchen table, a brown teapot between them, each one reading a book. She felt like an intruder. One of them asked perfunctorily if she had had a good time and she nodded, moving round to kiss them both briefly. Her mother's hair smelt of cold bacon fat; her father seized her hand in his and she tried not to recoil from the psoriasis which seemed to have worsened during her absence.

'Food,' her mother said vaguely, looking round. 'I expect you're hungry. There's some bacon in the fridge.'

'I don't want anything to eat,' Hannah said. 'But I'm awfully tired.'

'A hot bath,' said her father. 'You look done in. I should get off to bed if I were you.'

'I'll bring you up a tray of tea,' her mother said. She looked down at her book and with a faint sigh of regret, closed it.

'I'm afraid we're going out this evening,' said her father. 'Will you mind being left alone?'

She forced herself to smile at him. 'Not at all.'

Neither of them asked anything more about her time in Italy. Lying in bed, she tried to sleep but could not. It was early September and the clocks would not go back for another month; the sky was still bright even at nine o'clock. When her parents had left the house she got up and went into their bedroom. She dialled Anthony's number.

'It's me,' she said.

'Hannah!' He breathed her name with every evidence of desire. 'Where are you?'

'I'm at home.'

'But why didn't you tell me you were coming? I'd have picked you up at the airport.'

'Did you mean what you wrote?' she said. 'About wanting to marry me?'

'Of course.'

'The answer's yes.'

'Oh, Hannah,' he began. 'I swear to you I'll make you so happy—' but she cut him off because she knew that however hard he tried, he would not, that she no longer deserved happiness. Having taken a wrong turn, she would live with the consequences for the rest of her life. All she hoped, as she replaced the receiver, was that she would have the courage not ever to complain about what she had brought upon herself.

It was not for years that she understood how, in condemning herself, she had also condemned Anthony to unhappiness.

Her parents did not ask why she had returned so precipitately. Years later, after her father had died, on a visit to Hannah's house, her mother picked up a book on Tuscany and idly turned the pages.

'That summer you spent in Italy,' she said.

'Yes?'

'Something happened to you.'

'How do you know?'

Her mother stared down at colour photographs of tiled roofs, geraniums, a cobbled street. 'You looked so dreadful when you came home. So much older.'

'Why didn't you ask me?'

'It wasn't really any of our business.'

'What do you mean?'

'We just assumed,' said her mother, looking up, 'that you had lost your virginity.'

The cold words summed it all up for Hannah. She wanted to say, but I was your child, flesh of your flesh, of *course* it was your business. She longed to scream out her nightmares, to explain how that pale, blood-streaked face still haunted her, the remembrance of those sweet afternoons with Lucas still brought her close to tears. She wanted to shake her mother, force her to take notice, to care, just for once to be involved with her. But Lucinda came in at that point and afterwards, she simply thought, what difference would it have made?

NOW

22

'Hannah.'

She did not turn. Below her, on the surface of the pool, the outlined image of her head and shoulders was clear against the reflected sky. 'Yes?'

Tristan came up behind her and put his hands on her shoulders. 'We can't go on avoiding the truth,' he said.

'I know.'

'One way or another, it'll have to be laid bare.'

'Yes.'

She heard him sigh, felt his hands tighten. 'You were down here that night, weren't you? The night Lucas was killed?'

Hannah nodded.

'You saw him there, by the pool.'

'How do you know where I was?' She turned to face him.

'Was he dead when you found him?'

She did not speak.

'Or was he still alive, Hannah?'

Stepping back from him, she wrapped her arms across her body, as though to protect it from hurt. 'I've never been able to come to terms with it, Tristan. With what I did, how I behaved. I discovered I was quite a different person from the one I had believed myself to be.'

'Isn't that part of growing up?' he asked quietly.

'Is it? I only know that I was brought up with a certain code, with a strong sense of responsibility, even of honour – and that night I—' She broke off.

'You didn't kill him, did you?'

She looked at him then. 'Kill Lucas? Me? Of course not. How could you even think such a thing?'

'You had no difficulty in asking me the same question.'

'I – that was different.' But, she realised now, it was not.

'So what happened, Hannah?'

She hesitated. 'I've never told anyone . . . never even let myself think about it. All these years I've been so ashamed—'

'Tell me, Hannah,' Tristan said gently.

So she did. Describing those terrible moments seemed to dull the bitter colours of memory, reduce the facts of blood, of streaming hair, the harsh reality of dead flesh, to nothing more than wisps of long-vanished smoke. Her words fluttered and fell around them like crushed butterflies.

He said, 'I've always known you were involved in some way.'

'How?'

'Because, when you came into the kitchen that night, after Susie arrived and the alarm had been raised, and the police came, I couldn't help noticing your feet. You had such long, elegant feet.'

'What was wrong with them?'

'You were supposed to have gone straight up to your bedroom when we got back from Lew and Nancy's house. But when you came down, your feet were dirty, as if you'd been walking about in the garden. And don't you remember me picking a leaf out of your hair?'

He had leaned towards her and she thought he had touched her hair. 'Why did you do that?'

'Because you looked so frightened. Because I knew you had been lying when you said you wanted to go to bed.'

'How?'

'Oh, Hannah.' He smiled fondly at her. 'You're so bad at lying.'

'My whole life is a lie,' she said with bitterness.

'And also, I was with you, walking back from the Trevelyans, when Lucas called you. Remember? He . . . *summoned* you.'

'How did you—'

'He used to do it to Jane. She told me about it; I learned to recognise the signs.'

'Jane. You mean—'

'Marcus's wife. I was in love with her once,' Tristan said. 'We both were, Marcus and I. She chose him. Until Lucas came along.'

'Is that why you never married?'

'I never found anyone I wanted as much as I wanted her.' He put his arms around her waist and pulled her closer. 'Until now.'

'Even after what I did to you?'

'Yes.'

'Oh, Tristan. I'm so sorry.'

He laughed. 'It was a long time ago.'

'Nearly six months in prison while they tried to prove you guilty of something you didn't do.'

'The conditions were pretty primitive,' Tristan said, 'but they didn't treat me too badly.'

'The thing was, I didn't – I still don't – know whether you killed him. I mean, you could have.' She sighed. 'It doesn't seem to matter much now.'

'I told you when you came to Cornwall that I didn't.'

'Somebody did. And it wasn't Faustino, I'm sure. So who was it?'

'I've often wondered whether Jane herself—' Tristan let the words hang for a moment. 'After all, she was pregnant by him, she'd left her husband for him. And to discover that he was having it off not only with you but— Supposing she followed him that night and saw him with Marina. And when Faustino hit him and left him lying there, all her rage boiled over and she picked up that crowbar or whatever it was and smashed it down on his head.'

'It's possible, I suppose.'

'I've often thought that if that's what happened, and if Sophie saw her do it, it might explain the way she's turned out, poor girl. But I don't see how she could have – after all, it was in the middle of the night and she was only a little girl – she'd have been asleep for hours.'

'She wasn't,' Hannah said. 'She was there. Or at least, she was around, because I saw her.'

'Where?'

'Someone was hiding among the bushes when I first found Lucas. I just caught a glimpse in the light of my torch, though I don't know who it was. All I could see was pale hair, something –' it was coming back now, 'something which glittered. An earring. Or a tear.'

'Could have been Jane. Or Faustino.'

'But later,' Hannah said, remembering, 'after the police had interviewed me, after they'd . . . they'd taken you away, I was standing on the terrace and it came, the child – Sophie, I mean – came out of the shrubbery and then melted back into the bushes when she saw me.'

'Why would a child that age have been out of bed in the middle of the night?'

'I don't know.' Hannah looked up at him. 'She was everywhere, that summer, wherever I went, whatever I did. Like a ghost. Like . . . like nemesis. Tristan, do you think she saw what happened?'

'She certainly saw something. When Marcus sent me that book she wrote, I assumed she must have been told things by her mother, but now I wonder whether—'

'Can't we ask her?'

'Difficult, when we don't know where she is.'

'She's here,' Hannah said. 'I'm sure of it.' Suddenly convinced, she swung round, scanning the bushes all round. 'She's somewhere here. Lew Trevelyan saw her in the town yesterday. I told you.'

'How do you know it was Sophie?'

'It has to be her. Marcus told us she came to Italy at the end of last summer. Then she went to England and found me, got a job from me, with an idea of doing me some harm.'

'You hadn't harmed her.'

Not listening, Hannah continued: 'At first I thought it was the boy – her brother, who was trying to frighten me. Lucas's son. Have you met him?'

'Once,' Tristan said. 'Years ago, on a trip to the States. I went down to Arkansas or wherever Jane was living then. The marriage had broken up but she stayed on there, for various reasons. The boy – Orlando – must have been about fourteen then.' He paused. 'Seeing him, it was like being a boy again myself. He was the image of Lucas at the same age.'

'He is still,' Hannah said, 'uncannily so. The first time I saw him, I thought it was Lucas himself. Later I wondered if he had come to find me and avenge his father, because if I'd helped when I should have done, Lucas might not have died.'

'Isn't that a bit far-fetched? How would he possibly have known what you did or didn't do?'

'That's what I couldn't work out. But if Zoe – Sophie – was there watching that night, or Jane, either of them might have told him. You can see how it would have festered over the years. And then Sophie wrote that book, and he'd have been convinced of my guilt.'

'It's possible.'

'But it wasn't him,' Hannah said steadily. 'I know that now. It was Zoe. Sophie. She killed Lucinda.'

'Hannah.' Tristan shook her gently. 'If Sophie felt anything for Lucas, it must have been negative, not positive. After all, he had broken up her parents' marriage, caused her to be taken away from her father and landed in a strange house in a strange country where nobody took any notice of her. If she thought you were responsible for Lucas's death, wouldn't she have been glad rather than angry?'

'She's the only one who could have done it. She knew so much about Lucinda – I've been remembering all the questions she asked about me and my family. She could so easily have gone up to that cottage – I told her where it was – and made up some kind of story which would have persuaded Lucy to let her in. And after that—' She also had the opportunity, Hannah realised, to plant the brooch and the postcard under her pillow during the funeral, knowing that they'd be found. It would also have been easy for her to doctor the cassette-tape and put it in her car.

How could she have been taken in all these weeks? Why had she not realised that Zoe's consuming interest in her employer's affairs was unhealthy, dangerous?

'We're going to drive over to see the Trevelyans,' Tristan said.

'Check out this story of theirs about Sophie being here,' agreed Marcus.

'We won't be very long – keep the doors locked won't you, my dear?' Lightly, Tristan touched Hannah's shoulder. 'We'll have a drink when we get back: it'll just about be time.'

She smiled up at him. If it were not for Susie's arrival tomorrow, she would have left. She wanted to go home. She wanted to take up the reins of living again. She had wasted two-thirds of her life and it suddenly seemed imperative that she use what was left to the fullest advantage.

She would sell the shop, travel, do something, anything. The prospect had a curious flatness.

She went into the salon and stood looking out at the garden. Trees moved angrily against a leaden sky. Although dusk was falling, she felt a reluctance to switch on the lights. She needed to think but could not concentrate. Too much information had been fed to her in the past few hours. Although she was not much nearer to finding out what exactly had happened to Lucinda, the time she had spent here had been productive.

She sat down and leaned her head against the cushioned chair-back. Fatigue enveloped her: these last weeks had been tiring. As she closed her eyes, she tensed suddenly, sat upright. Inside her skull, the voice called.

'Hannah.'

She started up. Not Lucas. So who? Why? And then, as the minutes went by and the voice did not come again, she wondered whether she had really heard it or was simply caught up in a fold of time, trapped in the web of memory which pervaded this house. She waited – was it hours, or minutes? – not knowing which.

'Hannah. Help me.'

'Lucas,' she said aloud. 'No. Orlando.' Lucas's boy, calling her. What did he want? Where was he? But she had no need to ask the question: there was only one place he could be. She went into the hall and opened the front door.

Wind gusts; dead leaves circle, lifted by the wind and dropped again. She shivers. Down the steps, past the ivy-twined Pan, into the tunnels. It is darker here, the crowding evergreens blocking out what remains of the light, but she knows the way and where she has to go. This time, she will not shirk what is required of her.

Pushing aside the leaves, she does not allow herself to think of the stump of his arm, where the hand has almost literally been ripped off, clamped between the cruel teeth of the trap. She touches the knot of the silk scarf she wears: a tourniquet which, if need be, she will tie without flinching. The garden is so quiet that she can already hear the rustling bamboo.

Behind her, beside her, a voice says: 'Anna.'

Her pulses thump in an agitated beat. Did she really hear it? And if so, whose voice is it? Orlando's? Zoe's? Or is it Max's? Max, the alter ego, the wild thing, who makes mischief of one kind and another . . . 'I'm here,' she says quietly. She feels herself to be in mortal danger and wonders why she is not more afraid. Footsteps keep pace with her, somewhere beyond the leaves – or is it merely the beating of her heart? But when she puts her hand under her breast, she can feel no heartbeat, nothing.

Stone steps. Broken statuary. Evergreens dull in the dull light, massed against crumbling stonework. She slips, clutches, regains her balance. Below her now, she sees the bamboo grove.

'Anna.' Again she hears the soft androgynous whisper. Was it the voice on the tape in her car?

'Yes?' This is not happening, this is some mad dream.

'You have to pay,' the voice says. Is it inside her head, or coming from among the dripping leaves?

'I have.'

'Not enough,' says the voice and she wonders again with whom she is conducting this surreal dialogue.

'Enough,' she says. 'More than enough.'

'No.'

Time stretches in front of and behind her, twisted into thinness, attenuated. Now Time Present has folded into Time Past, so that the events of a summer evening long ago were simply what happened immediately prior to the events of this damp evening, now, part of a continuum, and all the time between immaterial.

How long ago it seems. Her body white in the black water, the slanting columns of sunlight, the murmuring bamboo and Lucas pushing through leaves to stand at the pool's edge, watching her.

She thinks, with a kind of sad surprise, how strange it is that while other things die – happiness, laughter, the sound of poetry in the ears – the call of physical longing should survive so strongly that even now, as she moves towards the stone-edged water, fleetingly she feels the same liquid desire as she felt then, the same shy anticipation of delight. Reaching the shallow flight of steps, mossy and leaf-choked, which leads down to the hidden pool, she sees something move behind the screen of stems. She starts to run, feet scrabbling for purchase. Something – someone – is lying there, beside the black water.

'Lucas.' She forces her way between the rattling stems. But it cannot be Lucas. 'Orlando!'

He is lying there in the almost-dark. Lucas's son, so like his father. His pale hair hangs just above the pool's surface as though, Narcissus-like, he strove to see his own beautiful reflection. He is hurt.

As she kneels beside him, feeling for his wrist, for a pulse, touching the back of his bloodied head with gentle fingers, she hears a sharp movement behind her. At least he is still alive, she thinks, as she turns to see a dark shape rearing above her, an arm swinging down against the mussel-grey sky of imminent night.

Faustino? Tristan? Marcus?

'Zoe,' she says. 'Stop. You've done enough,' but the words fail to halt the plunging arm or to stop the smash of it against her head so that she pitches forward, still holding the hand of Lucas's son, and hears between the swirling clouds of semi-consciousness, a voice say: 'Not yet.'

Immediately below her face, the water rocks gently against the edges of the pool. She can smell wet earth, a faint sweetness of mud; the marble edge cuts sharply into her leg. With surprise, she realises that although her head hurts abominably, she has not lost consciousness.

Footsteps. Something dragging. The wrist she still clutches is tugged from her hand as Orlando's body is pulled back from the edge of the pool. Someone is weeping. A voice – *the* voice – murmurs: 'Lucas—'

'Zoe,' Hannah whispers above the water. 'What did you see, what did you hear?'

But no sound emerges from her throat and if it had, the harsh sobbing behind her would have drowned it.

Moving slightly, she can just see a shape crouched on the marble paving. If she stays here, she knows she will be killed, as Lucinda was killed. Easy to tip an unconscious woman into the water, hold her under, wait. Part of her knows how Lucas must have felt when he said he would not mind dying: if it is inescapable anyway, why not welcome it? But far stronger is the will to live.

Hannah shifts again at the pool's edge, putting space between herself and Zoe. If only she were younger, more limber. Getting to her feet is no longer the single fluid movement it used to be. She is not young; she has lost elasticity. None the less, her desire to make up for the wasted years sends adrenalin pumping through her body.

Slowly she pulls her hands to her sides, rests her weight on them, draws her knees towards herself. At her side, Zoe slips an arm beneath the body of Lucas's son, murmurs.

Swiftly, Hannah crouches, pushes herself upwards, is gone, crashing through the leaves, racing towards the darkness of the garden, towards the boundary fence, the tunnels, the safety of the house. As she runs, she hears behind her a grunt of anger. Feet on the paving, breath swallowed to fill lungs.

She runs for her life.

She is not fast enough. As she reaches the foot of a flight of stone stairs overhung with ivy, half-hidden by rampaging box hedges, she sees someone ahead, above. She realises that Zoe, knowing this garden intimately, has taken a short cut.

The figure comes swiftly down the steps towards her and she turns, changes direction, cursing herself for heeding his voice: Orlando's voice. Lucas's voice. She should not be here. How long will it be before Marcus and Tristan return?

Branches. Clutching, grabbing. Evil twiggy fingers pulling at sweater, at jeans. The bruised smell of leaves, fingers streaked with green blood, hands scratched. Sweat on the soles of her feet, making her slip inside her shoes.

'Anna,' the voice calls. 'Anna,' and she runs onward, pushing through brushwood thick as jungles. How can she get back to the safety of the house; where can she hide?

She sees a hollow, a cave formed by years of mulch, leaf drifting down on to leaf, forming a natural roof among the heavy growth of intertwined bush and shrub. She drops to her knees and scrambles forward, burrowing into it like a hunted animal, a wild thing, pulling leaves around her as though they were a shawl, a cloak of invisibility.

'Anna,' comes the soft voice again, and sweat starts out along her shoulders, for this time her pursuer is nearer, much nearer, almost directly in front of her shelter. She squats, not daring to move, to breathe, while the painful blood leaps through her veins. She can smell sweat, a feral whiff of cruelty and danger, a wolf stalking its prey. Can the hidden stalker scent her fear? Hear the pumping of her body?

More movement, though scarcely audible, as though it is part of the wood which moves; leaves clash as relentless hands part them. After a while, she moves again, running silently through the garden, across the carpet-soft mould, away from the one who hunts her down. She stumbles, almost falling, down steps hidden by decades of leaf-drift, hard edges softened into slopes by the accumulation of fallen foliage. Sharply she catches her breath, feeling her ankle turn under her. Terror forces her onward, though she has no real idea where she is headed except that somewhere there must be sanctuary.

Sanctuary. She remembers the ruined building she had once thought to be a chapel. Is it still there?

'Anna,' the voice says, so softly that she nearly screams, for once again, it is very near, only inches from her head. She stands very still, her body pounding. Every corpuscle, vein, muscle, thrums with fear and exertion. Her nerves are stretched tight, almost to breaking. Is her breathing audible? She draws in shallow breaths through her open mouth, minimal breaths. On the other side of the box hedge, wildly overgrown, she can just make out a pair of shoes, tied with leather laces. Moccasins. Decksiders.

Are they Zoe's? She had been certain, now she is less so.

Zoe wears such footwear, but so do many people. At the back of her mind beats the question: does it matter *who* so brutally pursues her, or even *why*, when whatever happens when she is finally caught will be long-drawn-out and agonising?

Yet 'why' *does* matter. Perhaps if she knows why, she can somehow stop this mad pursuit – and into her mind come images of urns and timbrels, dancing delicate figures, black against terracotta, hands reaching for a fleeing nymph who does not wish to be loved and consumed by the fire of a god.

Lungs stretched almost beyond bearing, she breathes gently into the darkness, not daring to suck in greedily the gulps of air she so desperately needs.

'Anna,' she hears, and now the voice is beyond her, receding towards the house, swallowed by the leaves; for a brief moment she is safe.

If she closes her eyes and concentrates, sounds emerge from the night. Distantly, she can hear a car on the road outside the gates; a motorbike belches far away, winding up the side of the hill into the town. So safe, so useless, for she knows that were she to open her mouth to scream, the unknown hunter would be upon her long before help could arrive. She is trapped here, in the green garden, among the tendrils, the ramage and droop of vine and creeper. Tears fill her eyes; she dashes them away, for now is not the time for weeping.

'Anna?' The voice is fainter, questioning. Does her pursuer know that her name is not Anna, but Hannah. Is the misuse a deliberate provocation? She squats again, head hanging, perspiration trickling down between her breasts. On her neck, her hair is damp.

The one who wants to kill her must be tiring too. She hears the patter of leaves. It has begun to rain.

Carefully she moves down towards the pool again. The ruined chapel this side of the boundary fence will not help her if her hunter returns. The gazebo, the folly, the trysting place on the other side at least has a door. She can close it, push the table up against it, wait for Tristan to come.

She remembers the ghost in the glass, weeks ago, at the Festival Hall. It seems another world, another age. And fatally, she knows that if she is to die now, she will be, at the moment of death, more alive than she has been for all the years when the prospect of death was no more than the shadow she carried with her.

It was getting colder. In the dark, Hannah could not see her watch, but knew that it must be much longer than the promised hour since Tristan and Marcus left. Surely they would come looking for her the moment they found the house empty. She had managed to drag the table across the mosaic floor and push it up against the door. How long she could hold it there against determined shoving from the other side she could not tell. A faint grey light filtered through the windows, only marginally less dark than the shadows. Outside, something moved. Against her back, the table shuddered slightly as someone pushed at the door.

'Anna. Are you in there?'

If she answered, Zoe would know she was inside. Best to say nothing, to hope that the men would soon return. Seconds later, hands were scrabbling at the wall outside. A shadow appeared at one of the glassless windows. 'Anna?'

Hannah froze, every pulse drumming. In the darkness down by the door, she was probably not visible but if Zoe had a torch . . . Her mind went into overdrive. If the younger woman really wanted to, she would have no difficulty in forcing back the table. Hannah knew she was reaching the end of her strength. Where could she hide?

She thought about the other folly, the one whose floor she had so laboriously cleared. She remembered the line of brass in the floor, the brass ring set flush among the brilliant mosaic tiles. Was there a similar ring here? Another subterranean room? There had to be.

Zoe dropped again to the ground outside. Hannah could hear her moving about, muttering to herself. She was aware of madness. She moved cautiously forward on hands and knees, feeling with her hands for where the trap-door ought to be, guessing the position, hands sweeping across the floor. Nothing. Only the piece of mouldy carpeting, a few leaves.

She went the other way, towards the opposite wall, listening as she did so for movement outside. It would not take long for Zoe to work out how to get up to the window and then squeeze through. The only advantage Hannah had was that Zoe could not be certain that Hannah was in there.

As she thought this, her fingers found the brass edge of the trap-door let into the floor. She had known it must be there. She followed the line round to the ring. Was she being foolish? Would it not be easier to wait until Zoe was climbing through the window and then to make another dash for the house?

She knew she could not manage it. Energy was failing. The adrenalin supply had run out, leaving her drained. She got her fingers underneath the ring and pulled. Nothing. She moved round so that she crouched directly in front of it, and pulled again, muscles straining. When the door did not budge, she stood up and straddled it, leaned down, pulled once more. This time, she felt it move slightly. Desperate now, breath sobbing from her lungs, while outside she could hear Zoe trying to find a foothold in the stone wall below the window, she tugged again. The floor creaked upwards, swinging on some kind of fulcrum, and stopped halfway. There must be steps, she thought. A floor. Or did it go straight into some underground pit? She shuddered. Rats. Spiders. But it was that or . . .

Lying beside the hole, she felt around inside. Yes: steps. Quickly, she got up and pushed the table a little away from the door. If Zoe did get in, she would know at once that Hannah must be there if the door was blocked. She eased herself into the gap. She felt the underside of the trap-door and found another ring. Undoing her scarf, she threaded it through. If Zoe found her hiding place, at least she could pull downwards, which would take less strength than Zoe would need to pull up.

She went down two steps, four, five, then reached up and pulled the trap-door down, easing its passage so it would not thud back into place and so alert Zoe to where she was.

Sitting, she eased herself downwards until her feet touched the floor. Something rattled against her shoe; some round object rolled away from her. The blackness was impenetrable; it smelled musty, earthy and, beneath that, faintly nauseating as though something organic had slowly decayed. She had no intention of exploring the space, of finding

376

out how large it was. Nor did she wonder about the air supply, how long she might last here. She could always raise the door a little if she needed to, if she felt faint. Provided, of course, that Zoe gave up and went away. She sat hunched up on the steps, crouched just below the trap-door. Daylight would come. And, eventually, Tristan. She did not give thought to Marcus.

'Hannah!'
'Hannah!'
Tristan's voice, calling her.
'Where are you?'
In the darkness, she smiled. They would find her, they would save her.
There were footsteps above her head; the voices were louder now.
'Hannah, where are you?'
She bent her head and took the weight of the trap-door on her shoulders, pushing upwards. It was much heavier than she had expected. 'I'm here,' she said, as it moved upwards. She could see the light from torch beams. 'Tristan. Tristan.'
'My darling. Are you all right?' He was kneeling on the floor now, beside the gap. Above her head the trap opened fully and she could see Marcus's face.
Now that she was safe, she wanted to lie down and sleep. All strength seemed to have left her.
'Do you need some light?' Tristan flashed his torch down into the black space. The light caught something ivory-coloured at her feet.
She bent to stare more closely. A shred of yellow fabric, something which flashed and sparkled in the light. A human skull.
'Oh God,' she said, recoiling.
'What?'
'I think . . . I know what happened . . .'
She reached up and Tristan took her hand in his and helped her out. He flashed his torch again into the depths, held it steady for a long moment, put his arm around her.
'Poor Faustino,' he said.
'She was here all the time.' Hannah recalled that night, when she had passed the gazebo for the second time, and felt that something had changed. The table: it had been pushed across the trap-door, the carpet concealing the thin brass edge. Marina, hiding there from her angry husband, would not have been able to budge it. And no one had found her because no one had thought to look. How many people had even known the trap-door was there?
'Let's get you back to the house,' Tristan said. She followed the two men out of the door.
'Did you find the boy – Orlando?' she asked.

'He's all right; he came up to the Villa, arrived there just as we got back. We decided we'd better come and find you,' Marcus said.

'What about Zoe?' They were approaching the tunnelled paths now, walking in single-file. Marcus went ahead, Hannah, flagging, brought up the rear.

'What about her?' Marcus called back.

'I think she tried to kill me,' Hannah said.

'Are you sure?' said Tristan. 'She's—'

Something crashed through the leaves at the side of the mulched path, knocking Hannah to the ground. Feet kicked at her, a voice incoherent with some dark emotion swore and swooped, hands reached down to tear at her face. She felt the skin part, felt blood flow; she kicked in the darkness but could not find a target. A rock was smashed against the side of her head.

For a short moment, the two men did not realise what had happened. Then Tristan turned and they came running back to grab the arms of Hannah's assailant while Hannah herself lay on the ground, her head ringing.

'Zoe,' she said, into the darkness above her. 'My poor Zoe: I've suffered too, all these years.'

'Not enough!' her attacker screamed. 'Not ever enough.'

But when Tristan flashed his torch in her face, it was not Zoe they saw, face contorted, eyes wild, but Susie.

23

Lucinda is the worst thing.

How can Susie have done that?

For Hannah, that seemed the incomprehensible question. And the only answer lay in the madness which, looking back, she saw had always been there somewhere under the surface of Susie's ebullience. She remembered Tristan's friend – Geoffrey, was it? Or Brian? – who had referred to her as Stark Raving Susie. She herself had mistaken Susie's unbalanced behaviour for simple enthusiasm and zest for life, not recognising how close to insanity she sometimes steered. The sudden angers, the obsessions, the wildness: they should have been pointers. Might have been, except that one accepts one's friends for what they appear to be, without question.

With hindsight, it was easy to see that when Carlo, her husband, had died last year, there was no longer any brake on Susie's always overblown emotions. Left a very rich woman, she had given up her job at the university and instead had opted for a life full of meaningless activities – shopping, eating lunch, meeting her women friends – which helped to pass the days but did not engage either the heart or the mind.

Which left her too much time to brood. All she had ever wanted was money, children and Lucas. Without the last two, the first meant nothing.

Hannah realised that they might never know all the details of what exactly had happened the night of Lucas's murder. Frogmarched back to the salon of the Villa Giulia by Marcus and Tristan, Susie had at first been out of control, spitting, foul-mouthed, spewing out a bitter stream of almost incoherent verbiage. Her envy of Hannah, her desperation about not having children of her own, her grief at Lucas's death—

'I saw you,' she had screamed at Hannah. 'You murderous bitch, you just walked away and left him to die.' She had lunged forward, hands curved like claws, just as she had lunged twenty-five years before.

'Who killed him, Susie?' Hannah said.

'You, Anna. You did. You killed him.'

Hannah tried not to back away as Susie's spittle sprayed her face. Susie seemed to be losing her sense of reality; why otherwise confuse the real Hannah with the Anna who had featured in *Hurled by Dreams*? Hannah found it hard to conceal the disgust she felt at the physical deterioration of the woman she had until now considered her closest friend, closer even than her parents. The woman who had murdered Lucinda – for Susie admits it, explaining in rambling sentences and mumbled phrases how she had followed Lucinda to the cottage in the Dales, had knocked at the door and been invited in by a Lucinda who suspected nothing, who was delighted to see her godmother and readily accepted the explanation offered: that Susie had telephoned the shared house and been given the address by one of Lucinda's friends.

'I showed her the book,' Susie said, glaring at Hannah. 'I showed her just what kind of a slut her mother was. Just what kind of a whore, a cow, a fucking bitch—' and her voice had risen into accusatory shrieks.

'Yes, I killed her,' she said later. 'Knocked her on the head with a wrench from the tool kit in the boot of the hire car, and then threw her down from the steps in that tower thing, whatdoyoucallit, that dove-cote.' She had twisted her hands in her lap, then looked slyly up at Hannah. 'A life for a life, Anna, isn't that right? Isn't that morally acceptable? After all, you killed Lucas, so what else could I do but kill Lucinda?'

'Susie,' Hannah said gently. Why could Susie not admit the truth? 'It was *you* who murdered Lucas—' but again Susie had leaped from her seat, hands outspread, and screamed obscenities.

Hannah felt Tristan's hand on hers, but for the moment, she lacked the strength to look at him for the comfort she so badly needed. Lucinda, my daughter, my darling . . .

'And that boy, too,' Susie went on. Her lips were dry and cracked; she licked them with a tongue which looked as thick as a lizard's. 'That Daniel, the one who came to Italy with her.'

'But you said—' began Hannah, remembering how convincingly Susie had told her about Lucinda turning up with a woman friend, how she had bought them both an expensive frock.

'I had to deal with him too,' Susie said, a faint smile on her face. 'After he saw Lucinda lying there, obviously I had to deal with him too.'

And somewhere, in America, there would be parents to grieve, as Hannah grieved, a family who mourned as Adam and Anthony mourned. Hannah thought that when this was over, she would write to them, telephone them, explain that although she had never met him, Daniel had made Lucinda happy.

And yet, later that night, in the darkness of her room, Hannah acknowledges her own guilt and knows she will never be free again. For all three of them – Susie, Hannah and Zoe – that summer had changed their lives for ever. What happened then is the burden she must carry now. Useless to think that if only she had not . . . if Lucas had never . . . if, if, if. She had, and he had, and together they lit the fuse which led inexorably to Lucinda's death.

* * *

Piecing it together from her own knowledge and Susie's jumbled explanations while they waited for her to be removed to an expensive private clinic, Hannah realised that it was the book, *Hurled by Dreams*, casually bought at John F. Kennedy airport to read on a flight back to England, which had first set Susie's long-suppressed anger simmering.

She imagined Susie stretched out in Cabin Class, a courtesy drink in her hand, opening the first page of her book, and then the mounting disbelief, turning to consternation and finally rage, with which she read of a summer she herself had shared in, of people she had known, of a love affair she had suspected but been unable to prove, of the death she herself had caused. She was even able to read of her own unannounced return from Rome, how she had hidden her car, had followed Hannah down to the pool where Lucas lay bleeding, had, in a mindless fury, delivered the final blows to the man she loved while Hannah, best friend, Judas, ran for help.

And how, eventually, the fictional Anna herself met a hideous parallel fate, her musician's hands severed as she slowly bled to death. Susie knew that no such retribution had been handed out, that Hannah/Anna lived and grew, that she had a new life, a new lover, children, while Susie herself had nothing of what she had wanted.

It was Lucinda's visit in the New Year, accompanied by her American boyfriend, both of them so happy, which had finally caused Susie's rage to boil over.

Haunted by the richness of the things she did not have and could never, for all her money, hope to have, she had come over to England, hired a car and driven up to visit Lucinda at university. Staying in a hotel, she had spied on Lucinda – watching, following, studying – while the idea of an orchestrated programme of harassment had slowly taken shape in her mind. Lucinda was to become the instrument with which she would break Hannah.

It had been easy, in a student house, with poor security, people in and out all the time, to begin her campaign. Small irritations at first: the thefts, the ruined dress, the torn-up notes. A way of getting at Hannah, through Lucinda. A way of punishing Lucinda for being's Hannah's child and not her own.

Later, she told them how, suspecting Hannah's involvement with Lucas, she had returned from Rome early, going directly to the Villa Diana to confront Lucas with seducing her best friend. She had found him down in the folly, with Marina. Something must have snapped in her that night: seeing Lucas, knowing that her dreams were never going to come true, she had stormed out, only to hear Faustino crashing through the woods, raging in his turn.

She had watched Marina run into the darkness and the two men fight; when Lucas fell on to the mantrap, and Faustino ran off, calling his wife's name, she had watched him pitilessly as he wrenched and tore at his broken hand, desperate to release himself, already bleeding to death from the severed artery. She had seen with what pain he finally freed himself, and staggered over to the pool, but did nothing. If he was fucking Hannah – the phrase burst from her over and over again – then let him wait until Hannah came, let Hannah save him.

And then Hannah had indeed arrived. Susie had picked up the discarded iron bar, meaning to kill them both, but before she could do so, Hannah was gone again, and Marina had come instead, had seen Susie by the door of the folly, and shaking with terror had told Susie that Lucas had shown her a place to hide. Together the two women had uncovered the trap-door beneath the dining-table, and Marina, not knowing of Susie's obsession with Lucas, had gratefully descended into what she thought was the safety of the dark cellar. Above her head, Susie must have laughed as she covered the brass edge of the door with the carpet, had pushed the heavy table back into place, knowing that Marina, trapped, would not have the strength to push open the door.

After that, she had returned to the Villa Diana, called the police from there and then driven round by road to the Villa Giulia, to appear apparently innocent and uncomprehending, in Hannah's bedroom.

Hearing all this endlessly, repetitively, as Susie tore at her hair or plucked convulsively at the neck of her sweater, Hannah was reminded of something else.

'I think you will be my downfall,' Lucas had told her, and so she had.

For one thing was made very plain, during that long evening, while they waited for the discreet doctors from the clinic. Susie had understood about Marina, had even known about Jane. Both of them could be dismissed as serious rivals: Marina was married to someone else, she would never – so Susie reasoned – have Lucas, and Jane might well return to her husband, having realised that to Lucas she was nothing more than another notch on his gun. Part of Lucas's callousness towards Susie had manifested itself in telling her of his conquests, just as she told him about hers, both of them engaged in some dreadful contest of deliberate cruelty.

But Hannah . . .

Hannah was different. Hannah was Susie's friend. Hannah was young and eager and beautiful. Hannah was, above all, free. Unable entirely to blame Lucas, Susie had turned the full force of her hatred on Hannah, blaming her for the fact that Lucas was dead, her twisted mind refusing to accept that she herself had killed him.

It was Hannah's fault. However long it might take, Hannah must be punished.

Perhaps her resolve had weakened over the years. But the death of Carlo, leaving her rich and childless, had resurrected all the old flawed arguments. Hannah had left Lucas to die at the hand of an unknown assailant; never mind that it was Susie herself who was responsible: Hannah must be punished. In Lucinda, she had seen the perfect weapon.

In her bed that night, Hannah weeps. 'I think you will be my downfall,' Lucas had said, down by the pool where he was to die . . . he must have known how unstable Susie was, but could not have realised what kind of danger she might prove to be.

Most of Hannah's information had been gleaned that evening, with a police tape recorder whirring quietly on the table in front of them; the rest she had surmised. For more than an hour Susie had talked, repetitively, obsessively, sometimes shouting, sometimes dropping her voice almost to a whisper. And then, as though whatever engine was driving her had run out of fuel, she had lapsed into a semi-catatonic, barely functional state.

Listening to her, Hannah felt that she was hearing not new words but merely something she had always known. Only Susie could have done all that had been done that evening. Only Susie could have called the police; before pushing it into the storerooms of her memory, Hannah had often wondered how they arrived so soon after her own return to the house. And only Susie, she realised now, could, twenty-five years later, have put the doctored cassette into her best friend's car or played it over the telephone to her from the Villa Diana, the night before. Only Susie could have placed the brooch under her best friend's pillow.

Only Susie, too, could have telephoned the Mayor of the little town to complain about Hannah's arrival at the Villa Giulia and sworn him to secrecy about the complainant, or thrown the stones at the window. It had been done to terrify Hannah, alone in the house, just as she must have terrified Lucinda before murdering her.

Only Susie could have plotted with such care to demolish her best friend's security, her life.

Hannah refuses to think about Lucinda, alone in that cottage, and the moments during which she realised that her godmother was insane, was bent on killing her. The questions rear at Hannah: had Lucinda tried to run? To scream? To lunge for the phone? What had Susie done to her? How had she got her up those terrifying steps? Perhaps one day they will know, but perhaps not. Susie may take the information to her grave.

Nor can she bear to think about Daniel Pacino, whose body has been recovered from a shallow grave in remote woodland up near the Dale head, ironically, only a few miles from Marcus's house.

As for Zoe:
She sits crouched in a corner of the chesterfield in Hannah's

sitting-room. Next to her sits Marcus, her father, holding her hand. Behind, on the broad arm of the sofa, is Orlando.

So like Lucas, Hannah thinks, sitting opposite them, oh God, so like. And yet, close to, so unlike, so much his own man.

'I came to look for her,' he says anxiously. 'She's not entirely – she has problems.' His hands push the air in front of him, and Hannah envisages a small boy worrying perpetually about his big sister, taking on burdens too heavy for his shoulders. 'She shouldn't really be on her own – at least—' He looks with love at the sister who had saved his life, down by the pool.

'I'm sorry,' Zoe says. 'I'm sorry, I'm sorry.' She repeats the phrase insistently, on and on, while most of the others try to ignore her.

But Hannah takes the younger woman's hand. 'You were too little to understand. Now we've found out who really killed Lucas, you can start forgetting. You've paid a big enough price for something which wasn't ever your fault.' She smiles at Zoe and does what she had wanted to do before: smooths back the tender crop of her hair.

They have had time to sort things out, to listen to Zoe's incoherent account of what she saw that night, twenty-five years ago. At the time, nobody had thought to question her; she has chosen to block out the memories rather than try to live with them.

Piecing it all together, it was easy to see why she would do that. Why she had turned into someone who walked apart from those around her.

In the kitchen, fixing drinks for everyone, Tristan brings it up again. 'Lucas screwing her mother, and Marina, and you,' he says, looking for a corkscrew, not yet familiar with Hannah's places. He opens a bottle of wine, locates the whisky. 'She'd heard the phrase somewhere about the beast with two backs, she saw Lucas kill her puppy and talk about its back being broken in two, she—'

'She put it all together and came up with a nightmare she simply couldn't handle. I know.' Hannah pushes past him to take glasses from a cupboard and remembers Lew; he must have come to the Villa Diana that summer, must have used the words. She puts the glasses on a tray. The coarse wool of Tristan's sweater brushes her face.

'Lovemaking often seems to be quite the opposite of what it is,' Tristan says carefully. 'Easily misunderstood if you don't know what's going on, if you're a child, for instance. Especially when it's—' He fiddles with the cork from the wine bottle he has just opened, seeming embarrassed. 'When it's—'

'Noisy, do you mean?' says Hannah.

'Yes.'

'Are you?' she asks, trying not to smile. It was a question she would never have dreamed of asking in the past; now it seems no more than natural.

'Am I what?'

'Noisy. When you make love.'

She thinks he is not going to answer. Then he comes over to her and puts his arms round her. 'Why do you want to know?'

She pretends indifference. 'I just wondered.'

'When are you going to find out for yourself, Hannah?'

She touches his mouth lightly, leans her cheek against his. 'We're not in any rush, are we?'

'I am.'

'Soon,' she says. She means, when she has had a little more time to grieve for Lucinda, when it no longer seems wrong to go ahead with her own life, even though her daughter's is over. 'Very soon.'

Marcus comes into the kitchen. 'Can I help?' he says.

'We're fine, thanks.' Tristan fiddles with the tray, avoids Hannah's clear gaze, embarrassed.

Marcus's eyes find the whisky and, without asking, he pours himself a generous measure, raises it to his mouth. A pulse beats at his temple.

'I'm desperately hoping that now it's all been aired, things might be better for Sophie,' he says. 'She wants to go back to the States. Turns out she has some kind of a relationship – a man, a boyfriend – over there.' He has aged in the past week or so, he seems greyer and much less confident. Hannah feels sympathy for him; people are not often brought face to face with the painful consequences of their actions. If he had not neglected his wife, perhaps Jane would not have succumbed to Lucas's techniques of seduction and, in so doing, have traumatised his daughter.

'That's good,' Hannah says.

'Do you think so?' He does not sound convinced.

'Especially with you to help. And Orlando.'

'She's very fond of you, you know.'

'Is she?' Hannah is not sure how she feels about that. Zoe – Sophie – is very much an unknown quantity still. But though at one point she has suspected Zoe of responsibility for almost everything that has happened, including Lucinda's death, she is glad that, after all, Zoe did not betray her. Perhaps one day Zoe may come to take, in some measure, the place of Lucinda, lost child, beloved daughter. For Zoe, it now transpires, has done nothing more alarming than seek Hannah out in a muddled attempt to recover her past, just as Hannah seeks to rediscover her own.

Marcus stares sadly, resignedly at Hannah for a long moment. 'It's over, isn't it?' he says quietly.

'I'm afraid so.'

'It was so good,' he says, 'you and me, while it lasted. So good.'

'Yes,' Hannah agrees, because he is right, it had been good.

'Beginning like that, I suppose it was doomed from the start.'

'Look at it this way, old boy,' Tristan says cheerfully. 'You got the girl last time; I've got her this.'

Hannah smiles secretly. She thinks of Tristan's buttercup-yellow drawing-room, filled with the light from the sea; she thinks of him as a young man, naked against the leaves, Pan come to life.

Has he got the girl this time? Maybe. And maybe not. Either way, she has time to decide, plenty of time, really. The rest of their lives, in fact.

THE DIARY

. . . I think it's over now. After this, I shan't write in this diary again, but I want to put it all down, to set the record straight for the first and last time.

That evening, that night he died down there by the pool, I heard Jane weeping in her room, and I knew it was because of that man, Ivo, as I called him, like Evil, though his name was really Lucas.

I remembered the first time I pushed open the door of his room and saw the two of them, him and Jane, my mother, and how frightened I was when she began to cry out, beating at his back with her fists, turning her head on the pillow and saying stuff like 'Jesus!' and 'I can't bear it!' and 'No, no!'

I realise now they were just having sex, but at the time, I felt that same sense of things going wrong that I did when she and Father were having a row, or when he used to walk through the room without speaking to her, or ring up late in the evening and say he wasn't going to get back that night, because she said exactly the same things then: 'I can't bear it!' and 'No, no!'

She said them again when he hit her, that one time, just before we left.

But to get back to that summer, the other woman arrived to stay in the Villa Giulia. Hannah. He started to have sex with her too. I used to sit on the landing outside and pretend to play with the doll's house, the miniature house, and listen to them inside the room. I used to wonder why she came to him so often, when he was hurting her so badly. And not just her, but Jane too. I was too young to understand, but I could see how she – Jane – changed that summer. She was always watching him, slinking round corners, peering between shutters. She was always down by the pool, standing among the bushes; I saw her at that picnic, following him among the trees as it grew dark. And the more she watched, the thinner her face grew, the blacker the rings round her eyes, though her stomach got bigger and bigger.

And then, I was in the woods one evening – it was impossible to sleep in the heat – and I heard him again, saying the things he said to Jane and to Hannah. I looked in through the door of that little house in the woods, not a miniature house, but like a playhouse, a stone summerhouse. There was another woman, lying under him, screaming, sobbing, shuddering. The beast with two backs, like someone said that summer, one of the Americans, and that, of course, is what I thought he was doing to my puppy later, to my best friend.

But it's that night I'm trying to write about. That last night.

He was down in the summerhouse with the third woman. She was wearing a yellow dress, and I was watching, waiting for him to take her clothes off, the way he always did. And then the one who was his cousin, Susie, who didn't make the beast with two backs with him, though I think she wanted to, arrived, and shouted at them, and Ivo was horrid to her, speaking in a cold horrible voice, and she went raging out, and then a man came, an Italian, and he shouted at the woman in the yellow dress, and lifted the table up and threw it on the ground and Ivo got hold of his arms to stop him, and told the woman to run. He said: 'I'll get him out of here, Marina. You know where to hide. I'll come and get you when the coast is clear.'

The two men started hitting each other, punching, like a boxing match. They came outside and the Italian one had an iron bar which he kept swinging at Ivo. One time, I could hear his knee crack, and Ivo fell down, and the Italian man threw away the bar and started shouting, Marina, where are you?

Ivo crawled away and got caught in that thing which caught my best friend, my puppy. I watched him. I thought it served him right. And the other woman came back, Susie, and she watched too, and all the time she was kind of laughing to herself and muttering bad words about him and Hannah. And finally he got himself free and dragged himself over to the edge of the pool. And then Hannah came running through the woods, and the cousin disappeared. Lucas asked Hannah to help him but she wouldn't, she went away again, and then . . . and then . . .

Jesus this is really hard for me to write down—

. . . and then I picked up the bar and hit his head, lots of times, over and over again and pushed at him as hard as I could. I hated him because of what he did to my puppy, and then he fell into the pool.

I went back to the stone summerhouse and Susie was there with Marina, the woman in the yellow dress, and the two of them lifted up the floor, and Marina went down into a hole and Susie put the rug on the floor to hide the trap-door and then pushed the table over it.

A bit later, Hannah came back and saw Ivo in the pool and got him out and then she went away again. And I had a look at Ivo, and I could tell he was dead, because there was blood everywhere and he looked the same way my puppy looked so I knew he was dead and I was glad, but it was horrible, horrible, I couldn't bear to look at that blood and—

Face it, Zoe. You killed him.

Oh, God . . .
  It's the first time I've said it, the first time I've admitted that I am responsible for the death of another human being.
  How am I going to live with that?
  How am I going to live with anyone else? With T . . .

Then two men came, the Italian one and another one with white hair, and there was a lot of screaming and shouting and the police came and all sort of things and I went back to bed.

Should I tell someone? Father, for instance? Or Hannah? I feel so guilty about all the lies I told her. I liked her, I was happy with her. I think it's the first time I can remember being truly happy. The shop, those little doll's houses, Hannah and her family. I still don't know why I raced off to Italy, leaving the shop like that, things knocked over, a teacup smashed. I wanted to be where she was, to shield her, I guess. I had such a sense of danger hanging over her.

She thinks Susie killed Lucas: should I tell her what really happened that night? But if I did, she might hate me for it and then I would lose her. It's taken me all these years to see that I was not the only one who suffered that hot summer, but what possible use could it be to her to know that I killed Ivo – Lucas, I mean· What use . . .
  I guess I'm just going to have to live with it.
  I remind myself that I am an AUTHOR. That I have a contract to sign, other books to write.

But first I'm going to burn this. I don't ever want anyone else to read it.

I WANT TO LIVE.